The EU's Eastern Neighbourhood

The collapse of the Soviet Union has had profound and long-lasting impacts on the societies of Eastern Europe, the South Caucasus and Central Asia, impacts which are not yet fully worked through: changes in state–society relations, a comprehensive reconfiguration of political, economic and social ties, the resurgence of regional conflicts 'frozen' during the Soviet period, and new migration patterns both towards Russia and the European Union. At the same time the EU has emerged as an important player in the region, formulating its European Neighbourhood Policy, and engaging neighbouring states in a process of cross-border regional co-operation. This book explores a wide range of complex and contested questions related to borders, security and migration in the emerging 'European Neighbourhood' which includes countries of the Caucasus and Central Asia as well as the countries which immediately border the EU. Issues discussed include new forms of regional and cross-border co-operation, new patterns of migration, and the potential role of the EU as a stabilizing external force.

Ilkka Liikanen is a Professor at the Karelian Institute, University of Eastern Finland.

James W. Scott is Research Professor of Regional and Border Studies at the University of Eastern Finland.

Tiina Sotkasiira is a researcher at the Karelian Institute, University of Eastern Finland.

BASEES/Routledge Series on Russian and East European Studies

Series editor:
Richard Sakwa, Department of Politics and International Relations, University of Kent

Editorial Committee:
Roy Allison, St Antony's College, Oxford
Birgit Beumers, Department of Theatre, Film and Television Studies, University of Aberystwyth
Richard Connolly, Centre for Russian and East European Studies, University of Birmingham
Terry Cox, Department of Central and East European Studies, University of Glasgow
Peter Duncan, School of Slavonic and East European Studies, University College London
Zoe Knox, School of History, University of Leicester
Rosalind Marsh, Department of European Studies and Modern Languages, University of Bath
David Moon, Department of History, University of York
Hilary Pilkington, Department of Sociology, University of Manchester
Graham Timmins, Department of Politics, University of Birmingham
Stephen White, Department of Politics, University of Glasgow

Founding Editorial Committee Member:
George Blazyca, Centre for Contemporary European Studies, University of Paisley

This series is published on behalf of BASEES (the British Association for Slavonic and East European Studies). The series comprises original, high-quality, research-level work by both new and established scholars on all aspects of Russian, Soviet, post-Soviet and East European Studies in humanities and social science subjects.

The EU's Eastern Neighbourhood

Migration, borders and regional stability

Edited by
Ilkka Liikanen, James W. Scott and
Tiina Sotkasiira

Routledge
Taylor & Francis Group
LONDON AND NEW YORK

First published 2016
by Routledge

2 Park Square, Milton Park, Abingdon, Oxfordshire OX14 4RN
711 Third Avenue, New York, NY 10017

Routledge is an imprint of the Taylor & Francis Group, an informa business

First issued in paperback 2017

British Library Cataloguing in Publication Data
A catalogue record for this book is available from the British Library

Library of Congress Cataloging in Publication Data
Names: Liikanen, Ilkka, editor of compilation, author. | Scott, James
    Wesley, editor of compilation, author. | Sotkasiira, Tiina, editor of
    compilation, author.
Title: The EU's eastern neighbourhood : migration, borders and regional
    stability / edited by Ilkka Liikanen, James W. Scott and Tiina Sotkasiira.
Other titles: EU's eastern neighborhood | European Union's eastern
    neighbourhood | European Union's eastern neighborhood
Description: Abingdon, Oxon ; New York, NY : Routledge, 2016. |
    Series: BASEES/Routledge series on Russian and East European studies ;
    107 | Includes bibliographical references and index.
Identifiers: LCCN 2015037249| ISBN 9780415722865 (hardback) |
    ISBN 9781315858036 (ebook)
Subjects: LCSH: European Union countries--Foreign relations--Former
    Soviet republics. | Former Soviet republics--Foreign relations--European
    Union countries. | Former Soviet republics--Emigration and immigration.
Classification: LCC JZ1570.A57 F6648 2016 | DDC 341.242/20947--dc23
LC record available at http://lccn.loc.gov/2015037249

ISBN: 978-0-415-72286-5 (hbk)
ISBN: 978-1-138-47769-8 (pbk)

DOI: 10.4324/9781315858036

Typeset in Times New Roman
by Taylor & Francis Books

Contents

List of illustrations

List of contributors

Olga Brednikova is a Researcher at the Centre for Independent Social Research, Saint Petersburg, Russia.

Olga Davydova-Minguet is a Research Fellow at the Karelian Institute, University of Eastern Finland, Joensuu.

Olga Filippova is a Professor at V.N. Karazin Kharkiv National University, Department of Sociology, Kharkiv, Ukraine.

Paul Fryer is a Researcher at the Department of Geographical and Historical Studies, University of Eastern Finland, Joensuu.

Vladimir Kolossov is the Director of the Institute of Geography, Russian Academy of Sciences, Moscow.

Volodymyr Kravchenko is the Director of the Centre for Ukrainian Studies, University of Alberta, Edmonton, Canada

Ilkka Liikanen is a Professor and Docent of Political History at the Karelian Institute, University of Eastern Finland, Joensuu.

Anaïs Marin is a Marie-Curie Fellow at Collegium Civitas, Warsaw, Poland

Ihor Markov is Director of the Institute of Ethnology, Laboratory for Social Research of the National Academy of Sciences of Ukraine, Lviv.

Valeriu Mosneaga is a Professor at Moldova State University, Faculty of International Relations, Chişinău.

Oleksii Pozniak is the Head of the Migration Studies Department at the Ptoukha Institute for Demography and Social Studies, National Academy of Sciences of Ukraine, Kyiv.

Sergei Riazantsev is the Head of the Center for Social Demography and Economic Sociology, Institute of Social-Political Research, Russian Academy of Sciences, Moscow.

James Wesley Scott is Professor of Regional and Border Studies at the Karelian Institute, University of Eastern Finland, Joensuu.

Tiina Sotkasiira is a Researcher at the Department of Social Sciences, University of Eastern Finland, Joensuu.

Octavian Țîcu is Director of the Institute of History and Political Sciences, Free International University of Moldova, Chişinău.

Larissa Titarenko is a Professor at Belarus State University, Department of Sociology, Minsk.

Olga Tkach is a Researcher at the Centre of Independent Social Research, Saint Petersburg, Russia.

Sergey Rumyantsev is a Research Fellow at the Research Institute of Philosophy, Sociology and Law of the Azerbaijan National Academy of Sciences, Baku.

Furugzod Usmonov is a Senior Lecturer at the Department of International Relations, Tajik National University, Dushanbe.

Joni Virkkunen is a Researcher at the Karelian Institute, University of Eastern Finland, Joensuu.

Abbreviations

AEBR	Association of European Border Regions
ASSR	Autonomous Soviet Socialist Republic
BOMCA	Border Management in Central Asia
CARDS	Community Assistance to the Commonwealth of Independent States
CBC	cross-border cooperation
CEEC	Central and Eastern European Countries
CSO	civil society organisation
EaP	Eastern Partnership
EC Commission	Commission of the European Communities
EDM	European Dialogue for Modernisation
EEAS	European External Action Service
ENP	European Neighbourhood Policy
ENPI	European Neighbourhood Policy Instrument
ERDF	European Regional Development Fund
EU	European Union
EUBAM	European Union Border Assistance Mission
FRONTEX	European Agency for the Management of Operational Cooperation at the External Borders of the Member States of the European Union
GAMM	Global Approach to Migration and Mobility
IOM	International Organisation for Migration
LBT	Local Border Traffic
MID	Ministry of Foreign Affairs of the Russian Federation
NATO	North Atlantic Treaty Organisation
OHCHR	Office of the United Nations High Commissioner for Human Rights
OSCE	Organisation for Security and Cooperation in Europe
PCA	Partnership and Cooperation Agreement
PHARE	Poland and Hungary: Aid for Restructuring of the Economies
SIS	Schengen Information System
SSR	Soviet Socialist Republic

TACIS	Technical Assistance to the Commonwealth of Independent States
UNDP	United Nations Development Programme
UNESCO	United Nations Educational, Scientific and Cultural Organisation
WEI	Wider Europe Initiative (of the Finnish Ministry of Foreign Affairs)

The end of Wider Europe?

The EU, changing borders and spatial imaginaries of post-Soviet space

Ilkka Liikanen, James W. Scott and Tiina Sotkasiira

Introduction: concepts of Wider Europe and Neighbourhood

Ever since the collapse of the Soviet Union, the dramatic changes in the nature of post-Soviet borders have been the object of both grand political visions and violent conflicts in Eastern Europe and Central Asia. This book relates these changes to the emergence of EU policies of building a *regional neighbourhood*. The concept of European Neighbourhood has been a central element in policies of EU enlargement and the rearrangement of the Union's external relations. Much research attention has been focused on the development of the policy structures that define this Neighbourhood. However, beyond the technicalities of actual policies such as the European Neighbourhood Partnership (ENP), it is more seldom acknowledged that, either intentionally or inadvertently, the European Union (EU) is actually engaged in a struggle to piece together a new sense of (geo)political identity. This struggle for a meaningful and exceptionalist role in the world is apparent in narratives that suggest a new style of international relations in which partnership and the recognition of mutual interdependence will contribute to a transcendence of traditional interest politics. In many quarters, the EU's concept of Neighbourhood is furthermore based on the premise that the EU has exportable values, norms and models of social development that can assist in the social transformation of neighbouring states.

At the same time, post-Soviet transformation has not only necessitated a renegotiation of state–society relations but also led to a comprehensive reconfiguration of Soviet-era political, economic and social ties. The forces of change that impact on post-Soviet states and societies include complex social, economic and political processes as well as a differentiated exposure to globalisation pressures. These processes of change are an elementary part of a by no means finalised re-bordering of post-Soviet states; it is a difficult process, often punctuated by conflicting Soviet-time legacies and emerging nation-building strategies that have in extreme cases led to the resurgence of regional conflicts frozen during the Soviet period. On a more practical level, the reconfiguration of border regimes has been characterised by split communities, the shrinking of visa-free areas, fragmented border management and a

DOI: 10.4324/9781315858036-1

poor ability to control new migration patterns oriented towards both Russia and the European Union. Furthermore, the movement of people has had distinct effects both on sending and receiving countries, their policies and, of course, on the migrants themselves. Finally, we see an *internationalisation* of regional political contexts taking place; processes of European and Eurasian integration collide in the region, and Russia, the European Union, NATO (North Alliance Treaty Organization), Turkey and other actors have taken an increasing interest in energy-related and other strategic issues that are objects of (geo)political tensions. This is reflected in new, partly colliding spatial imaginaries attached to the region, the Russian discourse on Eurasia and the Near Abroad and the EU-inspired concepts of European Neighbourhood and Wider Europe (Averre 2011; Jones and Clark 2008). It is argued here that, with the spatial imaginaries of European Neighbourhood and Wider Europe, the European Union is itself actively engaged in re-configuring borders on its external frontiers and between post-Soviet states. It has been doing this in the following ways: first, by advancing a regional cooperation agenda that targets national modernisation and convergence to EU norms; second, by developing a new security area that aims at stopping undocumented immigration and addressing other perceived threats; and, third, through an implicit policy of creating a buffer zone between the EU and the Russian Federation's direct sphere of influence. These different objectives are contradictory and often problematic – they contain both progressive elements of potential regional partnerships but also exclusionary and discriminatory aspects. Finally, and with a view to future scenarios of deeper regional cooperation, there are discontinuities between domestic political agendas in neighbouring states and the EU's Neighbourhood Policy, especially in the form of border-transcending tasks set out in the 2003 Wider Europe document.

Wider Europe was one of the political catchwords and innovative spatial imaginaries that emerged in public debates at the turn of the new millennium as part of a new rhetoric of EU external relations and programmes of regional cooperation. Understood in progressive terms, the widening of the European community implied increasing openness and inclusionary politics where neighbourhood could be jointly negotiated between the EU and its regional partners. In the post-Cold War context, Wider Europe was seen to represent a new spatial imaginary that went beyond the old East–West divide. The means by which the EU utilised this concept in building relations to its eastern neighbours was perceived as an important part of the Union's campaign to profile itself as a new kind of international actor (Barbé and Johansson-Nogués 2008; Forsberg 2011; Haukkala 2008a; Jones and Clark 2008; Telo 2005). Yet the notion of Wider Europe was contested from the very beginning because of its inherent EU-centrism and has since continually lost ground as a political key concept, especially after 2007 when the Union began to formulate its common foreign and security policies in institutional terms.

In 2003, when the European Commission published its groundbreaking policy paper *Wider Europe – Neighbourhood: A New Framework for Relations with our Eastern and Southern Neighbours* (European Commission 2003), a systematic formulation of common external relations policies was made public (Browning and Joenniemi 2008; Gower and Timmins 2011). In the optimistic pre-enlargement spirit, the document laid the foundations for a reform of EU cross-border cooperation (CBC) programmes in tones reflecting the consolidation of a political Union with a constitutional mandate for common foreign and security policies that for a long time had been considered to lie outside the competence of EU institutions. In practical terms, it outlined the principal elements of the European Neighbourhood Policy that was to guide EU policies towards its neighbours during the coming years. More broadly, it can be understood as an attempt to balance the competing rationales of EU-internal consolidation and embryonic external relations with their conflicting logics of inclusion and exclusion (Scott 2005; Liikanen and Virtanen 2006).

With *Wider Europe*, the EU took a major step towards profiling itself as an international actor. The idea of the EU as a new type of security community whose policies would rely on normative soft power was officially added to the rhetoric of EU policies. This was reflected, for instance, in the objectives of avoiding drawing new dividing lines in Europe and promoting stability and prosperity 'within and beyond the new borders of the Union' (European Commission 2003: 4, 12). Importantly, *Wider Europe* introduced a reconfiguration of the territorial frames of EU policies even beyond its borders, especially in terms of promoting transborder regionalisation on the Union's external borders. These formulations revealed political innovation that combined new territorial imagination and new sovereignty conceptions. In this sense, they can be seen as an important element in the broader task of profiling the EU as a new kind of international actor and in building up policies of soft power as an alternative to securitised Cold War visions of conflict (Haukkala 2010). With the 2014 Ukrainian crisis in mind, the question can be raised whether we have come to the end of these policies.

Of old and new geopolitical conundrums

It is abundantly clear that the EU's European Neighbourhood Policy as expressed today in the Eastern Partnership, the Euro-Mediterranean dialogue and other regional cooperation fora is a geopolitical vision that remains unfulfilled. A certain consensus has emerged that, for a number of internal political reasons as well as policy setbacks, the EU has in fact resorted to a default mode of realist geopolitics (see, for example, Bialasiewicz 2012 and Follis 2012). Whether or not this represents a temporary situation, questions regarding the EU's transformative power outside its borders continue to be raised. It is indeed not altogether clear where the limits of the EU's regional influence actually lie. Furthermore, assuming that regional cooperation and increasing economic interaction are among the most important prerequisites for stability in the post-Soviet space, what are the prospects for dialogue? The events of 2014 in Ukraine have made these questions all the more salient; they have made it rather clear that the EU cannot unilaterally define its geopolitical identity and role, and even less impose a new geopolitical order. Instead, one major lesson that can be drawn from the Ukraine crisis and tensions in EU–Russia relations is that the EU's vision of regional partnership can only prosper through a mutually shared vision of social engagement and through greater knowledge of social contexts in neighbouring countries.

In fact, it is obvious that the Neighbourhood concept has from the beginning been appropriated by more traditional geopolitical thinking. To an extent it seems that projects of state- and nation-building have many times taken precedence over bridging borders. In other cases, attempts of newly independent states to widen their geopolitical options have generated conditions that do not encourage de-bordering. Indeed, as is sometimes the case with economic trade areas, the forging of new geopolitical alliances can work against wider and more open regional cooperation. As an increasingly important political actor on the regional and global scene, and as an actor that promulgates notions of open regionalism, the European Union has a potentially vital role to play in this complicated setting. A distinguishing feature of the EU has been that it has operated not only directly as a political actor but also indirectly as an economic and social or cultural power. Depending simultaneously on the tools of soft power and the realpolitik of conditionality, the EU has attempted to reshape political relations within Eastern Europe, Central Asia and the Caucasus and to promote democracy, peaceful coexistence and human rights in these regions.

To some degree, the emergence of the European Neighbourhood Policy could concurrently be read as a signal for a new form of regionalism based on the recognition of mutual interdependence and a manifestation of the EU's security concerns. The security concept of the EU has been significantly grounded in a fear of (unwanted) migration as a source of social and economic instability. It is thus not surprising that the EU has had an identifiable interest to impact the emergence of new border regimes and border-management practices in many post-Soviet states.

This book has grown out of two research projects. The first, 'Regional Stability, Borders and Migrations', was funded by the Finnish Ministry of Foreign Affairs' Wider Europe Initiative. Together with EU neighbourhood policies, the project has focused on migration and migration policies in the post-Soviet space. Special attention has been paid to topics such as migration law, educational migration, integration policies and practices and the effects of migration on the sending and receiving societies at both the macro- and micro-level. The second project, EUBORDERREGIONS, was supported by the European Union's Seventh Framework Programme for Science and Innovation and focused attention on relationships between cross-border cooperation, development and the promotion of a sense of 'European Neighbourhood'. EUBORDERREGIONS complemented the 'Wider Europe' perspective influenced by Finnish policy with scrutiny of the EU's Eastern Partnership (EaP), particularly with a view to relations with Ukraine, Moldova and Belarus.

The contributors to this volume investigate a range of complex and contested questions relating to EU policies on borders, security and migration in an emerging neighbourhood that includes countries as diverse as Ukraine, Moldova, Azerbaijan, Belarus and Tajikistan. Most notably, how consequent and successful have the policies of the EU and its member states been in promoting new border-spanning practices and spatial imaginaries of a shared Wider Europe? Furthermore, this neighbourhood is not only defined by policy agendas of cooperation with the European Union but also by processes of nation-building and the establishment of new state institutions in the post-Soviet context. This, coupled with security agendas and new border-management practices, has increased the significance of borders within the post-Soviet space and between the EU and its eastern neighbours.

The book develops these questions around five thematic areas that involve: the construction and changing political and social significance of borders in post-Soviet space; new forms of regional and cross-border cooperation; new patterns and policies of migration within changing political and economic spaces; migration and the everyday negotiation of borders; and potential roles and policy options of the EU as a stabilising external force. With the formulation of common foreign and security policies in mind, it can be questioned whether the EU is still pursuing the ambitious sovereignty-challenging policies of Wider Europe or whether we are actually witnessing a silent dismissal of opting for the role of a new kind of actor in international relations. In terms of politically innovative spatial imaginaries, are we facing the end of Wider Europe and a return to more traditional forms of conceptualising (common) foreign policies?

Since the fall of the Iron Curtain, many researchers have focused on the historical constitution of post-Cold War borders. They have most often tried to understand the origin and development of these borders either in terms of national development and nation-building or in terms of Western models of modernising social and political institutions, democratisation and the formation of civil society and state-structures based on the rule of law. In many cases, this search for original and natural borders has evolved into an examination of stereotypical historical patterns and models, Eastern and Western nationalism, European and non-European models of democracy, civil society, political institutions and values. It is argued here that in the study of post-Cold War borders these conceptualisations are not only clumsy tools of analysis but tend to reproduce spatial imaginaries that are politically hazardous. The following will be an attempt to apply an alternative approach that might better capture the multilayered historicity of the present borders. Particular attention will be paid to the ways in which the different historical layers, developed during different periods of time and mediated through different traditions, values and epistemic practices, are present in the formal and informal rules and norms concerning post-Cold War borders. Especially important are their inherent tensions and contradictions that should be recognised and addressed.

The question of Wider Europe largely concerns the policies of individual EU member states, too. Finland, for example, initiated its own Wider Europe Initiative (WEI) in 2009, at the same time that EaP was unveiled.[1] With the launching of the Initiative, defined as a bilateral and multilateral development cooperation programme for Eastern Europe, the South Caucasus and Central Asia, Finnish development policies were coordinated with the targets set by the EU's European Neighbourhood Policy. Since then, changes in the operational environment as well as in EU policies have, however, created a tendency to reconsider the relation of Finnish policies to the evolving EU policy frames and to sharpen the definition of the Finnish position in regard to the competing rationales and alternative options of developing the role of the EU in its neighbourhood. In the recently published policy paper for the second period of the Wider Europe Initiative (2014–2017), the European policy frame and innovative spatial imaginaries have given room to a more traditional framing of bilateral development cooperation between Finland and countries of Eastern Europe and Central Asia. In this sense there is a clear need to discuss the future of Wider Europe also in terms of policy choices of EU member states.

Beyond these specific issues, an attempt has, however, been made to highlight three more general concerns about migration and migration policy:

- the politicisation of migration and the fact that migration is increasingly being perceived as a source of controversy and a part of public policy requiring legislative and policy decisions as well as the allocation of resources (Guiraudon and Lahav 2000; Huysmans 2000; for an argument in favour of de-politicising migration, see Geiger and Pécoud 2010: 11);
- country-specific and EU-wide migration policies that are influenced by broader relations between the EU and non-member states, such as overall trade relations, geopolitical security issues as well as care regimes (Wunderlich 2012). These broader connections and their linkages with actual migration practices deserve serious scholarly attention.
- the need to give more prominence to the point of view of non-member states which are part of the EU's fluctuating sphere of influence. The perspective of these countries is relevant for everyday interactions as well as for policies; it needs to receive the proper emphasis in studies that focus on migration and demographic development.

One analytical tool employed here for a better understanding of these socio-political processes involves relating them to broader patterns of conceptual change in the political framing of borders and migration in the post-Cold War era. Thus, an approach will be pursued that addresses borders, migration and security issues from both a top-down geopolitical perspective and the vantage point of local societies, cross-border interaction and practical outcomes of cross-border cooperation policies. These reflections are based on the recognition that important relationships exist between social spaces and places, on the one hand, and processes associated with changing geopolitical spatial imaginaries, on the other. A focus on identity and place also makes it necessary to confront the very human propensity to construct negative or antagonistic *cultural others*, in this case of neighbouring states. This tendency can be exacerbated by political agendas set by unrepresentative elites and processes of nation-building or state consolidation. It should, however, be noted that stereotypical spatial imaginaries are not only characteristic of new emerging nation-states but can also be identified in the place-making strategies promoted through EU policies of cross-border cooperation. Reflection and constant revision of the political language of bordering embedded in EU policy documents are a vital precondition if the EU wants to live up to its promise to become a new kind of actor in international relations. A fall-back on images of deep dividing lines between East and West leaves post-Soviet states with poor alternatives, as the 2014 Ukrainian crisis demonstrates.

Ultimately, the question of Wider Europe affects not only the Union's relations with its eastern neighbours. In a broader sense, it involves the whole process of European integration. Wider Europe has offered the member states a common frame to customise their policies in line with a common European vision. Thus it concerns not only external relations of EU member states but also their relations to the EU and common European policies, as the case of the Finnish Wider Europe Initiative indicates. The fading vision of Wider Europe can be read as an indication of the problems that plague the whole process of European integration and as a sign of the EU giving up its vision of becoming a new kind of international actor. It is vital to see that, despite all the wailing about EU-level policies not passing the threshold of media attention, the EU is, deliberately and without any further debate, pushing ahead with a fundamental choice that has ramifications on the world scene at large. Changing visions of the EU's role also affect the expectations and strategies of other players, not just in the post-Soviet space but also in Syria, Israel, Darfur or elsewhere. The question of Wider Europe's future reflects a weakening vision of the EU as a new kind of international actor and more broadly of the European dream. As such it is a matter that should be urgently discussed not only on the level of the EU, the member states and their foreign policies but also by other political actors and citizens. Making choices about the future of Wider Europe raises the question what kind of Europe we want and what kind of role there is for Europe to play in the world.

The structure of the book

The main body of the book is divided into four parts. The first of these consists of a detailed investigation of EU policies and the resurgence of border-related issues in the post-Soviet context as well as of the problems of territorial sovereignty, national identity and state consolidation associated with them. The concrete cases discussed are Moldova and Ukraine. The second part is expressly focused on the uneasy relationship between emerging border regimes, the consolidation of border-management policies and regional cooperation.

Within this constellation, the European Union appears to have stressed issues of border and migration management to the detriment of broader socio-political cooperation. Parts Three and Four comprise eight contributions that discuss the migrants' place and role in various formal and informal settings within the European Union and in Azerbaijan, Belarus, Moldova, Russia, Tajikistan and Ukraine. All of these chapters emphasise the importance of local and regional migration trends and thus move away from the eurocentrism often prevalent in EU-related migration studies. In one way or another, all authors raise similar questions: what are the political aspects of migration? And how do the EU and partner states participate in constructing migration and especially migrants themselves as differently conditioned and positioned agents of social change? This is often done by considering the distinct effects of migration on both sending and receiving countries, their policies and the migrants themselves. Finally, based on the previous contributions, the last section will focus on scenarios for a more progressive EU neighbourhood approach to regional cooperation. At the heart of it will be the question whether, instead of giving up the ambitious goal of a new kind of international relations in Wider Europe, the EU could promote the principle of *co-ownership* of cooperation policies that might allow all participating states to equally share the benefits of greater economic, political and socio-cultural cooperation.

Part One: renegotiating borders in the post-Soviet space

The first section opens with a chapter by *Ilkka Liikanen*, which analyses conceptual changes in the definition of post-Soviet borders, their negotiation and the conflict over them from the point of view of EU policies. Liikanen examines how the rhetoric of cross-border cooperation promoted by EU Neighbourhood policies has been related to the political and social conditions of post-Soviet change and how the multilayered discussion about borders of former Soviet Republics has affected the development of the EU's external relations. The chapter analyses spatial imaginaries of EU CBC policies and strives to identify changes in the place-making strategies applied in EU external relations, especially towards its eastern neighbours. The focus of the study is on conceptual shifts in the ways of defining Europe and the European Neighbourhood, with special attention being paid to the sovereignty concepts that are attached to shifting spatial imaginaries. By examining the coexistence and clash of universalist rhetoric in EU policies of external relations (sometimes referred to as post-sovereignty) and competing rationales of EU cross-border cooperation programmes, Liikanen attempts to critically comment on and contribute to the broader discussion of post-Cold War EU policies in Wider Europe. He concludes that the spatial imaginaries and sovereignty concepts of the EU's CBC policy documents represent competing rationales connected to the internal logic of European integration and do not take into account the conflicting processes shaping post-Soviet borders, thus serving ill the aim of building up the EU's role as a new kind of international actor.

The following chapter, by *Volodymyr Kravchenko*, is a study of the formation of Ukraine's borders and the contradictory notions associated with it. According to Kravchenko, Ukraine, geographically located between Russia and the European Union, is still in the process of searching for its geopolitical and national identity. This process is connected directly with the disintegration and re-integration of (post-)Soviet and European political and cultural spaces. Ukraine's external borders sometimes acquire different cultural meanings within different regional contexts. From this point of view, the Ukrainian–Russian borderland seems to be the most problematic one. Kravchenko, moreover, argues that historical narratives, and various post-Soviet historical narratives in particular, serve as the main tool in the process of (re-)configuring the Ukrainian national space within the country's current political borders. The author asks how the national paradigm in this case confronts the Soviet paradigm in terms of producing different meanings of Ukrainian geopolitical identity. The chapter also investigates how Ukrainian regions with different historical experiences are being integrated into a single national narrative. In order to answer these questions, one needs to examine, among other things, how historical arguments are being used in the process of constructing Ukrainian symbolical borders as well as internal regional fault-lines. Thus far, Ukraine has remained hostage to its 'fatal geography', conceived in terms of a West–East binary opposition. Paradoxically enough, the author emphasises that it is precisely the Soviet historical and cultural legacy that serves Ukraine's internal political stability within its current borders. From that viewpoint, Ukraine's Soviet history is today counterpoised by its European geography.

Octavian Țîcu continues the discussion on the formation of post-Soviet borders by addressing questions related to Moldova's spatial imaginary and territorial integrity. The territory of the Republic of Moldova never formed an independent political entity until 1991; its historical fate was inextricably linked to that of the Romanian Principalities, the Ottoman Empire, the Russian Empire, Romania and more recently the Soviet Union, and its position was always a peripheral one. These territorial and political fluctuations have strongly affected the evolution and stability of Moldova in the twentieth century, and especially since 1991. Changes in the geographical and political landscape have often been portrayed as a constant shift from West to East and back. However, the clash over this territory can in fact be understood as a very specific form of nation-building based on the Soviet nationalities policies and the geopolitical confrontation between Romanian nationalism, which wanted to 'return home' its lost children, and Russian or Soviet imperialism, driven by geopolitical strategies to control Moldova. This complicated setting has left a particular legacy with regard to the current political and national physiognomy of the Republic of Moldova.

At least three different perspectives can be identified in approaching the issue of borders in the Republic of Moldova; all three have their supporters in politics, academia, the media, among NGOs and within society as a whole. The first has a Romanian orientation and essentially interprets the Republic of Moldova as a second Romanian state. The second strand is one of Moldovan nation-building and was formed during the interwar period by Soviet ideology and propaganda. This narrative gained consistency in the postwar period, when it became the official party line in both the Soviet Union and the Moldovan SSR. The third perspective on the issue of borders and the Moldovan state as a whole comes from the eastern part of Moldova (Transnistria), where a consistent majority of Russians live and consider themselves an integral part of the Russian political and cultural world. The chapter aims to address these tendencies historically and to determine the ways in which they presently and potentially influence issues of spatial imaginary and territorial integrity of the Republic of Moldova.

In the final chapter of this part, *Olga Filippova* develops a detailed analysis of different (re-)conceptualisations of borders in post-Soviet Ukraine. Filippova investigates the means by which borders in post-Soviet Ukraine have been reframed in the political and wider social debate and how they have been institutionalised in terms of border management, migration and cooperation with neighbouring states. Her examination refers to three dimensions: the reconsideration and reorganisation of Ukrainian borders as a reflection of EU policies and conditionality; the reframing of post-Soviet space and the reorganisation(s) of the borders in accordance with the views of the Ukrainian government and various other political actors; and the rethinking of border issues and the reconceptualisation of Ukrainian borders in terms of academic reflections. These different dimensions of thinking Ukrainian borders reflect the difficulties of Ukrainian nation-building in the post-Soviet context but also the complexities of Ukraine's attempts at greater regional cooperation with its Russian and EU neighbours.

Part Two: border management and cross-border cooperation

James W. Scott opens this section of the book with a contribution that develops a critical geopolitical perspective on the EU's external policies. Scott addresses tensions between idealistic notions of a progressive EU exceptionalism, political concepts of regional cooperation and partnership and more realist practices of securitisation and exclusion. The concrete focus is on the bordering effects of the EU's Neighbourhood Policy, and the Eastern Partnership in particular, as reflected in the perceptions of civil society actors in Ukraine and Belarus. One significant local perception of the Eastern Partnership is that of a buffer-zone policy for a territory situated between Core Europe and the geographically shifting Russian sphere of influence – a policy that extends the EU's political influence eastwards without providing commensurate concessions to neighbouring states. The EU has in fact received much attention as a promoter of new border-management techniques and restrictive migration policies that, while ostensibly targeted at third-country nationals, have had an impact on domestic debates on immigration, for example in Moldova and Ukraine. As the author claims, if the EU takes its political identity as a *force for good in the world* seriously, it should invest more political and social capital in promoting civil-society dialogue as a means to enhance regional cooperation.

The next chapter, by *Joni Virkkunen* and *Paul Fryer*, discusses border management and migration issues along the border between Tajikistan and Kyrgyzstan. In post-Soviet Central Asia, the demarcation and delimitation of borders inherited from Soviet times is a still ongoing process. The Ferghana Valley, one of the most densely populated and resource-scarce areas in the region, has the highest concentration of contested borders in the post-Soviet space and, as such, is one of the main sources of political instability. In this contribution, the southern border of the Ferghana Valley between Tajikistan's Sughd and Kyrgyzstan's Batken provinces is examined through the lens of border management. Although a joint border commission has been looking into the issue for a decade, no border agreement has been reached, a situation that has been contributing to feelings of marginalisation, insecurity and hostility amongst local communities on both sides of the border. The chapter focuses on the local phenomenon of creeping migration as an example of both states' questionable policies towards border management. Such migration is highly contested as it is generally identified with the illegal settling of Tajiks on Kyrgyz territory. Given such problematic issues, how do local inhabitants want to see border management implemented? How can the border be demarcated and delimited without restricting essential cross-border movements and communications that have existed in the area for centuries?

In her chapter, *Anaïs Marin* takes us to another post-Soviet context, that of the geopolitical situation of Belarus, and its ramifications for cross-border cooperation. Marin argues that Belarus's *borderscapes* are extremely dichotomous. On the one hand, Belarus's eastern border with Russia is virtually non-existent because of interconnections dating from the Soviet period and ongoing integration within the Eurasian Economic Space. By contrast, the borders with its EU neighbours – Poland, Lithuania and Latvia – can be seen as *borders of exclusion*. Several factors hamper the potential for CBC across these borders: historical enmities, Belarus's centralised territorial administration, lack of infrastructure, limited political dialogue and mutually constructed *bordering* practices on the part of Schengen countries and the Belarusian regime alike. Despite such unfavourable conditions, CBC has developed over the past years within the framework of four Euroregions and two European Neighbourhood and Partnership Instrument CBC programmes in which Belarus is participating. The chapter aims to analyse and compare the extent of this involvement, with a focus on the most consensual field for cooperation: the development of cross-border ecotourism.

Part Three: migration policies

Tiina Sotkasiira introduces this part with a discussion of migration issues as they relate to Europe's new borderland neighbourhood and efforts on the

EU's part to achieve political and social stability in the region. Her contribution provides an overview of policies that the EU has set up to manage migration and mobility in the Eastern Neighbourhood, and contrasts the migration-management approach of the European Union with the tendency towards a securitisation of migration, now prevalent not only in the EU but recurrently so in its eastern neighbourhood. To explain these contradictory developments, Sotkasiira reflects on the question how migration is articulated as a concern in the public debate of each region. The Eastern Neighbourhood is a geo-graphically broad region with a history of migrations and shifting political borders. Its diversity presents a challenge to the EU, which pushes for a common migration and asylum policy within the framework of the Eastern Neighbourhood.

Sergei Riazantsev's chapter discusses conceptual changes in recent Russian migration policies. In June 2012, President Vladimir Putin introduced a new approach to migration policy, which for the first time recognised migration not only as a risk, but also as a potential resource for Russia's development. However, this new concept of migration is subject to a number of contra-dictions and controversies. Thus, it does not address major issues such as problems related to emigration from Russia. It furthermore remains unclear whether or not this new policy concept can successfully transform Russia's rigid, inadequate and outdated migration regime. Modernisation in this sense would involve the development of an appropriate migration infrastructure, reduce corruption and put an end to the arbitrary treatment of migrants by the police and the administration. The chapter analyses these differences and suggests further ways to improve Russia's migration policy.

In her contribution, *Larissa Titarenko* raises a number of provocative issues with regard to Belarus and its migratory relationship with Russia and the European Union. According to official statistics, labour migration from Belarus to Russia is rather insignificant. However, independent experts and international organisations have estimated that Belarus is a country of origin for hundreds of thousands of migrants going both East and West, with roughly half a million of Belarusian temporary labour migrants working in Russia. As both countries are part of a customs union, Belarusian citizens face no legal restrictions if they wish to work in the Russian Federation. While the latter benefits from Belarusian migrant workers, this flow has in recent years started to raise con-cerns in Belarus about national labour shortages, especially in the agricultural and construction sectors.

Titarenko's chapter also provides a background to the complicated relation-ship between the EU and Belarus in the field of migration policy. She outlines recent developments in migration processes by examining migratory flows in and out of Belarus, with the focus on migration to the Russian Federation and the European Union. The chapter places the discussion on migration in the general framework of EU–Belarus cooperation and examines how factors external to migration come into play in defining the objectives of migration policies. The author argues that both Belarus and the European Union should adopt a more realistic approach for their migration policies. Belarus does not have readmission agreements and does not interact with the EU on a level sufficient for improving regional security and cooperation on border regulation and migration issues. The EU might contribute to solving the outlined problems by reconceptualising its attitude towards Belarus from one characterised by external governance to one of partnership.

Paul Fryer, Joni Virkkunen and *Furugzod Usmonov* end this section by discussing risks involved in migration from Central Asia to Russia. During the twenty years following the collapse of the Soviet Union, the phenomenon of international labour migration of citizens of the Central Asian states to the Russian Federation has been well documented and researched. Governments in the region not only accept this migration, but also encourage it as a strategy to increase their citizens' incomes in light of inadequate domestic employment opportunities. But this migration does not come without risks and pitfalls; over the years migrants have been subjected to trafficking, exploitation, poor working conditions and violence in host countries. At the same time, their home countries remain poorly developed and economically weak despite remittances, while family disruption has led to social problems. In this chapter, the international labour migration of Tajik citizens is examined from the perspective of migrants and their families. Why do Tajiks continue to send their family members abroad in full knowledge of the potential problems in Russia? Why is migration accepted as a cultural norm? Is it questioned at all? This chapter includes results from a small survey conducted amongst locals in Sughd province.

Part Four: migration and the everyday

The contribution by *Olga Tkach* and *Olga Brednikova* presents a practice-oriented case study of Russian migration policy in St Petersburg. It aims to show how the city administration has dealt with low-skilled labour immigrants arriving in Russia from post-Soviet states under a visa-free regime. The chapter provides a brief overview of migration policy in Russia since 2007; the authors indicate the main trends of this policy, the new migrant statuses that it has created, and the rules and regulations it has generated. It also deals with the main principles of administrative work with migrants on the regional level. Techniques of migration governance such as *barrier logics*, the principle of *total control*, the avoidance of face-to-face interaction with migrants, the treatment of migrants as guest workers and their social isolation are examined in some detail. The techniques mentioned reflect both processes of migration management and integration from above. These assertions are supported by empirical examples from research carried out by the authors within the framework of the project 'Labour Migrants in St Petersburg: Social Problems and Policy Recommendations' commissioned by the Russian Red Cross. The final part of this chapter focuses on the daily life of migrants and the problems they face in the fields of health care, housing and language. The authors demonstrate how various agents of integration act at the city level: locals, including employers, NGOs and grassroots initiatives, as well as migrants' networks that are evidence of a new consciousness of legal migrants and still weak attempts at organising themselves (e.g. trade unions). In concluding, Tkach and Brednikova conceptualise how governmentality works in the Russian migratory context. They argue that the Russian state monopolises all mechanisms of control and integration, while civil society and individuals work to compensate and overcome barriers and circumstances produced by the authorities.

In his contribution *Sergey Rumyantsev* analyses post-Soviet Azerbaijan's official attitudes towards circular migration and what can be termed *immigrant transnationalism*. Political elites as well as independent experts and academic communities in post-Soviet countries often pin hopes of change on students and young professionals with an education or working experience obtained abroad. The Azerbaijani government has adopted an ambitious plan for the years 2007 to 2015 to help students acquire higher education in EU countries. There, the expectation is that the experience of living abroad will give the younger generation the will and ability to create new conditions in their home countries that will lead to gradual changes in favour of democratisation processes. Rumyantsev provides a more nuanced understanding of educational migration from Azerbaijan to Russia, the EU and the United States. His analysis seeks to discover how the educational policies of Azerbaijan and the receiving states reconstruct the historical division between East and West. Rumyantsev then contrasts these essentialist discourses with the experiences and views of Azerbaijanis who have studied or are studying abroad. He places his empirical findings in an analytical field of postcoloniality, arguing that the opinions expressed by these (former) students largely reproduce the civilisational divide that has prevailed in Azerbaijani society already in Soviet times.

Amongst the post-Soviet countries, Ukraine and Moldova have much in common regarding migration. One of the recognised problems is the labour migration of their citizens to EU countries and to Russia. As *Olga Davydova-Minguet, Valeriu Mosneaga* and *Oleksii Pozniak* show, these migration flows have a strongly pronounced gendered character. In this chapter, recent migration tendencies in both countries are portrayed and analysed. Up-to-date statistical information about migration is used to contextualise the argument about gendered migration. In addition, the employment spheres of female migrants in targeted EU countries are discussed from the point of view of the structural organisation of care (models of the welfare state). In the target countries (Italy, Spain, Portugal and Greece) female labour is mostly used in the spheres of the organisation of elderly and child care. In classical conceptualisations of welfare-state regimes, three models are seen as ideal-types: the Scandinavian or social-democratic one, the liberal and the conservative. The so-called Latin Rim model is also discussed. Within these classifications the roles of the state, the market and the family as care providers differ significantly. Female labour migration of Ukrainians and Moldovans is targeted mostly at countries with conservative or Latin Rim types of organising care.

Therefore, the interconnectedness of female migrant labour and different types of welfare states and organisation of care needs to be acknowledged. The chapter brings to the fore the controversial character and outcomes of gendered migration not only at the source but also in target countries. It asks if a common EU welfare policy could contribute to alleviate some of the negative social effects of female labour migration from these two countries.

This discussion is followed by *Ihor Markov*'s study of the specificities of Ukrainian migration movements to EU countries and of the main factors that impact the elaboration of migration policies in the context of EU–Ukraine relations. In doing this the author also addresses problems related to the evolution of migration patterns during the past twenty years as well as changes in the forms of social life and the functioning of Ukrainian labour-migrant networks in both the EU and their home country. By analysing these issues, Markov examines several key factors that currently shape the process of migration between the EU and Ukraine as well as their migration policies. A central aspect of this contribution is its focus on networks of Ukrainian migrant workers. Particular attention is given to the transformation of the mobility space formed in recent decades. Markov shows that each successive generation of Ukrainian migrants has its own specificities in terms of cultural identity and geographic orientation, and also makes a different use of contemporary information and communication technologies. As in the case of the historically older Ukrainian diaspora, the formation of new communities of Ukrainian immigrants in EU countries takes place through self-organisation, with very limited, often only rhetorical support and sometimes hostility from the Ukrainian state. Cultural affinity and mental proximity appear to facilitate a relatively quick integration of Ukrainian immigrants into the socio-cultural space of the EU. On the other hand, the modern Ukrainian migrant is characterised by an attachment to Ukrainian everyday life: this involves constant contact with family life in Ukraine, an awareness of the economic conditions there and close attention to political, artistic and other events. In addition, Markov argues that Ukraine's migration policies are virtually non-existent, given that the country lacks: first, a strategic vision of the migratory processes and their regulation; second, the necessary legislative support to implement a migration policy as well as standards that define the legal status and rights of Ukrainian migrant workers and their families; and, third, specialised institutions that could perform a full range of administrative functions in the field of migration. As far as the EU is concerned, he pleads in favour of a greater liberalisation of migration policies and emphasises the strong need for a more decisive coordination and harmonisation of migration rules with Ukraine and other countries. In a wider sense, Markov suggests that a new migration policy model could be an important contribution to the development of more meaningful neighbourhood relations.

Conclusions: the future of Wider Europe

By way of conclusion, *Ilkka Liikanen, James W. Scott* and *Tiina Sotkasiira*, the volume's editors, summarise the arguments put forward in the previous chapters and analyse them through the lens of EU member state policies. Building on the experience of the Wider Europe Initiative of the Finnish Ministry for Foreign Affairs, they aim to provide a synthesis of insights that notably takes into account how member states and neighbouring countries perceive the role of the EU as a politically relevant actor in regional post-Soviet contexts. They discuss the ambitious policy goals set in the EU's Wider Europe document with regard to borders and migration and review these in relation to concrete outcomes at various locations. This will, on the one hand, serve to identify new, relevant research questions. On the other hand, it is vital to discuss the benefits and possible limitations of a wider European approach in this complex field of migration and border politics – and to ask if there is still a future for Wider Europe.

Acknowledgements

Finally, we would like to express our gratitude to all our contributors and those who helped us in putting this book together. We specifically thank the Ministry of Foreign Affairs of Finland for financing our research and thus enabling the cooperation upon which this publication is based. In addition, research was supported by the EUBORDERSCAPES (contract: SSH-2011-1-290775) and EUBORDERREGIONS (contract: SSH-2010-2.2.1-266920) projects, financed by European Union's Seventh Framework Programme for Research and Technological Development. We furthermore would like to thank our consortium partners, the Tampere Peace Research Institute (TAPRI) and the Aleksanteri Institute of Helsinki University, who provided valuable feedback for the development and refinement of our research. Thanks are also due to our colleagues at the Karelian Institute, especially Tatjana Lipiäinen and Lea Kervinen, for their active assistance in crafting the manuscript, and to our copy-editor Rupert Hasterok for his tireless efforts.

Note

1   Wider Europe in this context refers to the following Eastern European and Central Asian countries: Armenia, Azerbaijan, Belarus, Georgia, Kyrgyzstan, Kazakhstan, Moldova, the Russian Federation, Tajikistan, Turkmenistan, Ukraine and Uzbekistan. Although not officially part of the Wider Europe Initiative, the Russian Federation has been included in the present examination because of its key role in the migration and bordering practices and policies of the region.

Part One

Renegotiating borders in the post-Soviet space

1 Building regional stability through cross-border cooperation

Changing spatial imaginaries and sovereignty concepts of EU neighbourhood policies

Ilkka Liikanen

Ten years after the initiation of the European Neighbourhood Policy (ENP), the relations of the European Union with its eastern neighbours are more complicated and tense than ever. In the midst of the Ukrainian crisis it is time to look back and assess to what extent the European Union has managed to fulfil the great expectations raised by a policy that profiled the Union as an international actor. In the political rhetoric of 2004, the EU was, in the boldest visions, referred to as a force for good in the world and in more practical accounts of policy tasks as an advocate of regional stability in the European neighbourhood. Since the collapse of the Soviet Union, the will and ability of the European Union to promote peace and stability beyond its borders has been the object of intensive debates and visionary theorising. In discussions on the post-Cold War international order, the EU has been regarded as a new kind of international actor that, instead of using military force, is building its external relations on normative soft power (see, among others, Manners 2002). Instead of securitised notions of territorial integrity typical of the Cold War era, the EU has based its policies on programmes of territorial cooperation designed to create stability both within and beyond its boundaries (Scott 2005: 429–454; Telo 2005).

Through its policies of cross-border cooperation (CBC) the EU has, indeed, been actively engaged in spreading its influence beyond its external borders. On the one hand, it has promoted new spatial imagery of shared Europeanness or a common European Neighbourhood that goes beyond the geopolitical dividing lines and frigid national policy frames typical of the so-called Westphalian international order of the Cold War period. On the other hand, as part of its cross-border cooperation policies, the EU has adopted, and encouraged its neighbours to adopt, new thinking modes that diverge from traditional conceptions of sovereignty in terms of national interests and territorial integrity. Parallel to constructing internal supranational administrative structures, the EU has generated new practices of *shared* or *pooled sovereignty*. In its external relations, it has developed new sovereignty-challenging practices that have sometimes been seen as an opening towards a new era

DOI: 10.4324/9781315858036-3

of *post-sovereignty* (for a critical summary of this discussion, see Haukkala 2010). This type of visionary theorising on EU policies has not been limited to academic literature but can also be recognised in the political discussion that has schematised the EU as a peace project, most notably in connection with the granting of the Nobel Peace Prize to the European Union in 2012.

This chapter studies the role of the EU as an international actor by analysing the spatial imageries and sovereignty concepts applied in EU policies of CBC. It attempts to identify what kind of place-making (and *othering*) strategies have been attached to EU policies of regional cooperation, especially in relation to its eastern neighbours. The analysis is built on a close reading of the EU's CBC programmes, from the early INTERREG programmes to documents of the ENP and present-day formulations of common foreign and security policies. The focus of the study is on the sovereignty concepts that have been attached to the shifting spatial imageries of defining Europe and European neighbourhood.

What notions of pooled or shared sovereignty were attached to the first INTERREG programmes when the European Community was elaborating policies of CBC on its internal borders in the late 1980s? How and to what degree were these concepts later modified in documents defining the tasks of EU policies of pre-enlargement and the role of the EU in post-enlargement Wider Europe? Is it possible to uncover certain path dependencies or competing rationales, especially with regard to the Union's relationship with its Eastern Neighbourhood? How consistent has the formulation of EU policies been in this respect? By examining the coexistence and clash of novel sovereignty discourses (sometimes referred to as post-sovereignty) and the traditional geopolitical rhetoric of territorial integrity, this chapter attempts to critically comment on and contribute to the broader discussion on the role of the EU as a new kind of international actor and as a promoter of regional stability beyond its borders.

Shifting sovereignty concepts of making Europe and the European Neighbourhood

Through its cross-border cooperation programmes, the European Union has been actively engaged in reconfiguring borders in its immediate neighbourhood. Along and beyond its external boundaries, it has advanced shared European cooperation agendas that target political and social modernisation and convergence to EU norms. In the scholarly literature on post-Cold War international relations, EU programmes of CBC have often been seen as a key element in the shaping of a new type of normative, value-based foreign policies (see, for example, Bachmann and Sidaway 2009: 94–109). In contrast to military security-dominated Cold War policies, EU programmes of cross-border cooperation have been said to represent new (for some, postmodern) security thinking seeking to exercise soft or normative power calibrated to the new post-Westphalian realities. Emphasis on common Europeanness has been held to signify an alternative policy frame in which national borders and their integrity no longer are at the centre of international relations. Similarly, the introduction of the notion of a European Neighbourhood can be viewed as an alternative perspective to building clear-cut dividing lines between power blocs and civilisations in the sense of the traditional East–West juxtaposition (Browning and Joenniemi 2008: 519–551; Joenniemi 2008). In the study of EU–Russia relations this approach has sometimes been characterised as policies of post-sovereignty or as sovereignty-challenging practices. Lately, the main line of argument has been to set off EU policies of post-sovereignty against more traditional Russian policies that are thought to emphasise territorial sovereignty in a sense typical of a (bygone) Westphalian period (Barbé and Johannson-Nogués 2008: 81–96; Haukkala 2010; Kostadinova 2009: 235–255).

From the perspective of future-oriented policy analysis, such models, bound to certain time periods (Westphalian vs post-Westphalian), can in many instances hide as much as they reveal. Indeed, there is an obvious need for more nuanced approaches to EU policies and the relationship between cross-border cooperation and the broader architecture of international relations. Today, it is evident that parallel to its neighbourhood policies the EU has at the same time been developing a territorially fixed security area that aims, amongst other things, at stopping undocumented immigration and addressing other perceived threats through military potential provided by NATO. Clearly, these objectives are in themselves partly contradictory; they contain both elements of potential regional partnerships and exclusionary or discriminatory aspects. In terms of spatial imagery and sovereignty, it is obvious that the European Neighbourhood Policy is not just an implementation of post-Westphalian notions of post-sovereignty.

With regard to the elaboration of EU common foreign and security policies, scholars have questioned the one-dimensional models of normative soft power and traditional hard power and stressed the need for more sophisticated approaches to the relationship between cross-border cooperation and the broader architecture of international relations. In more nuanced terms, it has been asked whether normative policies can primarily represent an unequivocal new type of soft power and whether the tightened conditionality of the EU's normative policies actually comes close to traditional policies of regional hegemony (Haukkala 2009: 1757–1775; Jones and Clark 2008: 1–27; Kochenov 2008; Sasse 2008: 295–316; Scott and Liikanen 2011: 1–16).

In the case of the post-Soviet space it has been noted that actions undertaken by a neighbour, such as Russia's self-exclusion from the ENP, can easily reinforce the conditionality of EU policies in the name of shared European values. This has created competing joint agendas between ex-Soviet states and other relevant actors; indirectly, EU normative policies of cross-border cooperation have placed post-Soviet countries in a situation where there is an obvious tension between the attractions of the ENP and traditional cooperation with Russia (Averre 2011; Haukkala 2008a: 38). The 2014 Ukrainian crisis can partly be read as an ultimate expression of this tension.

However, this is not to say that the development should be characterised as a return to Cold War security-driven policies. As Derek Averre has noted, there are not just competing rationales behind the EU's normative policies and Russia's approach of territorial sovereignty but behind the EU policies themselves; tensions between elements of normative and structural power exist in the relations of both powers with the countries in their neighbourhood (Averre 2011: 5–29).

In this sense, the boundaries between traditional hard power and normative soft power are fuzzier than anticipated in the discussion about shared European values and common European neighbourhood policies, and the conception of the EU as a normative power can in many ways be contested. The distinct national preferences of (big) EU member states alone mean that the idea of the EU playing a new kind of role in international relations should be regarded with a lot of caution. Furthermore, EU external relations encompass a wide range of financial, legal, regulatory and environmental policies which go beyond classical foreign policy and are linked to various internal EU policy agendas and rationales (Averre 2011: 7). When considering EU programmes of CBC as tools of regional stability it is thus necessary to keep an eye on these competing rationales embedded in EU policies of external relations and especially in their relation to NATO. More importantly, the notion of competing rationales should also be extended to the long-term configuration of EU policies of CBC. The context and goal-setting of these policies have varied from internal economic and social cohesion to enlargement and pre-integration and finally to deepening institutional integration and the constitution of the political union of the Lisbon Treaty. In order to evaluate the role of the European Union as a new kind of international actor in relation to its neighbours, one obviously needs to analyse in detail what discursive layers can be recognised in the development of EU policies of CBC and what place-making strategies and sovereignty concepts are linked to these competing rationales: To what degree do EU documents of CBC reflect the post-Cold War perspectives of political innovation in international relations and the new constructivist approaches in academic discussions?

INTERREG: CBC as a tool of apolitical cohesion policies of the European Community

Roots of the common European CBC policies can be found in the so-called INTERREG initiative, designed in the late 1980s to stimulate cooperation between regions of the European Community. The first INTERREG programme (1989–1993) was financed through the European Regional Development Fund (ERDF) and was later continued as INTERREG II (1994–1999) and INTERREG III (2000–2006). The first INTERREG programme documents aimed at diminishing the influence of national borders in favour of an equal economic, social and cultural development of the entire territory of the European Community. In the Technical Fiche of INTERREG I, the main aim of the programme was defined as 'preparing the border areas for the opening of the Single Market, with an eye to the economic and social cohesion of the European Community' (European Communities 1990: 1). This was to be achieved by measures that exclusively concerned social and economic cohesion: (a) helping these regions to overcome problems arising from their isolation from the main economic and decision-making centres; (b) promoting administrative collaboration and the development of cooperation networks on both sides of internal borders as well as establishing links between these networks and wider Community networks; and (c) preparing external border areas for their new role in this integrated market by exploring possibilities for cooperation with third countries (European Communities 1990: 1). It is important to note that in the initial phase of EU common cross-border cooperation policies, even the measures concerning external border areas and third countries were targeted at promoting adjustment to internal integrated markets – a target quite far from the visions of a new kind of international order.

In a broad sense, this emphasis remained until the end of the INTERREG programme periods. This vein can be recognised even in the 2001 Communication of the Commission on INTERREG III, which defines its primary starting point by stating that 'the objective of interregional cooperation ... is to improve the effectiveness of policies and instruments for regional development and cohesion (European Commission 2001a: 1). This time the task of interregional cooperation is, however, explicitly broadened to include third countries:

> The Commission considers that interregional cooperation offers an additional dimension to the field of cooperation activity over and above that provided by cross-border and transnational programmes. It allows non-contiguous regions to enter into contact and to build up relationships, leading to exchanges of experience and networking which will assist the balanced, harmonious and sustainable development of the European Union and of third countries.
>
> (European Commission 2001a: 1)

During the whole INTERREG period, CBC along the external borders of the Union was mainly conceptualised in a similar manner, that is, in terms of regional development and cohesion policies. The 2001 Communication defined the main aim and added value of interregional cooperation as 'improving the effectiveness of policies and instruments for regional development and cohesion' (European Commission 2001a: 1). Typical for the Commission's documents was that they used an 'apolitical' language of regional planning which tended to bypass questions of sovereignty and to naturalise a liberal understanding of economic development. In terms of spatial imaginaries, the Europe of these documents referred primarily to the EU. At the turn of the new millennium, the preparation of the INTERREG III programme broadened the agenda and introduced tasks that were more closely connected to policies of pre-enlargement:

The overall aim of the INTERREG initiatives has been, and remains that national borders should not be a barrier to the balanced development and integration of the European territory. The isolation of border areas has been of a double nature: on the one hand, the presence of borders cuts off border communities from each other economically, socially and culturally and hinders the coherent management of eco-systems; on the other, border areas have often been neglected under national policy, with the result that their economies have tended to become peripheral within national boundaries. The single market and EMU are strong catalysts for changing this situation. Nevertheless, the scope for strengthening cooperation to the mutual advantage of border areas throughout the Community remains enormous. The challenge is all the greater when the future enlargement of the Community is considered, as this will increase the number of its internal borders and, progressively, shift the Community's external borders eastwards.

(European Commission 2004a: 23)

Targeted more specifically to address problems of the Union's external borders, the Communication from the Commission to member states on 28 April 2000 defined guidelines for a Community Initiative concerning trans-European cooperation intended to encourage the harmonious and balanced development of 'European territory'. It demanded effective coordination between INTERREG III and external community policy instruments, especially with a view to enlargement. Similarly, INTERREG III's General Principles, defined at the Cohesion Forum held in Brussels in May 2001, explicitly included in its task of 'economic and social cohesion' 'balanced and sustainable development of European territory' and 'territorial integration with candidate and other neighbouring countries'.

In terms of place-making strategies the first INTERREG programme clearly views the European Community as Europe. CBC and cohesion policies are discussed in a shared European frame but common Europeanness is above all emphasised in the context of building a stronger European Community understood in apolitical terms as a frame for economic progress and regional development. The same apolitical approach is typical of the sovereignty concept that can be recognised in the documents – if the question was raised at all. A certain internal sharing or pooling of sovereignty was evidently accepted as part of the goals of promoting regional development and cohesion. This apolitical approach, originally calibrated for internal development, was later – and without any deeper discussion – adopted for planning new programmes concerning the external borders. The question what kind of sovereignty concept this approach represented in regard to the broader architecture of international relations or EU–Russia relations was never raised in the policy documents. Nor did the first INTERREG programmes discuss how this apolitical approach to economic cohesion might fit in with the post-colonial features of developments in the prospective new eastern neighbour states of the Union: Belarus, Moldova, Russia and Ukraine.

INTERREG III: CBC as a tool of enlargement – and transition

During the INTERREG III programme period, the documents governing CBC came to reflect a rather clear pre-enlargement agenda. Under the title *Structural Policies and European Territory: Cooperation without Frontiers*, the Commission published in 2002 a brochure that explicitly defined preparations for the enlargement as the primary goal of CBC by stating that aid to Central and East European countries (CEEC) and regions bordering the Union was 'providing them with a real opportunity to become acquainted with the methods and rules of Community programming'. The brochure also referred to the task of deepening integration of the so-called candidate countries by advocating accelerated preparations for post-enlargement programmes of cross-border cooperation and regional development (European Commission 2002).

It was understood early on that the planned 2004 enlargement would create a completely different setting for cooperation across the new external borders of the Union. After the accession of Finland in 1995, the EU had come to share a border with the Russian Federation and initial cross-border cooperation programmes had been started and received rather positively on the Russian side, especially on the regional level (Liikanen and Virtanen 2006: 113–130). Now, there would be new neighbours and, with the Baltic countries seeking membership of both EU and NATO, a neighbouring Russia that might no longer have a positive attitude towards cross-border relations. This setting called for action to create better preconditions for effective cooperation on the external borders, e.g. in terms of coordination between INTERREG programmes and the EU Technical Aid Programme for Countries of the ex-Soviet Union (TACIS). In 2001 the European Commission published *A Guide to Bringing INTERREG and TACIS Funding Together*, a booklet which rather enthusiastically re-assessed the tasks of CBC on external borders:

> This guide reflects our joint determination to ensure that cross-border cooperation with Russia is a success today. ... At the cross-border level between the EU and CIS countries, the ultimate aim is to create new opportunities for the population living in border areas, to promote the spirit of cooperation and to foster trust between the authorities on each side of the border. At the wider regional level (i.e. the Baltic region), there is a need to promote interstate and interregional cooperation with a view to assisting the development of the Northern Dimension and moving towards enlargement.
>
> (European Commission, 2001b: 3, 5)

With TACIS CBC, a new programme was designed to offer support to partner states undergoing transition. At this point the EU officially set as its goal to accelerate the transformation process in partner states through their cooperation with border regions in the European Union or CEEC. This could be seen as a starting point for giving CBC policies new tasks aimed at influencing domestic developments in neighbouring countries – not just the prospective member states but also neighbouring states that had joined the new CIS. In this sense TACIS CBC meant introducing a new kind of sovereignty thinking that linked the old aid programme to EU-defined goals of the INTERREG programme:

> Objective: TACIS CBC is one of the multi-country programmes of TACIS and covers four partner states: Belarus, Moldova, Russia and the Ukraine. The TACIS regulation defines the purpose of cross-border cooperation as:
>
> – assisting border regions in overcoming their specific development problems;
> – encouraging the linking of networks on both sides of the border, e.g. border-crossing facilities;
> – *accelerating the transformation process in the partner States through their cooperation with border regions in the European Union or Central and Eastern Europe;*
> – reducing trans-boundary environmental risks and pollution.
>
> (Council of the European Union 1999, Article 2.
> Emphasis added)

Ultimately, the coordination of CBC policies and the nascent policies for external relations was given a more systematic formulation in the major policy document *Wider Europe – Neighbourhood: A New Framework for Relations with our Eastern and Southern Neighbours* (European Commission 2003). The document laid the foundations for the reconfiguration of EU CBC programmes in more ideological tones than in the case of the administrative streamlining of INTERREG and TACIS. Summarily, it defined the main goals of policies towards the EU's post-enlargement neighbourhood. The Union was to avoid drawing new dividing lines in Europe and, instead, to commit itself to promoting stability and prosperity 'within and beyond its new borders'. Furthermore, it was to develop a zone of prosperity and a friendly neighbourhood (a 'ring of friends') with whom the EU would enjoy close, peaceful and cooperative relations. In addition, Russia, the three western newly independent states (Belarus, Moldova and Ukraine) and the Southern Mediterranean countries were offered the prospect of a stake in the EU's Internal Market. This was to be accompanied by 'further integration and liberalisation to promote the free movement of persons, goods, services and capital', also known as the four freedoms (European Commission 2003: 4, 12).

In this sense, *Wider Europe* continued the reconfiguration of new sovereignty-challenging principles that had started already a year earlier at the Copenhagen European Council, which had decided that the Union should take the opportunity offered by enlargement to enhance relations with its neighbours on the basis of 'shared values' (Council of the European Union 2002). Behind this alignment of EU policies, it is possible to recognise a logic that is crystallised in the concept of transition, commonly used at the time to designate post-Soviet change. The concept promotes the idea of a clear-cut shift in social organisation towards a goal known in advance: from communism to capitalism, from totalitarianism towards a Western model of political democracy (Neumann 1996; Prozorov 2006). EU programmes of CBC were thus tied to a goal of promoting a particular pre-given economic model beyond its boundaries. The Wider Europe that the EU was building was consequently comprised not only of the candidate countries but also of Russia and the neighbouring ex-Soviet states, at least as far as they were progressing on the path of transition. In terms of spatial imaginary, a new vision of a Wider Europe, a shared European space of cooperation, was initiated – but not without conditions.

Wider Europe describes an emerging hegemonic political project, an EU striving for the redefinition of both its external political agenda and the territorial frames of its policies. It is possible to discern here conceptual shifts and political innovation both in terms of territorial imagination and new sovereignty conceptions. There is a strong vision of shared European neighbourhood as a frame for a new kind of policies of regional cooperation. The transition logic-based conditionality was, however, still present, though in a new form. According to the new programme rhetoric, the EU saw itself as the force for good in a world where other players were stuck in old notions of territorial sovereignty and integrity. The new language of common Europeanness introduced the notion of shared European norms and values which in hindsight can well be recognised as tools of pre-enlargement and an identity-political project of a hegemonic EU at the height of its appeal to the neighbouring post-communist countries.

European Neighbourhood policy: CBC as a frame of pooled sovereignty and soft power

Preparations for the accession of ten new member states initially led to the drafting of new regional cross-border programmes and amendments to upgrade the existing programmes to include the candidate countries. The primary aim at this point was to coordinate INTERREG with the instruments for accession and programmes concerning third countries, i.e. TACIS, PHARE and CARDS (see, for example, European Commission 2004b). This practical task should, however, be placed in the context of a broader reconfiguration of EU policies of external relations. With *Wider Europe*, the idea of the EU as a new type of security community using normative or soft power was officially added to the rhetoric of EU documents. This was reflected, for instance, in the objective of avoiding drawing new dividing lines in Europe and promoting stability and prosperity 'within and beyond the new borders of the Union'. The document was based on the idea that interaction could itself be a means to promote stability, security and sustainable development (European Commission 2003: 4). These formulations of *Wider Europe* can be understood as an important element in the broader discussion on building up the EU's policies of soft power as an alternative to securitised Cold War visions of conflict.

In the new rhetoric, institutional streamlining was accompanied by new notions of European values and conditionality which have since become important tools of EU external relations. Already, *Wider Europe* referred to the need of establishing a strong partnership based on historic links and common values expressed in earlier Partnership and Cooperation Agreements in effect with Russia, Ukraine and Moldova (European Commission 2003: 6). The idea of common values was, however, not only promoting place-making strategies of common European space but was from the beginning linked to the notion of conditionality: 'In return for concrete progress demonstrating shared values and effective implementation of political, economic and institutional reforms, including reforming legislation in line with the Acquis, the EU's neighbourhood should benefit from the prospect of closer economic integration with the EU' (European Commission 2003: 4). And:

> The setting of clear and public objectives and benchmarks spelling out the actions the EU expects of its partners is a means to ensure a consistent and credible approach between countries. Benchmarks also offer greater predictability and certainty for the partner countries than traditional "conditionality". Political and economic benchmarks could be used to evaluate progress in key areas of reform and against agreed targets. Beyond the regulatory and administrative aspects directly linked to market integration, key benchmarks should include the ratification and implementation of international commitments which demonstrate respect for shared values, in particular the values codified in the UN Human Rights Declaration, the OSCE [Organization for Security and Co-operation in Europe] and Council of Europe standards. Wherever possible, these benchmarks should be developed in close cooperation with the partner countries themselves, in order to ensure national ownership and commitment.
>
> (European Commission 2003: 16)

With the introduction of the European Neighbourhood Policy in 2004 this normative commitment to shared values was in practice adopted as a key element of EU policies of CBC (European Commission 2004e). The explanatory memorandum introducing the Commission's proposal on the European Neighbourhood and Partnership Instrument (ENPI) opens, however, rather prosaically with a reference to the Commission's earlier communication on financial perspectives (European Commission 2004c: 2). This blunt opening is well justified by the fact that the necessity of creating the new instrument was, indeed, first introduced in the Commission's communication *Building Our Common Future: Policy Challenges and Budgetary Means of the Enlarged Union 2007–2013* (European Commission 2004d), targeted at streamlining administration in the field of CBC. The Commission committed itself to adopting the principle, strongly highlighted in the text, of one instrument per policy area and one fund per programme. It stated that 'EU funding instruments will, as far as possible, be consolidated and rationalised so that *each policy area* responsible for operational expenditure has a *single funding instrument* covering the full range of its interventions' (European Commission 2004d: 30–32; original emphasis). A connection to the broader streamlining of the political architecture of the Union is set out by underlining the importance of developing an area of prosperity and close cooperation involving the European Union and the neighbouring countries 'as recognised in the draft Constitution' (European Commission 2004c: 2). Whereas the reference to the Constitution is here limited to a single sentence, it is more visible in the work of the so-called Peace Group, which first put forward the idea that the European Union's framework for external assistance should be rationalised and simplified by a reduction in the number of legal bases, budget lines and programmes. More precisely, it recommended that 'the complex structure of existing aid pro-grammes ... covering a wide range of interventions ... should be significantly streamlined' and that European Community and Member States policies and implementation should be harmonised' (European Commission 2004c: 39).

The European Neighbourhood Programme laid the groundwork for a pooling of sovereignty in EU policies of external relations for the coming years. In addition to defining a common policy frame, the objective was to create a single policy instrument. This task of administrative streamlining can be connected with the topical aim of consolidating EU administration that crystallised in the unsuccessful constitution project. In this sense, the elaboration of policies of neighbourhood and pooled sovereignty were intimately linked with the creation of the EU as a political union. The new spatial imagery of European neighbourhood had a sovereignty-challenging dimension in terms of external relations. At the same time, the conception of European neighbourhood was vital for the consolidation of the EU as a stronger international actor and it can even be interpreted as an attempt to institutionalise the hegemonic posi-tion that the EU enjoyed at the time (Liikanen and Virtanen 2006: 113–116; Liikanen 2013: 58–69).

In the 2007 review of the ENP, it was insisted that 'a motivating framework should be established, based on agreements with ENP countries which respect fundamental European values, are willing to integrate more closely with the EU and demonstrate objective performance in terms of ENP action plan implementation' (European Commission 2006a). With its emphasis on European values, the ENP constitutes perhaps the starting point for the institutional and discursive Europeanisation that has fuelled later discussions in the neighbouring countries about national sovereignty and territorial integrity (Scott and Liikanen 2011: 4–7). Obviously, the introduction of the concept of European Neighbourhood brought a new layer to the sovereignty-challenging policy definition of earlier CBC programmes. This neighbourhood was not only a frame for a certain type of economic development and interaction but an area of cooperation under EU normative soft power with conditional perspectives for collaboration based on EU-defined European or shared values.

Common foreign and security policy: post-sovereign responses to a changing European Neighbourhood?

With the Lisbon Treaty establishing the political union in 2009 and the formulation of EU common foreign policies, tasks of earlier CBC policies have been completed to a large extent. This has, however, not led to a thorough redefinition of the CBC policy frames, although individual documents signalling changes in the institutional architecture of EU common foreign policies have been published. A policy paper, 'A New Response to a Changing Neighbourhood. A Review of European Neighbourhood Policy', was published in spring 2011 as a Joint Communication by the High Representative of the Union for Foreign Affairs and Security Policy and the European Commission (European Commission 2011c). It provides a topical short-term analysis of the current state of the EU's external relations. Perhaps the most interesting fact is that this brief review also offers the first official account of the role of cross-border cooperation policies in the design of EU common policies for foreign affairs.

The document gives, however, a rather thin account of the connection between EU external relations and the promotion of regional and intraregional cooperation. This connection is taken as a self-evident starting point rather than an object of serious analysis. The paper concentrates on reviewing EU policies in the context of current topical events along the EU's eastern and southern borders. Important self-critical observations are made in regard to the application of CBC policy instruments as tools for promoting common foreign policy goals. These observations are, however, more a reaction to external impulses, most notably the Arab Spring, than a profound analysis of earlier programmes of regional and intraregional cooperation and their significance for the formulation of common foreign policies. In the assessment of the changes that occurred in the European neighbourhood, the specification of the ENP's tasks remains unrelated to broader discussions concerning the role of the EU as a foreign political actor:

> The new approach must be based on mutual accountability and a shared commitment to the universal values of human rights, democracy and the rule of law. It will involve a much higher level of differentiation allowing each partner country to develop its links with the EU as far as its own aspirations, needs and capacities allow. For those southern and eastern neighbours able and willing to take part, this vision includes closer economic integration and stronger political cooperation on governance reforms, security, conflict-resolution matters, including joint initiatives in international fora on issues of common interest.
>
> (European Commission 2011c: 2)

The European values that earlier might have been seen as part of a hegemonic ideological project are now described as universal or shared values. In this sense, they can perhaps better be understood as a foreign policy argumentation that different parties are individually expected to recognise than as part of place-making strategies of building a Wider Europe and common Europeanness. In addition, references to conditionality are now more naked, without appeals to shared European values. 'Increased EU support to its neighbours is conditional. It will depend on progress in building and consolidating democracy and respect for the rule of law. The more and the faster a country progresses in its internal reforms, the more support it will get from the EU' (European Commission 2011c: 3). Together with downgrading European values to tools of conditionality, spatial imageries and space-making strategies, too, are recalibrated to a less ambitious level. Instead of emphasising common Europeanness and a shared European neighbourhood, the aims are now defined more modestly:

> The EU will propose to neighbouring partners to work towards the development of a Common Knowledge and Innovation Space. This would pull together several existing strands of cooperation: policy dialogue, national and regional capacity-building, cooperation in research and innovation, and increased mobility opportunities for students, researchers and academics.
>
> (European Commission 2011c: 10)

The concept of Eastern Partnership introduced in 2009 as a new frame for recalibrating the European Neighbourhood Policies can be interpreted as a further step back from the sovereignty-challenging features of the notion of European Neighbourhood. Eastern Partnership is again more clearly something agreed between distinct international actors without aspirations towards post-sovereign spatial imageries:

> The establishment of the Eastern Partnership (EaP) has strengthened mutual relations with partner countries in Eastern Europe and the Southern Caucasus. It has helped to initiate and consolidate a difficult process of change. The region has seen general progress towards democracy over the past decade, including situations of regime change. The region continues to face major economic challenges – it is poor, with significant differences between individual countries, and susceptible to external factors and influences.
>
> (European Commission 2011c: 13)

The rise of the Eastern Partnership to the status of a new key concept of EU external relations had already started at the time the Lisbon Treaty entered into force in 2009. In a speech given in February 2009, the Commissioner for External Relations and European Neighbourhood Policy, Benita Ferrero-Waldner, introduced the Eastern Partnership as an ambitious project for twenty-first-century European foreign policy. Using as a starting point security threats stemming from Russian policies, she set out to formulate classical foreign policies in a traditional geopolitical context with rather little hints of searching for a new role in international relations (*Statement by European Commissioner for External Relations and European Neighbourhood Policy, Benita Ferrero-Waldner, on the Eastern Partnership* 2009). Here, Russia is clearly the *other* of European Neighbourhood and not anymore a part of this space. This return to a more traditional security-based foreign policy rhetoric was also evident in the 2009 Joint Declaration of the Prague Eastern Partnership Summit. The EU was clearly distancing itself from the most far-reaching tasks attached to the European Neighbourhood and allowing for a reconsideration of how far it wanted to engage itself:

> The pace of progress is determined by the degree to which partners have been willing to undertake the necessary reforms, and more has been achieved in the economic sphere, notably trade and regulatory approximation, than in the area of democratic governance. However, the pace of progress also depends on the benefits that partners can expect within a reasonable time frame. Here the extent to which the EU has been willing to engage itself with the partnership has also had, and will continue to have, a significant effect.
>
> (Council of the European Union 2009)

Thus, it is possible to discern in this formulation of common foreign and security policies a certain duality. On the one hand, spatial imagery of a shared European Neighbourhood is prevailing as a kind of long-term task of shared post-sovereign space. On the other hand, the EU is now clearly building external relations to distinct international actors in a context defined in rather traditional geopolitical terms. One might perhaps speak of a certain type of selective sovereignty notion attached to the definition of common foreign and security policies. In his study on the limits of post-sovereignty, Hiski Haukkala concludes that in contrast to the internal pooling of sovereignty, 'in its external policies the EU has a more variegated logic whereby it advocates a host of sovereignty-challenging practices while seeking to preserve its own sovereign prerogatives in full' (Haukkala 2010: 24).

The formulation of common foreign and security policies has more openly brought to the fore separate concepts for inclusive policies concerning internal borders and exclusive policies of securitised external relations. This can probably be explained in part by changes in the external environment. Since the Georgian war in 2008, and especially with the Ukrainian crisis of 2014, policies towards Russia have been sustained by geopolitical rhetoric that hardly leaves room for visions of a shared European space. At the same time, the turn reflects the EU's internal problems and the economic crisis that has been weakening the hegemonic position the Union was occupying in the eyes of its neighbours. The securitisation of borders, tight migration policies and the increased conditionality of ENPI agreements can be seen as means of building a Europe with a more clear-cut spatial image under the NATO umbrella. It remains to be seen whether this means an end to the conceptual innovation and vanguard spatial imagery of the earlier documents of CBC policies that introduced notions of a Wider Europe and a European neighbourhood as symbols of a shared European space of cooperation.

Conclusions: CBC and sovereignty-challenging spatial imaginary in the European Neighbourhood

Through its cross-border cooperation programmes, the EU has been engaged in promoting regional stability beyond its external borders, in its immediate neighbourhood. It has adopted and encouraged a new spatial imagery of shared Europeanness or of a common European Neighbourhood that goes beyond the frigid dividing lines of the Cold War period. At the same time, the EU has elaborated new policies of shared or pooled sovereignty that diverge from traditional conceptions of sovereignty in terms of national interests and territorial integrity. There are, however, clear differences in what form and to what extent these sovereignty-challenging notions have been included in EU policies of CBC during different periods. Shifts in EU policies of CBC can be linked to changes both in the internal and external political environment (especially Russia's ambitions), to tasks concerning deepening integration and institutional consolidation of the political union, as well as challenges to border control by migration and smuggling. These changes have also affected the position of the EU's eastern neighbours and the way that sovereignty-challenging features of EU policies have met the realities beyond the border.

The first cross-border cooperation programmes (INTERREG I and II) were initially targeted at promoting interregional cohesion within the EU (at first the European Community (EC)) and based largely on an apolitical vision of (economic) cross-border regionalisation. In this respect, the sovereignty concept of the initial policy frames and instruments were not calibrated for tackling the problems of post-colonial and post-communist transition and barely suitable for promoting regional stability on the external borders. In terms of spatial imagery, INTERREG did not at first offer groundbreaking geopolitical visions to the neighbours. It promoted a supranational idea of Europe but this referred mainly to the existing EC or EU. For neighbours, this image of Europe appeared at worst as an exclusive concept and at best as a model for developing economic and political institutions in order to solve problems of post-communism. The first INTERREG programme did not include sovereignty-challenging practices in regard to the external borders. However, the apoliticised vision of regional development and economic cohesion naturalised the liberal models of EU internal policies and thus indirectly offered neighbours a model for solving problems of transition.

The INTERREG III programme (2000–2006) was modified significantly to meet post-communist conditions, although the logic of transition and the idea of Western models remained part of the document's architecture. INTERREG III introduced a new place-making rhetoric and sovereignty-challenging policy formulations that mainly served as a tool for enlargement and pre-integration. At the same time, the concepts of Wider Europe and European Neighbourhood introduced new spatial imaginary of a shared European space of cooperation that went beyond the EU's boundaries. The programme language, that openly emphasised cross-border regionalisation even on external borders, was in this regard imbued with notions of shared European values. This added to the document a rather strong dimension of identity-political Europeanisation targeted primarily at easing the accession of Central and Eastern European countries. The elements of conditionality embedded in this rhetoric were at the time broadly discussed in the candidate countries and have later been openly criticised, especially in Russian political debates. With the souring of EU–Russia relations, this has exposed other countries of the ex-Soviet Union to pressures stemming from competing rationales contained in the policies of the Russian Federation and the EU as the case of Ukraine sadly testifies.

The ENP created a separate agenda for cross-border cooperation on the external borders and introduced country-specific agreements for implementing it in the neighbouring countries. At the same time, the beginnings of the ENP were closely linked to the institutional streamlining of the EU and the project of establishing a constitution, which later led to the Lisbon Treaty. With its emphasis on European values, the ENP promoted institutional and discursive Europeanisation that later fuelled discussions in the neighbouring countries, especially in the context of Russia's refusal to join the programme. The introduction of the concept of European Neighbourhood brought a new layer to the sovereignty-challenging policy definition of earlier CBC programmes. This neighbourhood was not only a frame for a certain type of economic development and interaction within the future enlarged Europe but a broader area under EU normative soft power with conditional perspectives for cooperation based on EU-defined European or shared values.

In the later formulation of EU common foreign and security policies it remains possible to discover the spatial imagery of a shared European Neighbourhood as a new kind of post-sovereign space. At the same time, the EU is clearly building external relations to distinct international actors in rather traditional geopolitical terms. Increased conditionality of the individual ENPI agreements carries ideas of European models that can be seen to hinder the neighbours to find their own paths through post-communist social change, nation-building and democratisation. In fact, a certain type of selective sovereignty notion attached to the definition of common foreign and security policies can be detected here. In contrast to the internal pooling of sovereignty, the EU is pushing forward with a more variegated logic in its external relations that advocates sovereignty-challenging practices for its neighbours while seeking to preserve its own sovereignty in rather classical terms.

Moreover, the formulation of common foreign and security policies has brought to the fore separate concepts for inclusive policies concerning internal borders and exclusive border policies of securitised external relations. The securitisation of borders, tightening migration policies and the increased conditionality of ENPI agreements can all be seen as means of building a Europe with a more clear-cut spatial image – and perhaps an end to the sovereignty-challenging spatial imagery that was introduced in documents of CBC with notions of Wider Europe and European Neighbourhood.

Obviously, the direction EU policies have taken in terms of place-making strategies and sovereignty-challenging practices is not unequivocal at the moment. There are palpable tensions embedded in the political rhetoric and even institutional practices originating from earlier layers of CBC policies and especially from the growing tensions in relations with Russia. Their careful analysis and open discussion is a precondition for developing a common foreign policy in line with the task of making the EU a new kind of actor in international relations capable of promoting stability beyond its borders.

2 Ukraine

History confronts geography

Volodymyr Kravchenko

Studying the Ukrainian borders is a serious challenge for any scholar, as the name of the country, derived from a word meaning 'borderland', already suggests.[1] In many ways, Ukraine's space and its perceptions need be explained by the very nature of the huge Eurasian landmass stretching from the Pacific to the Atlantic. This space has been involved in a permanent process of reconceptualisation and renaming in terms of geographical (geopolitical) and historical (national) identities which largely depended on whether its function was to divide or to unite East and West. The symbolical border between these two imagined entities was and continues to be in a state of flux, subject to changing geopolitical situations in the region. Over the centuries, it has consequently been shifting from the Danube River towards the Dnieper and Don Rivers and up to the Ural Mountains (Bassin 1991: 1–17) and then, in the opposite direction, to the western border of the former German Democratic Republic. Its present-day representations can be expressed in a variety of definitions, inspired most notably by the 'European', 'Eurasian', 'Russian', 'Soviet' or 'New' rhetoric.

After 1991, national frameworks became the main intellectual tool employed in the process of reconceptualising the territory of the former Soviet Union. However, it appears that the nation-building processes in the post-communist republics have raised new questions. What kind of nationalisms are they producing? Are these different from Western templates and, if so, is it possible to apply existing theories and concepts of nationalism to them? These questions, in turn, have necessitated a rethinking of the Soviet experience and its role in nation-building processes.

The classical imperial model defining the Soviet historical experience ('a prison of people') has been challenged recently by a new model, that of an 'affirmative action empire' (Martin 2001), which in turn entails the issue of non-classical nationalism(s) of the former Soviet people(s). This has resulted in an inevitable process of revising the most influential concepts of nation-building processes on the territory of Eastern Europe, initiated by scholars, such as Hans Kohn, Miroslav Hroch and Ernest Gellner, interested in the former Soviet area (Brubaker 2011; Kuzio 2000, 2001, 2002b; Szporluk 1997, 2002). Among those who have pursued this line of research many are prominent figures in Ukrainian Studies.

DOI: 10.4324/9781315858036-4

As J. Arnason has put it, 'the reemergence of Ukraine on the map of Europe is a major event, significant enough to prompt rethinking of some broader issues concerning Europe, its internal divisions and its boundaries' (Arnason 2006b). Ukraine's importance for defining both European and Russian geopolitical identities is well known (Garnett 1997; Hajda 1998). Depending on the observer's perspective, Ukraine can be seen either as the eastern part of Europe or the western part of Asia (Szporluk 1991: 466–482). Ukrainian space shares almost all the particularities and the historical fate of the entire East European borderland, its ever-changing political configurations, cultural heterogeneity, polycentrism, amorphousness and transparency.

Ukraine is definitely not a classical nation-state. Its nation-building process is nothing like those that have taken place in the West. A long-standing stateless-ness is one among Ukraine's many historical paradoxes. It is only episodically that a sovereign Ukrainian nation has made its appearance on the historical map, generally in the context of major geopolitical upheavals and wars along Europe's eastern frontiers. The Ukrainian lands always played the role of a periphery in the polyethnic states whose centres of influence were located beyond Ukrainian territory: Vilnius, Warsaw, Istanbul, Moscow, St Petersburg, Vienna and Berlin. Consequently, all border regions of present-day Ukraine have been involved in a variety of competing projects of constructing an imperial nation-state or attempting modernisation.

The Ukrainian borders offer a vivid example of the social construction of borders. For the first time in its history, Ukraine has acquired more or less stable external borders, although the process of their demarcation and delimitation is being far from completed. Before, external borders easily became internal ones and vice versa when border regions acquired or lost their significance in times of geopolitical cataclysms. No wonder that the territory of present-day Ukraine has been crisscrossed by ever-shifting political and symbolical boundaries that resulted in a conglomerate of historical regions known under a variety of names: Rus', Ukraine, Little Russia, New Russia and so on. As a rule, these names and others derived from them had no permanent associa-tion with a given territory. In some cases, they were interchangeable, in others, competing designations.

The successive symbolic and political configurations of what came to be the present-day Ukrainian national space each added additional layers, resulting in an ever more complex cultural heterogeneity. As Yaroslav Hrytsak has explained, Ukraine 'is firmly located in several regional/national/international/ supranational landscapes. ... Ukraine belongs not to one, but to several nested geographies' (Hrytsak 2004a: 252). Consequently, perceptions of the Ukrainian space have been expressed through a variety of metaphors – 'grey zone', 'warlands', 'bloodlands' or even 'no place' – most of which suggest vagueness, ambiguity and paradox.

Nested geographies are supplemented by nested historical legacies, those of the Soviet Union, the Polish Rzeczpospolita, the Russian and Habsburg empires and Kiev Rus'. Until today, all attempts at reshaping the Eastern

European borderland by the various border polities – empires as well as nation-states – seem to be highly contradictory. Under the cover of political innovation imposed from above, only a few basic values and even fewer institutional structures of the borderland societies were changed, and only slightly at that. It is therefore hardly surprising that Ukraine sometimes looks like a living museum of history. It is also the reason why history always plays a leading role in the construction and reshaping of Ukrainian national space(s), borders, regions, and identities.

Any historical narrative is directly related to the formation of national identity (Friedman 2001: 41). The latter also has a spatial dimension on the local, regional, national and transnational level. Thus, depending on the political conjuncture, historical narratives can either establish a symbolic border between spaces of different identity or, conversely, eliminate barriers that have separated them. In modernisation and nation-building processes, history either contradicts or supports geography.

What follows is an overview of various approaches to the intellectual mapping and conceptualisation of Ukrainian national space within its current external borders. Its focus will not only, and indeed not very much, be on political borders but rather on the process of mentally constructing and symbolically representing Ukraine's present-day territory in contemporary historical narratives. How is Ukraine's geopolitical identity being conceptualised? How is history used to legitimise Ukraine's integrity and outer borders? How do historians approach Ukraine's multiple historical legacies and its regional cleavages? In which ways are Ukraine's physical borders invested with 'soft' symbolical meanings? To sum up, is Ukrainian history compatible with Ukrainian geography in present-day intellectual representations?

This chapter is largely based on historical narratives of Ukraine produced over the last two decades within the broad interdisciplinary field of Ukrainian Studies. Its theme is approached from two perspectives: an external one, associated with geopolitical changes and the development of state-building projects on the territory east of Europe, and an internal one, associated with the consolidation of various kinds of national identity and the 'erasing' of the internal borders separating the main historical regions located on contemporary Ukraine's territory. The chapter will make use of several published and unpublished texts by the author that are related to the theme of historical writing.

Defining national space

Challenging historical legacies

In the twentieth century, Ukraine has occupied a quite particular place on the political map of the world in the form of a Soviet republic that combined the external attributes and symbols of a modern nation-state with the mummified remnants of imperial and, later, Soviet nation-state projects. The Soviet era has not only consolidated the boundaries of the Ukrainian Soviet Socialist Republic founded in 1922 but also preserved Ukraine's earlier multifaceted historical and cultural legacy. Neither the national revolution of 1917–1920 nor the Soviet modernisation succeeded in establishing a Ukrainian unified national space as both only created the façade of one and covered it with the corresponding symbols. Relicts of previous historical epochs and social structures were preserved under the Soviet shroud. After the collapse of the Soviet Union, all of them became active again.

The political fissures that in the late 1980s and early 1990 led to the dissolution of the Soviet Union coincided with the boundaries of Soviet republics that had emerged in the 1920s on the basis of the contemporary understanding of an ethno-cultural nation. Simultaneously, they revealed the weak legitimacy of these boundaries. Indeed, the territory of the Ukrainian Soviet Socialist Republic was never a coherent whole. It was disrupted by Russian Soviet enclaves in the form of particular regions (the Crimea, the Donets Basin) and large enterprises of 'All-Union' status under the direct control of Moscow. By contrast, the modern 'Ukrainian' national tradition that took shape in the twentieth century was declared nationalist and fascist, and its manifestations were consequently prohibited. As a result, the trappings of a nation-state conferred by the USSR merely served to conceal the phenomenon of 'Little Russianism', well known from the times of the Russian Empire. Together with the Russians, ethnic Ukrainians and Belarusian 'Little Russians' constituted the so-called Orthodox Slavic core of the USSR.

The political and ideological fiasco of the communist regime brought about the erosion of Soviet identity, which by that time had not even been fully constructed, and led to a return to pre-Soviet historical and cultural legacies. As a result, curious layers of a previous immaterial project of social development began to resurface from behind a façade of Soviet unification. The symbols of a modern Ukrainian nation- and state-building project were now added to the structures of the Soviet empire, mixed with the frozen leftovers of the Russian empire.

The shaping of present-day Ukraine's symbolic space and the legitimisation of its integrity have, above all, been carried out on the basis of historical mythology, that is the idea of a revival of the nation-state. The conceptualisation of the historical unity of Ukraine's national territory within its existing boundaries has, among other things, been inspired by teleological ideas of irredentism or *sobornist'* (Kuras and Soldatenko 2001), as well as by concepts of colonisation (in the sense of settlement), the moving steppe frontier (The Great Steppe border), the changing geography of the main centres of the Ukrainian national movement, or 'gathering peripheries of peripheries' (Szporluk 1997: 85–119). The symbolical space of the Ukrainian nation-state territory was being re-marked by Cossack and other ethnic-folk symbols.

However, the paradigm of a national revival soon revealed its weakness and contradictions. The political nation of Ukraine has yet to be constructed from different pieces. The traditional national narrative openly challenged almost all other national, post-national and pre-national narratives created by Ukraine's neighbours. Real Ukraine appeared to be a multiethnic, multicultural country more similar to the late Soviet Union than to a homogeneous nation-state (Kaganskii 2001). As a result, Ukrainian political and symbolical space(s) turned into a battlefield of different collective identities (Kohut 2001). All political attempts aimed at establishing a single dominant identity or at eclectically combining them into a single and coherent narrative have failed and led to the further marginalisation of the entire Ukrainian discourse (Ishchenko 2011: 369–395; Kappeler 2009: 217–232; Portnov 2010: 54–59).

Challenging geopolitics

The emergence of the nation-state paradigm in Ukrainian historical writing has been accompanied by the postulate of Ukraine's imminent joining of the European Union, expressed in the rhetoric of a 'return to Europe' or by geographical metaphors that describe Ukraine as 'the geographical centre of Europe', 'the crossroads of Europe' and so on (Hnatiuk 2005; Portnov 2010; Zhurzhenko 2010: 58–60). Other interpretations of Ukraine's geopolitical identity include 'New European', 'Eastern European', 'Intermarium', and 'New Eastern European' concepts (Arnason 2006a; Michnik, Grudzińska-Gross and Czarny 2011; Plokhy 2007; Portnov 2009; Troebst 2003). In this regard, Ukrainian intellectuals might be following the footsteps of Polish, Czech and Hungarian dissidents of the post-war period.

However, the postulate of Ukraine's European identity is often perceived to operate as an axiom, based primarily on the country's geographical position, and is poorly conceptualised in terms of shared social values and the European Union's founding mythology (Zaleska-Onyshkevych and Rewakowicz 2009). The European paradigm in Ukrainian national narratives also contradicts that of a national revival, since past Ukrainians heroically struggled precisely against those imperial or quasi-imperial polities which heavily supplied Ukrainian history with symbolical markers of Europeanness, namely the Polish Rzeczpospolita, the Austro-Hungarian and Russian empires. At the same time, European policy towards Ukraine (Gawrich, Melnykovska and Schweickert 2010: 1209–1235; Pentland 2008: 129–146) is not supported by historical conceptualisations: Ukraine figures in some western synthetical accounts of European history but not in others (Bideleux and Jeffries 1998; Davies 1996). Generally, historians can only trace the changing political configurations of the Eastern European borderland and try to explain them retrospectively.

More traditional schemes of geopolitical identification in terms of an East–West paradigm are still present in the current intellectual debate (Lysiak-Rudnytsky 1987; Ševčenko 1996). They represent Ukraine as the arena of a centuries-old historical struggle between East and West, Europe and Asia, or a crossroads of two civilisations that have their origins in postulates going back to the times of Romantic nationalism and of the geopolitical cataclysms of the twentieth century (Yakovenko 2002: 333). Efforts to find a place for Ukraine between East and West are based on implicit notions of Ukraine as a transitional zone or refer to the possibility of synthesising Western and Eastern traditions in the Ukrainian lands.

Interestingly, there are historians in the Ukrainian academic community whose works may, with reservations, be regarded as representing Ukrainian Eurasianism (Zhurzhenko 2010: 43–74). If the existence of a Ukrainian embryonic Eurasianism is accepted hypothetically, then it should be associated with the integration of Oriental components into the national narrative. The origins of such an intellectual tradition are evidently to be sought in the Cossack-centred historical narratives of the eighteenth and early nineteenth century associated with the doctrine of Polish Sarmatism. In recent times this current of Ukrainian historical thought has been represented in works whose authors try to integrate the Turko-Tatar heritage of the northern Black Sea littoral and especially the Crimean Khanate into the national narrative (Halenko 2004).

Consequently, the model of a civilisational conflict between East and West on Ukrainian territory has acquired a third spatial dimension in the form of the Steppe or the 'South'. The North–South framework of Ukrainian geopolitical identity looks like an underestimated intellectual or even political alternative to the East–West paradigm. Theoretically, this could help to fit the Turko-Tatar as well as the Russian imperial and Soviet legacies of the South region into the Ukrainian national narrative while contributing to the emerging concept of a Black Sea historical region (Adams *et al.* 2002: 120–147; Erkut and Mitchell 2007).

The difficulties historians are facing in their efforts to reinterpret the historical legacies of the South are obvious. The nation-state paradigm which relies on notions of the heroic struggle of the Ukrainian people against Turko-Tatar aggression would appear to be only one of the obstacles along that path. No less significant is the fact that the southwestern regions of present-day Ukraine have already been woven into the Russian national narrative, which emphasises the civilising mission and the military glory of the Russian empire in the region. Last but not least, the North and the South are even less elaborate notions than the elusive West and East.

Dividing national space

The geographical projection of historical legacies

The difficulties of conceptualising the integrity of a Ukrainian national space have paved the way for intellectual fragmentation. The geographical projection of historical legacies has resulted in concepts of several Ukraines – two, three, four or even more – imagined on the basis of geopolitical or regional identities which have appeared on the symbolical map of Ukraine. The East–West paradigm, for instance, presented itself in the form of Two Ukraines, each an extension of the two competing – European and Russian – visions of the Eastern European borderland.

Thus, Samuel Huntington has divided Ukraine into two parts: a Western, Greek-Catholic and pro-European one and an Eastern, Orthodox one that has remained within the gravitational field of Russian civilisation (Huntington 1997: 165–168). His paradigm's influence on historians has probably turned out to be much greater than the author himself ever could have imagined. Actually, the symbolic boundary between those two imagined parts of Ukraine keeps shifting with successive political conjunctures. All that remains constant is the image of a divided country whose western regions are said to be oriented towards a Ukrainian national idea while the eastern regions supposedly gravitate towards a different – Russian or Slavic Orthodox – national idea.

The Ukrainian political analyst Mykola Riabchuk, for example, describes the nine southeastern oblasts of present-day Ukraine as a geographical, economic and cultural entity shaped by the combined influence of history and geography (Riabchuk 2007a, 2007b). To give weight to his argument, he refers to civilisational differences between the Polish Rzeczpospolita and Moscow Czardom: the southeastern oblasts had come under the influence of the latter and thus did not experience the civilising influence of the West, therefore differing widely from the rest of Ukraine's territory. According to Riabchuk, the population of this region has a vaguely expressed ethnic identity and a mentality characterised by a high degree of Sovietisation and Russification and by the absence of the national collective historical memory and traditions, which turns it into pliable material in the hands of local oligarchs, criminal clans and corrupt communists.

Generally speaking, this intellectual mapping of post-Soviet Ukraine, emanating from the High Castle Tower of Lviv, reveals its immanent connections not only with the concept of a West–East slope or Huntington's clash of civilisations but also, and more precisely, with a Polish intellectual tradition of portraying the Eastern borderland as a battlefield between a civilised Europe and a barbarian Asia. The concept of Two Ukraines sparked off heated debates which do not seem to have abated since. Tatiana Zhurzhenko referred to this approach as the 'huntingtonisation' of Ukrainian political discourse (Zhurzhenko 2002) and other authors for the most part agree with her (Hrytsak 2004b: 216–228; Szporluk 2002). Nevertheless, further 'Orientalisation' and even alienation of the eastern and southern regions of Ukraine became popular among some Ukrainian intellectuals (Yuri Andrukhovych) and national-minded publicists in the context of the 2004 and 2010 elections in Ukraine.

A similar yet opposite paradigm of Two Ukraines is being promoted on the other side of the country: the geopolitical concept of a Russian World (*Russkii Mir*) (Sidorov 2006: 317–347). In the eyes of its adherents, the space of this Russian World is essentially defined by the extent to which have been propagated the historical legacies of Kievan Rus', the Russian Empire and the Soviet Union. Russian political and cultural elites make extensive use not only of the Russian language and Orthodox religion but of Stalin's Great-Patriotic-War historical mythology to contrast a 'Russian' heroic East with a 'Ukrainian fascist' West.

In many ways, the rhetoric used by adherents of the Russian World is tributary to the conception advanced by Samuel Huntington. Additional support comes from the works of Russian orthodox nationalists, starting with a nineteenth-century ideologue, Nikolai Danilevsky, and continuing with twentieth-century Russian émigré Eurasianists and our contemporary Aleksandr Dugin. It seems like their ideas have been incorporated into the political doctrine of President Putin for practical use.

The Eurasian doctrine can be considered as yet another version of an imperial geopolitical model projected by Russia onto the Ukrainian political and symbolic space (Laruelle 2008). It has been designed to promote the reintegration of the former Soviet republics under the aegis of Russia and in opposition to the West, although it is hard to fathom how the religiously inspired doctrines of an Orthodox Slavic Russian World could be reconciled with the imperial (secular) doctrine of Eurasianism, which includes the non-Orthodox and non-Slavic regions of the Caucasus and Central Asia. As the nature and direction of Russian nation- and state-building is getting more nationalistic, the future of the Eurasian doctrine remains unclear.

In the mental geography of contemporary Russian nationalist discourse, Ukraine is conceived in terms of an eternal East–West confrontation. The alien notion of modern Ukraine, incomprehensible to adherents of Holy Rus', is countered with that of Orthodox pro-Russian or even just Russian regions. While 'Ukraine' is moving towards the West, the 'Russian' part of Ukraine has become a rather vague entity designated by a variety of names, such as Little Russia (*Malorossia*), New Russia (*Novorossia*) and South-East Ukraine. In fact, each of these regional labels has different historical connotations and the regions thus referred to have different symbolical boundaries: the first one consists of the central Ukrainian districts associated with Cossack times; the second is a product of the Russian Western-inspired modernisation project of Catherine the Great; and the last definition has been coined only recently to describe the predominantly Russian-speaking regions that vote for Soviet-type policies.

To all appearances, the adherents of both Europe and the Russian World consider their part of Ukraine to be more civilised, more enlightened and more modernised. If so, then, for all the differences in their interpretations, it is hard to avoid seeing the common denominators of their publications, namely a dualistic, even Manichaean approach to the cultural borderland and vigorous efforts to remap its nested geography and re-imagining its entangled history according to particular national projects. It should be noted that both concepts, *Russkii Mir* and that of a Russian-dominated Eurasia, are mainly confined to political and public discourse, as very few professional historians in Ukraine subscribe to them.

With the further disintegration of the Soviet identity and its symbolical space, new political and geopolitical divisions have provided impetus to the phenomenon of Ukrainian regionalism (Hughes and Sasse 2002; Barrington and Herron 2004) and, correspondingly, to the development of regional studies (Vermenych 2003). The latter have produced a huge volume of literature on the past and present of certain Ukrainian lands defined either by current administrative divisions or on the grounds of historical legacies, linguistic criteria, collective identities and political geography.

As a result, Samuel Huntington's Two Ukraines gradually have given way to the Three Ukraines of more insightful observers who have postulated the existence of a Western, Southeastern and Central region by referring to a correlation between history, electoral geography and identity (Korostelina 2013; Melnykovska, Schweickert and Kostiuchenko 2011; Osipian and Osipian 2012; Shulman 2004). However, some adherents of this scheme, turning to history, have not been able to resist the temptation of 'huntingtonisation'. In their view, Ukraine's western regions, for example, seem to be an embodiment of 'individualism, freedom, democracy and tolerance' while the central regions are proof of a mixed Soviet identity and the southeastern regions 'highlight the values of collectivism and patrimonialism' (Melnykovska, Schweickert and Kostiuchenko 2011). Needless to say that the Three Ukraines paradigm represents by no means an improvement on its ideological predecessor since the third Ukraine, located between the two extremes, remains hard to define in terms of its geography and history.

Challenging borders

Border issues gained considerable momentum early in the 1990s, immediately after the proclamation of Ukraine's independence. The institutionalisation and legitimisation of Ukrainian *hard* state borders have been explored in numerous publications whose authors privilege the functional aspects of borders. In the early years of Ukraine's independence, historians played the most active role in justifying the validity and legitimacy of the current state borders by retrospectively tracking, or reconstructing, their existence in the past or by focusing on ethnic–cultural external boundaries and stressing the necessity of making them coincide with the political borders of present-day Ukraine. To make their case for hard state borders, historians have invoked the Kyivs'ka Rus', the early modern Cossack polities and the modern Ukrainian statehood of the early twentieth century.

The representation of Ukraine's external border in the current edition of the Ukrainian historical encyclopaedia is noteworthy. Looking at a black-and-white photograph of dark watchtowers rising towards a cloudy sky, with sombre border guards at their battle stations observing the cleared space that separates them from the barbed wire, it is hard to shake off the impression that this is the impregnable state border of the USSR during the Cold War era, a border under lock and key, hostile not only to foreign influences but also towards the country's own citizens. If indeed it has a symbolic foundation of some kind, then only in the sense of a holy ground protecting the spiritual purity and innocence of those professing the true faith from the corrupting influence of the West.

In recent years, however, research on the history of Ukraine's borders, its national territory and regions has come under the growing influence not only of geopolitics but also of cultural and mental geography, which considers such problems in the context of constantly changing forms of collective identity. Scholars are beginning to apply such concepts as *imagined boundaries* and cultural border spaces to the medieval, early modern and, to some extent, the modern period of Ukrainian history. Their publications project an image of historical Ukraine that resembles a palimpsest of various boundaries that have given rise to hybrid collective identities. Accordingly, metaphors such as 'kaleidoscope' or 'mosaic' seem more appropriate than notions of a homogeneous Ukrainian national space.

The historian Natalia Yakovenko, for instance, proceeds from the representation of Ukrainian territory as 'a sharply defined contact zone with a rather variegated spectrum of sociocultural phenomena and constantly shifting internal boundaries between linguistic and ethnic groups, states, religions, political and cultural systems, economic arrangements, and so on' (Yakovenko 2009: 117–148). Political scientists and sociologists work on concepts of 'junction areas' (Siargey Yaromenko) and boundaries of identity (Tatiana Zhurzhenko). If the publications of Western scholars – Timothy Snyder, Kate Brown, Daniel Beauvois, Tanya Richardson, and Hiroaki Kuromiya – are added to these Ukrainian productions, then the list of those studying various aspects of Ukrainian boundaries and borderlands looks quite impressive.

Clearly, concepts of a cultural borderland, while still requiring more and better theoretical and methodological foundations, already present the most realistic alternative to the centralist nation-state paradigm prevalent in post-Soviet space. To all appearances, the humanities in Ukraine urgently need to further conceptualise border studies to successfully achieve the latter's status as an independent academic discipline. To develop these kinds of studies, an interdisciplinary approach must not remain an exception but become the norm, thus creating a space for a dialogue between historians, political scientists, sociologists, philologists, ethnologists and scholars of regional studies, ethnic relations and other disciplines related to the subject.

An interdisciplinary approach to Ukrainian borders is the only way to explore their multidimensional nature. Ukraine's western border with the EU has succeeded the formerly Soviet hard border, heavily charged with historical memories and symbolical meanings; progress in its transformation will depend on overcoming the old nation-state paradigm on both sides of the border. To the east, the border with Russia is gradually turning from an inner, administrative boundary of the Ukrainian Soviet Socialist Republic into a real, hard political border; progress here will be determined by the outcome of the specific nation-building process in both Ukraine and the Russian Federation.

Wherever Ukraine's western state border coincides with that of the former Soviet Union, one may speak of its firm institutional character, due to an historical symbolic foundation. An open dialogue between historians from both sides of the border could, in some cases, endow the latter with a unifying function and lead to the notion of a cultural borderland, notably on the border with Poland. In other cases, the border functions are primarily divisive. The dialogue between Ukrainian and Romanian historians is practically non-existent and a similar situation prevails with regard to the Ukrainian–Turkish borderland.

The Ukrainian–Russian dialogue looks far more complicated. Here, the hard, institutionalised border has few symbolic foundations. Ukrainian and Russian territory are hard to separate either in historical narratives or in the collective social memory. However, Ukraine and Russia now pursue different concepts of nation-state building: the former one that is coloured by notions of an ethnic–cultural nation and the latter one that is firmly based on the Orthodox religious–imperial tradition. Hence, the dialogue appears as one in which the Ukrainian side attempts to emancipate itself from a shared historical and cultural legacy and the Russian side to completely erase the border with Ukraine. This explains the presence in Ukrainian public discourse of both unifying and divisive images of the Ukrainian–Russian borderland, which has been subject to interpretations not only in terms of a cultural and geographic phenomenon but also of a particular – historical, national or ethnic, linguistic and territorial – border identity.

Conclusions

In the author's opinion, the material presented in this chapter supports the idea that Ukraine can serve as a perfect model for studying the concept of borderland in terms of a particular historical, cultural and geographic meso-region and confirms the validity of this approach. Practically all the basic features of a borderland, with its characteristic dialectics of unity and regional variety, ambivalence and polycentrism, hybrid cultural identities, shifting borders etc., are already present in the Ukrainian post-Soviet historical narrative.

The Ukrainian borders lend themselves poorly to linear characterisations and conceptualisation. There are no stable, clearly defined dividing lines here. Instead, one sees particular enclaves in a disrupted sociocultural space with elusive boundaries. Ukraine is best characterised as a zone of cultural contacts that, in times of violent conflict, occasionally produces a human catastrophe. The problem of Ukraine's cultural heterogeneity and its (in)compatibility with the project of building a nation-state has remained an unsolved historical puzzle to this day.

Notions of 'a periphery of peripheries' and 'from a periphery to a sovereign state', proposed by Roman Szporluk, aptly accentuate the particularities of the historical process in Ukraine. It is another matter that the notion of periphery calls for a conceptualisation in its own right. The study of this borderland requires the development of a particular methodology. Once this will have been accomplished, it may become possible to grasp how the universal doctrines of nationalism and modernisation have acquired their particular local characteristics in the borderland.

External influences on the territory of the Ukrainian borderland have so far overwhelmed its internal efforts towards self-organisation. Ukraine generally resembles a battleground of various modernisation projects planned and carried out by distant political and cultural centres. In relation to these, Ukraine has remained a periphery, moving within a symbolic space of the borderland but never beyond it. With the Ukrainian lands belonging simultaneously to a variety of political, cultural and symbolic spaces, the result has been a kaleidoscopic series of geopolitical images and definitions of the Ukrainian borderland that have varied in accordance with changing cultural and political contexts.

Geography retains its influence on present-day Ukraine's geopolitical identity, although it is hard to assess this unambiguously. On the one hand, fundamental differences between models of political cultures, social values, as well as the palpable gap that separates the standard and quality of life in the two geographic centres of influence – the European Union and Russia – have created tensions and the risk of Ukraine breaking apart. On the other hand, the possible convergence between them offers Ukraine's political elites limited room for manoeuvering to work out a formula of internal consolidation. From that viewpoint, Ukraine has remained hostage to its fatal geography, perceived in terms of a binary opposition of East and West.

History, in turn, determines the process of consolidating the Ukrainian space in terms of the conflict between tradition and innovation. Paradoxically enough, it is precisely the Soviet historical and cultural legacy that until now has served to guarantee Ukraine's relative internal political stability after the dissolution of the Soviet Union. From this viewpoint, Ukraine's Soviet history is counterpoising its European geography. Now, when the Soviet historical legacy is almost exhausted and is giving way to both Russian and Ukrainian nationalism, it is impossible to predict what kind of historical legacies will be chosen as the main foundation for the further development of Ukrainian nation-state building. From that viewpoint, Ukraine with its prolonged statelessness remains hostage to its 'fatal history' in addition to its 'fatal geography'.

The Ukrainian borderland is the result of a regional version of modernisation that has generally divided society along sociocultural lines. In Ukrainian intellectual history, a superficial and weak modernisation has led to the continuing dominance of mythological over rational thinking in the description of Space and Time, without which the process of collective identification is impossible. The popularity of civilisational schemes for interpreting the historical process and, more particularly, their use in Ukrainian historiography indicate the reliance of many authors on mythological or religious traditions. The sacralisation of the national territory and its external borders (the Land) along with the people inhabiting it is, first and foremost, an indication of its affinity with Russian and Soviet historical narratives. The desacralisation of national boundaries in the new historical narrative is an acknowledgment of their instability, transparency and weakness. It is also a symbolic mapping of the cultural divide brought about by the contradictions of modernisation on the eastern frontiers of Europe.

Ukraine's symbolic space in historical narratives is most often a projection of its present-day administrative and political space onto the past. But the various regions constituting that space are inadequately represented in those narratives with regard to their current place and role in the life of the Ukrainian state. Ukraine's border regions, especially those adjacent to Russia, usually resist symbolic reconfiguration by finding ways to make their ethnic and political boundaries coincide.

Attempts to 'Europeanise' Ukrainian history by means of a contrived rhetoric and facts taken out of context are unlikely to convince anyone. For this reason, one possible way to come to terms with Ukrainian historical – or rather living – legacies would be a complete reinterpretation of the Russian and the Soviet past as an integral part of a new national narrative. These historical legacies, and above all their reformist and Western aspects, contain the potential of facilitating modernisation, a potential that a renewed Ukrainian national discourse could appropriate and even turn to its advantage in order to integrate all Ukrainian regions within the current political borders.

The time has come to discuss the phenomenon of Orthodox nationalism in a comparative perspective, to rethink Ukrainian history in terms of values, oppositions between sacred and secular, tradition and innovation. Last but not least, a new spatial framework, promoted by authors such as N. Baron, M. von Hagen, S. Kotkin and R. Suny, and the 'entangled histories' model seem far more promising attempts of further conceptualising Ukraine and its borders with the aim of rationalising the elusive space of Eurasian time.

Ukraine's permanent and, after all, boring uncertainty in time and space most frequently appears to be a deviation, something abnormal for any observer used to operating within the normative language and classical rhetoric of the nation-state: 'For anyone writing about Ukraine, language is always a problem. Not the Ukrainian that is favoured in the west of the country, nor the Russian that is still spoken in the east, but the language used to describe the country's politics. The usual terms simply do not apply.'[2]

The language problem mentioned here clearly indicates a shortage of concepts in the Western discourse on Ukraine, reflecting the limitations of existing theories of nationalism and national space and their very applicability to the post-Soviet terrain, and specifically the Ukrainian case (Hrytsak 2004b). The lack of a new and more suitable language and of intellectual tools prevents EUropean politicians from understanding Ukraine's geopolitical and cultural identity as being simultaneously non-European and non-Russian. Obviously, no proper understanding can be achieved without redefining European identity itself on a non-historical basis (Berger 2009: 21–36).

The same could be said of Russian identity. It remains an open issue whether the possible rationalisation and secularisation of the Ukrainian borderland will be of some use to the re-identification of neighbouring Russia. In one still plausible scenario Russia could involve Ukraine, as well as Belarus, in its process of nation-state building and this could result in the appearance of new boundaries and borders of a post-Soviet Eurasia. In this case History, once more, would prevail over Geography.

Notes

1 At other times, the meaning is given as 'outskirts', 'border district' or 'land at the edge'.
2 'Linguistically challenged', *The Economist*, 6 April 2013. Online. Available at: www. economist.com/news/europe/21575786-how-ukraine-falls-between-political-economic-and-linguistic-camps-linguistically-challenged (last accessed 3 August 2013).

3 Borders and nation-building in post-Soviet space

A glance from the Republic of Moldova

Octavian Țîcu

The territorial space of a nation is often given a meaning beyond its definition as an area of land under the political control of a state or ruler. The history of a nation, its struggles, conflicts, defining moments and tragedies all happen in particular places that are seen not only as shaping their character but also that of the nation. Consequently, territory is a vital component of national identity as an emotive source of imagining what the nation is all about. Scholars working on questions of territoriality have pointed out that understanding territory as a 'space to which identity is attached by a distinct group who hold or covet that territory and who desire to fully control it for the group's benefit' (Knight 1982: 526) is fundamentally problematic since such a conception tends to encourage the social construction of national boundaries that do not necessarily match state borders.

Until 1991, the present territory of the Republic of Moldova never formed an independent political entity. Its shape and borders are the result of successive projects of nation- and state-building: from that of the medieval Moldovan state to those of the Romanian Principalities, the Ottoman, Habsburg and Russian Empires, Greater Romania and to the affirmative nationality policies of the Soviet Union. As a result, perspectives on borders and territory in post-Soviet Moldova are deeply intertwined with competing visions of national and state identity and the imaginary geography that Moldovans attach to their republic's current boundaries. This chapter approaches the question of Moldova's borders and territorial situation by taking into consideration the historical implications of and interferences from the various processes of state- and nation-building which have modelled the present shape of the Moldovan state as well as its configuration and crystallisation in the geopolitical context of the *longue durée*. Prior to 1812, the territory of Moldova was part of the Romanian Principality of Moldova, which is said to have emerged in 1359 and which later, in the sixteenth century, came under the suzerainty of the Ottoman Empire. In 1775, the Habsburg Empire annexed the northern part of the Moldovan state and renamed it Bukovina, while the eastern part, historically known as Bessarabia, became part of the Russian Empire after the Russian–Ottoman war of 1806–1812 and remained so until 1917.[1] In 1859, the core area of the Romanian Principality of Moldova became attached to

DOI: 10.4324/9781315858036-5

Wallachia as part of the modern Romanian state. After the Great War, Bessarabia was returned to Romania. This situation lasted until the 1939 Molotov–Ribbentrop Pact, which added the region to the Soviet sphere of influence, and the subsequent occupation of Bessarabia by Soviet troops in 1940. On 2 August 1940, the Soviet Union created the Moldovan Soviet Socialist Republic (SSR), comprised of Bessarabia and the Moldovan Autonomous Soviet Socialist Republic (ASSR), which had been established in 1924 within the Ukrainian SSR. With the exception of a period of temporary reoccupation by Romania between 1941 and 1944, the Moldovan SSR was part of the Soviet Union until 27 August 1991, when the Republic of Moldova, on the eve of the Soviet Union's dissolution, proclaimed its independence. The Declaration of Independence condemned the 1812 and 1940 annexations, thereby emphasising Moldova's territorial unity and historical continuity with Romania.

These territorial and political fluctuations, to which must be added the effects of Moldova's peripheral (and landlocked) location in regard to the powerful states that shaped its history, have often been portrayed as a constant shifting between East and West that still affects the new Republic of Moldova. In their more recent expression, they can more precisely be understood as a confrontation between Romanian nationalism, which wants its historical province of Bessarabia to 'return home', and Russian imperialism and Soviet nationalities policies that were driven by geopolitical strategies aimed at controlling Moldovan territory. This confrontation has left a particular legacy that continues to shape the current political and national physiognomy of the Republic of Moldova. The remaining part of the chapter will examine more closely the issue of Moldova's borders and identity in the context of the main geopolitical challenges the country has been facing since independence.

Soviet nationality policies and the shaping of Moldova's borders

The Moldovan SSR was the first state in history to be formed on the basis of an ethno-political unit, or nationality in Soviet parlance. Confronted with growing nationalisms, the Soviet authorities responded by systematically promoting the national consciousness of these nationalities and by creating for many of them institutional forms that are specific to nation-states (Martin 2001; Suny 1993; Slezkine 1994). The logic and the content of the Soviet nation-building policy was mainly focused on four attributes: the creation of national territories; linguistic indigenisation; the creation and promotion of native elites; and support for national cultures.

The Soviet understanding of nationhood was based on the Stalinist linkage between nationality, territory and an indigenous political elite. Following Stalin's definition of the nation, Soviet authorities promoted the idea of a nation attached to a particular territory. The major ethnic groups were assigned officially recognised territories and organised into an elaborate administrative hierarchy, in which the fifteen Soviet republics represented the highest rank of statehood accessible to a Soviet nationality (Motyl 1992: 33–35).

The case of the Moldovan SSR constituted an exception in the western part of the Soviet Union in that Soviet Affirmative Action (Martin 2001) here aimed to create a nation where national sentiments had barely existed or only in the sense of a regionalism at a time when the territory was part of the Russian Empire or Greater Romania. Whereas other western republics had a strong sense of identity, the Moldovan SSR resembled more the republics of Central Asia in the 1920s, during the early stages of the indigenisation policy (see Akiner 1997 and Pipes 1964). More particularly, the four attributes of the Soviet nationalities policy mentioned above were being promoted in Soviet Moldova to emphasise Moldovan primordiality and its distinctiveness from the Romania one.

According to the pattern described by George Schöpflin (1993: 28–30), the Baltic countries, for instance, can be considered as traditional societies which preserved what they could from the past despite their Soviet experience and which only changed in largely unperceived ways during the Soviet period, while Moldovan society had been a Soviet creation *ex nihilo*, which means that it owed to the Soviet nation-building policy its very existence, its political status and even its ethnic identity.

The roots of the current Republic of Moldova go back to the Soviet Union's decision, in 1924, to establish an autonomous Moldovan SSR within the Ukrainian SSR. The Moldovan Autonomous SSR was formed on the basis of what Terry Martin has called the Soviet 'Piedmont Principle': by creating a 'homeland' for Moldovans living beyond Romania's border, the Soviet leadership hoped to advance their claims on Romanian territory. Even though the Piedmont Principle played no general role in Soviet policies of nation-building, it was, in the exceptional case of the MASSR, the main reason for the creation of the republic (Martin 2001: 9, 274).

The Soviet Union never recognised the attachment of Bessarabia to Romania and, in response to it, created the Moldovan ASSR as part of the Ukrainian SSR, calling it, in the words of Volodymyr Zatonsky, 'our own Moldovan Piedmont' (quoted in Martin 2001: 274). Despite its small size and its dubious ethnic make-up – Moldovans represented 31.6 per cent of the Moldovan ASSR's population and Ukrainians 49.6 per cent (Gosstatizdat 1926: 24) – the newly created area received the status of an autonomous republic in view of an eventual annexation of Bessarabia.

When the Moldovan SSR was established by the Supreme Soviet on 2 August 1940, allegedly upon the initiative of a majority of the region's working population (Repida 1977: 246–247), it was composed of historical Bessarabia and parts, but not all, of the Moldovan ASSR, as only six out of the Moldovan ASSR's thirteen *rayons* were attached to it.

The Soviets did not follow any precise ethnic, historical or cultural logic in the creation of the new republic but rather used strategic considerations. As a result, three counties of the historical Bessarabia (Cetatea Alba, Ismail and Hotin) were annexed to the Ukrainian SSR in exchange for parts of the Moldovan ASSR (Verhovnogo Soveta 1940: 183). In addition to destroying the territorial integrity of historical Bessarabia, Soviet officials pursued a strategy that would secure the Soviet Union access to the Danube River via a politically reliable Slavic republic, thereby transforming the Moldovan SSR into a landlocked entity. The Ukrainian lobby, too, played a major role in the transfer of these territories. Historical documents attest that it was Nikita Khrushchev who suggested to the Central Committee of the Communist Party of the Soviet Union that the new Moldovan Soviet Republic should be created by unifying the 'Moldovan population only' and not unite the territories of Bessarabia and the Moldovan ASSR (Cioranescu *et al.* 1967: 163; Lazarev 1974: 524). Attaching the disputed territory between the Nistru and the Prut Rivers to Ukraine meant that Bessarabia ceased to be an officially recognised territory. It was expected that this would bar any future attempt to have the area returned to Romania.

In the long run, the unification of the two formerly distinct entities, known as Bessarabia and Transnistria or the Left and Right Bank of the Nistru River, into a territory that had never existed before in any sense, was critical for the further evolution of both the Moldovan SSR and the Republic of Moldova. It not only changed the ethnic balance in the Moldovan SSR, but the Soviet policy of colonisation generated the premises of the future Transnistrian separatism. Indeed, the powerful 14th Guards Army was installed on the left bank to guarantee national security and Soviet influence in the region. On 2 September 1990, the area, with political and military support from Moscow, proclaimed its independence as the Pridnestrovian Moldovan Republic (PMR) and ceased to take orders from the central government of the Republic of Moldova.

Since achieving sovereignty in the wake of the Soviet Union's collapse, the Republic of Moldova has been embarking upon a process of state- and nation-building. When looking at the complex realities that characterise Moldova's border and identity, the reader should therefore always bear in mind that this process, as well as Moldovans' sense of state and nation, is inextricably linked with Moldova's former imagined and real place within the Soviet Union. The Soviet era forms the main foundation on which independent Moldova has to build its own political and national identity.

Post-independence historical–political narratives of Moldova's borders

The two decades of the Republic of Moldova's post-Soviet history have witnessed the rise of three projects of state- and nation-building. All are strongly influenced by the historical discourses present at the time of the Declaration of Independence or emerging in its immediate aftermath and all refer to earlier projects of state- or empire-building. Each of these projects has been directly stimulated and influenced by actors outside the country, mainly Romania and the Russian Federation. Moldovan citizens have supported them with varying intensity and not always consistently.

The Romanian option

The first narrative has a Romanian orientation. It identifies the Republic of Moldova as a second Romanian state and its history as part of the wider history of Romanians. Accordingly, Moldova's current borders are thought to be the result of Russia's imperial policy, which led to the annexation of Bessarabia in 1812, and later of Soviet expansionist policies during and after the Second World War. Supporters of this view can be found in both Romania and the Republic of Moldova. For them, 'anti-Romanism' and Russification were part of Moscow's arsenal designed to ensure the denationalisation of Romanians living in the Moldovan SSR. The latter's resistance against these policies as well as the later disintegration of the Soviet Union are seen as proofs of the impossibility of 'Moldovenism', as the majority of the republic's citizens is thought to have preserved an attachment to the Romanian language and identity. The independence of the Republic Moldova has been interpreted as a step towards reunification with Romania, along the lines of what happened in Germany in 1990. Finding a powerful echo in the late 1980s and early 1990s, the arguments advanced by Romanian-oriented political leaders and intellectuals were reflected in the Republic of Moldova's Declaration of Independence, adopted on 27 August 1991. The declaration proclaimed the independence of the Republic of Moldova from the Soviet Union, condemned the annexations of Bessarabia by the Russian Empire in 1812 and by the Soviet Union in 1940 and emphasised the Romanian character of the new state (Republica Moldova 1991). The Romanian tricolour became the state flag, the Romanian coat of arms the state emblem, the Romanian anthem 'Wake up, Romanian!' the national anthem, and the basic unit of the national currency was named *leu*, as in Romania.

The narrative lost its political force after the 1992 war in Transnistria and with the subsequent arrival of the Moldovenisation policy, but intellectuals and large parts of the population that identify themselves as Romanians still find it attractive. 'Bessarabia is Romanian land' (*Basarabia – pământ românesc*) is their well-known credo. Proponents of the Romanian option perceive Russia as the historical enemy and as the main threat to the independence and territorial integrity of the Republic of Moldova. They are also very critical of the cession of the former territories of Bessarabia to the Ukrainian SSR and argue that Transnistria, never a part of Moldova in their view, should be exchanged for the southern and northern part of Bessarabia, now part of Ukraine.

While its adherents were being persecuted during the government of the Party of Communists (2001–2009), the Romanian current became once more intellectually attractive and politically powerful after the 2009 parliamentary elections and the street riots which led to the overthrow of the Communist government and the establishment of the democratic Alliance for European Integration. However, the political union with Romania is no longer on the agenda or rather has been postponed until the Republic of Moldova will eventually have joined the European Union, a goal that has become increasingly popular.

The 'Moldovan' stance

The second narrative is a Moldovan one. Its origins go back to the Soviet ideology of the interwar period, gaining consistency in the post-war period as the official party line in both the Soviet Union and the Moldovan SSR. In this version, Moldovans and Romanians are two different peoples who speak two different languages, and their histories, even if they sometimes intersected in the past, have taken different routes since the common ethnogenesis. Considered historically obsolete when the Soviet Union collapsed, the narrative has, however, survived Moldova's independence and even gained prominence during the Communist Party rule (2001–2009), which was justified in the name of Moldovan statehood.

It reached its apogee in the context of the 1994 parliamentary elections and, more precisely, on 5 February 1994, when President Snegur, during the congress Our House – the Republic of Moldova, denounced the Romanian orientation and accused pro-Romanian intellectuals of denying 'the legitimacy and historical foundations of the right to be a state and to call ourselves Moldovans' (Şarov and Cuşco 2011: 739). The former Soviet argument of a Moldovan language distinct from Romanian was reiterated and ushered in by the congress as the official ideology of the Moldavian state to be reproduced afterwards by the Democratic Agrarian Party and Communist governments. The theory of Moldovenism and the notion of a 'secular Moldovan statehood' promoted by the Soviet ideology and propaganda were thus adapted to new political circumstances and once more seen as central elements of state-building and the national identity.

The return of Moldovenism also had an impact on the new constitution, adopted on 29 July 1994, that replaced the anthem 'Wake up, Romanian!' and defined the 'Moldovan language' as the official language of the state. This policy of Moldovenisation continued during the second presidency of Petru Lucinschi, who insisted on the idea of a 'millennial' continuity of the Moldovan people and state (Fruntaşu 2002: 375). Its importance can largely be explained by the lacking historical legitimacy of the new Moldovan state, which has resulted in the reappearance of Soviet-style historical arguments, promoted especially by the Party of Communists. After coming into power in 2001, the Communist government took vigorous actions to formalise a Moldovan ideology, which culminated in the adoption of the Concept of National Policy of the Republic of Moldova on 19 December 2003. The state thus attempted to assert its authority over the discourse on national identity, aimed at 'continuing a centuries-old political and juridical process of the Moldovan people towards statehood' (Legea privind aprobarea concepţiei politicii naţionale a Republicii Moldova nr. 546-XV din 19.12.2003 2003; author's translation).

According to the Moldovenist narrative, the history of the Republic of Moldova can be traced back to the medieval Moldovan Principality of 1359 and all subsequent changes have left legacies that are reflected, for instance, in the particular shaping of Republic of Moldova's present borders. This thesis is, however, very hard to defend since the heart of the medieval Moldovan state was located in present-day Romania and the Transnistrian region was never a part of ancient Moldova.

The supporters of post-Soviet Moldovenism have frequently accused Romania of interfering in the internal affairs of Moldova and sometimes of having imperialist ambitions, while attributing a positive character to Russian and Soviet influence. They are highly critical of Romania's hesitation to sign the main border treaty with the Republic of Moldova. Whereas the Romanian authorities consider the border a consequence of historical injustices created by the 1939 Germano-Soviet Pact, their Moldovan counterparts, especially during the Communist governments, detect behind this statement a hidden agenda aiming at reclaiming a former Romanian province.

The idea of Moldovenism has been supported by the Russian Federation through various strategies that continue to turn any attempt of a rapprochement between Chişinău and Bucharest into a sensitive issue. The anti-Romanian stance of the Communist government reached its climax in the context of the 7 April 2009 protests when the Romanian ambassador in Moldova was expelled and Romania accused of organising the disorder 'to wind up Moldovan statehood'. The rejection of neo-Communist Moldovenism by large segments of the population and an overwhelming majority of intellectuals and students can be recognised as a manifestation of Romanian identity.

The Transnistrian trend

The third narrative comes from the eastern part of Moldova, from Transnistria, where a majority group of Russians identify themselves as being part of the Russian political and cultural world. *Pridnestrovie – russkaya zemlea* ('Transnistria is Russian land') is their slogan, although Moldovans, or Romanians, represent one third of the population and Ukrainians another third. The emergence of the Pridnestrovian Moldavian Soviet Socialist Republic on 2 September 1990, supported by the Soviet power and later the Russian Federation, divided the Republic of Moldova into two parts and led to a war that both parties have interpreted as one of independence, that of Chişinău from the Russian Federation and that of Tiraspol from the Republic of Moldova.

Transnistria, over which the Republic of Moldova has no longer any control, has developed a particular perspective on Moldovan statehood. It is argued that its beginnings go back to the creation of the Autonomous Republic of Moldova within the Ukrainian SSR, since the area had never been part of the medieval Moldovan state. The Transnistrian regime therefore has refused to acknowledge any historical connection with the Republic of Moldova and claims to subscribe to the condemnation of the 1812 Russian and 1940 Soviet occupations that forms part of the Moldovan Declaration of Independence of 1991, thereby legitimising the existence of a Transnistrian state which had not been occupied. The authorities of the PMR consider themselves to be the authentic heirs of the Moldavan SSR and the Moldovenism created in 1924. They have preserved the emblem and flag of the former Soviet Republic but also introduced symbolic elements that have no historical connection with the territory, such as the image of the Moldovan ruler Dmitrie Cantemir on the Transnistrian one-hundred-ruble bill.

The authorities of the PMR see no future for a united Moldovan state and have been promoting the idea of a distinct Transnistrian people (*Pridnestrovskii narod*), made up from a melting pot of Moldovans (more than one third of the population), Russians and Ukrainians (each almost one third). The Transnistrian border and identity construction shows many affinities with the Soviet pre-war conception of Moldova: Transnistrians are distinct from Moldovans as Moldovans were held to be distinct from Romanians.

Adherents of this narrative see the Republic of Moldova and Romania, as well as Ukraine since the 2005 Orange Revolution, as the main threats to the integrity and security of Transnistria, with the Russian Federation as the guarantor of its existence. Although Russia officially recognises the territorial integrity and independence of the Republic of Moldova, it has remained the main ally of the Tiraspol administration and given it political, economic, financial and military support (Vrabie 2009: 79–88). Despite allowing Transnistria to function as a pseudo-state, the Russian Federation has, however, been unwilling to confirm its independence. Thus, when the Tiraspol authorities, during the Russian–Georgian war, asked the Russian Federation to recognise the PMR on similar grounds as those invoked for Abkhazia and South Ossetia, Moscow rejected their demand. Russian diplomacy rather seems to pursue the Transnistrisation of the Republic of Moldova by promoting a federal state in which Chişinău and Tiraspol would have equal status. Such a solution would ensure Russia's influence over political decisions made by Chişinău, the maintenance of its military base in Transnistria and the recognition of Russian as the official language of the new state.

Of the three projects of state- and nation-building presented above, the first and the last are radically opposed and incompatible historically, ideologically and politically. Points of convergence can be observed between the first and second projects, which plead respectively for 'Romanisation' and 'Moldovenisation': both recognise Moldova's territorial unity but differ on the prospects of a political union. The Romanian option stresses the unity of Romanians on both banks of the Nistru River, while the second postulates the existence of a multi-cultural and bilingual Moldovan people. At the same time, both the Moldovan and Transnistrian projects promote Moldovan–Russian bilingualism and refer to Soviet Moldovenism. However, the Communist presidency of Vladimir Voronin has demonstrated that Moldovenism could not bridge the gap between Chişinău and Tiraspol even in times of great ideological proximity.

Borders and neighbours

Three states have shown a strong interest in the issue of the Republic of Moldova's borders. Two of them, Romania and Ukraine, are geographical neighbours whereas the Russian Federation has legitimised its interest in terms of the historical past and by invoking the presence of a large Russian minority. At the same time, two other important actors have voiced concerns about the future of the Moldovan state, the European Union and the United States.

Romania

Romania was the first state to recognise the independence of the Republic of Moldova. The Romanian government interpreted Moldova's independence as the 'proclamation of an independent Romanian state on the territories forcibly annexed as a result ... of the Molotov–Ribbentrop pact and a decisive step toward a peaceful solving of its fateful consequences for the rights and interests of the Romanian people' (Ministry of Foreign Affairs of Romania 1991; author's translation).

A declaration by the Romanian Parliament on 3 September 1991 stated that:

> The decision of the Moldovan Parliament establishes a deep longing for freedom and independence of the Romanians on the other side of the Prut River. ... The new conditions created by the Declaration of Independence of the Parliament of Moldova have opened good prospects for developing cooperation and multiple ties between the two neighbours who descend from a single trunk of the Romanian people, as it was formed historically.
>
> (Ministry of Foreign Affairs of Romania 1991)

Ever since Moldova's accession to independence, the slogan 'one nation, two Romanian states' has been part of the rhetoric employed by Romanian politicians of various political parties. In Chișinău, the Transnistrian conflict and Russia's growing influence as well as the reappearance on the political scene of the former Soviet political elite led to an exacerbation of Romanophobia and anti-Romanian sentiments. Accordingly, the political dialogue between Bucharest and Chișinău gradually deteriorated into altercations, especially during the time when the Communist Party was in government.

Both capitals' positions during the negotiations on the Basic Political Treaty and the Border Agreement revealed a completely different understanding of the issue of statehood with regard to the Republic of Moldova. Thus, while in Bucharest's vision, the Basic Political Treaty was to establish a European partnership with Chișinău and enshrine the status of Romanian advocacy for Moldova's integration into the European Union, Chișinău wanted – at least until 2009 – an ordinary treaty of partnership and a form of collaboration that would not only avoid any reference to an historical, ethnic and linguistic unity between Moldova and Romania but expressly refer to the Paris Peace Treaty of 1947, considered a sequel of the past by Romanian politicians and 'a barrier against Romanian irredentism' by the successive governments in Chişinău. Things came to a head during the rule of the Party of Communists (2001–2009). Romania considered the Peace Treaty obsolete and the resulting border demarcation a consequence of the 'unjust and aggressive Molotov–Ribbentrop pact' whereas the Moldovan president Vladimir Voronin denounced Romania as the last 'empire' in Europe and exposed to the international community 'the Romanian hidden agenda regarding the Moldovan state'.[2]

Until recently, the two countries had a very different take on the issues of Moldova's European ambitions and Romania's involvement in resolving the Transnistrian conflict. With regard to the first, Bucharest emphasised the principle of 'one nation, two Romanian states', while Chişinău stressed the formula 'two peoples, two different states'. And whereas Romania pleaded for a political solution of the Transnistrian conflict through negotiations, Chişinău wanted Bucharest to play a passive role, namely by signing the two agreements that would strengthen the international status of Moldova, the Basic Political Treaty and the Border Agreement between Moldova and Romania.

In the context of the radical political change that occurred after the 2009 parliamentary elections, the newly created Alliance for European Integration succeeded in getting the Border Agreement signed in November 2010, but not the Basic Political Treaty, an outcome that many political actors in Chişinău, especially the communists, have attributed to a Romanian lack of good will in regard to the future of the Moldovan state. Relations between the Republic of Moldova and Romania, including in view of Moldova's European aspirations, have, however, greatly improved and a sort of rapprochement has taken place.

Ukraine

Diplomatic relations between the newly independent states of Ukraine and Moldova found their first expression in the Treaty of Good Neighbourhood, Friendship and Collaboration signed in 1992. The most sensitive issue in the relations between the two countries is the Transnistrian question, which has given rise to concerns about the security of Moldova's eastern border – the delimitation and demarcation of the Ukrainian–Moldovan border has not yet been completed (Boian 2009: 40–48). Until a new border treaty enters into force, the boundary between the Republic of Moldova and Ukraine follows that which existed between the Moldovan and Ukrainian SSRs. On 18 August 1999, a border agreement (Republica Moldova 2002) was signed in Kiev that launched the process of delimiting the final demarcation. The most contentious issue was the cession to Ukraine of seven kilometres of the Odessa–Reni road near Palanca village in exchange for a one-kilometre-long strip of land that gave Moldova access to the Danube River. After another border agreement, signed by the Moldovan authorities in July 2001, the first territory was passed to Ukraine where it now forms an enclave on the territory of the Republic of Moldova.

Ukraine is also involved in the so-called '5 + 2 Talks' that try to settle the Transnistrian question, and President Yushchenko was the initiator of a plan, the so-called Yushchenko Plan, which stipulated the democratisation of the breakaway region as a prerequisite for its reintegration into the Republic of Moldova (Boian 2009: 45).

The period of the Orange Revolution (2004–2010) has shown that a pro-European Ukraine with democratic aspirations can contribute to regional stability and help contain Russia's influence on the European post-Soviet space in a manner greatly beneficial to the Republic of Moldova. After the election of President Yanukovych in 2010 and the success of the Party of Regions in the parliamentary elections of 2012, the regional context was, however, deeply affected by the growing influence of Russia in Ukraine, a situation that has closely linked the question of Moldova's territorial integrity to that of Ukraine's autonomy vis-à-vis Russia.

The Russian Federation

> Georgia, Ukraine, Moldova and Kyrgyzstan are lost; Adzharia has fallen; Transnistria is under siege. Enemies have engaged in subversive activities in Uzbekistan and Kazakhstan and are approaching the gates of Belarus. Minsk is standing firm, but if it falls the road to Moscow will be widely open.
>
> (Furman 2006: 68)

This statement by Dmitry Furman, one of the leading figures of the Russian Academy of Sciences' Institute of Europe, reflects a common perception of the Russian political and intellectual establishment as well as the majority of Russians. Russian geopolitical discussions have always focused on the Russian Near Abroad as a place with special historical and cultural meanings for Russians, just as the West has regarded this semicircle of countries surrounding Russia of similar strategic value because of its potential for containing Russia. For Russia, the Near Abroad is not simply an area that must be controlled for strategic reasons but is also composed of territories that are intimately linked to Russia through historical, economic and cultural ties. In this sense, Russian territorial consciousness extends beyond the country's present borders and neither Russia nor Russian identity are confined to the space occupied by the present Russian Federation. After all, Russia's international political history has always been dominated by action on its frontiers (O'Loughlin and Talbot 2005: 29).

In the context of post-Soviet politics, the relations between the Russian Federation and the Republic of Moldova are marked by many contradictions. As described above, Russia combines its official recognition of Moldova's territorial integrity and its involvement in the settlement of the Transnistrian question with its political, economic, financial and military support for the separatist regime in Tiraspol (Vrabie 2009: 79–88), justifying its interest in the Republic of Moldova on historical grounds and by emphasising the presence of a large Russian minority there.

With the intention of safeguarding its interests, Russia has introduced two plans for settling the issue of Moldova's territorial integrity: the 1997 Primakov Memorandum (Memorandum on the Principles of Normalisations of the Relations between the Republic of Moldova and Transnistria), signed the same year by Petru Lucinschi and the Transnistrian president Igor Smirnov, and the so-called Kozak Memorandum (Vrabie 2009: 83), which was supposed to have been signed in 2003 but was rejected by the Communist government in Moldova after massive public protests and foreign pressure. Both aimed at the federalisation of the Republic of Moldova in the expectation that maintaining a military base in Transnistria would allow Russia to exercise its influence over the new republic.

The Russian Federation's interests in Transnistria are based on the following strategic needs: to maintain the strategic positions of the Russian Federation in southeastern Europe; to defend in Moldova the interests of the Russian minority and other nationalities that consider Russia as their historical motherland; to maintain the strategic links with Transnistrian enterprises, many of which occupy a unique position within the military–industrial complex; to solve the conflict in the interest of Russia's own stability and of the consolidation of Russia's relations with the states in the Near Abroad that have a Russian minority; to establish stable and predictable relations with Romania and to reverse the latter's growing influence on Moldova (Țîcu 2011: 111–112).

Good bilateral relations have prevailed between Moldova and the Russian Federation as long as the Chișinău leadership has been receptive to Moscow's wishes, whereas policies contrary to Russian interests have been followed by sanctions, as in 2003 when the refusal to sign the Kozak Memorandum led to gas and wine 'wars' against the Moldovan state.

The war with Georgia and the recognition of the separatist republics of Abkhazia and South Ossetia formed the first, at least partially, successful attempt by Russia to use the issue of territorial integrity in a strategy that combined the question of national security, neo-imperial ambitions and the desire of being internationally recognised as a regional and world power. But the attempt has also been seen as proof of the incapacity of the Russian political elite to transform the post-Soviet space in accordance with contemporary principles of influence and power. Should a similar scenario be expected in regard to the Republic of Moldova? The logic at work in Russian political action suggests that the Russian Federation has no other strategies at the moment than those aimed at undermining the territorial integrity of neighbouring states in order to achieve its geopolitical goals (Țîcu 2011: 113).

Russia's attitude and behaviour towards the Near Abroad attest that the Kremlin seems content to grant internal sovereignty and territorial integrity to the Republic of Moldova, as long as the latter does not become a threat to

Russia's interests and challenges the perception of the Near Abroad as Russia's vital space. Obviously, the Russian Federation uses the issue of territorial integrity to influence policy-making in the Republic of Moldova. At the same time, Russia's position on the Transnistrian question remains something of a puzzle and may have to be explained in terms of the great power game between the Russian Federation, the European Union and the United States.

The European Union

The relations between the European Union and Moldova have evolved in the highly complex international environment that emerged in the early 1990s and are in several ways archetypal of the geopolitical tensions and political identity politics that have played out in both East and West since the collapse of the Soviet Union. As Soitu and Soitu (2011) have indicated, EU–Moldova relations cannot be clearly separated from the Moldova–Romania context. However, overarching processes of diffusing European Union regulations, norms and values did promote a struggle for distinct geopolitical orientations among Moldovan political elites. Moldova thus lived through a number of alternating periods of pro- and anti-EU sentiment that was also linked to questions of Moldovan national identity. Those siding with Russian Eurasian geopolitics understood Moldova as an inherently different culture, more closely linked to the Russian and Soviet past than to the West. These elites mistrusted what they saw as attempts to create EU hegemony and to weaken Moldovan sovereignty. The counterargument of EU-friendly elites, who gradually became stronger after 2009, placed Moldova at the heart of Europe, with close historical, linguistic and cultural links to Romania and Western nations.

The Republic of Moldova has thus, for understandable reasons, not been as coherent as the EU in defining its foreign policy priorities. Successive shifts can partly be explained by the effects of Transnistria's secession and Russia's increasingly assertive influence in the region, forcing Moldova to achieve a certain balance in its foreign relations and even to adopt at times a neutral stance to safeguard its fragile statehood.

In regard to Moldova's relations with the EU, three periods can be distinguished. The first (1991–2001) could be considered a period of missed opportunities because Moldova at the time failed to join the movement towards EU integration along with other East European countries, including the Baltic countries. The second coincides with the years in which the Communists governed (2001–2009) and the European Union introduced its Neighbourhood Policy. The increasing interest of the EU in its neighbourhood after the 2004 enlargement, together with other external and domestic factors such as the resolution process of the Transnistrian conflict, then made both parties more willing to advance their bilateral relations. The third period starts with the 2009 parliamentary elections in Moldova and the launching of the Eastern Partnership by the EU the same year. Since then, EU–Moldova relations have mostly been about Moldova's future prospects in Europe.

A few days after the fifth enlargement wave of May 2004, the EU launched its European Neighbourhood Policy, which marked a revision of its policy approach towards sixteen countries in its neighbourhood. In March 2005, the EU appointed a Special Representative (EUSR) for Moldova whose mandate was to participate in the resolution of the Transnistrian conflict. Since October 2005 the EU has the status of an observer in the 5 + 2 negotiation process (Chirila 2009: 168).

Following the signing of the Memorandum of Understanding on the EU Border Assistance Mission to Moldova and Ukraine (EUBAM) in October, the official opening ceremony of EUBAM took place on 1 December 2005. EUBAM at first received a two-year mandate, extended in 2007 for another two years (Chirila 2009: 169). Officials in Tiraspol perceived EUBAM as an attempt to install an economic blockade against the PMR in order to impose the Moldovan plan for reintegration.

The EU has offered to both parties, on the left and right bank of the Nistru River, the benefits of European integration and EU officials have repeatedly expressed support for Moldovan territorial integrity under the control of Chişinău. The Transnistrian question was on the agenda of several high-level meetings of European and Russian leaders between 2010 and 2012. Finally, German Chancellor Angela Merkel, during an official visit to the Republic of Moldova in August 2012, underlined her intention to provide support for Transnistria's reintegration into the Republic of Moldova and to extend the benefits of future visa and free trade agreements to the region.

Conclusion

The independence of the Moldovan state is based on the heritage of various mixed state- and empire-building processes with the Soviet nationality policy as the main foundation for national identity. In today's complex geopolitical context, this has led to diverging and conflicting trends in approaching the issue of borders, territory and state integrity, each supported by a specific historical narrative: a Romanian orientation, which sees the Republic of Moldova as a second Romanian state and its history as part of the general history of Romanians; a Moldovan one, according to which Moldovans and Romanians are two different peoples speaking different languages and having a different history despite a common ethnic origin and a partly shared past; and a third perspective, from Transnistria to the east, where a majority of Russians have taken control and consider themselves an integral part of the Russian political and cultural world.

Perhaps more importantly, these projects have been directly stimulated and influenced by actors outside Moldova, mainly by Romania and the Russian Federation, and have received support of various intensity and consistence from Moldovans. All three projects are more or less incompatible historically, ideologically and politically and have led to internal political strife (and even to war and secession in the case of Transnistria). They also strongly diverge in terms of Moldova's geopolitical orientation between West and East. For these reasons, the future of Moldova's political and territorial identity remains uncertain. Based on the positions taken by the various internal and external actors in the recent past and the present, several scenarios can, however, be imagined. The first one would result in a single Moldovan state that accords a large autonomy to Transnistria; the second outcome would be a confederation composed of Chişinău and Tiraspol (plus the Gagauz region), each of them with an equal status; the third would be the integration of the Right Bank (i.e. the present Republic of Moldova minus Transnistria) into Romania on historical grounds that emphasise a Romanian unitary state which includes the historical territory of Bessarabia; the fourth outcome would mean the attachment of Transnistria to the Russian Federation along the lines of the two consecutive referendums voted in Transnistria, where this proposal was supported by a majority, albeit under circumstances marked by great irregularities; a fifth scenario could be of Transnistria joining Ukraine, a possibility suggested by history – Transnistria had been part of Ukraine between 1917 and 1940 – and demographic factors (ethnic Ukrainians represent 28 per cent of the region's population); sixth, Transnistria could become an independent state, as its officials and inhabitants have advocated numerous times.

However, similar historical experiences, such as that of Ukraine, suggest that post-colonial or post-imperial contexts are hard to predict when a newly formed state's political and territorial identity is fragile and collides with great power ambitions of the former imperial centre. Since 1991 Moldova has often been perceived as being caught between two civilisational models: the Western world, represented in the eyes of Moldovans by the European Union and NATO, and the Russian one, with its Community of Independent States and various Eurasian supranational political and economic unions. But the basic dilemma of finding a balance between East and West appears to go back to 1812. Today, it is frequently presented in terms of a strong alternative: the Republic of Moldova could become a European state, with Transnistria an integral part of it as a result of European integration, or a confederation of Moldova and Transnistria under Russian control that would participate in the Eurasian projects of the Russian Federation. In both cases, the selected pattern would reflect not only internal preferences of Moldovans, influenced by various state- and nation-building projects, but also the general context of conflicting or consensual relations between the European Union and the Russian Federation regarding this issue. For these reasons, the most likely outcome in the short and medium run seems to be the maintenance of the present status quo.

Notes

1   The 1856 Treaty of Paris returned the southern part of Bessarabia to the Principality of Moldova, but the area was ceded to the Russian Empire during the 1878 Berlin Congress.
2   'Preşedintele Vladimir Voronin consideră că România trebuie să înceteze intervenţia în Republica Moldova'. Online. Available at: www.azi.md (last accessed 23 December 2003).

4 Reconceptualisations of borders in post-Soviet Ukraine

Between EU regulations, the Soviet legacy and internal political strife

Olga Filippova

The notion that post-Soviet borders would be more or less permanent was cruelly challenged by Russia's annexation of Ukrainian territory – the Crimean peninsula – in March 2014. This dramatic event served to accelerate a process of what might be called a 'hard bordering' between Russia and Ukraine. Shortly after the annexation of the Crimea, the Ukrainian government announced plans to construct a 'Maginot Line' on its border with Russia and thus prepare for possible further Russian incursions.[1] The long-term geopolitical significance of Ukraine–Russia border conflicts is difficult to foresee, but it is most likely that border-related issues will increase in visibility as political relations between Russia, other post-Soviet states and the European Union become more complex.

It is against this background, that the present chapter will attempt to investigate reconceptualisations and re-institutionalisations of post-Soviet Ukraine's borders by focusing on three dimensions: external geopolitical impacts on the reconfiguration of Ukraine's borders; the rethinking of borders and border issues in academic debates; and the reframing of post-Soviet space and perceptions of borders by the Ukrainian government and various other political actors, in particular with regard to the question whether the country's borders should be understood within a European or Eurasian framework. The following analysis will be based on three assumptions: the diverse nature of Ukraine's borders; the different functions that derive from this diversity; and the significance of Ukraine and its border issues for the EU.

International law and politics have traditionally ascribed a triple function to borders: that of demarcating state territory, guaranteeing state sovereignty and consolidating a sense of nation. However, in the recent past, both understandings of state border functions as well as the nature of borders themselves have undergone considerable transformation and, as David Newman (2003) has pointed out, the social sciences now operate under the assumption that boundaries are characterised by multidimensionality. Several contributions to this volume (particularly those of Kravchenko, Liikanen and Scott) emphasise, for example, the symbolic nature of borders in which often competing notions of national, European or Eurasian identity are communicated. In the case of post-1991 Ukraine, border issues have emerged not only in terms of

DOI: 10.4324/9781315858036-6

traditional border functions but also as an important factor of nation-building where historical, symbolic and geopolitical issues are closely intertwined. This is not of mere academic curiosity as similar situations have often led to conflicts and inconsistent political strategies.

Since Ukraine's western borders have become the eastern border of an enlarged EU, the issue of security (i.e. where it exists and where it does not) has become central to the perception of Europeanness (Browning and Joenniemi 2008). However, there are other less evident but nonetheless important facets that are linked to the construction of a European identity. As Christiansen, Jorgensen and A. Wiener (2001: 14) have asserted, the construction of Europe 'has depended on parallel constructions of the "other" ... against which a separate European identity is seen as being constructed, created or invented'. In this sense Ukraine and its borders constitute for the EU a 'closed other' that serves as an element within the process of European identity construction.

At present, Ukraine shares borders with seven other nation-states and the frozen-conflict zone of Transnistria. These borders are characterised by different border-crossing regimes, are of varying political and economic importance and are therefore being perceived differently by the wider public. Ukraine's western borders (with Poland, Romania; Hungary and Slovakia) have been stable external borders for decades, once dividing the Soviet Union from its allies in Central and Eastern Europe. After 1991 they gradually opened up and offered a considerable measure of free movement to people living in the borderlands until the EU's eastern enlargements in 2004 and 2007 led to an increasing number of restrictions. Several of the country's borders have, since independence, become external ones: with Belarus and the Russian Federation to the north and east and with Moldova in the southwest. These borders are of great political concern to both the EU and Russia. Not only are there a number of ongoing border disputes with neighbouring countries, the occupation and annexation of Crimea by Russian forces has driven home the interrelatedness of borders, strategic concerns and questions of national identity. Meanwhile, the border with Transnistria continues to be seen as a potential threat to the European security system and has remained under special surveillance in accordance with EU border policy regulations.[2]

This chapter deals with the post-Soviet context before the 2014 Russian incursions into Ukraine. It is in fact perhaps too soon to measure the impact of the conflict with Russia in terms of reconceptualisations of Ukraine's borders. Nevertheless, political discourses of borders that have emerged since independence reflect the centrality of borders and geopolitical thinking to Ukraine's nation-building project.

Border issues in Ukraine: examples from political discourse

Inevitably, Ukrainian political discourses on border issues are closely connected with nation-building and the independence of the state. Borders are seen as a guarantee to ensure territorial integrity and a hands-off policy towards Ukraine, as clearly demonstrated by the following extract of former President Yushchenko's speech on Independence Day in 2008:

> No one ever will give us direction in which way to choose. No one ever will measure off our borders, islands and peninsulas. ... We must speed up our work to achieve membership of the European system of security and raise the defence capabilities of the country. Only these steps will guarantee our security and the integrity of our borders.[3]

With the collapse of the Soviet Union, the prospect of contesting and renegotiating state borders has become everyday reality. This, in the case of a newly independent state such as Ukraine, seeking to secure national cohesion and territorial integrity, is of existential importance. Ukraine shares borders with seven *de jure* states and one *de facto* state (see Table 4.1). And since independence in 1991, there has been no dearth of challenges to Ukraine's territoriality. There remain, for example, a number of latent border disputes and 'frozen conflicts'. In October 2003 Russia claimed that the island of Tuzla, a sandy split located between the Crimean peninsula of Kerch (Ukraine) and the Taman peninsula (Russia) was part of continental Russia and had therefore not been transferred to Ukraine in 1954. Although the press service of the Ukrainian Foreign Ministry announced in July 2005 that Russia had recognised Tuzla as part of the Ukraine, this was not confirmed by the Information and Press Department of the Russian MID.[4] In July 2010, President Yanukovich signed a law on the demarcation of the common border in order to resolve remaining disputes on segments of the common border. This gave rise to a public debate and has been criticised by the opposition. As the events of 2014 have shown, these issues were not resolved; they were rather kept 'alive' for future strategic use by Russia.[5] Another problematic case is that of the unrecognised quasi-state of Transnistria (or Pridnestrovian Moldovan

Table 4.1 The new borders of post-Soviet Ukraine

State	Length of border
Russian Federation	2295.04 km (incl. 321 km of maritime border)
Republic of Moldova	1222 km (incl. 267 km of river border)
– Transnistria	452 km
Republic of Belarus	1084.2 km (incl. 325.9 km of river border)
Romania	613.8 km (incl. 325.9 km of river border)
Republic of Poland	542.39 km (incl. 187.3 km of river border and 33 km of maritime border)
Republic of Hungary	136.7 km (incl. 85.1 km of river border)
Slovak Republic	97.852 km (incl. 2.3 km of river border)

Source: Zagal'na kharakterystyka derzhavnogo kordonu. Online. Available at: http://mil.in.ua/encyclopediya/pravoohoronci/prykordonnyky (last accessed 18 September 2010).

Republic), located between the Dniester River and Ukraine. With the collapse of the Soviet Union, Transnistria declared its independence from Moldova, an act which led to armed conflict in March–July 1992. As a result, the question of borders between Ukraine and Moldova has yet to be fully resolved.

Perhaps more than in many other European cases, Ukraine's border and borderlands play a significant role in the definition of nation, whether conceived as part of a wider European or a Slavic identity. In this respect, it hardly matters whether individual politicians adopt a pro-European or a pro-Russian stance, although they may emphasise different aspects. Indeed, all of them have to take into account the influence of Ukraine's two most powerful neighbours, the EU and the Russian Federation. During a conference on Europe's borders, Hryhoriy Nemyria, a former deputy prime minister, thus addressed the issue of Ukraine's borders in the context of Europeanisation: 'The borders of Europe are not a question of geography. Ukraine belongs to Europe geographically, but it is very significant for us to belong to Europe politically and economically.'[6] Ukraine's political leaders constantly have to convince their Western partners that their country does have a European choice and that, after it will have completed certain reforms, it will be 'at the centre of the Euro-Atlantic world'.[7] However, as V. Zigalov has pointed out, given Russia's influence, Ukraine's situation could only change if the United States and Europe would be prepared to make considerable investments in order to 're-orient Ukraine'; otherwise the country would remain a 'borderland' between the West and Eurasia.[8]

In political discourse, borders are closely associated with potential threats and national security. Unlike Russia's official discourse, Ukrainian political rhetoric generally remains vague about the nature of these potential threats, simply underlining that a 'state border must become a border of good neighbourhood, partnership and little hostility between friends ... but at the same time it must be impenetrable for those who have bad intentions'.[9] The most notable concern voiced is illegal migration. In this perspective, Ukraine's borders are viewed as a barrier against threats that challenge the stability of the European continent. Thus, the EU–Ukraine Readmission Agreement, which was signed in 2006 and entered into force on 1 January 2010, regulates the return of undocumented Ukrainian nationals and third-country citizens who entered EU territory via Ukraine. Indeed, Ukraine's northeastern border is relatively open and illegal immigrants tend to concentrate along the neo-European border in the west, a situation reflected in a distinction between the two borders' functions. Yuriy Lutsenko, a former Minister of Interior Affairs, has thus stated that 'as a politician, I want the EU's doors on illegal [migrants] to be closed on the eastern rather than on the western border of Ukraine'.[10] He proposed that the border should be considered as an instrument for implementing a policy that enforces the protection of the state.

The border issue becomes a borderland issue as soon as the focus is on cross-border cooperation which is targeted at promoting ties with partners in neighbouring countries and seen as vital 'to achieve national goals and fulfil national interests'.[11] On the regional level, cross-border cooperation aims at attracting investments, creating jobs through the introduction of new technologies and facilitating cultural exchange. At the same time, it offers an opportunity for Ukraine's administration to demonstrate how much progress the country has made towards the Europeanness of the country. During the Yushchenko presidency, participation in EU projects was high on the political agenda and relations between the border regions and European partners were considered a 'key to solve economic, humanitarian, social, cultural and other problems'.[12] Border issues also had a higher public visibility. Yushchenko's policies were strongly oriented towards European integration and border issues thus played a significant role in promoting the European vector. Moreover, Yushchenko's presidential term coincided with the EU's eastern enlargement, which strongly affected the status of Ukraine's borders. After the Orange Revolution and the second EU eastern enlargement, issues concerning the Ukraine–Russia border received much greater attention, not least because the EU gave them a high priority (Zhurzhenko 2007).

Victor Yanukovych's government has privileged the economic dimension of borders, with more pragmatic goals. It has introduced key legislation that has brought the country's border and migration management closer to European standards. According to an analysis prepared by Marta Jaroszewicz for the Centre of Eastern Studies, a Polish think-tank:

> [the] strategy of integrated border management has been prepared and passed through the parliament at express pace. This is the main strategic document that prepares Ukraine to leave behind the post-Soviet system of border control and join the four-tier model of border management operational in the EU.[13]

Ukraine's recent official discourse has stressed not only the country's 'European choice' but also affirmed and even claimed its European identity. In an interview given on 13 October 2010, Prime Minister Mykola Azorov not only stated that the 'most important thing for us is to do for ourselves the work necessary to bring Ukraine closer to European standards'.[14] Asked whether the free-trade agreement with the EU or a customs union with Russia was more important, he insisted: 'We are in Europe geographically, just look at the map. Ukraine is the largest European country in territory and the fifth in terms of population. Not to notice Ukraine on Europe's map is just impossible. Or else, one would have to have zero political outsight [sic!].'[15]

At the same time, the theme of 'Slavic brotherhood' has received a new reading in today's political rhetoric of belonging, mainly for pragmatic reasons. Ukraine and Russia are said to have mutual interests and Ukraine is indeed an important market for Russian products. Over the last decade, President Kuchma's 'multi-vector foreign policy' thus gave way to the 'European vector politics' under Yushchenko, which has since been replaced by Victor Yanukovych's politics of 'the most favourable regime from both the EU and

Russia'. The official discourse no longer opposes or views as contradictory Ukraine's relations with Russia and the EU.[16] Even more, it is claimed that this approach is beneficial for the EU:

> European integration remains a priority of our foreign policy. For the first time in the years of independence we have approached the Association Agreement with the European Union … It is obvious that normalisation of our relations with Russia does not stand in the way of our European integration, but helps it. The United Europe needs an economically strong, democratic Ukraine, which together with Russia contributes to strengthening stability in Central and Eastern Europe, as well as throughout the Eurasian space.[17]

The framing of border issues in academic discourse

Research on border issues by Ukrainian scholars have taken one of two forms: policy-oriented analyses and 'pure' academic research. The first category of studies is generally produced by research institutions that resemble think-tanks and include the National Institute for Strategic Research, the Institute for Euro-Atlantic Cooperation, the Centre for Peace, Conversion and Foreign Policy of Ukraine and several regional centres, such as the Center of Regional Research in Odessa and the Center of Inter-Regional Borderland Cooperation, created by Kharkiv oblast (Ukraine) and Belgorod oblast (Russia). Analyses mostly focus on the processes of Ukraine's European and Euro-Atlantic integration and its position in the wider world, producing comments, recommendations and forecasts.

One main theme has been the question how the Ukrainian government's proclaimed multi-vector, non-bloc foreign security policy can be reconciled with the need to continue reforms that would result in the adoption of Euro-Atlantic standards of the rule of law, transparency and accountability. As one author has stated, unless Ukraine implements these standards, it will not be able to become even a 'security bridge' between the West and Russia but will find itself in a growing security vacuum that will create a perfect environment for the further marginalisation of the country in regional and global politics (Sushko 2010: 6). Several reports, often produced thanks to various international grants, have attempted to evaluate the Ukrainian government's efforts to move closer to European standards (see, among others, 'Borders of Ukraine')[18]. Other research has tried to assess the impact of EU policies on Ukraine. After examining EU geopolitics and EU policies for Ukraine with regard to borders, regulations and standards, Mitriaeva (2007), for example, has concluded that political and security issues play a much greater role than economic questions.

Academic research has a different research focus, methodology and even readership, which can be post-Soviet for publications in Ukrainian or Russian or international for those in English. Pavliuk (1999), for instance, has ana-lysed how border issues are linked to the mutual interests of Ukraine and its western neighbours (Poland, Hungary, Romania and the Slovak Republic). By studying successive bilateral agreements between Ukraine and countries of Central Europe[19] since 1992, he has shown that for the latter, Ukraine's borders guarantee to a certain extent geographical 'detachment' from Russia, less direct influence of the Russian Federation and therefore a lack of a direct external threat to national security. Moreover, the political and cultural dia-logue between these countries is strongly informed by the presence of national minorities living on the territory of neighbouring states.

The impact of the EU's eastern enlargement on Ukraine's borders was first studied by Mrinska (2006), while Zhurzhenko (2004, 2005, 2010) has focused on various aspects of the institutionalisation of the Ukraine–Russia border and largely contributed to make this border and its borderlands one of the best-studied in Ukraine. Zhurzhenko has emphasised the simultaneity of seemingly contradictory processes, leading on the one hand to greater physical barriers, higher tariffs and a stricter surveillance regime and, on the other, to cross-border cooperation and the development of programmes that promote greater regional economic integration. Kononov (2010) and Khobta (2010) have investigated everyday life in these borderlands, particularly in the oblasts of Rostov (Russia) and Lugansk (Ukraine). Filippova (2010) has studied the role of the border for identity politics. Cross-border cooperation has also been examined through the lens of economic geography, but these studies generally lack a theoretical framework and have been hampered by the little interest regional authorities have shown in the development of regional cross-border cooperation.[20]

Finally, it should be noted that Ukraine's border issues have attracted a number of western scholars. Bojcun (2005) has examined the problems of migrants and refugees along the Russian–Ukrainian border and the EU's attitude towards them in the light of its 2004 enlargement. Zimmer (2008) has produced an analysis of Ukraine's asylum policy by focusing on migrants and refugees in the 'buffer zone'. Vermeersch (2007) has been interested in the impact of the EU's eastern enlargement on the situation of the Ukrainian minority in Poland. Several EU Border Monitorings have resulted in academic research (Border Monitoring Project Ukraine 2010; Buzalka and Benč 2007). Allina-Pisano (2009) has published an excellent ethnographic case study of a Magyar village divided between Ukraine and Slovakia, which concludes that:

> As the softening of internal borders and harmonisation of domestic policy have brought about a degree of denationalisation within EU member states, EU eastward expansion, with its attending technologies of border control and economic inequalities, has driven processes of nationalisation in its outer borderlands.
>
> Allina-Pisano (2009: 290)

The European Union: a focus on border management

Since the European Union prioritised engagement with the newly independent states of the former Soviet Union, it has been setting agendas with specific priorities for particular countries that are intended to promote further political dialogue and cooperation. The key document for the EU's policy towards non-EU members is the European Neighbourhood Policy (ENP), viewed as the main instrument to target sustainable development and approximation to EU policies and standards as agreed upon in the ENP Action Plan. Although the document is comprehensive, EU enlargement policy privileges certain tasks and reflects differently in various national contexts. For the period 2007–2013, the EU has set up the European Neighbourhood and Partnership Instrument (ENPI) to support the development of an area of prosperity and good neighbourliness encompassing the European Union and the partner countries covered by the ENP.

With regard to the countries of the Eastern Region[21], five strategic areas, reflecting the EU's main priorities, have received support: networks, and in particular transport and energy networks; environment and forestry; border and migration management, the fight against international crime, and customs; people-to-people activities, information and support; and anti-personnel land mines, explosive remnants of war, small arms and light weapons (European Commission 2006a: 2). Resources under the ENPI are allocated on a national basis according to country-specific priorities defined by a Country Strategy Paper (CSP) and a National Indicative Programme (NIP). For Ukraine, both such documents were published in 2006 (European Commission 2006b, 2006c). The first, adopted by the Commission in March 2007, offers a comprehensive overview of proposed EU assistance priorities. The second contains three Priority Areas (European Commission 2006c):

- Support for democratic development and good governance. Targets are public administration reform and public finance management; rule of law and judicial reform; human rights, civil society development and local government. Education, science and people-to-people contacts/exchanges.
- Support for regulatory reform and administrative capacity building. Targets are: promoting mutual trade, improving the investment climate and strengthening social reform; sector-specific regulatory aspects.
- Support for infrastructure development. Targets are: (non-nuclear) energy; transport; environment; border management and migration including readmission-related issues.

More particularly, Ukrainian border issues are considered under two headings: security and infrastructure development (European Commission 2006c: 4). They are conceptualised within their strategic contexts and in view of their long-term impact (Sushko 2006). One of the main ideas of EU policy is that borders should be transparent as well as secure, not create obstacles to the movement of people, but also serve as a 'secure fence' to effectively deal with international threats such as illegal migration, trafficking in human beings and organised crime. The most significant issues related to the 1,418-km-long border between Ukraine and the EU are Ukraine's incomplete legal frameworks, ongoing processes of border delimitation and demarcation, the lack of efficient infrastructure and a boundary with the frozen-conflict zone of Transnistria (Sushko 2006).

EU border assistance to Ukraine is implemented on a technical and a political level. Technical assistance is mainly aimed at the upgrading and modernisation of border crossings and the strengthening of Ukraine's eastern border. To improve border management the EU supports reform of the State Border Guard Service (SBGS), which also implies new legislation, infrastructure and personnel training. To this end, the SBGS cooperates with the European Agency for the Management of Operational Cooperation at the External Borders of the Member States of the European Union (FRONTEX), primarily through joint operations along the EU's external border within the framework of the Five Borders joint pilot project (FRONTEX 2008: 63).

Political and geopolitical aspects play a significant part in the EU's border policy. Reinforcing the Ukraine–Russia border means not only the creation of a 'secure fence' but is also aimed at weakening Russia's geopolitical role and influence in the region. As the eastern enlargements have brought Transnistria closer to the EU's eastern border, this conflict zone has become of special concern because of actual and potential threats.[22] Over the recent years, the Union has launched several initiatives to provide political ground for the conflict-resolution process there, the most important being the EU Border Assistance Mission (EUBAM) set up in 2005. According to the EU, the mission is technical and advisory; its mandate is to help improve the capacity of the Moldovan and Ukrainian border and customs services to prevent and detect illegal activities (smuggling, customs fraud etc.).[23]

Security-related concerns are strongly linked to migration issues, that is, Ukrainians moving to EU countries and third-country citizens trying to enter the EU via Ukraine. The control of these flows are considered a priority in the cooperation between Ukraine and the EU. EU visa regulations are mostly determined by the stipulations of the Schengen Agreement and Convention that provides common ground for regulating the movement of people and goods both inside the Schengen area and between the contracting parties and other countries. In January 2008, agreements between the Ukraine and the EC on granting visas and on readmission entered into force. Moreover, the 2008 EU–Ukraine Summit in Paris has launched a dialogue with the long-term perspective of establishing a visa-free regime between the two partners.[24] Migration and visa regulations have also been one of the priorities of the EU–Ukraine Association Agenda for 2010 (Delegation of the European Union to Ukraine 2010). With five neighbouring EU countries, Ukraine remains a major transit country for irregular migrants. Already ahead of the EU's eastern enlargement, the Söderköping process was launched in 2001 to address problems of cross-border cooperation and to promote a dialogue on issues related to asylum seekers and irregular migrants between countries located on the EU's future eastern border. Since 2004, the Söderköping process has specifically focused on sharing experiences about asylum, protection, migration and border management between Estonia, Latvia, Lithuania, Hungary, the Slovak Republic, Poland and Romania, on the one hand, and Belarus, Moldova and Ukraine, on the other.[25]

Thus, European standards for border management and enforcement require Ukraine to develop a certain migration policy, introduce migration controls, strengthen the border with Russia, better control the issuing of passports and to make use of biometric data. In response, Ukraine has unilaterally adopted a visa-free regime for EU citizens and a two-phased action plan that will allow Ukrainians to freely enter EU countries. The plan has a political component – Ukraine has to sign the Council of Europe Conventions – and a technical one – reinforcing its eastern border. Achieving both seems highly unlikely in the near future, given external and especially internal factors (mainly political instability). And while the institutionalisation of the Schengen zone may have made significant contributions towards a unified Europe – the issue is still being debated (see, for example, Lacroix and Nicolaïdis 2011) – Ukraine has been facing new obstacles or at least challenges. For several years, Ukraine enjoyed a visa-free regime with its western neighbours until Hungary, Poland, Slovakia and Romania joined the EU. Since then, experts and journalists have often stressed that the dialogue between the EU and Ukraine about visa regulations has been rather one-sided and sometimes has become the source of discriminatory measures against Ukrainian citizens, distancing or even isolating them from the rest of Europe.[26]

At the same time, demands to enforce borders are motivated by EU concerns about security threats from outside the Union. Since the EU's eastern enlargements, its new external borders are located in regions characterised by poverty and political tensions. Although concerns about organised crime, smuggling or illegal migration are well-founded, experts have emphasised that a rapid expansion of the Schengen regime to the new EU members serves short-term interests by creating a barrier against crime but 'may work against the Union's long-term security interests' (Batt 2003: 5).

Infrastructure development has been implemented through several initiatives. Increased cross-border cooperation, for example, is a major component of the ENP. Thus, the ENPI aims at supporting cross-border contacts, as well as cooperation between local and regional actors and civil society. For the period 2007–2013, EUR1.18 billion have been allocated for activities of this kind along the EU's eastern and southern borders, with the objective of developing partnerships that jointly address common challenges in fields such as the economic and social development of border areas, environment and health (communicable diseases), illegal immigration and trafficking, efficient border management and people-to-people contacts. For Ukraine, the EU has been the major funding source of cross-border cooperation. The ENPI financial envelope under the National Indicative Programme amounted to EUR494 million for the period 2007–2010 (European Commission 2009a). In accordance with the ENPI for cross-border cooperation, financial support was given to multi-country (including the Neighbourhood Investment Facility) and regional programmes. Ukraine is participating in three cross-border cooperation programmes adopted in 2008 for the period 2007–2013: Romania–Moldova–Ukraine, with a budget of EUR126.718 million, Poland–Belarus–Ukraine (EUR186.201 million) and the Black Sea Basin (EUR17.306 million). The programmes have been designed to foster sustainable development and enhance human contacts.[27] The EU also supports imports initiatives on small-border movements (Eastern Partnership Panel on Migration and Asylum 2007, 2009). However, questions have been raised over the effective operation of all these programmes.

Conclusions

In post-Soviet Ukraine, border issues manifest themselves in several domains: nation-building, the construction of a national identity, state security and geopolitical dialogues. This can be linked to two diachronic dimensions: the unfinished process of nation- and state-building, which the majority of European countries achieved in the late nineteenth and early twentieth century, and the country's geopolitical aspirations to become part of Europe and the EU since the end of the Cold War. But Ukraine also has a Soviet legacy of Slavic brotherhood that has produced a particular political language and particular geopolitical orientations, as well as internal political strife leading to ambivalent and inconsistent politics.

Despite their significance, border issues are underestimated in academic and public discourse. Although researchers have become more interested in studying borders, their methodologies are mostly inappropriate for the post-Soviet space. Post-colonial conceptualisations have not only failed to stimulate a debate but have hardly found an echo with Ukrainian scholars. For these reasons, the academic discourse has had only a minimal impact on public debate, political language and political decision-making. In the media, border issues are generally covered in a way that stresses negative connotations. Other topics, such as Ukrainian cooperation within the ENP framework, are hardly present.

Border policies implemented by Ukraine's political authorities bear the stamp of Ukraine's two powerful neighbours, the EU and Russia. In the political discourse, border-related themes are actualised with every new round of EU monitoring of Ukrainian reforms and every time the geopolitical and economic relationship between Ukraine and Russia has to be redefined. It is difficult to find a comprehensive long-term concept of borders and border management, since there has been no political continuity. Every political force that accedes to power has advanced different priorities and acted situationally. Yet border issues have been conceptualised within the framework of a European and

Eurasian space. The lack of a consistent conceptualisation of borders and border management, together with the EU's disappointment about the implementation of democratic reforms and the rule of law, could lead to Ukraine losing its status as a 'security bridge' between the West and Eurasia.

The security of Ukraine's borders has been one of the main targets of the ENP. However, it is far from clear whether this is enough to integrate non-EU countries, and particularly Ukraine, into the European space. It seems that Ukraine is a good illustration of EU geopolitics as 'contested projects of re-territorialisation and bordering' and of core–periphery dynamics (Scott 2009). Paradoxically enough, EU border policies and the absence of adequate and effective EU geopolitical models to deal with the wider Neighbourhood have led to rather exclusionary practices, which have created a perfect environment for worsening socio-economic inequalities and widening cultural differences.

Notes

1 'Ukrainians build "Maginot Line" to repel Russia', *Financial Times*, 31 March 2014. Online. Available at: www.ft.com/intl/cms/s/0/38e1f6bc-b8e9-11e3-98c5-00144fea bdc0.html (last accessed 31 October 2014).
2 See 'EU Border Assistance Mission to the Republic of Moldova and Ukraine' (European Commission 2005).
3 See 'Promova Prezidenta Viktora Yushchenko z Nagody Dnia Nezalezhnosti Ukrainy', *Press office of Viktor Yushchenko*. Online. Available at: www.uaoc.in.ua/ 2008/08/blog-post_341.html (last accessed 10 December 2010).
4 See Victor Yanukovich's presidential address pronounced on Independence Square in Kyiv in 2010. Online. Available at: www.president.gov.ua/en/news/5534.html (last accessed 1 December 2010).
5 Other border disputes have included that over Zmeinyi Island (also known as Snake or Serpent Island) between Romania and Ukraine. This dispute was eventually resolved by an International Court of Justice decision in 2009. A dispute with Moldova over a land-border segment near the village of Palanka, on the road between Odessa and Reni, was decided in 1999.
6 See G. Nemyria 'Derzhava potrebue 'bil'she Evropy', *Uriadovyi Kur'er*, 17 December 2008. Online. Available at: www.ukurier.gov.ua/index.php?articl=1&id=2 (last accessed 10 December 2010).
7 Prime Minister Yanukovich in a statement published in The Washington Post on 5 October 2006. See 'Yanukovich (The Washington Post): Vybor Ukrainy – v Napravlenii Evropy', *Podrobnosti-TV*, 5 October 2006. Online. Available at: http://podrob nosti.ua/power/intpol/2006/10/05/354591.html (last accessed 1 December 2011).
8 See V. Zigalov 'Yushchenko Peretvoryvsia na Komvelia, ale chi Bude Vin Tak Samo Poslidovnym Dali? (Ogliqd Evropeis'koi Presy)', quoted in a press review of *Radio Svobody*. Online. Available at: www.radiosvoboda.org/content/article/ 961930.html (last accessed 10 December 2011).
9 Victor Yushchenko 'Vitannia Presidenta Ukrainy Viys'kovosluzhbovtsiam, Pratsivnykam ta Veteranam Derzhavnoi prikordonnoi Sluzhby (2009) President Victor Yanukovich, official website. Online. Available at: www.president.gov.ua/news/ 13850.html (last accessed 10 December 2010).
10 See 'Yak Polituk Ya Pragnu, shchob Dveri ES vid Nelegaliv Zakrylysia na Skhidnomu, a ne na Zapadnomu Kordony Ukrainy', Interview with Yuriy Lutsenko,

UNIAN, 26 June 2009. Online. Available at: http://eunews.unian.net/ukr/detail/ 191471 (last accessed 3 December 2010).

11 'President discusses border cooperation', *Press office of Viktor Yushchenko*, 6 March 2007. Online. Available at: www.president.gov.ua/en/news/5534.html (last accessed 1 December 2010). In December 2006, the Ukrainian government launched a pro-gramme of cross-border cooperation, which has since then been further developed and extended for the period 2011–2015. The programme concerns eight Euroregions, border regions shared with both EU member states and newly independent states (Russian Federation, Belarus and Moldova). For more information, see the official website of Ukraine's Cabinet of Ministers at: http://zakon.rada.gov.ua/cgi-bin/laws/ main.cgi?nreg=1088-2010-%EF.

12 'President discusses border cooperation', *Press office of Viktor Yushchenko*, 6 March 2007. Online. Available at: www.president.gov.ua/en/news/5534.html (last accessed 1 December 2010).

13 See M. Jaroszewicz, 'EU-Ukraine visa liberalisation: an assessment of Ukraine's readiness', *EurActiv*, 4 February 2011. Online. Available at: www.euractiv.com/east-mediterranean/eu-ukraine-visa-liberalisation-assessment-ukraine-readiness-analysis-5019181918 (last accessed 5 July 2014).

14 See 'Ukraine Prime Minister: "We are against South Stream"', Interview with the Ukrainian Prime Minister Mykola Azarov, *EurActiv*, 14 October 2010. Online. Available at: www.euractiv.com/en/east-mediterranean/ukraine-prime-minister-we-are-against-south-stream-interview-498806 (last accessed 5 July 2014).

15 See note above.

16 See endnote 2 of this chapter.

17 'President's Independence Day Address at the Independence Square in Kyiv', *Press office of Viktor Yanukovych*, 24 August 2010.

18 'Borders of Ukraine', Project supported by the Freedom House Partnership for Reform Program and funded by the United States Agency for International Development. Online. Available at: http://cpcfpu.org.ua/en/projects/borders/ (last accessed 5 December 2010). Unless indicated otherwise, all translations are by the author.

19 For the debate on the definition of Central European countries, see Zamfirescu (1996).

20 See, for instance, the publications of the Center of Inter-Regional Borderland Cooperation and the Center of Regional Research, which are available online at: www.euroregion.ru/ and http://crs.org.ua/ru/18.html (last accessed on 29 November 2010).

21 The Eastern Region includes Armenia, Azerbaijan, Belarus, Georgia, Moldova, the Russian Federation and Ukraine.

22 Major perceived threats include illegal migration, organised crime, smuggling and the trafficking of human beings, weapons and drugs. For more details, see FRONTEX (2008).

23 EUBAM was established in response to a joint letter by the presidents of Moldova and Ukraine, calling for additional support to improve capacity-building in border management, including customs, along the border between Ukraine and Moldova (and Transnistria). The mission works closely with the team of the EU Special Representative for Moldova on political border issues and has field offices in Kyiv, Chisinau and Odessa. For more information, see European Commission (2005). The current mandate expires on 30 November 2015.

24 The main focus has been on document security (including biometrics), illegal migration (including readmission), public order and security, as well as external relations.

25 This pro-active initiative is supported by the European Commission, the Swedish Migration Board, the United Nations High Commissioner for Refugees and the

International Organisation for Migration. For more information on the Söderköping process, see the website www.soderkoping.org.ua.
26 For more information, see, among others, 'The Schengen Acquis: A view from Ukraine', published by the Centre for Peace, Conversion and Foreign Policy of Ukraine. Online. Available at: http://cpcfpu.ru/en/projects/foreignpolicy/papers/01 2005/Russia-Belarus (last accessed 31 October 2014).
27 For more information on these programmes, see the websites of the Joint Operational Programme Romania–Ukraine–Republic of Moldova 2007–2013. Online. Available at: www.ro-ua-md.net and the Hungary–Slovakia–Romania–Ukraine ENPI Cross-border Cooperation Programme 2007–2013. Online Available at: www.huskroua-cbc.net (both last accessed 31 October 2014).

Part Two

Border management and cross-border cooperation

5 Eastern Neighbourhood as a political divide

EU policies of regional cooperation and 'selective visibility' in the case of Ukraine

James Wesley Scott

Conceptualisations of the EU as a geopolitical actor reflect a variety of disciplinary, philosophical and critical approaches as well as rather different normative understandings. In this regard, new geopolitical perspectives and the question of whether Europe is engaging in postmodern, post-colonial or, in the most critical reading, neo-imperial statecraft, inform much critical debate on the EU's external policies (Anderson 2007; Bialasiewicz 2012; Browning and Joenniemi 2008; Klinke 2012; Kuus 2007). Some readings of the 'Europe as Empire' metaphor are rather benign, if not outright positive, such as the suggestion by Jan Zielonka (2006) that a 'post-modern' European empire without immutable and excluding borders can generate a hybrid multi-level sense of governance, citizenship and identity. On the other hand, more normative International Relations understandings of EU geopolitics rely on 'objective' criteria with which to assess the EU's actual or putative ability to act internationally (Tocci 2012).

As different as these interpretations of 'Europe in the world' are, they all explicitly raise questions regarding the EU's ability to balance security prerogatives with improved regional cooperation and conflict resolution. Since the end of the Cold War, the European Union has been engaged in attempts to promote cross-border and regional cooperation with its immediate neighbours. Various programmes and policy initiatives have, for example, accompanied the process of EU enlargement and external engagement with the former Soviet Union. Starting with TACIS (Technical Assistance for the Commonwealth of Independent States) in 1991, the EU's external policies have acquired considerable institutional complexity and are now defined, among others, by a Partnership and Cooperation Agreement with the Russian Federation and the European Neighbourhood Policy (ENP), which structures cooperation with a number of former Soviet republics. More recently, the Eastern Partnership (EaP) has signalled greater EU engagement with eastern neighbours such as Ukraine. Inaugurated in 2009 during the Czech EU presidency, the EaP is a logical consequence of the EU's push for a more central geopolitical role in the post-Soviet space. In all of these initiatives the EU has sought to create a clear geopolitical identity for itself by putting a distinct stamp on the nature of regional cooperation. This has been attempted through an insistence on

DOI: 10.4324/9781315858036-8

common values and acceptance of the EU's Acquis as a basis for political partnership. In addition, however, the EU has engaged in a rather selective framing of common Neighbourhood concerns in its concrete cooperation practises. While the ENP and EaP are labelled as comprehensive and inclusive platforms for regional dialogue, the last decade has seen a prioritisation of security issues and institutional cooperation at the expense of social needs and an engagement with civil society. In what I argue resembles an Arendtian 'politics of visibility', the EU has selectively drawn attention to issues that address its specific short-term needs while marginalising other areas of cooperation. This also includes using human rights as political leverage in regulating the intensity of political interaction.

Perhaps inevitably then, the ENP, the Eastern Partnership and the strategic partnership with Russia have formed a backdrop for political and cultural contestations that are often laden with tension. This has become particularly evident given the heightened sense of crisis that has followed the Crimea annexation of March 2014 and Russian incursions into East Ukraine. However, even before these events EU–Russia relations, and by extension the Eastern Partnership, have been characterised by a geopolitical competition for normative power (Steinkohl 2010) partly based on different understandings of sovereignty and state–society relations (Haukkala 2010). However, there is also evidence that relations between the EU and its neighbours, Ukraine in particular, are similarly characterised by discomfiture regarding the issue of conditionality, or convergence with EU norms (Korosteleva 2012). Of particular interest is the degree to which the EU is seen to offer an inclusive platform for the development of political dialogue and whether its notion of partnership elicits positive reactions. Here it has been important to obtain information on the ways in which civil society actors view the EU (and EU member states) in terms of providing opportunity structures for the implementation of domestic agendas, organisational development and learning good practices from EU member states. Furthermore, it is important to know more about the perceptions of local civil society actors regarding the openness and inclusiveness of the EU in terms of engaging local concerns and opinions.

Within broad debates in the literature regarding the EU's ability to balance security prerogatives with improved regional cooperation and conflict resolution, this chapter will, first, in somewhat general terms, explore external perceptions of the EU as a political actor on the international scene and, secondly and more specifically, evaluate the regional cooperation policies the EU has developed with regard to its eastern neighbours in terms of their local reception by civil society actors. This also includes perceptions of the evolving quality of the EU's social and political influence within post-Soviet contexts.

Rather than apply a top-down approach that presupposes a specific geopolitical role for the EU within the so-called Neighbourhood, this contribution will emphasise perceived contradictions and contested political and socio-cultural underpinnings of EU cooperation policies. Crucially, the chapter will also indicate the ways in which local actors interpret the EU as a potential promoter of greater intercultural dialogue and social transformation.

This chapter is based primarily on a Ukrainian case study but is supported by evidence from work carried out in Russia, Belarus and Moldova. The empirical material used consists largely of interviews with representatives of civil society organisations but also reflects the perspectives of academic researchers, policy experts and international organisations.[1] The research confirms the EU's impact on social transformation in post-Soviet states. However, it also gives evidence of a considerable cooperation divide between the EU and its neighbours. On the positive side, the EU's Neighbourhood policies are praised in the sense that they have established a new platform for political, technical and social cooperation that has assisted in institutional capacity-building and social agenda-setting. On the other hand, the ENP–EaP policy complex is regarded as paternalistic, inflexible and insensitive to local needs. However, these more general assessments do not provide the whole story. While programmatic and technical issues are important conditioning factors of regional cooperation, assessments of the more ideational aspects of EU cooperation policies reveal a rather complex picture. Indeed, the EU's desire for a visible political identity as a sovereign actor and cooperation practices that derive from it are also critically reflected in local interpretations of Neighbourhood policies. In its dealings with Ukraine the EU has, however, applied a selective 'politics of invisibility' that highlights mainly those aspects of Neighbourhood that conform to the EU's more immediate agenda of regional cooperation while marginalising important social issues that condition post-Soviet transformation. Patterns in the perceptions and opinions voiced by interviewees (and to an extent in the research literature) will be elaborated below in terms of dominant narratives. These include: perceptions of EU unilateralism; the issue of 'common values' as an ideational basis for regional cooperation; the borderland complex which emerges as a subtext of EU cooperation, particularly with Ukraine; and a lack of commitment and support to representatives of civil society. Given the future challenges facing regional cooperation in the EU's Neighbourhood and given the potential role of the EU as a conditioner and agenda-setter of socio-political transformation, the concluding section suggests the need for a cooperation philosophy that bridges political, cultural and administrative divides between the EU and its eastern neighbours.

Regional cooperation and the emerging EU geopolitics of neighbourhood: a possibilistic perspective

Cross-border relations between the EU and post-Soviet states have evolved rapidly during the last two decades with cities, regions, states and civil society opening new avenues of communication with their neighbours. One major conditioning factor underlying this cooperation is the EU's desire to assume a stabilising but also transformative role in the post-Soviet context (Browning and Joenniemi 2008).[2,3] Evidence for redoubled EU efforts to promote cooperation with its immediate neighbours is provided by the European Neighbourhood and Partnership Instrument (ENPI), which in the programming period 2007–13 undertook investments in promoting cooperation and integration between the EU and neighbouring countries, advancing good governance and sustainable socio-economic development in the respective states, and promoting cross-border cooperation.[4] The ENP has thus complemented the EU's attempts to develop a closer relationship with the Russian Federation based on bilateral 'Common Spaces' – i.e. areas of mutual interest and where common values ostensibly form a basis for cooperation. An economic space, a common space of 'freedom, security and justice', a common space of external security and, finally, a common space of research, education and culture were defined within the framework of the 1997 Partnership and Cooperation Agreement. More recently, with the EaP, the EU has prioritised cooperation with its eastern neighbours Armenia, Azerbaijan, Belarus, Georgia, Moldova and Ukraine. The priorities of the EaP suggest an ambitious regional cooperation agenda that seeks to develop more comprehensive free trade and to promote democracy and good governance, energy security, public sector reform and environmental protection.[5] Importantly, the precondition for the EaP is a willingness on the part of the neighbouring countries to be open to greater political cooperation and economic integration with the EU. In effect, the EaP is a security, stability and development package that aims to increase the EU's overall influence in these countries. It has also offered the promise of easier travel to the EU through a gradual process of visa liberalisation, accompanied by measures to tackle illegal immigration.

Given the above, it can be argued that regional cooperation with neighbouring states is an important element of the EU's political identity; the ENP, EaP as well as the EU–Russia Common Spaces are informed by discourses of partnership, co-development and mutual interdependence that are part of the ideational and visionary foundations of EU political community. However, more than two decades after the collapse of the Cold War political order, it is clear that characterisations of the EU as a geopolitical actor are as controversial as they are heterogeneous, a situation that reflects the ambiguities inherent in EU policies. Part of the problem are the rather disappointing results that the ENP has achieved to date. More substantial, and as will be elaborated in greater detail below, is the asymmetric and paternalistic nature of EU–Neighbourhood relations (Korosteleva 2012). With its geopolitical vision of Neighbourhood, the EU has attempted to export well beyond its borders not only its principles of democracy and good governance but also its security concerns. At the same time, the ENP can be seen as a means by which to unilaterally promote the values and external influence of the EU in third states such as Ukraine without offering prospects of direct membership or easier access to the Schengen area (Kostadinova 2009). Indeed, with mid-term and long-term perspectives of future enlargements clouded by political and economic uncertainty, the promise of potential EU membership has, for many neighbouring states, been replaced by a somewhat ambiguous offer of 'special partnership'. Some recent critiques of the EU are more pointed, suggesting that the EU's relations with its neighbours are increasingly characterised by a 'hard territoriality' that privileges security issues, border management and sovereignty (Bialasiewicz 2012). This resonates with concerns voiced by Follis (2012), Scott and Liikanen (2010) and others that obsessions with undocumented migration, cross-border crime and terrorism as well as continuing visa restrictions on non-EU citizens could reinforce obstacles to cooperation, conjuring up fears of an emerging Fortress Europe that effectively divides the continent.

As a consequence, it is difficult to comprehend the ENP strictly in either objective or normative terms of foreign policy. The notion that there can be a geopolitical vision free of historical prejudices and without a sense of political or cultural exceptionalism and mission is unrealistic. The human geography perspective is generally critical in this respect, as geographers have made it their business to uncover how geographic knowledge is created and manipulated for political purposes. Chastened by the memory of geo-determinism and its bitter legacy, critical geographers tend by nature to be sceptical of 'grand' cartographic imaginations and generalisations as these are thought to legitimise hegemonic control of territory through borders, visas, as well as military and ideational projections of power (Agnew 2009; O'Tuatheil and Dalby 1998; Parker 2008). Furthermore, according to Kuus (2007), geopolitics and culture are closely interlinked and, in the case of EU securitisation policies, these links raise questions related to the borders of Europe and definitions of Europeanness. In this view, the EU acts with respect to its neighbours as a border-confirming and border-consolidating agent, inscribing 'otherness' between Western, Central and Eastern Europe (Kuus 2004).

However, in addition to drawing attention to the EU's bordering practices as part of the construction of political community, EU–Neighbourhood relations should also be understood in terms of encounters between different political identities and the political and cultural contestations they involve. There is an inherent tension between attempts to consolidate and thus 'border' the EU on the one hand, and to enhance the EU's presence beyond its immediate borders through regional cooperation, on the other (Scott and van Houtum 2009). The wilful and strategic consolidation of a supranational European space provides the Union with increasingly sharpened territorial characteristics (Bialasiewicz, Elden and Painter 2005); as articulated in the (Reform) Lisbon Treaty, the EU is actively promoting an agenda of social, economic and territorial cohesion in order to strengthen the basis for political community and economic integration, which in turn enhances the status of territorial aspects within EU policy-making (Fritsch 2009). As a result, we are currently witnessing processes of Europeanisation in the ways policy-makers and researchers conceptualise (and subsequently attempt to organise) the EU-European territory as an increasingly unitary and integrated space. Regarding the cultural contestations which will be developed in more depth in this chapter, the ENP and other aspects of EU–Neighbourhood relations should be understood not only as an outcome of internal processes of negotiating external policy priorities, but also as a function of the identity politics of the EU – both as an ideational projection of European exceptionalism (and European values) and as a mechanism of differentiation between the EU and its neighbours. Unquestionably, the hard territoriality, border securitisation policies and restrictive practices of the EU with regard to asylum seekers and undocumented migrants are serious issues (Levy 2012; Rosière and Jones 2012). They give sustenance to the idea that, far from representing a new form of political community, the EU is developing into a supranational institution that has itself acquired traditional state functions and that exercises de facto state violence and a neoliberal politics of exclusion (Aalto 2006; Anderson 2007; Smith 2005).

Ironically, the view of the EU as a new type of Westphalian state does not necessarily resonate on the other side of the European divide. Here, the EU is rather understood as a disjointed project of 'post-national' and 'post-sovereign' political identity construction that through its discourses, practices and mere appearance suggests a variety of possible state–society relationships; national interests appear to be present only in diffused form. Much debate has suggested a confrontation between a supposed 'post-modern' EU project of shared sovereignty against post-Soviet nation-building reminiscent of a 'past' era in European history which in itself posits a sense (perhaps perception) of civilisational difference (Prozorov 2007). In the case of EU–Russia relations, Haukkala (2008b, 2010) has also highlighted the role of political identity in terms of differing normative understandings of sovereignty. This goes beyond the dynamics of normative power rivalries (Niemann and de Wekker 2010; Steinkohl 2010); as Haukkala argues, the EU has normatively challenged Russian notions of sovereignty through a unilateral definition of European values – values that emphasise universalistic rights transcending state and nation. Russia in turn has become increasingly defensive of its domestic politics. While the EU–Russia rivalry only partly helps interpret the quality of EU–Ukraine relations, there are similar tensions at work here. In the case of Ukraine, Kravchenko (this volume) confirms that state-centred understandings of sovereignty and the ongoing project of post-Soviet nation-building serve to differentiate the EU's and Ukraine's outlooks on Neighbourhood cooperation agendas. The political priorities of Ukraine's political elites are very much (and understandably) focused on nation-building, the consolidation of a political identity and the formal institutionalisation of state institutions. Because of the difficulty – or, as Gallina (2011) argues, the failure – to create functioning state structures, there is heightened political sensibility to criticisms of statism. As Kravchenko also states, there is at the same time a tension between the notion of Ukraine as a borderland between the EU and Russia and more traditional understandings of Ukraine as a historical nation.

While not trying to lessen the importance of critical interpretations, the approach adopted here develops a possibilistic alternative to a priori conceptualisations that imply an almost historical inevitability of a civilisational or neoliberal EU geopolitics. As Zielonka (2006) and Marciacq (2012) suggest, it is difficult to pigeonhole the EU as a specific kind of political actor. The possibilities for a progressive post-Westphalian politics of regional cooperation exist; there is no geopolitical determinism that leads to neo-Westphalian realism or to immutable and foundational understandings of where Europe begins or ends. Radchuk (2011) and Stegniy (2012) thus argue that the geopolitical and cultural boundaries between the EU and its eastern neighbours are in a simultaneous process of confirmation and negotiation. They also suggest that, while the eastern neighbours are more ready than the EU to transform the rigid Schengen boundaries erected by the EU, bordering processes are not unilateral; the EU and its neighbours actively seek to 'construct and maintain distinctions but also to delineate potential grounds for their reconciliation' (Radchuk 2011: 22). Arguably, the frustration of slow European advances in the Neighbourhood and Russian contexts has led to the EU's responding with a short-term approach that favours interaction with government elites over civil society, but this situation might not be permanent. Going beyond the present contingencies of border management and security policies, this author supports the notion that Neighbourhood regional cooperation is open-ended and as yet indeterminate (Tassarini 2005). To paraphrase Putnam (2004), he contends that social progress in regional cooperation, while by no means inevitable, is possible. Nielsen, Berg and Roll (2009) have alluded to this possibility in suggesting the mutual processes of learning and political socialisation that have been initiated across the EU's external borders by civil society actors. The following section will present evidence of this in the case of Ukraine and other neighbouring countries.

Perspectives on the EU as a political actor: narratives of neighbourhood and policy divides

The research upon which this section is based had a twofold purpose: on the one hand to identify major societal issues influencing socio-political change and stability in the post-Soviet context and, on the other, to critically assess the potential of the EU to positively influence socio-political transformation in post-Soviet states and thus to enhance regional stability. Rather than involving a normative notion of convergence to EU norms, this research largely privileged local perspectives with regard to the societal impacts of the EU and its policies, such as the ENP and EaP. The results suggest socio-political and socio-cultural perceptions that partly reflect a civilisational divide as well as disillusionment with the EU. At the same time, these perceptions of the EU are frequently positive in the sense that the EU is seen to offer alternative and more progressive understandings of state–society relations and social issues. Co-development is also understood to take place through societal interaction rather than only through formal policies themselves. Furthermore, criticism of local situations is given greater focus through interpretations and engagement with EU values. The picture that emerges is one of a policy divide that nonetheless provides spaces for social engagement and dialogue.

Most of the material discussed here is based on case studies of Ukraine and Belarus, although this chapter will primarily deal with the former.[6] The material is organised according to major thematic narratives that emerged during the course of the project: perceptions of EU unilateralism; the issue of common values as an ideational basis for regional cooperation; the borderland or buffer-zone complex which emerged as an important subtext of EU cooperation; and ambiguities regarding support for civil society activities and cooperation, particularly with Ukraine. This cross-section of civil society perceptions does not aim for a comprehensive representation of opinions regarding the EU and its role in the Neighbourhood. Instead, it presents important critical insights from civil society actors with a clear stake in international cooperation and who welcome a more progressive EU engagement in local social affairs.

Perceptions of EU unilateralism

One main criticism that has emerged from most interviews and background research is that the EU has imposed a unilateral and top-down cooperation model that is counterproductive to more open working partnerships. This is perhaps the least surprising result of this research as it confirms a pattern that has emerged since the inauguration of the ENP in 2003. EU policies such as the ENP and EaP are thus seen to offer too little to neighbouring states such as Ukraine in order to be taken fully seriously; the 'partners' keep giving in to EU demands without receiving commensurate recognition or reward, such as prospects for candidacy or the lifting of visa and mobility restrictions. Countries such as Ukraine see themselves forced to accept an inherently asymmetric relationship with the EU and this has resulted in a reduced level of genuine local engagement. As Korosteleva (2012) confirms for Moldova, this engagement is often of a symbolic nature, which in turn frustrates the EU's cooperation agendas, hindering real progress in the promotion of partnership and integration.

The asymmetric nature of EU–Ukraine Neighbourhood Policy interaction is more directly reflected in a lack of sensitivity on the part of the EU towards social sensibilities and developmental needs of neighbouring states. Instead, the EU is perceived as more intent on imposing its own cooperation agenda. As one Ukrainian interviewee directly stated: 'With its focus on border management, the EU seems to ignore development issues in Ukraine that exacerbate security, migration and other social issues.'[7] The principle of joint ownership of policy agendas, which initially motivated neighbouring states to participate in the ENP and EaP, is now seen to have been replaced by the language of 'mutual commitments' that more strictly correspond to the EU's security interests in border controls, migration and crime management. At the same time, by creating these policy issues for Ukraine with regard to the EU and its borders, unfunded mandates have emerged that require legislative changes regarding immigration on the Ukrainian side. The International Organisation for Migration has been called on to help out; one of its main remits is capacity-building in terms of migration management and counter-trafficking policies, labour migration and assistance to refugees.[8] There are initiatives in terms of 'soft' border management as well, including a labour migration project funded by the EU, the World Bank and Portugal that facilitates seasonal migration and projects that promote communication between families of labour migrants.

The framing of undocumented migration as a security issue has given right-wing groups in Ukraine ammunition to engage in xenophobic and anti-European activities.[9] This shortcoming is thought to weaken the EU's claims to be a credible force for good and limits the overall positive effects of the ENP and EaP. Within this context, the issue of the EU's restrictive Schengen visa regime is critical and affects perceptions of the EU in a profound way. The visa issue also reveals tensions in neighbourhood relationships as it openly exposes EU mistrust of the institutions and policies of neighbouring states, for example regarding their ability to issue legitimate travel documents and carry out reliable passport controls and border checks.

Dissatisfaction and disappointment with the rigidities of the ENP and EaP notwithstanding, interaction with the EU is seen to bring benefits to Ukraine, some perhaps of an unintended nature. The ENP in fact bolsters the state- and nation-building project of Ukraine by institutionalising borders and border controls and sharpening the contours of Ukraine's political identity as a 'borderland' (see Filippova in this volume); as one interviewee stated: 'Having demarcated and controlled borders is a normal process of becoming a real state, a political partner.'[10] At the same time, Ukrainian political elites gain legitimacy by reconciling the consolidation of national sovereignty and territorial integrity with the EU's 'post-national' regional cooperation project (Kravchenko in this volume). Perceptions of EU unilateralism and paternalism are thus attenuated by Ukrainian identity politics and the harder line taken by the Yanukovych government, which appeared to be following a strategy of balancing EU and Russian influences in order to create a stronger Ukrainian state. As one respondent stated in rather blunt and self-critical terms: 'Ukraine's main problems with the EU and its borders are internal. The EU's perceived discrimination is highly exaggerated and used as political capital for specific groups within the country.'[11]

'European' values as arenas of political and social contestation

Perceptions of EU unilateralism – and the sense of paternalism associated with such perceptions – negatively affect the political image of the EU. However, the question of EU–Ukraine relations within the ENP and EaP framework raises deeper issues regarding European values and the extent to which they are recognised to be shared or contested. Ukrainian and Belarusian respondents were especially pointed in their criticisms. As one outspoken Ukrainian interviewee stated:

> Cultural distance between the EU and post-Soviet states like Ukraine is a problem; the EU would clearly like partners that are similar to it and has

problems understanding the local situation. It simply doesn't trust Ukraine as a neighbour. This lack of trust is mutual – Ukraine has learned not to expect very much from the EU and the EU has become very cautious in advancing mobility and visa liberalisation for Ukrainians.[12]

On the basis of such observations, it would appear that the EU often understands cultural difference as an obstacle to cooperation that must be overcome. The interviews conducted have also revealed a perception that processes of differentiation between post-Soviet states (among others) and 'EU-Europe' are taking place through discourses that emphasise domestic internal crises, corruption, political divisions as well as the thorny issue of potential proclivities towards partnership with Russian. Frequently embedded in the EU perspective is the perceived duality of Ukrainian, Belarusian and Moldovan identity in which Russian and European orientations are apprehended as antagonistic opposites. The interviews similarly indicate that the EU's ambitious value-laden agenda can be understood to partly alienate potential partners in neighbouring states in that it suggests different categories of 'Europeanness' based on the degree of local convergence to proclaimed EU standards.

However, despite these critical observations, respondents signalled overall acceptance of the notion of common European values as well as a basic set of principles that facilitates positive interaction and a sense of joint purpose. As one interviewee stated: 'Values can indeed unite us. We can see Europe as a success story in terms of social development and welfare; this is not only an important demarcation but also a bridge between the EU and neighbours like Ukraine.'[13] While they take umbrage at the idea that they are citizens of a second-class country, Ukrainian civil society organisations (CSOs) working in newer areas of social concern (e.g. gender, migrant and minority rights) stress that they are supportive of the EU's ideals and are more 'Western' than 'Eastern' in orientation. This was specifically emphasised by representatives of international women's rights organisations in Ukraine, which, by the nature of their remit, are focused on international cooperation.[14] For them European values promote human rights and more progressive understandings of the social issues that post-Soviet transformation has generated. Nevertheless, the idea that democracy and respect for human rights are somehow specific to the EU – and that the EU enjoys 'moral hegemony' – is rejected. Basic rights, the rule of law and social solidarity are understood to be much more general in nature; they do not in themselves constitute a unique European identity or sense of purpose.[15] EU-Europeanness in their view is mainly seen in terms of specific attitudes towards efficient governance, the value of work (e.g. reliability!) and related issues.

International exchange and intercultural learning have helped people who grew up in the Soviet Union and who are only familiar with local conditions to think about women's rights, minority rights and other social issues that in the past did not receive much local attention. Returnees from the EU have also experienced change in their social attitudes and have become important factors in Ukraine's overall social change – indeed: the word Europeanisation as an expression of this change is explicitly mentioned. As one interviewee stated: 'It is important to have European values, and I am not afraid of the EU, I am more afraid of the Russian Empire, the influence of the Orthodox Church and their values.'[16]

The respondents emphasise that cooperation with international organisations (the EU, the Council of Europe, the UN) is essential for Ukraine's democratisation. At the same time, they suggest that the international community should be more active in supporting groups in Ukraine that prioritise human and gender rights as the Ukrainian state neglects these issues. Indeed, several actors decried what they saw as a lack of substantive political commitment of the EU to support citizen's movements and rights in neighbouring states. This also applies in the case of Belarus where the EU is accused of being too restrictive, making it difficult, for example, for journalists to obtain visas and thus hindering dialogue with precisely those whom the Commission and EU states they should be working with.[17]

However, criticisms of the EU's policy practices do not mean that civil society actors are uncritical of their own governments. There are obvious tensions within Ukraine, Moldova, Belarus and Russia, where political liberalisation is contested by different groups and often hampered by political elites. CSO representatives point out, for example, that Ukraine is tough on foreigners and does not deal well with ethno-cultural differences. Non-traditional immigrants (for example, from Africa and Asia) face many barriers in Ukraine in terms of employment, obtaining residence papers, housing, and suffer from everyday discrimination. Despite the fact that immigration has constantly declined in the last years, tougher legislation was introduced in 2011, making it difficult for dependents of migrants to obtain residence permits.

The borderland and buffer-zone complex as contextual issues

Another related issue that has emerged from this work is that of a perceived social, political and cultural construction of geopolitical boundaries between the EU and its eastern neighbours. This is, however, a mutually constitutive rather than unilateral process as the EU–Ukraine case study bears out. This bordering narrative is difficult to characterise as it is both understood in deeply negative terms and as a rather positive alternative notion of Ukraine within Europe. On the one hand, EU cooperation policies are widely understood by civil society representatives to represent a cordon sanitaire between the EU and Russia. Examples of this are visa regulations that are seen as discriminatory and the border security regime promoted by the EU.[18] On the other hand, the notion of 'borderland' or 'bridge' between East and West has been put forward as a more legitimate characterisation of Ukraine's political identity, given the country's history of shifting borders and multi-ethnic composition (Kravchenko in this volume).

In the estimation of most of the interviewed persons, one buffer-zone discourse prevalent in Ukrainian media and public debate has clearly negative connotations as it goes hand in hand with exaggerated reports of illegal immigration and of Ukraine being used as a platform for illegal activities. In this reading of Ukraine as a borderland, visa and migration issues have also been used by anti-EU interests as proof of the EU's discriminatory practices and its humiliation of Ukrainian citizens.[19] There are even voices demanding the reinstatement of visa requirements for EU citizens. In addition, the readmission agreement signed by Ukraine and the EU is similarly used to denounce the EU and to discredit the EU's policies. This all adds up to a very negative image (promoted by some political forces) of the EU as not really trusting, liking, wanting Ukraine.[20]

The geopolitical role of Russia is also an important buffer-zone issue with regard to EU–Ukraine cooperation. Implicit in the information collected through interviews, reports and background research is that Russia plays a central role in conditioning the EU's geopolitical strategies. It is not completely surprising, for example, that Ukraine partly interprets the EaP as a political strategy that aims to limit Russian influence and increase dependence on the EU. Ukraine (along with Belarus and Moldova) are seen as contested countries between the EU and Russia (see Radchuk 2011) and find themselves in a situation of (geo)political flux. This magnifies the border issues in these countries. In addition, the EU is applying direct pressure on Ukraine in terms of policies that directly or indirectly affect border management.

In terms of understanding Ukraine as an extended security perimeter for the EU, visas, introduced in 2003 for Ukrainian citizens, have become critical. Strict Schengen visa regulations reinforce perceptions of 'Fortress Europe' in the minds of Ukrainians and expose tensions in the EU–Ukraine relationship.[21] As interviewees attest, migration from Ukraine is clearly not (or should not be) the issue, as it has become in the last fifteen years a well-organised circular process based on contracts (labour movers rather than immigrants) that do not burden the social welfare systems of the host countries. Despite the abundance of cheap opportunities to travel, the EU has discouraged Ukrainians from applying for visas through tough conditions and financial obstacles – interestingly, approval and rejection rates for Ukrainians seeking a Schengen visa do not show up in official statistics.[22] It was feared that the maintenance of the present visa regime might also translate into an EU mistrust of the citizens of neighbouring states. In addition, the visa regime is held to create a travelling elite with the resources to obtain multiple-entry and long-term visas; this discriminates against younger and less well-off citizens of neighbouring states. One important change has taken place: in July 2009 a regulation on local border traffic went into effect which allows for passport-free travel within designated 30-km border zones.

With its security and border-management agenda, the EU has inadvertently succeeded in exacerbating negative migration myths as part of the buffer-zone syndrome.[23] In 2009 the EU and Ukraine signed an agreement governing the re-admission and processing of third-country nationals attempting to enter the EU illegally. This catalysed anti-immigrant media campaigns although the actual numbers of remitted foreigners was very low. Scenarios of huge 'concentration camps' in border regions, harbouring large numbers of refugees, and problems related to drugs, terrorism, crime etc. were depicted in the media. In reality, only several hundred undocumented persons targeted by the agreement were apprehended at the border.[24] According to one respondent: 'Illegal immigration is exaggerated and constructed by the media as a threat, and this also encourages xenophobic attitudes. There are xenophobic, racist groups (Patriota Ukrajna, Stop-Migration) operating in the country that, while illegal, are not really hindered in their activities.'[25]

While the buffer-zone notion serves to politicise EU–Ukrainian relations and suggests a form of neo-imperial relationship between the two countries, the concept of a borderland, often used in conjunction with popular geographic imaginations of Ukraine as a bridge between East and West, was suggested by interviewees as something positive.[26] Civil society actors active in social affairs generally viewed debates over 'competing sovereignties' as a Ukrainian rather than an EU problem, claiming that many of Ukraine's ruling elite 'seem to live in the nineteenth century with their national focus'.[27] Ukrainian academics such as Volodymyr Kravchenko (this volume), Olga Filippova (this volume) and Tatiana Zhurzhenko (2006, 2010) have at least partly corroborated this notion of borderland, in which a reconceptualisation of Ukraine as a cultural borderland, rather than as a nation-state, would better reflect entangled transnational histories.

Civil society – a neglected development resource

Since the emergence of the ENP and the EaP, which have replaced previous support mechanisms for local and regional cross-border cooperation, the EU's engagement with civil society in Ukraine (and neighbouring states, including Russia) is seen to be altogether insufficient. CSOs working in the area of migration and immigrant rights have been openly critical of the EU's Technical Aid Programmes because they work through state structures and do not involve CSOs. For example, EU-funded projects of the International Labour Organization, the United Nations Development Programme and the Council of Europe do not include CSOs, as their main partners are ministries and public agencies. Furthermore, while the EU demands clear migration-management policies from Ukraine, its focus is on 'hard' measures of border and migration management and not on the more social aspects or 'soft' measures needed to deal with the basic problems.[28] Migrant holding centres ('accommodation centres' for six-month detention) are funded by the EU as part of a EUR30 million package for financing readmission measures. Integrated border management is also embedded within the EaP cross-border cooperation projects funded by the European Neighbourhood and Partnership Instrument.

The de-emphasis of civil society participation is seen to indicate a clear shift to a more structured foreign policy dialogue between centres of power in the EU and neighbouring states. However, the fact that this dialogue is evolving at the expense of cross-border cooperation in local or regional development is seen as a major policy error. Material support for cross-border cooperation (CBC) is meagre in comparison to other priorities and lacks effective focus. In addition, there is a neglect of civil society as a CBC actor, despite rhetorical claims to the contrary.

The policy divide that the ENP and the EaP are held to have propagated is a particular vexation to civil society actors who have been striving for more than two decades to stabilise cooperation with EU partners. Civil society organisations have been key players in the area of social development, inter-cultural dialogue, social-welfare policy, capacity-building and in the strengthening of community institutions in post-Soviet states (Laine and Demidov 2012; Scott and Liikanen 2010). Civil society networks are perceived as crucial for shaping the quality, thematic focus and dynamics of cooperation activities in ways that are sensitive to local concerns. Such networks have also enabled different actors to pool resources, share their knowledge and reduce CBC transactions costs for smaller local organisations. Thanks to civil society networks between the EU and neighbouring countries, shortfalls in the public provision of social services have been partially compensated, while notions of social equity, welfare and group rights have been reframed as policy concerns in new member states and neighbouring states. As CSO representatives inter-viewed within the scope of this research confirm, their activities have been highly influenced by social values central to the traditional social democracies of Europe and that are embodied by EU policies.

Upon closer scrutiny, it furthermore becomes clear that there are not only distinct policy gaps between internal EU development and external cooperation with neighbouring states. Berg and Ehin (2006) and the Finnish Foreign Ministry (2011) have alluded to the more general situation of a fragmented policy process in which a jumble of rules defined by EU agencies for regional development, justice, external affairs and development aid create uneven conditions for regional cooperation. In general terms, the complexity of different policy logics operating within the context of Neighbourhood tends to privilege formal areas of bilateral cooperation, such as border management, large infrastructure projects and interagency technical assistance, while it marginalises cooperation between civil society actors (Scott 2011).

In addition, the EU's focus on budgetary control and administrative standard-isation has promoted bureaucratic practices and policies of conditionality that tend to complicate CSO cooperation. The EU has, for example, developed a systematic framework for implementing cross-border civil society projects that involves a laborious implementation process channelling support for civil society projects largely through state structures. Here, the EU demands certain types of bureaucratic discipline, such as budgeting (including matching funds), auditing, monitoring and evaluating civil society projects, which often sub-ordinate CSOs to state agencies on the national, regional and local level. This approach largely determines the types of CSOs that are capable of practicing such discipline and of accessing EU financial support. It also contributes to the emergence of a privileged CSO elite, particularly in the neighbouring countries, that is separate from other CSOs and from its potential constituents and whose agenda and priorities may differ from those of the EU and other western donors.

Conclusions

Within ongoing debates on the role and nature of the ENP, this chapter has considered external perceptions of the EU as a political actor on the international scene. More specifically, it has focused on the responses of local civil society actors to EU regional cooperation policies. Similar to the observations of Darbouche (2008), Klitsounova (2008) and Kostadinova (2009), the research presented here suggests that despite the EU's strong rhetorical commitment to regional partnership and multilevel cooperation, these goals are often subordinated to the dictates of geopolitical expediency. It might appear, in fact, that the EU's idealist notions of regional cooperation have been confronted with the realities of socio-political change, post-Soviet transformation and the recent Ukraine–Russia conflict over Crimea. This idealism is also a victim of EU indecision and lack of societal engagement. In the case of Ukraine, EU policies have been attacked as creating a new buffer zone between East and West. The EU is thus seen as neglecting Ukraine despite this county's attempts to adhere to EU conditionality. While highly exaggerated, fears that Ukraine will end up as a host country for unwanted immigrants, refugees and asylum seekers help cement EU–Ukraine divisions. At the same time, this research indicates that the EU has not been projecting its ideas very clearly – and thus is subject to misrepresentations. It is perceived as too aloof and distant and thus portrayed in very negative terms by nationalist groups. However, the EU also resonates for many as a model of a more open and tolerant society and has in fact promoted new social agendas and new ways of thinking about Ukrainian social and political transformation.

The EU might, ironically, be reproducing what it explicitly seeks to avoid: the creation of new divisions in welfare, social opportunity and political dialogue. Having achieved its ambitious enlargement agenda, and now securing its eastern borders, the EU appears to have lost sight of the material and symbolic significance of regional cooperation. Civil society struggles to receive greater recognition and support from the EU even though its political salience continues to increase. Based on the above discussion, three main conclusions can be drawn:

– Developing and implementing a pragmatic understanding of neighbourhood and partnership

The EU's ENP and EaP strategies appear to suffer from their own ambitions and assumptions. One of the more problematic assumptions is that the EU as a large political community can directly influence developments in neighbouring states. There is no doubt that the EU has had transformational impacts on the societies of the former Soviet Union and has, in its own way, contributed to more open and empowered societies. However, this normative power does not automatically provide the EU with the influence to elicit institutional and policy convergence given the different interests and state–society relations that exist between EU member states and eastern neighbours. The EU should also aim for gradual – if often slow – institutional change based on intercultural dialogue rather than technocratic conditionality. More recent EaP strategy documents of the European Commission (2012c) might signal a shift in this direction.

Another point to be made here is that the EaP could be exploited more effectively as a platform for transnational cooperation and development. In order to achieve stability and create the conditions for democratic development, certain issues such as migration must be seen in a greater regional and international context and in terms of a long-term focus on the causes and consequences of increasing migration, rather than merely in terms of border security and the policing of individuals. EU platforms for regional cooperation would also improve the level of policy dialogue between post-Soviet neighbours. This goes hand in hand with a greater degree of inclusion of civil society organisations and actors.

– Increasing support of multilevel cooperation between the EU and post-Soviet states

The clearest long-term contribution of the EU to social modernisation in post-Soviet states has been that of reframing social and welfare issues. Furthermore, considerable potential exists for horizontal, non-hierarchical institutional learning that involves motivated sectors of the population and strengthens their social impact locally and regionally (Scott and Laine 2012). In particular, almost all informants agreed that the EU has been missing important opportunities to develop neighbourhood partnerships by neglecting the role of civil society. Working with and through civil society actors helps promote new forms of policy learning outside formal institutionalised policy channels by creating a pragmatic rather than normative environment of transnational communication and exchange.

– Engaging socio-political and socio-cultural transformation

One critical point that can be made is that of the EU's attempt to construct a geopolitical identity based on a set of European values and its own Acquis communautaire. Such attributes of Europeanness as democratic, liberal and progressive are, on the one hand, essential to the definition of an EU exceptionalism that can be projected outside the confines of the EU-27. On the other hand, this exceptionalism can only be promoted through 'soft power', conditionality, incentives and prospects of political and economic benefits. As several observers have noted, the EU has not been terribly successful in promoting regional cooperation based on partnership and conditionality (Korosteleva 2012; Marin 2006). Part of the problem is the complexity of EU geopolitical identity construction; the other is an inability to understand and operate within contexts of socio-political and cultural transformation. The ENP can be seen to involve a clash of cultures and values based on a notion of post-national citizenship and post-sovereignist notions of human rights. At the same time, the EU through its policies appears to confirm and institutionalise statist notions of nation and bordered territoriality.

Given the critical discussion of EU regional cooperation policies that has unfolded in this chapter, what might signal a way forward in terms of a more progressive understanding of Neighbourhood? In taking up Hannah Arendt's (1958) position in thinking about things political, a progressive notion of Eastern Partnership, and Neighbourhood in more general terms, would address the plurality of human needs and capacities. Openness towards a plurality of interests could allow for new and often unforeseen spaces for action whereas (often hubristic) adherence to normative models as guides for political action tends to limit choices and marginalise groups distant from policy elites (Borren 2008; Hammer 1997). With visibility comes the potential for recognising the existence of and giving political voice to certain situations, groups, persons, needs and concerns. An Arendtian 'politics of visibility' would thus entail an acceptance of the contingencies of accommodation rather than a regulated and orchestrated political scenario, privileging diversity and civic participation in political life.

In a similar vein, Radchuk (2011: 22) suggests that a 'reconciliation lies in two-way positive perceptions of the various polities, and more importantly in certain cultural values that pertain to the EU but are seen by these countries' citizens as being important for their own societies'. This would in any case support the idea that greater engagement with civil society is necessary and that the construction of a European Neighbourhood must, despite the EU's leading role, be a mutual and reciprocal undertaking.

Notes

1 The research documented here was funded by the Finnish Ministry of Foreign Affairs – which itself has taken a stake in exploring the potentials for enhancing the stabilising role of the EU in post-Soviet national and regional contexts – and the EU. Reference is made here to the Security and Development Research within the 'Wider Europe Initiative Security Cluster', funded by the Finnish Ministry of Foreign Affairs (contract: HEL 8207–75), which specifically funded fieldwork in Ukraine, Moldova, Belarus and other post-Soviet states. In addition, critical insights on EU–Russia and EU–Neighbourhood cooperation were provided by work supported by the international research project 'EUBORDERREGIONS: European Regions, EU External Borders and the Immediate Neighbours. Analysing Regional Development Options through Policies and Practices of Cross-Border Cooperation' (contract: SSH-2010–2.2.1–266920), financed by the European Union's Seventh Framework Programme for Research. More information about this research project is available at: www.euborderregions.eu (last accessed 13 May 2013).

2 According to the ENP strategy paper (European Commission 2004e: 3), 'the privileged relationship with neighbours will build on mutual commitment to common values principally within the fields of the rule of law, good governance, the respect for human rights, including minority rights, the promotion of good neighbourly relations, and the principles of market economy and sustainable development'.

The document then states: 'The level of ambition of the EU's relationships with its neighbours will take into account the extent to which these values are effectively shared.'

3 The countries involved in the ENP are: Algeria, Armenia, Azerbaijan, Belarus, Egypt, Georgia, Israel, Jordan, Lebanon, Libya, Moldova, Morocco, the Palestinian Authority, Syria, Tunisia and Ukraine. While not part of the ENP process in the strict sense, Russia participates in cross-border programmes funded through the European Neighbourhood and Partnership Instrument (ENPI–CBC). No agreements have been established to date with Belarus, Libya and Syria.

4 Article 2 of the ENPI Regulation reads as follows: 'Community assistance shall promote enhanced cooperation and progressive economic integration between the European Union and the partner countries and, in particular, the implementation of partnership and cooperation agreements, association agreements or other existing and future agreements. It shall also encourage partner countries' efforts aimed at promoting good governance and equitable social and economic development.'

5 See the website http://eeas.europa.eu/eastern/index_en.htm (last accessed 3 October 2013). EU funding for the eastern partner countries within the scope of bilateral programmes between 2007 and 2010 was as follows: Armenia (EUR98.4 million), Azerbaijan (EUR92 million), Georgia (EUR120.4 million), Moldova (EUR209.7 million), Ukraine (EUR494 million).

6 The study involved interviews with 27 representatives of civil society and research organisations based in Kyiv, Kharkiv, Minsk and Vilnius. The case study is part of a wider project that also covered Russia and Moldova. Where relevant, information from these case studies will be drawn upon. All interviews were anonymised and are referenced in the text according to a chronological and geographical interview key number.

7 Interview in Kyiv (Ukraine), 2 June 2010. Interview Key: UKR 11.

8 For information regarding the border security implementation projects, see the EU Border Assistance Mission to Moldova and Ukraine (EUBAM) website. Online. Available at: www.eubam.org/ (last accessed 4 February 2013).

9 Interviews in Kyiv (Ukraine), 31 May 2010, with representatives of organisations that monitor hate crimes and different types of xenophobia in Ukraine. Interview key: UKR 2.

10 Interview in Kyiv (Ukraine), 31 May 2010. Interview key: UKR 1.

11 Interview in Kyiv (Ukraine), 2 June 2010 with sociologist (and representative of a migration rights organisation). Interview key: UKR 9.

12 Interview in Kharkiv (Ukraine), 15 October 2011. Interview key: UKR 13.

13 Interview in Kyiv (Ukraine), 2 June 2010 with sociologist (and representative of a migration rights organisation). Interview key: UKR 9.

14 Ukrainian interviewees (IDs UKR 2, 5, 6–8, 9, 12) voiced concern over the deeply conservative, traditional and 'introverted' nature of domestic politics. The European Union is seen as an important potential counterbalance.

15 In the specific case of Belarus, the concept of European values has in fact led to a general rejection of much of the ENP agenda; here, the political regime insists on stability and economic development rather than convergence to international norms as societal priorities. This particular situation is, of course, difficult for the EU to navigate – although the interviewees have suggested that a less pointedly political strategy on the part of the EU might have enhanced ENP's effectiveness (Interviews in Minsk on 4 June 2010: BEL 1, 3, 6 and Vilnius on 21 August 2011: BEL 7, 11).

16 Interview in Kyiv (Ukraine) with representatives of a women's rights organisation, 2 June 2010. Interview key: UKR 12.

17 Interview in Minsk (Belarus) on 3 June 2010 with representatives of an organisation that monitors migration issues and EU–Belarus relations. Interview key: BEL 6.

18　See Follis (2012) and Korosteleva (2012).
19　As emphasised, for example, in interviews conducted on 1 June 2010 in Kyiv (Ukraine) with representatives of organisations lobbying for the easing of visa restrictions for Ukrainian citizens. Interview key UKR 7, UKR 8.
20　This was emphasised quite strongly by representatives of international as well as Ukrainian immigration organisations (interviews in Kyiv on 2 June 2010. Interview keys: UKR 9, 10,11,12).
21　See Ukrainian Europe Without Barriers. Online. Available at: http://novisa.com. ua/en/ (last accessed 4 February 2013).
22　Interview 1 June 2010 in Kyiv (Ukraine). Interview key: UKR 7.
23　This was substantiated by interviews with representatives of Ukrainian and international organisations, 31 May 2010 (UKR 1, 2), 2 June 2010 (UKR 11, 12) in Kyiv and 16 October 2011 (UKR 15) in Kharkiv.
24　See note 10.
25　See note 18.
26　Interviews in Kyiv (Ukraine) on 1 June 2010. Interview keys: UKR 6, 7, 8.
27　See note 18.
28　Interview with a representative of an international immigration organisation in Kyiv (Ukraine) on 2 June 2010. Interview key: UKR 11.

6 Bordering in post-Soviet Central Asia

Two tales from Tajikistan

Joni Virkkunen and Paul Fryer

In post-Soviet Central Asia, the process of demarcating and delimiting the borders inherited after the collapse of the USSR is still ongoing. This chapter portrays post-Soviet Tajik bordering through two examples: the city of Tursunzoda on the Tajik–Uzbek border and the patchwork border dividing the ethnically troubled Ferghana Valley between Tajikistan and its neighbour, Kyrgyzstan. Both illustrate different aspects of a post-Soviet bordering process that is contributing to regional instability, with serious socio-economic and political impacts on the border region. At the same time, the movement of Tajik citizens across the southern Ferghana Valley border has been inducing angry reactions from the country's neighbours; ethno-nationalist conflicts have often erupted on the local level. The two examples demonstrate the wide range of contemporary bordering in post-Soviet Tajikistan and highlight some of the future challenges to Tajikistan as a whole.

In this chapter, two field sites are examined. Tursunzoda is a small city in the west of the country, some 60 kilometres from the national capital, Dushanbe, but only a few kilometres from the border with Uzbekistan. Originally known as a productive agricultural area, Tursunzoda is now more famous for its industrial capacity. The Tajik Aluminium Company (TALCO) was founded in the early 1960s, following the establishment of the nearby Nurek Hydroelectric Station on the Vakhsh River. Built at a time when the internal borders of the Soviet Union did not impede its development, the factory grew to be one of the largest aluminium producers in the world despite the local absence of raw materials; the city grew on the cheap hydropower. After the collapse of the Soviet Union, the city's location on the border next to an independent Uzbekistan left it vulnerable as relations between the two neighbours worsened over the years. Today, the border crossing between the two countries at Tursunzoda remains open, though it is often closed unilaterally by the Uzbek authorities, with the result of disrupting trade and preventing necessary imports for the factory to reach their destination.

The situation of the second site of research – the border between Tajikistan and Kyrgyzstan in the southern Ferghana Valley – is quite different. While both countries make great efforts to maintain good relations and local infrastructure is closely integrated, the situation is complicated by the existence of several

DOI: 10.4324/9781315858036-9

territorial enclaves and the absence of a final agreement on border delimitation and demarcation. This has encouraged especially Tajik citizens living in the densely populated Sughd province to begin making use of lands on the Kyrgyz side of the border and in some cases to move there permanently. This creeping migration has alarmed many people in the Batken region of Kyrgyzstan, one of the country's most marginalised provinces that continues to suffer from outmigration. As Tajiks and Kyrgyz compete for land and scarce resources, conflicts often take an ethnic nature, raising the spectre of ethnic violence as witnessed in the Kyrgyz city of Osh in 2010.

On the basis of the collected materials, the authors argue that a stable long-term solution to Tajikistan's border questions requires a multifaceted under-standing of the country's complex and varied boundary issues. The problems of Tursunzoda and its factory are fundamentally different from those of the Ferghana Valley, but a discussion of borders cannot be removed from more general problems, such as unemployment and extreme poverty, rapid popula-tion growth, poor management of cross-border infrastructure etc. Despite these differences and their ambivalent nature in domestic politics, Tajikistan has called on the international community to take a significant role in resolving the problems. There is a clear request for the more active involvement of trusted foreign governments, such as the Russian Federation and joint regional and international organisations, in resolving contemporary border-related chal-lenges. The European Union and some of its member states, too, could take a more active role in mediating peace and creating social and interethnic stability.

Borders of Tajikistan: Soviet and post-Soviet developments

The borders of Central Asia are contested for many reasons. Before the October Revolution, the area was commonly known as Russian Turkestan, divided into several provinces and khanates that were loyal to Moscow. These internal borders were artificial creations of the tsarist authorities and did not reflect ethnic realities on the ground. The only borders with a historical foundation in the region were those between the Russian Empire and its neighbours – China, the British in Afghanistan and Persia. With the revolution, the new Bolshevik authorities sent commissions to evaluate the ethnic situation and make recom-mendations on how to support the creation and development of new Soviet nations (see Smith 2013).

The commissions were to propose borders between ethnic groups, but in reality this aim could not always be achieved – the populations were mixed – and economic considerations sometimes outweighed ethnic ones. By the 1930s, the boundaries between the Central Asian Soviet Socialist Republics were largely fixed as we know them today. But in the carefully controlled and highly centralised Soviet Union they meant very little outside the context of collecting administrative statistics and the region remained integrated within the overall Soviet planned economy (Rahimov and Urazaeva 2005).

Though the routine of everyday life did not alter drastically with the drawing of Soviet borders, the new administrative self-determination, which was intertwined with Soviet nationality policy, meant that, for the first time, the peoples of Central Asia began to conceptualise themselves in terms of separate nations, with national consciousness developing over the decades (Kaiser 1995). In both western Tajikistan and the Ferghana Valley, this resulted in locals developing a strong regional identification with certain territories while earlier mixed populations had shared historical and Islamic identities. It is this administrative development of the Soviet state that has set the ethnic, historical and territorial background for the border situation that the Central Asian states found themselves in after independence, in 1991. Increasingly, as in the case of Tajikistan, these borders became contested.

It should be noted that the former external borders of the Soviet Union, specifically those with China, Afghanistan and Iran, do not pose the same challenges to the Central Asian states. These borders were clearly demarcated and securitised by the Soviet regime and, after independence, it only remained for the newly independent states to confirm the former treaties with their neighbours. In the case of Tajikistan, the border with China is poorly accessible and the border area sparsely settled, while the more complicated Afghan border, for reasons related to the current security situation in the country, is the focus of much attention today. However, as both of these borders were demarcated years ago, they fall outside the scope of this chapter.

Map 6.1 indicates the authors' fieldwork sites in the Ferghana Valley and the Tajik–Uzbek border zone. Fieldwork, carried out during the period 2010–2012, consisted of a visit to the Tajik Aluminium Company in 2012 and numerous interviews in the Tajik and Kyrgyz capitals Dushanbe and Bishkek. Border villages in the Ferghana Valley were visited with Tajik and Kyrgyz colleagues on several occasions, when semi-structured interviews with local experts and activists were conducted and informal interviews and discussions took place with local residents on the streets. The majority of interviews were conducted in Russian but some meetings were held in the Tajik or Kyrgyz languages, especially in more remote villages where locals were less fluent in Russian. Only very few educated specialists and representatives of international organisations were able, or willing, to share their views in English. Most of the interviews were recorded digitally and later transcribed. However, due to the very sensitive character of borders and centralised administrative traditions in post-Soviet Central Asia, some individuals refused formal interviews, requested to remain anonymous and asked that the conversation not be recorded.

Tursunzoda: a tale of TALCO and the Uzbek border in Central Tajikistan

The history of the small city of Tursunzoda on the Tajik–Uzbek border is a rather common one in the post-Soviet context. The establishment of the Tajik

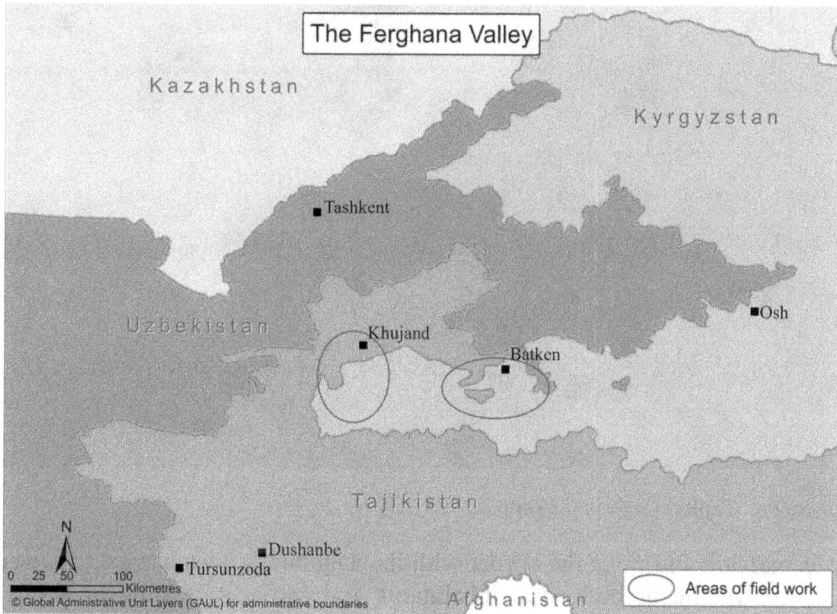

Map 6.1 Sites of fieldwork: Tursunzoda and the Ferghana Valley

Aluminium Company, an All-Soviet industrial project, turned a small village, formerly known as Regar, into one of the major industrial centres of Tajikistan.[1] Relying heavily on energy, the plant could only start its production after the development of the Nurek Dam hydroelectric power station on the Vakhsh River in western Tajikistan, about 125 kilometres from Regar and 75 kilometres east of the republic's capital of Dushanbe. After the plant's formal opening in 1975, the growing settlement was renamed Tursunzoda in 1978, in honour of the Tajik national poet Mirzo Tursunzoda, an event that marked the town's departure along the same path as many of the mono-industrial towns in the Soviet Union.

Today the Tajik Aluminium Company dominates the cityscape with dozens of factory chimneys. It represents a legacy that was established on the basis of the Soviet division of labour and company-run social and economic infrastructure (see Figure 6.1). Constructed along the Tajik–Uzbek border to make use of abundant labour resources in both republics within the All-Soviet production network, TALCO and Tursunzoda not only illustrate the overall difficulties of post-Soviet Tajik transformation. Significantly, the case study also demonstrates the 'Uzbek question' in post-Soviet Central Asian bordering. This refers to the recent unpredictability of the Uzbek authorities towards the state's borders and of the very concrete local-level impacts of the deteriorated interstate relations in general.

After Islamist attacks on Uzbek territory in 1999, the Uzbek government restricted cross-border movements and communications, and unilaterally started

Figure 6.1 Tajik Aluminium Company TALCO

to demarcate and mine the border with its neighbours. This has led to injury and loss of life of both local inhabitants and cattle. According to Kamar Ahror (2012) from the Institute of War and Peace Reporting (IWPR), a total of 76 persons have died and 81 have been injured along Tajikistan's northern border since 2000. While the border crossing at Tursunzoda suffers only occasional disruptions and relations in this sector are more 'normalised', this is not the case along some sections of the border in the Ferghana Valley, e.g. around the Tajik exclave in Uzbekistan. Yet, for a major industrial company like TALCO, all interruptions on the border cost money and may seriously hamper production.

The following section will analyse the Tajik–Uzbek border issue in Tursunzoda by exploring TALCO's narratives about the situation, as the border is only a few kilometres from the production site. An interview with the company's press secretary Igor Sattarov, conducted during a site visit in May 2012, is combined with external secondary sources, which reveal the company's very particular perspective on contemporary Tajik bordering. After emphasising the significance of the company for the national economy, Sattarov presents the border from three perspectives: the importance of the border and of good economic ties with Uzbekistan for the company and the Tajik economy; the critical role of the controversial Roghun Dam (and of cheap available energy) for the company's survival; and the possible role of international organisations in solving the troubled interstate relations that have a direct impact both on the company and the Tajik economy in general.

TALCO's full integration into the All-Soviet planned economy was its main advantage and, yet, one of its early weaknesses. The state provided the company with locally produced cheap energy and raw materials from other parts of the Soviet Union, while the company guaranteed its employees a high standard of living through a comprehensive social infrastructure such as schools, kindergartens, hospitals, shops and recreational facilities. As in many similar industrial towns of the former Soviet Union, the collapse of the Soviet system and its economic networks had a direct impact on the company: 'The main problem emerged because of the disrupted economic ties', Sattarov notes.[2] The supply chain of raw materials from other parts of the Soviet Union was interrupted, while taxes, transport and energy costs increased along with, and significantly, political instability (especially the Tajik civil war of the 1990s) that led to a rapid decrease in production: despite a capacity of 517,000 tonnes of aluminium per year, the output amounted to less than 200,000 tonnes by the mid-1990s (Interview with Sattirov, May 2012; see also Coulibaly 2012).

What makes the Tajik Aluminium Company significant and worth studying in detail in this chapter is its location on the Uzbek border and the fact that it is a product of the Soviet division of labour adjusting to a new context of nationalising states and the global market economy. Despite the sudden decrease of production after the collapse of the Soviet Union, the company is still the largest tax payer in Tajikistan. It contributes up to 70 per cent of Tajikistan's official GDP and is responsible for about 75 per cent of all foreign currency that officially enters the country. The company consumes up to 30–40 per cent of all the energy generated in Tajikistan, provides 70 per cent of the total income of the main electricity producer Tajik Energy Holding and mobilises about forty other companies as direct subcontractors. In other words, the company is a great regional and national player (see also Jacoby 2013). From this perspective, 'about 400,000 people are in one way or another dependent on the enterprise (and) should the enterprise collapse, about 400,000 people would be affected immediately. ... We take care of all the social infrastructure, housing for elderly people, kindergartens, hospitals, schools, houses for the handicapped, everything. Should the enterprise collapse, nobody would take care of the social infrastructure' (Interview with Sattarov, May 2012).

Amongst post-Soviet cities, this form of company-based social infrastructure is common. In Tursunzoda, this means a great reliance on the company successfully keeping its position in the wider global economy. The success mirrors not only the company's adaptability in the new global context but also the policies that national governments exercise while enforcing their post-Soviet state sovereignty through borders, customs, taxation systems etc. The economic performances of Tajikistan, as a landlocked state between Afghanistan, China, Kyrgyzstan and Uzbekistan, and of TALCO are heavily dependent on well-functioning borders and cross-border economic corridors, as well as on the pricing and transit policy of its neighbours. Yet, as 'Tajikistan is located in a place where it cannot operate without Uzbekistan' (Interview with Sattarov, May 2012), any interruptions in these economic corridors running through Uzbekistan have a direct impact on the surrounding city of Tursunzoda.

Related to the above, the second main theme emphasised by TALCO's public relations officer was the central role of the internationally controversial

Roghun Dam, the construction of which has led to 'Cold War'-like relations between Tajikistan and Uzbekistan (Jacoby 2013; Juraev 2012). In Tajikistan, Roghun has been turned into a major national strategic project, a symbol of state sovereignty, designed not only to end frequent energy shortages but to make the country energy-independent (Peyrouse 2009). Within this context, the dam has been promoted through extensive propaganda campaigns (see Figure 6.2) and attempts to increase citizen ownership of the project. In 2009, the Tajik president Emomali Rakhmon called on 'every son of the nation, every patriot and our countrymen abroad to support Tajikistan through financial and moral help' and organised a 'voluntary-compulsory' investment programme for private individuals.[3] All citizens were compelled to purchase nearly USD700 worth of shares, a sum exceeding most Tajiks' annual income, in order to collect the USD600 million for construction to continue. Despite setbacks – the state originally hoped to start producing electricity in 2012 – and the controversial nature of the project, the construction of the dam is still ongoing (see Demytrie 2010).

From the company's perspective, the construction of the Roghun Dam is necessary: 'We have to solve this problem as we don't have any other sources of energy – no gas, no oil. We need to build Roghun' (Interview with Sattarov, May 2012). To reduce internal and external risks in the fragile economic environment, TALCO has produced an extensive risk analysis. The main risks for the company are: permanent fluctuations of transport and transit prices in Uzbekistan (Uzbek transit and pricing policy), insecure physical importation of cargo across the border from Uzbekistan (border policy) and, internally, unfavourable public attitudes and the possible increase in the costs of electricity, taxes and other domestic fees that weaken the company's position in the global market.

Figure 6.2 Roghun propaganda in Tajikistan

From its perspective, the company links all of these risks directly to the construction of Roghun and to Uzbekistan's recent attempts to limit cross-border interactions and trade between the countries: 'Uzbekistan has its own opinion about the construction of Roghun, and if they see something suspicious amongst the cargo, they stop it on their territory' (Interview with Sattarov, May 2012). Uzbekistan has closed most of its border-crossing points with Tajikistan, exited the Central Asian energy grid in 2009 to ensure its own energy security and, in 2011, stopped hundreds of freight railcars with food, construction materials, gasoline and humanitarian aid on the way to Tajikistan. Moreover, referring to the 'completion of contract obligations' (Juraev 2012: 2; see also Kozhevnikov 2012) and the need to provide gas to China, Uzbekistan repeatedly blocked all cargo and natural gas exports across the border to Tajikistan in 2012. Since TALCO, for technical reasons, cannot halt its production at any time and has remained fully dependent on Uzbek gas, the embargo forced the company to invest in an extensive new coal-operated back-up power plant, to prevent damage to the machinery in case of future interruptions of the gas supply and, thus, to decrease dependence on the scheduled cross-border gas deliveries.

As the present problems have their roots in domestic and international politics and have ended in a deadlock situation in which the two governments are not able to solve the problem by themselves, it has been proposed (see, amongst others, Juraev 2012) that the international community should act as a mediator, e.g. by creating an independent expert commission. Indeed, the European Union, the United Nations or the OSCE have in many cases proven able to alleviate tensions. However, in this particular Central Asian political environment, these organisations need to balance between development and political correctness and, therefore, to avoid becoming involved in politically sensitive matters such as conflicting interstate relations. Despite good intentions and a detailed strategy for Central Asia, the European Union has not been a very active player in the region (see Virkkunen, Fryer and Satybaldieva 2015; see also Boonstra and Denison 2011). Its Border Management in Central Asia Programme (BOMCA) aims for well-functioning border management between the states in the region, but has few resources and clearly avoids political issues such as the poor relations between Tajikistan and Uzbekistan.

As both Tajikistan and Uzbekistan are strategic partners of the Russian Federation, it has been proposed that the latter should play an increasing role in solving the conflict. Both countries also belong to the same regional organisations, namely the Central Asian Cooperation Organisation (CACO), the Euro-Asian Economic Community (EurAsEC), the Commonwealth of Independent States (CIS) and the Shanghai Cooperation Organisation (SCO), all operating in Central Asia. Perhaps one of these bodies could be capable of providing a format for resolving the crisis, which, if further politicised, may have an impact on the entire region, including the Ferghana Valley.

Borders in the Ferghana Valley

The border issues in the Ferghana Valley of northern Tajikistan are considerably different from the one in Tursunzoda. Instead of high-political bordering and a strong politicisation of matters such as the Roghun Dam, the border situation is predominantly defined by the local specificities of the valley: a very complicated border design, including multi-ethnic communities, exclaves or enclaves, and poorly managed and only partly delimited and demarcated post-Soviet borders that deeply affect everyday life in the border area. By providing local Tajik and Kyrgyz voices from the field, the following section aims to understand the conflicting character of the Ferghana Valley's borders and to compare it with the central Tajik circumstances of Tursunzoda. Like elsewhere in the region, the borders of the Ferghana Valley gained importance along with post-Soviet nationalism that has combined with failed delimitation of state boundaries, large ethnic minorities, gradually increasing dissatisfaction with poverty, the lack of natural resources (land and water in particular) and poor prospects for development.

As Madeleine Reeves (2005: 67; see also Reeves 2009) notes in her article about ethnic conflict in the Ferghana Valley, the region is often cast as 'dangerous' and 'crisis-ridden' as it fails to fit into normative accounts of what constitutes a 'proper' nation-state – territory, ethnicity and citizenship. Local narratives, by contrast, stress the importance of territorial delimitation through state-imposed barbed-wire fences, improper border controls and passport checks as major sources for increasing interethnic pressure and, thus, potential conflicts, that is 'the attempt of states to "state" the region, bringing it within a discursive regime of citizenship and citizenship controls, of "civilised" borders and territorial clarity, which is not merely resented, but seen as the real source of danger' (Reeves 2005: 69). Much of this can be explained by the very particular historical and social context of the valley.

The Ferghana Valley is a small 300-km-long and 170-km-wide valley in Central Asia. It consists of three provinces in Kyrgyzstan (Osh, Jalal-Abad and the recently created Batken), three provinces in Uzbekistan (Andijan, Ferghana and Namangan) and the Sughd (formerly Leninabad) province in Tajikistan. Until the creation of the Soviet Union, the valley between the northern Tian-Shan and southern Gissar-Alai mountain ranges remained a single administrative unit. In 1924, the creation of national republics in the developing Soviet state divided the multi-ethnic valley into three administrative areas, all containing large populations of non-titular nationalities (Uzbeks in Kyrgyzstan and Tajikistan, Tajiks in Uzbekistan etc.).

With the collapse of the Soviet Union and the establishment of new nation-states in the early 1990s, the formerly internal administrative lines between Soviet republics became international state borders. As the borders took on a new meaning as the limits of state sovereignty, they were forced upon locals. As the 1990s progressed, several factors forced the Central Asian states to reassess their border policies, including security threats from Islamist groups both within the region and from Afghanistan; environmental threats due to water and arable land shortages; and internal instabilities resulting from migration and economic dislocation.

Map 6.1 not only indicates fieldwork sites, but also illustrates the great challenges faced by the Ferghana Valley. Eight enclaves[4] and multiple minuscule land strips, a few kilometres in length or width, advancing into the territory of neighbouring states and the division of this 20,000-square-kilometre valley between three independent states characterise the entire valley as a borderland. In this post-Soviet nationalising context, borders not only define people's everyday lives and interactions in the valley, but also create a certain risk for the entire region's peaceful development.

Objectively, many of the existing conflicts in the region could be defused if the confusion over border delimitation and demarcation were to be addressed. In addition to the very complicated ethno-territorial setting, the three countries in the region all have border disputes with each other. While some progress in defining the borders has occurred since 1991, many important questions remain. As recently as March 2013, the Kyrgyz government was reporting that 371 kilometres of the border with Uzbekistan remained disputed, while 452 kilometres of the Tajik–Kyrgyz border are not subject to any agreement, in both cases especially near enclaves such as Vorukh, Sokh and Barak.[5] Despite the interstate relations between Uzbekistan and Tajikistan described above, only about 25 per cent of the border between the two countries remains delimited, mainly in the sections of Sughd province in the Ferghana Valley.[6]

Just as the Tajik–Uzbek border at Tursunzoda, the borders of the Ferghana Valley are products of the Soviet regime. Along with sudden independence, they turned from meaningless marks on Soviet administrative maps into unpredictable closed barriers representing new statehoods (Megoran 2006). In the multi-ethnic Ferghana Valley, they have become signifiers of the new territorialities, creating an unexpected break in the long tradition of joint Islamic identities and cultural ties, everyday regional interaction and transnational trade. They also meant a great change to a long tradition of openness inherited from the Silk Road era when traders transferred goods between China, the Middle East and Europe.

In the peripheral and densely populated Ferghana Valley, the turn from territorial openness to state-imposed bordering had a severe impact on (formerly borderless) infrastructure and strong interethnic contacts. Apart from economic failure, the collapse of the Soviet Union led to serious incidents of interethnic violence and long-lasting conflicts among the population, in addition to introducing several structural obstacles and dissatisfaction in people's daily lives. The Saferworld report on conflict prevention in the Ferghana Valley identifies six commonly agreed key factors behind the conflict dynamics in the valley (Hiscock and Paasiaro 2011): poverty; ethno-nationalist sentiments; shortage and mismanagement of natural resources (particularly of land and water); border (mis-)management and border crossing procedures; drugs, extremism, organised crime and weapons; and (weak) governance on national and local levels.

In other words, borders in the post-Soviet Ferghana Valley relate to different everyday concerns and conflicts, as well as to poor governance, rather than to diplomatic state-level threats such as in Tursunzoda for diverse conflict dynamics (see, amongst others, Smith and Satybaldieva 2015; Virkkunen, Fryer and Satybaldieva 2015). The rest of this chapter will give a platform to local voices from the Tajik–Kyrgyz and Kyrgyz–Uzbek border areas in the Ferghana Valley. It is argued here that neither the Ferghana Valley nor its borders can be understood solely through a traditional approach to (state or border) security.

Here the understanding of the concrete local impacts of post-Soviet bordering, unclear border delimitation and demarcation, and the politicisation of ethnicity through everyday developments is crucial. Understanding this reality helps us recognise and formulate specific security-related policies for this very particular, and politically very challenging, border region. It is these that will be explored in the rest of the chapter.

Border delimitation and demarcation in the Ferghana Valley

Borders have become an important local political issue. Two decades of weak state control have made the task of governments sitting down together to discuss the needed demarcation and delimitation difficult. Nowhere is this more evident than in the Tajik–Kyrgyz borderlands of the southern Ferghana Valley, a densely populated area with a historically mixed population of Tajiks, Uzbeks and Kyrgyz that is undeniably volatile due to the acute shortage of resources, highly mobile populations and non-demarcated borders. As one resident of the Kyrgyz border town of Tash-Tomshuk observed: 'We don't have a border. Whoever is Kyrgyz is a citizen of Kyrgyzstan. Whoever is Tajik is a citizen of Tajikistan. The same goes for the property. If a Kyrgyz lives there, it's Kyrgyzstan. If a Tajik, it's Tajikistan' (Yefimova-Trilling and Trilling 2012). And in Ak-Sai, similar sentiments are expressed: 'In many villages, Tajiks and Kyrgyz live side by side and all are convinced that they live in their respective country!' (Interview Ak-Sai, November 2011).

Discussions with local residents – for the most part – indicate a strong desire to formalise the borders and their border-crossing regimes. And at least Kyrgyzstan and Tajikistan have publicly declared their commitment to bringing to a successful conclusion the border demarcation talks that have been ongoing for many years. But as the intergovernmental commission for border delimitation has not been able to make any progress because of the highly sensitive character of the matter, mistrust in central government is increasing and encouraging local residents, frustrated young men in particular, to take the initiative to protect 'their territory' by themselves. So with all the momentum in favour of demarcation and delimitation, it is perplexing that a solution has not been found already. The next section largely addresses the issue from the point of view of people living in the Kyrgyz–Tajik border area located between the Sughd (Tajikistan) and Batken (Kyrgyzstan) provinces.

The past decade has heightened anxieties over creeping migration, which is the process whereby citizens of Tajikistan illegally purchase land and houses in Kyrgyzstan, partly with the aim of using contested border lands for pasture, water and agriculture (Fryer, Nasritdinov and Satybaldieva 2014; Reeves 2009). Two patterns have developed that have contributed to the situation. In Tajikistan, high birth rates have put considerable strain on land resources, as one official from Chorkukh district stated:

> You know, the population of Chorkukh is growing fast and last year, in the Chorkukh *jamoat*, 1600 infants were born, but 142 people died; each year about 400 households appear, which equals the population of a small district. We have small parcels of land and it is impossible always to provide families with lands for orchards and for building houses.
>
> (Interview Chorkukh, June 2012)

In Kyrgyzstan, years of large-scale outmigration from many Batken villages to other parts of the country and to Russia have emptied the Kyrgyz border zone, which Tajik citizens interpret as an invitation to move into the area. Despite the Kyrgyz authorities' efforts to keep creeping migration at bay, for example through legislation, such as the 2011 law on border regions that gave a special status and funding to 46 villages in an attempt to, in the words of a former Deputy Minister for Social Protection, 'keep people there' (Interview Bishkek, November 2011), Tajiks[7] continue to settle in the area.

Because of unclear borders, the area suffers from increasing cross-border conflicts that have been ethnicised – clashes have occurred between Tajiks and Kyrgyz in 2002, 2004, 2006, 2008 and 2011 over land disputes and most recently over the construction of a road on contested territory (Fryer, Nasritdinov and Satybaldieva 2014; Jamoat Resource Centre of Vorukh 2011; Safarov and Rizoev 2010; Trilling 2013).[8] This has caused especially Kyrgyz to demand a stricter border regime and a better border delimitation, with commonly heard slogans and statements such as 'wire fences to protect us' (Interview Sogment, June 2012), 'demarcation to be carried out by the UN' (Interview Ak-Sai, June 2012) and 'the border is a disease' (Interview Samarqandyk, June 2012). Locals blame the Tajik side for not pursuing the normalisation of the border: 'Everyone here is waiting for demarcation, but not all the Tajiks want it. They see the chance to grab land and they have a green light now.' – 'Tajiks come into our land and when we complain, they say that it is contested – will stay here until demarcation forces them out.' (Interviews Ak-Sai, November 2011 and June 2012) The authorities in Batken go as far as to point the finger at the 'Tajik authorities: '(They) support creeping migration with documents and registration; it's not official policy, local authorities are not in a hurry to define the borders, this will only come from above.' (Interview Batken, November 2011)

The Tajik authorities, for their part, do not have a clear position on demarcation and delimitation. Dushanbe is far away and local officials do not strive for delimitation, although they emphasise that local residents are aware of the border and answerable to local informal administrative associations, or *mahallas* (Interview Qistaquz, June 2012). From the local Tajik perspective, the non-demarcated border is confusing and many residents do not understand why they cannot use territories across the border when they have been doing so for decades. As one informant stated in Chorkukh:

> Before, the states were defined as separate countries, (now) we face misunderstandings. We have joint roads; there are thirty small and big rivers that cross the territories of Tajikistan and Kyrgyzstan. It is difficult to understand how these natural resources and roads are going to be divided between two states.
>
> (Interview Chorkukh, June 2012)

An official of the Tajik Ministry of Foreign Affairs stressed the importance of creating new maps of contested areas to help with delimitation (Interview Dushanbe, May 2012), but a representative of an international organisation in Khujand played down this fixation with maps, suggesting that it showed the Tajik government's intention not to deal with delimitation anytime soon (Interview Khujand, June 2012). The European Union recently announced technical support for the mapping process by offering satellite imagery of border areas, but other international representatives suggest that this programme is misplaced or 'backwards', as the political dialogue over delimitation needs to move ahead further before technical assistance with demarcation can proceed (Delegation of the European Union to the Republic of Tajikistan 2012). One local expert laughed at the EU's efforts: 'The EU programme will not help, because satellite images will not help choose which map to use!' (Interview Bishkek, May 2012) It seems that the delimitation and demarcation of the borders between Tajikistan and Kyrgyzstan cannot solve all of the region's problems. Instead, the international community should focus its efforts and support on getting each government to address the weak institutions of governance and the endemic and widespread social and economic problems local inhabitants are facing rather than blame the absence of 'lines on the ground'. An advisor to the governor of Batken province remarked that 'people don't feel as though there is a border – there wasn't before, so why now?' (Interview Batken, November 2011). If the international community wishes to support the process between these two neighbours, its help must fit the existing socio-political context to be successful.

Conclusion

This chapter has focused on Tajik borders and the redefinition of economic and political space in two contexts: the situation in the town of Tursunzoda with its company TALCO, close to the Uzbek border in central Tajikistan, and the Tajik–Kyrgyz border in the Ferghana Valley. The two examples illustrate simultaneous but different bordering processes in contemporary Tajikistan, the serious economic impacts of an unstable and unpredictable border regime with Uzbekistan, resulting from the collapse of Soviet production networks and deteriorated interstate relations, and the ethno-territorial instability connected to creeping migration that is particularly significant on the Tajik border with Kyrgyzstan.

The case of Tursunzoda raises one of the most difficult issues of Tajik and, more generally, Central Asian post-Soviet bordering: the great importance of interstate relations and de facto interest in solving evolving disagreements. In Tursunzoda, this finds its concrete expression in the 'Cold War'-like relations between the Tajik and Uzbek states and the related unstable prices of transit and for raw materials, together with occasional interruptions at border crossings. Despite economic integration into the global market, these nationalised policies form some of the major risks for both TALCO and the Tajik economy in general. In the Ferghana Valley, the new situation has led to increasing poverty, the lack of, or poor (domestic and cross-border) management of natural resources, frustration over the secretive border delimitation process as well as associated everyday insecurities and local ethnic conflict. This, of course, relates to the battle over economic resources, repositioning in regard to economic flows, rising nationalism and domestic policy-making that are central to the bordering processes in Ferghana valley as well. Despite the integrated history and multi-ethnic character of local societies, the states aim for increased territorial integration and, additionally, for intensive ethnic othering. In a region with one of the most complicated borders (e.g. numerous enclaves), these have resulted in a social instability that may, as many experts and local inhabitants fear, spiral out of control.

Politically, the two areas studied present something of a challenge. New nationalising states like Tajikistan and Uzbekistan are struggling with the economic reorganisation of Soviet-time production and political space. Power and sovereignty are being negotiated through intensive bordering and nationalised mega projects like the Roghun Dam. On the one hand, the two countries call on the international community to provide assistance in solving their difficult issues and in normalising their relations. On the other hand, no international attempts have succeeded in improving the situation. From the perspective of the Tajik Aluminium Company and the Tajik state, any international attempt to mediate would be welcome. Here, international organisations such as the United Nations and the European Union, as well as the Russian Federation and the CIS, could take a more active role. A successful mediation will, however, not succeed without a true commitment of all participating states to a meaningful dialogue.

In the Ferghana Valley, a political solution for border regularisation and stabilisation would be more complex, requiring an entire set of actions by local, national and international actors. Many of the problems stem from frustrations about poverty and the ethnicised policies of late and post-Soviet power changes, the lack of water and land in a context of very strong population growth. In order to manage migration and avoid the further politicisation of natural resources, as well as of ethnicity, the region needs long-term (and cross-border) development. Most of the informants in the region have stressed that only limited improvement can be made without better economic conditions and, thus, economic investment. This in turn necessitates, however, a more stable and predictable business environment based on the rule of law (including serious measures against corruption) and a more inclusive society. To make use of the traditional multi-ethnic and formerly borderless character of the region for development and to avoid further ethnic and cross-border conflicts, serious consideration should be paid to border delimitation, the local impacts of the recently introduced state border and local-level conflict management.

Here, international organisations such as the United Nations Development Programme (UNDP) and the EU's Border Management in Central Asia (BOMCA) do play an important role. They give national administrations technical support and provide local actors with the ability to cope with different conflict situations. Yet, less focus should be put on top-down training and international consultancies, which are not respected by locals due to their lack of engagement, and more attention should be paid to a long-term commitment to good governance and the rule of law, to structural and economic development, to supporting the delimitation and management of national borders and maintaining good practices in local-level conflict management.

Notes

1 For a detailed self-produced history of the company, see Kabirova *et al.* (2011).
2 For a discussion on the phenomenon of so-called 'monotowns', see World Bank in Russia, Russian Economic Report, No. 22, June 2010, 21–27. Online. Available at: http://siteresources.worldbank.org/INTRUSSIANFEDERATION/Resources/305499-1245838520910/rer_22_eng.pdf (last accessed 9 June 2013).
3 See Platonov 2010, Tolipov 2012 and 'Tajikistan: Rogun Hydropower Plant to be Supported by Poor?', *Ferghananews.com*, 13 November 2009. Online. Available at: http://enews:fergananews.com/news.php?id=1465&mode=snews (last accessed 9 June 2013).
4 The eight enclaves of the Ferghana Valley are: Vorukh and Kairagach (Tajik enclaves in Kyrgyzstan); Sarvan (Tajik enclave in Uzbekistan); Sokh, Shakhimardan, Chon-Kara (or Qal'acha) and Jani-Ayil (or Dzhangail) (Uzbek enclaves in Kyrgyzstan); and Barak (Kyrgyz enclave in Uzbekistan).
5 See 'Kyrgyzstan Pushes Uzbekistan to Discuss Border Demarcation', *Ferghananews.com*, 16 March 2013. Online. Available at: http://enews.ferghananews.com/news.php?id=2507&,ode=snews (last accessed 9 June 2013).
6 See 'Tajik-Uzbek Intergovernmental Commission of Delimitation and Demarcation Border to Resume in February', *Avesta*, 27 January 2012. Online. Available at: www.avesta.tj/eng/security/1557-tajik-uzbek-intergovernmental-commission-of-delimitation-and-demarcation-border-to-resume-in-february.html (last accessed 9 June 2013).
7 While it is clear that the citizens of Tajikistan moving into Kyrgyzstan are of various ethnic origins, the terms Tajik and Kyrgyz (rather than Tajikistani or Kyrgyzstani) are used here to highlight the ethnicised nature of the conflict.
8 A number of violent border clashes also have taken place along the Kyrgyz–Uzbek border, especially along that of the Sokh enclave (Megoran 2004 and 2012; Myrzabekova, Sikorskaya and Khaldarov 2013; Reeves 2014).

7 Of barriers, breaches and bridges

Cross-border ecotourism and the prospect
of horizontal governance acting as a bridge
in Belarus–EU Neighbourhood relations

Anaïs Marin

Post-Soviet Belarus defies the assumption that in progressing eastwards Europeanisation, together with the EU enlargements, will pave the way for a Europe free of dividing lines. Much to the contrary, Belarus, a paragon of a borderland country, is located as Eurasia's buffer on the fault line of a new 'clash of civilisations' between the EU and Russia. Since 1994, Alexander Lukashenko has confidently rejected democratic values and the EU's governance model alike, favouring instead reintegration with Russia, his main ally and sponsor. Regardless of the EU's efforts to attract Belarus into its 'ring of friends' through policies such as the European Neighbourhood Policy (ENP), the Eastern Partnership (EaP) and, lately, the European Dialogue on Modernisation (EDM), Minsk has shown no genuine interest in a rapprochement with Europe, at least not within the normative framework that Brussels tries to impose on neighbours not applying for EU accession. Whereas Brussels conditions its cooperation and support on the respect of democratic principles, the Belarusian government is interested in a pragmatic relationship limited to matters of joint economic interest. Hence, Minsk has responded selectively to the EU's offer, extended in May 2009, to participate in the Eastern Partnership. It has called on the EU to comply with the principle of 'joint ownership' contained in the EaP's founding documents while dismissing that of democratic conditionality also encapsulated in the EU's policies.

By arguing that Belarus's non-candidate status makes EU interference in its internal affairs illegitimate, the Belarusian leadership highlights a drawback of the EU's neighbourhood policies that has long been criticised in academic debates (Browning and Joenniemi 2008; Kochenov 2008; Tulmets 2006). Used outside its initial pre-accession context, conditionality indeed appears to be a questionable practice. The liberal reforms demanded by the EU entail serious costs for undemocratic leaders, yet the incentives to compensate for these losses are not attractive enough. Applying to non-candidate countries a principle transferred from the enlargement toolbox (i.e. democratic conditionality) even denotes hegemonic and arrogant behaviour. However condemnable the values the Belarusian regime claims to be defending, those promoted through the EaP are obviously not shared but EU-centric ones (Bosse 2008). This conceptual shortcoming, a feature underpinning the ENP, has not been solved

DOI: 10.4324/9781315858036-10

by the EaP initiative, which merely added a new layer to an already contested policy: a relationship in which one partner unilaterally dictates the rules of the game and imposes its values is an ill-defined partnership. This, critics argue, amounts to 'sending a signal that, all the pro-active rhetoric notwithstanding, the EU is not ready to be wholeheartedly engaged with the ENP partners' (Kochenov 2009). Belarus's reluctance to take part in this unbalanced relationship should therefore come as no surprise. It shows that boundary-building (or bordering) is actually a mutually constitutive process whereby Eastern neighbours respond to the EU's normative ambitions by erecting their own barriers to cooperation (Bosse and Korosteleva-Polglase 2009).

Notwithstanding Minsk's reluctance to cooperate with the EU on Brussels' terms, Belarus is not totally disconnected from European sub-regional integration dynamics. There appear to be breaches in the wall. In spite of the numerous obstacles to decentralised cooperation, several cross-border cooperation (CBC) initiatives are readily being implemented with the support of actors from various levels of governance – the EU-level and national and local levels within EU member states and in Belarus. No less than four of the five border regions (*oblasti*) of Belarus are involved in a Euroregion operating with partners from an EU country (Poland, Lithuania and Latvia): Neman, Bug, Country of Lakes and Belovezhskaya Pushcha (see Table 7.1).[1] Against the current geopolitical background, the very existence of Euroregional projects shows that the regime is not completely impervious to cooperation with the EU. The Belarusian leadership even authorised local administrations from the Grodno, Brest, Vitebsk regions and part of Minsk region to get involved in two programmes funded under the EU's neighbourhood and partnership instrument for cross-border cooperation. Identifying the fields in which local stakeholders consider CBC projects as best practices of cooperation could thus help EU policy-makers improve their partnership offer towards Belarus, thereby creating a bridge between the EU and its eastern neighbour.

This chapter attempts to demonstrate that the multiplication of cross-border interactions with EU neighbours could help socialise Belarus within the European realm. In the current circumstances, socialisation is the most realistic goal the West can aim for. Track One diplomacy, that is efforts to use top-down leverage through political conditionality, is obviously failing to induce the Belarusian regime to adopt democratic reforms. Track Two diplomacy – support for the democratising forces of civil society, aka 'linkage', a term used in the literature on the EU's 'external governance' (Lavenex 2011) – also appears to have a limited impact. In fact, Belarus belongs to the category of non-candidate countries where authoritarianism pre-emptively obstructs and slows down the societal changes expected from the EU's enhanced cooperation with civil society organisations (CSOs) and the political opposition (Lavenex and Schimmelfennig 2011). Lacking the necessary autonomy and freedom of manoeuvre, the latter are not reliable in-country channels for promoting democracy. Hence, Belarus qualifies as a good candidate for Track Three diplomacy (Marin 2011b), intended to encourage democratic governance in

Table 7.1 EU–Belarus Euroregions in a nutshell

	Bug	Neman/Niemen/Nemunas	Country of Lakes /Aziorniy kray/Ezeru zeme/Ežeru kraštas	Belovezhskaya pushcha/Puszcza białowieska
Date of creation	September 1995	6 June 1997	29 January 1999	25 May 2002
Belarus	Brest oblast'	Grodno oblast'	Braslav, Glubokoje, Miori, Postavi and Verhnedvinsk districts (Vitebsk oblast').	Kamemets and Pruzhany districts (Brest oblast'); Svisloch district (Grodno oblast')
Poland	Lublin voivodship	Suwałki and Białystok voivodships	–	nine districts (gminy) of Podlasie voivodship
Ukraine	Volyn and L'viv oblasti		–	–
Lithuania	–	Alytus, Mariampole and Vilnius counties.	Municipalities of Ignalina, Svencionys, Utena, Zarasai and Visaginas.	
Latvia	–	–	District or city councils of Daugavpils, Krāslava, Rēzekne and Preili.	–
Russia	–	Chernyachovsk, Krasnoznamensk, Gusev, Oziorsk and Nesterov districts of Kaliningrad oblast'		–
Website	www.euroregion bug.pl	www.niemen.org.pl	www.country-of-lakes.de	euroregion-puszczabialow ieska.prv.pl/

the conduct of public policy through functional cooperation with selected third-sector partners (CSOs, epistemic communities, business circles, but also public administration) in a restricted number of consensual fields. This governance model emphasises sectoral horizontal cooperation as a channel for gradual liberalisation along with network contacts between people (socialisation) as an instrument for values transfer. Given the Belarusian realities, it is the most promising model for democracy promotion, and cross-border cooperation the best tool for implementing it.

Looked at through a constructivist lens, the multiplication of cross-border flows of goods, people and ideas across Belarus's EU borders since the end of the Cold War entails hopes for a mental de-bordering and socialisation of Belarus in Europe. An institutionalist perspective reveals, however, a darker picture: the border-breaking efforts of ongoing CBC projects are being hampered by the autocratic boundary-making responses of the Belarusian central government. Yet, for lack of better instruments for democratic rule–transfer, the EU should sustain its efforts of socialising Belarusians through principled, not conditional cooperation, starting with fields and issues where a minimal consensus between the state and society in Belarus could be brokered.

The rest of the chapter is composed of four sections. The next will provide an overview of the historical, domestic and external obstacles, or barriers, to CBC with the EU. Building on the empirical findings of field research conducted in Euroregion Neman in 2010, the second section will highlight the breaches which allow for CBC and transborder region-building. The third section will assess their border-breaking potential in a field of cooperation which is a traditional driver of confidence-building initiatives across EU borders: environmental protection. In particular, projects aiming at the sustainable development of transboundary ecosystems (forests and waterways) and their transformation into green-tourism destinations, along the lines of the model offered by the Augustów Canal across the Polish–Belarusian border, have an unexplored potential to bridge the existing gap in neighbourhood relations. This is because the prospect of an influx of foreign investment and tourists in Belarus's western borderlands is attractive enough not to alienate the state authorities. The fourth and concluding section thus will advocate that the EU further encourage green-label CBC projects as part of a wider geopolitics-of-bridging strategy towards Belarus. By facilitating the emergence of horizontal governance networks, which experts previously identified as indispensable for the Europeanisation-by-socialisation of Belarus (Bosse and Korosteleva-Polglase 2009), such an approach could even contribute to opening up Belarus, or at least its western borderlands, to the influence of democratisation from below, a long-term objective that Western linkage policies have until now failed to achieve in Belarus.

Barriers: evidence of boundary-making in and with Belarus

Of all post-Soviet countries, the Republic of Belarus is arguably the most impermeable to globalisation and its alleged perforating impact on borders.

Under the iron hand of Alexander Lukashenko, Belarus has since 1994 shown an astonishing resistance to the call of market democracy and European integration alike. Its Soviet-type command economy has remained largely unreformed. In spite of its pivotal role as a transit corridor for Russian energy exports to Europe, Belarus remains a rather closed economy. As for Belarusian society, it can be described as closed, too – in the Popperian sense of the term. With its autocratic leadership, hypercentralised governance structure and contempt for fundamental freedoms, the regime has consolidated an unchallenged control over the Belarusian population. These features negatively impact on the potential for CBC. Yet the EU's isolation policies have contributed to mutual alienation as well.

Belarus as a borderland: shifted, relict and crystallised boundaries

Conditions for border life and border-crossing in Belarus differ dramatically according to the quality of diplomatic relations with the respective neighbouring country. As a result of border changes in the twentieth century, neighbourhood relations are particularly strained with Poland and Lithuania. For three centuries, the present territory of all three countries constituted a single state, the Union of Two Nations, until the Polish–Lithuanian Commonwealth was partitioned by neighbouring empires in the late eighteenth century. The most visible relict boundary left by border shifts in the cultural landscape is, however, a legacy of the westward translation of Polish territory after the Second World War (Sobczynski 2006). The former Kresy Wschodnie (a Polish term for 'Eastern borderlands') became part of the Soviet Union. An ethnic minority of about 300,000 Catholic Poles still live in the Hrodna region in western Belarus. Poland's nostalgia for its lost territories and concerns for the fate of this Polish minority imply that initiatives promoting increasing CBC are seen in Belarus as irredentist moves. This, in turn, crystallises the exclusionary function of Belarus's borders with the EU.

Belarus's borderscape is extremely differentiated. The eastern border with Russia is one of interdependence. Functional (re)integration is accelerating within the Union State of Belarus and Russia, the Customs Union (between those two and Kazakhstan) and the Eurasian Economic Space. Hence, this border fits perfectly into the 'border of inclusion' category described by Oscar Martinez in his famous taxonomy of borders (Martinez 1994). To the south, the border with Ukraine is one of coexistence, with residual elements of interdependence. The same can be said of the northern border with Latvia and, to a lesser extent, of the one with Lithuania. Conversely Belarus's border with Poland is an ideal-typical border of alienation.[2]

The whole borderscape has experienced a double swing over the past two decades. Following the fall of the Iron Curtain, the Polish–Belarusian border reopened, while the demise of the Soviet Union led to the transformation of Belarus's administrative borders with Latvia, Lithuania, Ukraine and Russia into international borders. Throughout the 1990s, Belarus's formerly closed border with Poland evolved into a more open one. Similarly, the borderlands with Lithuania and Latvia became spaces of inclusiveness and cooperation, as important flows of goods and people (commuter workers, shuttle traders, tourists, smugglers etc.) were crossing the border daily. However, when these three neighbours started preparations for joining NATO (between 1999 and 2004), the EU (2004) and the Schengen space (2007), their borders with Belarus progressively became increasingly exclusive. The Schengen enlargement in particular led to the closing down of the border between Belarus and the new EU member states: in December 2007; economic, socio-cultural and family ties were abruptly disrupted as a more restrictive visa regime was imposed on Belarusians. In the absence of a bilateral agreement with the EU – the process of signing it had been frozen in 1996 as part of Brussels' isolation policy towards Lukashenko's regime – Belarusians are the only Europeans who pay as much as 60 euros for a Schengen visa. However the biggest obstacles to CBC stem from the Belarusian regime's own boundary-building practices.

Domestic obstacles to cross-border cooperation

Much like in Soviet times, twenty-first-century Belarus is a centrally administered polity with no free and fair elections, no political pluralism and no separation of powers. Authoritarian consolidation means that all powers are concentrated in the president's hands. The political opposition, independent media and autonomous CSOs are virtually excluded from the public arena. In fear of some Western-funded 'colour revolution', the regime 'preemptively' has been discrediting political opponents by accusing them of acting as a fifth column on a Western payroll.[3] The omnipresent populist propaganda resembles an Orwellian attempt to justify encroachments of fundamental freedoms, notably free speech, association and assembly. All this objectively obstructs CBC in fields where at least some devolution to sub- and non-state actors would be necessary.

First, local administrations (municipalities and regional authorities) in Belarus lack constitutional prerogatives and autonomy. Their legal status is still regulated by the law On Local Government and Self-Government dating back to 20 February 1991. The executive committees of each of the seven Belarusian *oblasti* have neither tools nor means for self-government. Heads of administration are appointed by and personally accountable to the president himself, a subordination which deprives them of any right to take initiatives, the less so in international affairs.

Second, centralisation and bureaucratisation complicate socio-economic interactions across EU borders. Whereas the existence of individual entrepreneurship, SMEs and private investment has been acknowledged as an essential driving force for implementing CBC projects, especially when public funds are lacking, third-sector actors in Belarus are powerless. This shortcoming limits the channels, if not the very need for CBC. The legal climate for cooperating with foreign partners is highly unpredictable. This is a disincentive for business and civil society actors to get involved in EU-led CBC projects.

Third, Lukashenko's paternalistic autocracy builds on what he abusively calls his 'social contract' with Belarusians. This implies that civil society remains weak, unconsolidated and thus vulnerable. All pro-democracy civil society actors are prevented from working freely, and opposition-minded CSOs closed down altogether as soon as the authorities become suspicious of their relations with Western partners. Restrictive legislation[4], the repressive use of administrative resources and intimidation by secret services are called upon to outlaw opposition-minded CSOs and media outlets and to imprison their leaders.

In order to maintain contacts with Western donors, many pro-European civil society activists retract behind youth, education and charity organisations. Recreational, sports and environmental associations can also operate in Belarus more easily as long as they remain apparently apolitical. Yet young Belarusians' expectations in terms of social comfort, culture, environmental protection and access to basic consumer goods for leisure activities are comparable to those found in EU countries. A by-product of globalisation, this homogenisation somehow cements the need for CBC with EU neighbours. Yet the foreign policy preferences of the Belarusian leadership consistently deny this social demand, thought to carry with it calls for liberalisation which are considered tantamount to regime sabotage or attempts aimed at overthrowing the regime in the longer run.

The impact of geopolitics: Belarus's (self-)exclusion from the West

Since 1996, Lukashenko's regime has been the target of blaming and shaming as well as of 'restrictive measures' (sanctions) from the West. After the 2008 Russia–Georgia war, the EU softened its Track One isolation policy in an attempt to tame the regime with promises of rewards in exchange for – finally unkept – promises of democratic elections. Contrary to claims that Lukashenko's dictatorial ways alone led him to being self-excluded from the West, EU isolation policies contributed to alienate Belarus from the rest of Europe.

The Belarusian regime remains a reluctant partner in most of the EU's regional integration initiatives, notably the Eastern Partnership (EaP), a cooperation platform established by the EU in May 2009 as a means to draw its six eastern neighbours closer. The Belarusian authorities' response to the latest EU cooperation offer to date, the European Dialogue for Modernisation (EDM) launched in March 2012 by the European Commission, has been equally cold. Since the last rigged presidential elections on 19 December 2010, the regime has backslid into authoritarianism and the West subsequently has renewed its sanctions. Swapping carrots for sticks, the EU failed to take into account its insufficient leverage over Minsk to impose its democratic conditionality, especially in comparison to Russia, which provides significant subsidies to Belarus almost unconditionally. For this reason, the EU's policy of offering a partnership to Belarus while sanctioning the country's leadership was doomed to be met with scepticism; given the cost of the reforms requested by

Brussels, it comes as no surprise that the Belarusian leadership has remained reluctant to participate in the EaP.

Yet the (re)construction of boundaries is a two-way, mutually constitutive process fuelled by the West's own isolation policies. Upon shifting its borders eastwards, the enlarging EU itself became 'subject to the boundaries enacted by neighbouring states' (Bosse and Korosteleva-Polglase 2009). These boundaries can be symbolic, taking the form of anti-Western narratives for example, as well as physical, as illustrated by the recent evolution of the border and the Belarusian government's policy of migration control. In retaliation for the visa ban imposed by the EU against over 240 Belarusian officials in 2012, Lukashenko's regime expanded its own black list of undesirable foreigners and re-enacted the Soviet-era practice of forbidding some of its own citizens to leave the country. Under these conditions, the EU's external governance model (Lavenex 2008) might hold better prospects for democratising Belarus than previous attempts at isolating the regime or entering into a 'critical engagement' (2008–2010) with it.

Breaches: transborder region-building processes in Belarus

In spite of unfavourable geopolitical and domestic conditions for CBC, a closer look at grassroots developments reveals signs of a partial de-bordering across Belarus's EU borders.

The Euroregional model

Four Euroregions operate across the EU–Belarus border. Most transborder regions are mere rhetorical creations, if not empty shells, notably when they involve non-EU countries.[5] With the exception of a single micro-Euroregion (Country of Lakes, with Lithuania and Latvia), Euroregions involving Belarus result from Polish initiatives motivated by a mix of nostalgia and irredentism. Restoring ties with borderlands 'lost' to an eastern neighbour has actually been a common way for Germany, Finland, Poland and Romania to heal the 'stump syndrome' caused by border shifts that have occurred in the aftermath of the Second World War (Popescu 2008). Nations are feeling ethically responsible for their kin, that is the ethnic minorities left on the eastern side of a border. Moreover, once some of these countries had joined the EU, they wanted to share with their eastern neighbours – Ukraine, Belarus, Moldova – the experience of CBC that they made on their own western borders, as Germany has done with Poland (Mezhevich 2009).

The idea to transfer the Euroregional model to Poland's eastern borders was first aired by Cezary Cieślukowski, the governor of the Suwałki voivodship and later head of the Assembly of Euroregions of Poland (Kotskaya 2006). His initiative was endorsed by the signatories of the closing Declaration of the Third Baltic Economic Forum in February 1995 (Urząd Statystyczny we Wrocławiu 2007) and, on 6 June 1997, representatives of the governments of

Poland, Belarus and Lithuania thus signed the founding statutes of the Euroregion Neman.[6] This Euroregion, which now covers a population of over 3.6 million in four countries (Poland, Lithuania, Belarus and Russia), has been the first to involve during its very beginnings a Belarusian administrative unit, namely Hrodna *oblast'*. Two years earlier the Ukrainian Volyn *oblast'* and four neighbouring Polish voivodships had established the Euroregion Bug, to which Brest *oblast'* adhered in June 1998 and L'viv *oblast'* (Ukraine) later on, thereby turning this Euroregion into one of the largest in Europe, with almost five million inhabitants. In 2002 another, two-tier only, Euroregion was established on the Polish–Belarusian border, Belovezhskaya Pushcha, named after the Belovezh primeval forest, a UNESCO-listed transboundary natural World Heritage Site.[7] Just as Country of Lakes, situated in the Braslaw lake area northeast of Minsk, Belovezhskaya Pushcha is a micro-Euroregion created with the main objective of enhancing cooperation in the field of sustainable development and green tourism.

Marginalised in their respective national settings, Eastern European peripheries increasingly rely on tourism as a driver of economic growth. With EU support, the Polish secretariats of Euroregions have published multilingual booklets and maps to advertise the borderland as a 'cultural heritage' and 'green tourism' area, emphasising such landmarks as the Augustów Canal and the Białowieża (Belovezh) primeval forest, both attractive for alternative forms of tourism, whether nostalgic or green. Cross-border group excursions to the untamed Belarusian part of the Belovezh forest are now being organised thanks to easily obtainable one-day visas (Marin 2013). Euroregions participated in drawing up itineraries and creating cycling tracks for these new tourists.

Belarus's participation in CBC projects with the EU remains however limited. This in turn hampers the institutionalisation of cooperation, thus limiting the performance of Euroregions and their potential to let these regions gain visibility on the European level.[8] Belarusian civil servants usually lack the experience and the knowledge crucial for conducting CBC projects. Their poor knowledge of English often disqualifies them from access to EU sources of funding for which they might be eligible, namely the Technical Aid Programme for Countries of the ex-Soviet Union (TACIS) CBC, before the EU's eastern enlargement, and the European Neighbourhood and Partnership Instrument (ENPI) CBC funding since 2007. The centralised management from Minsk of local administrations' activities results in lengthier procedures for endorsing an initiative or implementing a project (Pazdnyak 2006; Popławski 2010). Moreover, local elites tend to hijack the Euroregion brand – as a concept, logo and platform – for their own business interests. The great majority of the population is unaware of living in a Euroregion or at most perceives CBC as the framework for a mayor's cross-border tourism or a playground for business circles merely interested in cross-border trade. Only during the Neman or Bug Euroregion Trade Fairs are Euroregions mentioned by the local media. Borderlanders seldom identify with Euroregions: the societal dimension is usually missing in CBC. Another legitimacy problem stems from the frequent apprehension that Euroregions are instruments of Poland's ambitions for regional leadership.

The inhabitants of micro-Euroregions seem, however, to identify more closely with the Euroregional project in cases where CBC programmes positively affect the life of borderlanders in such fields as public health, education, cultural and school exchanges and sports competitions. But underfunding limits the added value of all Euroregions: their budget comes from membership fees, which poorer administrations cannot afford to pay. Central governments usually perceive Euroregions as a challenge to their sovereignty and refuse to subsidise them. From a Belarusian viewpoint, CBC generally implies a threat to territorial statehood and regime stability, given the potentially subversive impact of social networking across EU borders. Yet the participation of Belarusian local administrations in Euroregions would not have been possible without the consent of Lukashenko himself. The very fact that the authorities support transborder region-building, albeit only on paper, provides evidence that the regime is showing interest in developing CBC, especially because if offers the prospect of attracting EU funding.

European Neighbourhood programmes (ENPI CBC)

Building on the INTERREG IIIA/TACIS CBC 2004–2006 Neighbourhood programmes, fifteen new programmes for cross-border cooperation have been established under the European Neighbourhood and Partnership Instrument (ENPI CBC) for the period 2007–2013. Two of them involve Belarus, one together with Latvia and Lithuania, the other with Poland and Ukraine. The funds earmarked for co-financing them amount respectively to EUR41.737 million and EUR186.201 million.[9] The Poland–Belarus–Ukraine programme has been designed to support CBC projects with a potential impact in three priority fields: increasing the competitiveness of the border area; improving the quality of life; and encouraging networking and people-to-people cooperation. The priorities of the Latvia–Lithuania–Belarus programme are formulated a bit differently ('promoting sustainable economic and social development' and 'addressing common challenges') but the overall objective is the same: socialising borderlanders through daily practicing of CBC, which is seen as both a tool and an end of the EU's neighbourhood policy.

It is too early to assess the achievements of ENPI CBC programmes since they have been effectively launched only in 2009 and are meant to end in 2016. However, two preliminary findings are worth mentioning. First, Belarusian civil society actors (NGOs, schools and universities, cultural and sports associations etc.) have a chance of getting involved much more actively in the preparation and implementation phases of ENPI CBC projects than is usual within the framework of Euroregions.[10] Second, projects relating to the protection of the borderlands' natural environment form the bulk of ENPI CBC projects currently being implemented. For Minsk, environmental protection is indeed a sufficiently apolitical and consensual common good to let local administrations get involved. As the next section illustrates, pragmatism has also led the Belarusian authorities to admit that cross-border tourism and the shuttle trade can provide economic benefits and to acknowledge that the prospect of less restrictive border-crossing regimes has met with a highly favourable reaction from the Belarusian population.

Local Border Traffic agreements

Since Belarus does not fulfil the democratic conditionality requirements allowing it to develop full-range institutional relations with the EU, the signing of a visa facilitation and readmission agreement has been postponed for the time being, a situation seen as both unfair and counterproductive (Marin and Titarenko 2011). Experts have long advocated a unilateral liberalisation of the Schengen visa regime in order to enhance pro-EU moods in Belarus (Melyantsou and Silitski 2008). However, only neighbouring countries eventually waived national-visa fees for Belarusians in 2011 as part of Track Two diplomacy in support of civil society. Another positive development for people's mobility has been the signing of Local Border Traffic (LBT) agreements between Belarus and its three EU neighbours that offer hundreds of thousands of borderlanders a chance to visit these countries without having to apply for a visa (see Table 7.2).

The LBT regime was negotiated by Central and Eastern Europe's new EU members with the aim to lessen the negative impact that their joining of the Schengen space has had on people's mobility across their own eastern borderlands. Rules for defining reciprocal conditions related to visa-free local border traffic were laid down in a 2006 Regulation amending the Schengen convention.[11] They grant certain categories of people residing in a 30-to-50-km zone on either side of the Schengen external land borders the right to obtain from the neighbouring country a simplified document that allows them to travel within the perimeters of this zone. Applicants must show that their journeys have a legitimate purpose (family ties, cultural and economic reasons) and sign a declaration that they will not work in the neighbouring country. This exceptional regime only applies to *bona fide* travellers who have been legally residing for at least one year (three in some cases) in the border zone and who have not been the subject of an alert in the Schengen Information System (SIS). Permits cost no more than a short-term multiple-entry visa (20 euros) and are delivered for up to five years, although the maximum duration of a single stay must not exceed ninety days within a period of six months.

The new regime owes its existence mainly to humanitarian and socio-economic considerations: most eligible areas, especially in the Belarusian borderlands, are home to a rural elderly population that partly relies on selling home-grown agricultural products and self-picked berries and mushrooms for survival. They also host a high concentration of minorities, people who have been separated by the new border from their families or who had formerly worshipped at places across the border. For them, the visa-free regime is

Table 7.2 Local Border Traffic agreements with Belarus

	Poland	Latvia	Lithuania
Date of signature	12 February 2010	23 August 2010	20 October 2010
Date of ratification by Belarusian Parliament and by neighbour country	17 November 2010 22 June 2010	10 December 2010 9 November 2010	22 December 2010 28 June 2011
Date of endorsement (signature of the ratification law by the President of Belarus)	1 December 2010	31 December 2010	10 January 2011
Date of exchange of diplomatic notes	Withheld for political reasons	1 December 2011	Withheld for political reasons
Municipalities and rural settlements (within the 30–50 km border zone) concerned – in Belarus	Brest, Hrodna, Vaukavysk, Skidziel, Pruzhany, Zhabinka, Malaryta, Vysokaje, Kamieniec	Braslau, Verkhnyadzvinsk, Mijry and Vidzy	Hrodna, Lida, Astraviec, Ashmiany, Miadziel, Braslau, Pastavy Voranava, Iuje
– in neighbouring country	Biala-Podlaska, Michałowo, Sejny, Sokółka, Suchowola, Siemiatycze, Zabłudów, Supraśl	Daugavpils, Dagda, Zilupe, Krāslava	Vilnius, Druskininkai
Approximate number of people eligible for a LBT permit – in Belarus – in neighbour country	920,000 600,000	64,000 180,000	700,000 800,000
Entry into force	postponed	1 February 2012	postponed
Permit delivery authority – in Belarus	Polish consulates in Brest and Grodno	Latvian consulate in Vitebsk	Lithuanian Embassy in Belarus (Minsk)
– in neighbouring country	Belarusian consulates in Białystok and Biała-Podlaska	Belarusian consulate in Daugavpils	Belarusian Embassy in Lithuania (Vilnius)
Total number of travel documents issued between 1 February and 31 October 2012 – in Belarus – in neighbouring country	n/a n/a	ca. 200 ca. 9,500	n/a n/a

Source: Belarus-Lithuania LBT. Online. Available at: www.pravo.by/main.aspx?guid=3871&p0=H11100239&p2.

meant to simplify daily life... and has been welcomed for this reason by the local population. According to a December 2012 survey by the independent Vilnius-based IISEPS pollster, no less than 37 per cent of Belarusian respondents said they were aware of the existence of LBT agreements with EU neighbours and one out of two would like them to be implemented.

Only the LBT agreement with Latvia has come into force so far, on 1 December 2011, after the parties had exchanged written notifications about the completion of necessary internal procedures, such as compiling lists of eligible residents and defining the perimeter within which permit-holders are entitled to travel.[12] Belarus has signed similar agreements with Poland and Lithuania, but technical difficulties as well as recent diplomatic tensions have delayed their implementation until now.[13]

Bridges: transboundary ecosystems, a cornerstone for CBC

Shared concerns for environmental protection – a common good *per se* – was early on identified as the least common denominator for launching confidence-building measures. Within the Communist bloc, cooperation between neighbouring countries on managing transboundary parks and waterways long remained very limited. Although Poland and the Soviet Union signed an agreement in 1964 on the use of shared water resources, each country continued to control the water quality of border rivers, such as the Bug River, according to its own standards and methods, and information on the sources of pollution were seldom exchanged (Landsberg-Uczciwek and Zan 2003). After the collapse of the Soviet Union, border management was transferred from Moscow to the capitals of the newly independent republics. For the Polish leadership, this opened a window of opportunity for addressing neighbourhood issues directly with its Lithuanian and Belarusian counterparts.

Environmental protection, a consensual common good

In these contested borderlands, CBC appeared to be the most efficient instrument for consolidating good neighbourhood relations. Common goods have the ability of raising awareness about cross-border interdependence, whether negatively – as a result of transboundary air or water pollution, for example – or positively, when border communities realise that they can join forces for turning the borderland into a wealth-multiplier or a tourist attraction.

In March 1992 representatives of central and regional authorities from Poland, Lithuania, Belarus and Ukraine met near Lake Wigry to sign a declaration proclaiming the Augustów and Belovezh primeval forests in their common borderlands to be 'green lungs of Europe'.[14] The Wigry Declaration, a first step towards the sustainable management of joint ecosystems, also turned out to be a cornerstone for future CBC and Euroregional projects. In the late 1990s, the ideal of environmental protection evolved as new CBC initiatives were launched in other low policy sectors. Local authorities in particular realised that transboundary ecosystems could be valorised and become an asset for attracting Western and international donors, including the UNDP and UNESCO, as well as foreign investors and tourists.

Interestingly enough, nature conservation and, more particularly, the sustainable management of shared water resources have been presented as the founding stone of all Euroregions operating on Belarus's borders. The existence of a transboundary ecosystem was probably the smallest common denominator for coalescing border regions around CBC projects. The Euroregions Neman and Bug were actually named after local transboundary rivers: the Neman River (Niemen in Polish, Nioman in Belarusian and Nemunas in Lithuanian)[15] and the Western Bug.[16] Building symbolic bridges across these rivers, which only decades ago had been battlefields, was from the outset the main motor for CBC. The Euroregion Country of Lakes involves border municipalities of the Dvina (Daugava) River basin, which irrigates Belarus, Lithuania and Latvia. Here again, sustainable water management and related spatial planning were the drivers for CBC, together with the development of cultural tourism through SME cooperation and the revival of folk culture. With EU support and under the leadership of Daugavpils, the most internationalised of Latvia's participating cities, the Euroregion developed new concepts for self-promotion.[17] The most emblematic of these are a culinary-heritage label for all restaurants located within the Euroregion (Belarus included) and the upstream development of training activities at the Latgale vocational culinary school. The aim is to improve SME cooperation and to create jobs by promoting the traditional regional cuisine, an immaterial common good for all border-landers, which can enhance the attractiveness of this land of lakes for tourists.

The growing interest of international tourists in alternative (green-sustainable, agro-ecological, cultural, nostalgic etc.) forms of tourism has not gone unnoticed in Belarus, which, like eastern Poland, has a lot to offer in this field. The medieval city of Grodno (Hrodna), for example, is a major cultural attraction for nostalgia tourism from Poland but also World War-related tourism from Germany: the Molotov line used to run nearby, and several military cemeteries, some dating back to the Great War, are now sites of pilgrimage. The 'untouched' natural heritage of the borderland, too, can be turned into a commodity. This makes CBC ever more necessary for Belarus: cooperating with Polish neighbours on upgrading the local ecotourism offer is a good way to obtain external funding and loans. Belarusian actors are readily learning from their EU neighbours how to replace a Soviet-style services culture with customer-friendly tourist services. They are cooperating with EU companies to obtain the necessary technologies and investments for modernising Belarusian tourism infrastructure. In the process, they also learn the canons of touristic image-branding, a subject now taught at Hrodna University. All these interactions contribute to the diffusion of a European business culture and of some EU principles and values (liberalism, subsidiarity, democratic governance, budget transparency, accountability etc.). This Europeanisation-by-socialisation could contribute to change the mindset of the Belarusian population.

Best practices: the Augustów Canal, from sustainable water management to the development of cross-border ecotourism

The renovation and reopening to (cross-border) navigation of the Augustów Canal is the most emblematic environment-related CBC project launched in Belarus so far (Marin 2011a). The canal, a 100-km-long masterpiece of hydrologic engineering, was built in the 1830s, when the Kingdom of Poland formed part of the Russian Empire. The westward shift of the Polish–Soviet border during the Second World War left twenty kilometres of the canal upstream the Neman river on Belarusian territory. In Poland the canal area became a famous recreational site for water sports adepts because it connects with the Masurian Lakes, famous in the whole of Europe among amateurs of biking and water sports (sailing, kayak and fishing). On the Belarusian side however, the Soviet authorities let the canal's state deteriorate.

In 2004, the Belarusian government, inspired by the Polish success of branding the Augustów Canal as a tourist destination, decided to renovate it and designed ambitious investment and marketing plans to turn the whole area into a green-tourism complex. Conscious of the growing demand by Polish, German, Scandinavian, British and North American consumers for alternative forms of tourism, the Belarusian authorities understood that the local economy could earn a lot from getting nostalgic tourists and agro-ecotourists to come and visit the Belarusian segment of the canal as well as cultural attractions in nearby Hrodna.

Building on the precedent of the Belovezh forest, Lukashenko's ambition was to apply for the inclusion of the Augustów Canal on the UNESCO list. For that purpose, the Belarusian regime had to renovate the locks situated in the border zone and the no man's land, which had been left unattended for decades. In the process, Belarusian stakeholders learnt from their Polish neighbours the best practices of ecotourism promotion. In 2007 the Kurziniec cross-border lock was eventually reopened to navigation: although no steamboat operates cruises across the border yet, kayakers with a 'cruise visa'[18] are now entitled to cross the border at the Kurziniec sluice to reach the Neman River. A similar border-crossing point on the river should be reopened on the Belarusian–Lithuanian border, allowing kayakers to pursue their route down the Neman to Kaliningrad and the Baltic Sea.

The example of the Augustów Canal shows that CBC projects have a great potential for opening up Belarus as they play a role in empowering civil society actors: environmental NGOs, advocacy groups, sports and youth associations, schools and universities, SMEs etc. Cross-border networking in turn participates in the emergence of new horizontal cross-border governance patterns. In spite of the many obstacles to CBC, this transboundary scope of action and the institutional regimes taking shape in this context contribute to drawing Belarus and Belarusians closer to Europe.

'Geopolitics of bridging': the emergence of network governance patterns

The network governance model typical of Euroregional cooperation and trans-boundary World Heritage Site management can indeed favour the emergence of new institutional regimes, and the harmonisation of Belarusian legislation with EU standards in this field contributes to reinforcing Europeanised elements in the values scale and the business culture of Belarusians. This hypothesis builds on the work of Sandra Lavenex, who has stressed the potential of governance-type democracy promotion to affect domestic developments in countries that are not candidates for EU accession, notably when other models, mainly leverage and linkage, fail to bring about positive changes.

A number of prerequisites are, however, needed to make this work. According to Lavenex, 'new forms of horizontal flexible integration' may appear between the EU and its neighbours through the 'flexibilisation of the modes of policy-making within the EU', at least in some relevant policy fields (Lavenex 2008: 938). One policy field where the EU is already privileging functional (horizontal) regulatory structures over territorial (vertical) ones is actually that of transboundary water management: the 2000 Water Framework Directive,[19] for example, has been 'the first instrument of Community legislation to implement the principle that regulations should not be organised along jurisdictions but also along functional lines' (Lavenex, 2008: 948–949). Lavenex has shown that the directive is being implemented by functional cross-border networks of the competent (border) authorities that naturally emerge for the purpose of integrated river basin management, including beyond the EU's borders.

Scholars interested in transborder region-building on the EU's eastern borders have actually identified a similar trend in several Euroregions or equivalent working communities. In Eastern Central Europe, cross-border institutions are often initially established for the purpose of environmental protection and the joint management of shared water resources, once more in line with EU regulations (Roll 2001). In a case study of the Lake Peipsi (Chudskoe) Basin on the Estonian–Russian border, Gulnara Roll uses an institutional effectiveness model to show that the incompatibility of Estonian and Russian legislations and pollution measurement criteria led to the emergence of a 'distinct international water quality management regime' that was nonetheless connected to the implementation of the EU Water Framework Directive (Roll 2001). She has stressed that this original regime was shaped not only by governmental actors (central ministries and the Estonian–Russian inter-governmental Transboundary Water Commission) or that it had come into being simply because Estonia had to harmonise its regulations with those of the EU. Rather it seems that local stakeholders (universities, municipal authorities, fishermen, farmers and their unions) lobbied for flexible institutional arrangements to address practical problems locally and in spite of an unfavourable diplomatic context. This is but one illustration of how environmental safety, as a common good per se, may offer a consensual platform for decentralised, horizontal CBC with non-EU countries.

Conclusion: from de-bordering to Europeanisation-by-socialisation?

This chapter has highlighted the institutional dynamics at work in EU–Belarus cross-border relations. Building on an empirical assessment of local practices, it has tried to demonstrate that CBC aiming at the sustainable transformation of borderlands into ecotourism destinations has fostered horizontal, functional networking among civil society actors across the 'Schengen curtain'. This has facilitated the emergence of new governance patterns across otherwise 'alienated' borders. By encouraging dialogue and promoting interdependence, these networks may well be the best, if not the only, platforms for the socialisation of Belarus in Europe.

The findings of this chapter illustrate that attempts at influencing an authoritarian regime 'from outside-in' have better chances to succeed in low policy fields, such as environmental protection, public health and education, where the involvement of civil society actors, NGOs and individuals is a key to success. More particularly, CBC projects in the field of sustainable ('green') tourism encourage horizontal networking, which, against the background of Belarusian authoritarianism, is currently the best and possibly only pattern for the EU to exercise its soft power on domestic developments in Belarus. CBC projects that the Belarusian government deems worthy of supporting, such as Euroregions or turning the Augustów Canal into a transboundary World Heritage Site, quickly and easily create opportunities to open a Third Track in relation to Belarus, and to implement the principle of joint ownership contained in the Eastern Partnership. Network-based transborder region–building dynamics give the EU a chance to reach its long desired goal of supporting the democratisation of Belarus without alienating the current political leadership. In addition, network-based projects contribute to socialising Belarusian civil society actors in Europe. Since they necessitate some devolution within the Belarusian administrative system and are able to mobilise civil society at the grassroots level, CBC networks can enhance, at least locally, the diffusion of European values and the Europeanisation of business culture in Belarus.

These findings should inspire policy-makers in charge of the Eastern Partnership in their drafting of more inclusive policy models. On other EU peripheries where transboundary natural spaces, and notably waterways, are a central element of the border landscape, such as the Prut River, which marks the border between Romania and Moldova, cross-border networks established for the joint sustainable development of borderlands have the potential of serving as cornerstones for building bridges across the eastern borders of the EU and the Schengen space. Although political relations between Minsk and Brussels are currently constrained by the official position of the EU Council towards

Lukashenko's regime, the Eastern Partnership may provide a basis for a practical rapprochement along the Third Track. This, in turn, should facilitate the evolution of the Eastern borderlands' status of alienation or benign neglect (coexistence) towards one where some degree of positive interdependence may allow for a partial socialisation of Belarus within the dynamics of Europeanisation.

Notes

1 Dniepr, the fifth Euroregion with Belarusian participation, has been labelled 'Slavic only' because it involves, alongside Homel Oblast (Belarus), neighbouring oblasti in Russia (Briansk) and Ukraine (Chernihiv).
2 Martinez has classified borders into four categories, depending on the level of conflict and cooperation contained in human interactions across them: an 'alienated' borderland is thus characterised by territorial disputes, ethnic conflicts and the absence of CBC. As conflicts diminish, a borderland may become one of 'coexistence', or even 'interdependence' as socio-economic interactions develop across it. Finally, a border is 'integrated' when the regions adjacent to it are functionally merged, such as the few successful Euroregions within the EU, notably EUREGIO on the German–Dutch border and Euregio Basilensis, centred on the Basel conurbation.
3 The notion of 'preemptive authoritarianism' was coined by a Belarusian political scientist, the late Vitali Silitski, to characterise Lukashenko's preventive arsenal to deal with the threat of democratic contagion entailed by the so-called colour revolutions (Silitski 2005). For a more up-to-date overview of these measures, see Korosteleva (2012).
4 See, for instance, the infamous article 193.1 of the Criminal Code, which engages criminal responsibility for activities conducted by unregistered public associations, political parties, as well as religious organisations and foundations.
5 Transborder region is a generic term referring to 'a territorially integrated unit comprising contiguous sub-national units (from two or more nation-states) that promote political cooperation, economic development and people-to-people contacts for the benefit of local civil society'. This definition, initially advanced by the Council of Europe, was subsequently appropriated by the Association of European Border Regions (AEBR), which comprises over 120 'transborder' members (Euroregions, cross-border associations, working communities or communities of interests), among them three Euroregions involving partners from Belarus. For more information see the association's website (www.aebr.eu).
6 The founding statutes can be consulted (in Polish) on the website of the Polish association Euroregion Niemen. Online. Available at: http://niemen.org.pl/index.php?option=com_content&task=view&id=82&Itemid=27.
7 The Polish part of the 2,500-square-km-large Belovezh forest (Puszcza Białowieża in Polish) was included in the UNESCO World Heritage list already in 1979. In 1992, the Belarusian part of the forest was added to the list and the entire area became one of the world's six transborder biosphere reserves and the first to be recognised in the post-Soviet space (Marin 2013). The Belovezh forest is also a nominee for the New Seven Wonders of Nature (see www.bialowiezaforest.eu).
8 This visibility significantly increased in 2012 after the Belarusian government had created a bilingual website presenting all Euroregions with Belarusian participation (see http://beleuroregion.by/); an interactive map is available on the website's main page.
9 Detailed information about these ENPI CBC programmes can be found on their respective websites at: www.pl-by-ua.eu; and www.enpi-cbc.eu.

10 Interview with Auksė Bernadišienė, Director of the Joint Technical Secretariat of the ENPI CBC programme Latvia–Lithuania–Belarus in Vilnius, 15 June 2010.

11 Regulation No. 1931/2006 of the European Parliament and the Council of Europe adopted on 20 December 2006 (see http://europa.eu/legislation_summaries/justice_ freedom_security/free_movement_of_persons_asylum_immigration/l14506_en.htm).

12 The Consulate of Belarus in Daugavpils and the Latvian Consulate in Vitebsk started issuing permits on 1 February 2012. On that day alone, 200 residents of Belarus and 4,000 of Latvia applied for a permit.

13 See Paula Borowska 'Belarus Wants to Keep its Western Border Locked Shut', *Belarus Digest*, 29 March 2013. Online. Available at: http://belarusdigest.com/story/ unclear-future-local-border-traffic-poland-13511 (last accessed 12 August 2013).

14 The Augustów primeval forest (puszcza) stretches from the Biebrza valley to the southern edges of the eastern Suwałki Lakeland and, further east, to southern Lithuania and northern Belarus. It covers a total area of about 1,600 square kilometres, 70 per cent of them located in Poland, making it the largest forest area of the country and the best-protected, along with two national parks, Wigry and Biebrza. Together with Puszcza Białoveża, it forms the largest and wildest primeval forest of Europe. Both are home to several protected species of flora and fauna, including the reacclimatised wild bison (zubr) and the European wild horse (tarpan).

15 This 937-km-long river starts in Belarus, enters Lithuania territory at 360 kilometres south of Alytus and then drains into the Curonian Lagoon at Klaipeda. Over a course of 116 kilometres, it forms the border between Lithuania and the Russian Federation, in the northeastern corner of Kaliningrad Oblast. The River Neman does not irrigate Polish territory but is connected to it by the 100-km-long Augustów Canal.

16 The Western Bug, with a length of 830 kilometres, flows from central Ukraine westward into Poland, where it empties into the Narew River, a tributary of the Vistula. Over a course of 291 kilometres, the Bug constitutes Poland's eastern border with Ukraine, and a 176-km-long segment forms the border with Belarus. The Bug also marks the border between Orthodox and Catholic peoples and was a front line between German and Soviet forces during the Second World War, in whose aftermath the Polish city of Brest-on-the-Bug was transferred to Belarus. Hence Brest, like Grodno and L'viv, is a focal object of nostalgia for the Polish collective memory of the lost Kresy Wschodnie.

17 See, for example, the Euroregion's Development Strategy adopted in 2000. Online. Available at: www.country-of-lakes.de/cgi-bin/cgi.pl?id=108&l=2.

18 So-called cruise visas are delivered by a consular office opened by Belarus in the town of Augustów, the starting point of most kayak excursions in Poland. The office operates during the navigation season only (Marin 2011a).

19 Formally known as Directive 2000/60/EC establishing a framework for Community action in the field of water policy, this directive, adopted on 23 October 2000, prescribes steps for EU member states to achieve good quantitative and qualitative standards for water bodies by 2015. For a presentation of this common EU 'water policy', see http://ec.europa.eu/environment/water/water-framework/index_en.html.

Part Three
Migration policies

8 Where ideals and anxieties meet

The EU and migration policy in Wider Europe

Tiina Sotkasiira

Writing at the time of the launch of the European Neighbourhood Policy (ENP) in 2004, Sandra Lavenex and Emek M. Uçarer (2004: 433) evaluated cooperation between the EU and neighbouring countries, in contrast to the comprehensive 'Europeanisation' strategy pursued toward candidate countries, as quite occasional, sectoral and rather inspired by short-term interests on both sides. Since then the situation has changed. Thus, in the field of migration policy, which is the focal area of the present and following chapters, the EU has placed growing emphasis on attempts to manage migration together with its neighbours. Cooperation has progressed, for example, in the fields of asylum policy, irregular migration and visa policy as a means to better control the movements of people within 'Wider Europe', i.e. the regions to the EU's east and south (European Commission 2011a, 2011b and 2012b).

Migration is an exemplary terrain to discuss challenges to social and political stability. The movement of people has been said to be 'at the heart of the political debate in Europe' and EU-induced cooperation on migration is being considered 'one of the strategic priorities in the external relations of the Union' by the European Commission (2006d). The Commission has also affirmed that the careful management of migration can be a positive factor for growth and success both within the Union and in neighbouring countries. This optimistic discourse on migration is, however, usually accompanied by an 'anti-illegal immigration discourse', which William Walters (2010), along with many others, perceives as the second elementary part of the Union's migration management project.

This two-tier discursive strategy towards migration can be found in the document, in which the Commission first outlined the rationale of the ENP in 2003, namely its Communication 'Wider Europe – Neighbourhood: A New Framework for Relations with our Eastern and Southern Neighbours' (European Commission 2003). First, it is stated there that 'the EU and the neighbours have a mutual interest in cooperating, both bilaterally and regionally, to ensure that their migration policies, customs procedures and frontier controls do not prevent or delay people or goods from crossing borders for legitimate purposes'. Secondly, it is maintained that 'threats to mutual security, whether from the trans-border dimension of environmental and nuclear hazards, communicable

DOI: 10.4324/9781315858036-12

diseases, illegal immigration, trafficking, organised crime or terrorist networks, will require joint approaches in order to be addressed comprehensively'. Thus, right from the beginning, the EU discourse on the eastern neighbourhood has distinguished between two kinds of migration, one legitimate and the other illegal, both requiring definite policy responses from the Union and its neighbours.

Barbe *et al.* (2009: 379) argue that a relative consensus has been reached in the scholarly literature on the ENP that the European Union, with its neigh-bourhood policy, has promoted its own system of rules abroad. They also claim that this premise often assumes a coherent set of norms or rules that the EU communicates through its programmes and initiatives. However, as far as migration policy is concerned, it is apparent that the EU's policy approach is rather based on a set of contradictions. To quote but one example, the logic of the market is concurrently weighed against welfare protectionism, and demands for a qualified yet, from the market's perspective, affordable work-force and concerns about national needs and resources against transnational rights. In many circumstances discrimination and exclusion of migrants exist alongside strong assertions of equal treatment (Boswell and Geddes 2011; Morris 1997).

This chapter will focus on discursive strategies and policies developed by the EU in its efforts to manage migration in the eastern neighbourhood and beyond, in the so called Wider Europe, by analysing the EU's communications on the ENP published between 2003 and 2013 (EEAS 2014). More particularly, the chapter will examine the EU's migration policies in the context of five eastern neighbourhood countries, namely Azerbaijan, Belarus, Moldova, Tajikistan and Ukraine. It will consider them from the theoretical perspective of the securitisation of migration and set off this approach against the conceptual framework of migration management, another relatively new term for under-standing and rethinking worldwide migration flows (Arango and Martin 2005; Martin, Abella and Midgley 2004; Omelaniuk 2005). In addition to documents concerning the ENP and migration, the analysis will make use of the Partnership and Cooperation Agreements (PCAs) and Association Agreements concluded with these countries.

Migration management and the EU

The 2004 and 2007 enlargements of the European Union led to the incorporation of twelve new member states and the creation of a new borderland with resurgent flows of goods, people and capital (Wallace and Vincent 2009: 144). Until then, the EU's institutional involvement in the South Caucasus and Central Asia had been relatively modest in comparison to relations with other international, European and Euro-Atlantic, actors. However, in the early 2000s, the EU Council (2003) recognised the need to take a stronger and more active interest in its neighbouring regions and to bring them closer to the Union. In 2004, the EU thus launched the European Neighbourhood Policy, which targeted the southern Mediterranean countries and, in the east, Belarus, Moldova, Ukraine and three states of the South Caucasus. With regard to Central Asia, the EU's position was outlined in the EU–Central Asia Strategy adopted in 2007. In addition to more general policy statements, these policy instruments introduced significant changes in the migration policy defined for the Union and the neighbouring regions.

Andrea Wierich (2011: 225) argues that EU migration policies first and foremost address the so-called internal dimension of migration, that is, aspects directly relevant to the EU member states, perceived in the documents as countries of destination, and to their citizens. Here, efforts have concentrated on managing migration through practical cooperation, information sharing and the synchronisation of national migration policies. For the period 2007–2013, for instance, almost EUR4 billion were allocated to the General Programme 'Solidarity and Management of Migration Flows', with the intention that EU countries share the financial burden arising from the integrated management of the Union's external borders and from the implementation of common asylum and immigration policies (European Commission 2013d).

But, as Wierich (2011: 228) states, the EU's migration policy also has an external dimension, which concerns the migrants' countries of origin, transit countries and the reasons for migration. In this respect, the management of migration and related policy areas, such as border control and the prevention of human trafficking, have been identified as key areas for cooperation between the EU and its neighbours. Projects that involve eastern partners are funded through geographically defined instruments, such as the European Neigh-bourhood and Partnership Instrument (ENPI), and more short-term targeted interventions under the Thematic Programme for the Cooperation with Third Countries in the Areas of Migration and Asylum (European Commission 2012b). Furthermore, the EU has declared that it would be seeking to enhance dialogue and cooperation on migration with regions of transit, origin and desti-nation through its Global Approach to Migration and Mobility (GAMM) (European Commission 2011b). As part of the GAMM, the EU has proposed a dialogue on migration with its eastern and southeastern neighbours that focuses on 'four pillars': legal migration and mobility; irregular migration and trafficking in human beings; international protection and asylum policy; and the maximisation of the developmental impact of migration and mobility. Bilateral policy targets, of which some concern migration and border issues, are specified in Partnership and Cooperation Agreements negotiated between the EU and governments of individual non-member states.

The approach that the European Union increasingly applies in migration policy can be described as migration management. This approach is not unique to the EU; the need to govern migration more effectively has also been emphasised by governments in Central and Eastern Europe, the Caucasus, Central Asia and that of the Russian Federation, as well as by intergovern-mental organisations that play a major role in shaping migration policies in this region, such as the United Nations, the Organisation for Security and

Cooperation in Europe (OSCE), the Council of Europe and the International Organisation for Migration (IOM). On a practical level, this has led to calls for increased cooperation between the respective governments to better tackle illegal or unregulated migration flows, produce up-to-date information on population movements and improve border controls, for example through training and by introducing new technologies (IOM 2005).

In the scholarly literature, migration management is being understood as an alternative to conventional approaches to migration which emphasise national interests and a need to control migration rather than effectively managing it. As Martin Geiger and Antoine Pécoud (2010: 1–2) argue, migration management is not a technical term but a particular set of discourses and practices concerning the movements of people, which are used by a multitude of actors and are intertwined in a complex, heterogeneous and often conflictive manner. Table 8.1 presents key differences between the migration management approach envisaged by Geiger and Pécoud and more conventional approaches to migration.

Geiger and Pécoud (2010, 2012) view migration management in a fairly positive light. Despite a critical undercurrent found in their work, they choose to promote migration management as a kind of 'third way' between states' proclaimed zero-immigration policy and an ideal of open borders which, if put into practice, could have unforeseen consequences for both sending and receiving societies. In Geiger and Pécoud's (2012: 12) opinion, adequately managed migration would have the potential of serving the interests of both sending and receiving societies, implying genuine international cooperation and the necessity to engage in mutual collaboration. This said, Geiger and Pécoud also point to critics that see migration management as a technocratic invention that disguises the continuation of restrictive and control-oriented migration policies with the purpose of enabling powerful receiving states to steer migration flows according to their political and economic interests (Geiger and Pécoud 2012). Migration management can thus be understood as

Table 8.1 Major differences between conventional approaches to migration and migration management

	Conventional approaches	*Migration management approach*
Focus	state sovereignty	intergovernmental cooperation
Perception of migration	migration as a problem	a normal process in a globalising world
Key aim	to control the movement of people	to be proactive
Key notion	security vs labour	a more holistic approach, including development and human rights

the embodiment of a managerial approach that negates the fundamental political issues raised by migration. Critics argue that the management approach ultimately threatens the core principles of internationally acknowledged human rights, such as the right to seek protection under the Geneva Convention, and undermine attempts to create a consensus on new principles of regulating migration.

Within the EU, the notion of management has gone hand in hand with the idea of – at least gradually – including a more comprehensive approach to migration, cooperation and common decision-making on migration policy. Such a shift towards a more holistic management discourse occurred in the early 2000s and was explicitly articulated in the 2006 Communication on migration and mobility from the Commission to the European Parliament and the Council:

> Among these policy developments, those referring to migration and development and to legal economic migration are probably destined to exert the more innovative effects. This goes in parallel with the fact that *until recently the external dimension of the migration policy has been prevalently built around the objective of better managing the migratory flows with a view to reducing the migratory pressure on the Union.* Although this remains a valid goal, the additional *challenge today lies in the development of policies which recognise the need for migrant workers to make our economies function* in those sectors where the EU is facing labour and skills shortages and, at the same time, which maximise both for the migrants and for their countries of origin the benefits triggered by the migration. This presupposes *an approach which goes beyond the questions of border control and fight against illegal immigration,* to incorporate other dimensions of the migratory phenomenon, in particular development and employment
>
> (European Commission 2006f, emphasis added)

The document thus claims that, while in the past the external dimension of migration policy had been about managing migratory flows with a view to reducing immigration, a more recent policy shift was triggered by the demand for migrant workers in specific sectoral labour markets. The Communication argues that in order for this change to take place, and for the EU to become an attractive destination for qualified labour migrants, cooperation on migration policy should be based on a more comprehensive approach to the issues at hand. In addition, the declaration also contains components of more traditional approaches to migration, based on the principle that each sovereign state govern and control its borders and the movement of its citizens in the name of state security. In practice, a traditionalist standpoint has been expressed for example in the negotiations concerning visa facilitation, which have systematically been tied to or, to use the European Commission's expression (2006e: 6), negotiated 'back-to-back' with agreements on the re-admission of irregular migrants.

Conventional wisdom in and outside the academic community claims that contradictions in the EU's migration policy result from multilevel factors, such as the globally felt economic crisis, heightened nationalism and security concerns, which in the European Union are counterpoised by factors such as an increased awareness of the demographic challenges faced by the majority of the member states. The economic crisis, together with the rise of anti-immigration sentiments, has been used as a rationale for developing more restrictive migration policies, especially towards irregular migrants and asylum seekers (Yuval-Davis, Anthias and Kofman 2005: 515). Moreover, migration in Europe is more and more associated with security issues, as criminal and terrorist acts are invoked as threats to the public order and stability (Huysmans 2006). In the scholarly literature, these tendencies are usually discussed as securitisation, which refers to a process through which these issues become recognised and then represented as 'existential threats', calling for and justifying extreme measures (Wæver 1995: 55). Michaela Ceccorulli (2010) argues that this is a particularly prevalent point of view when the focus is placed on the EU's eastern neighbourhood, which many scenarios identify as a staging area for illegal immigration, the drugs trade and the trafficking of human beings (see also Christou 2010).

The EU's migration policy towards Wider Europe

On paper, developing cooperation on migration policy between the European Union and countries in Wider Eastern Europe appears as a linear step-by-step process: Partnership and Cooperation Agreements are followed by Association Agreements, which will then led to the signing of visa facilitation and readmission agreements that will eventually result in a visa-free travel regime for short stays. This ideal progress of the EU-sponsored migration management project for neighbours is summarised in Figure 8.1.

In practice, the process has, however, been less smooth, as most commentators agree that the EU's neighbourhood and external migration policies have only led to a qualified success. The following country-by-country analysis will bring some of the controversies to the fore.

The EU's 'critical engagement' with Belarus

The case of Belarus demonstrates several major difficulties in the EU's attempts to manage migration in the wider eastern neighbourhood, despite jointly agreed principles. While Belarusian commentators have pointed towards the EU's unwillingness to engage in a real and equal partnership, the EU has taken the view that dialogue and cooperation with Belarus is being hampered by the general political situation there and in particular the negative attitude that the Belarusian authorities have assumed towards the EU and those of its member-states that have taken an interest in the country's internal matters. With respect to migration, the major debates in Belarus have

| Technical cooperation | Bilateral and/or regional cooperation | Mobility partnership | Visa facilitation and readmission | (Short term) visa liberalisation |

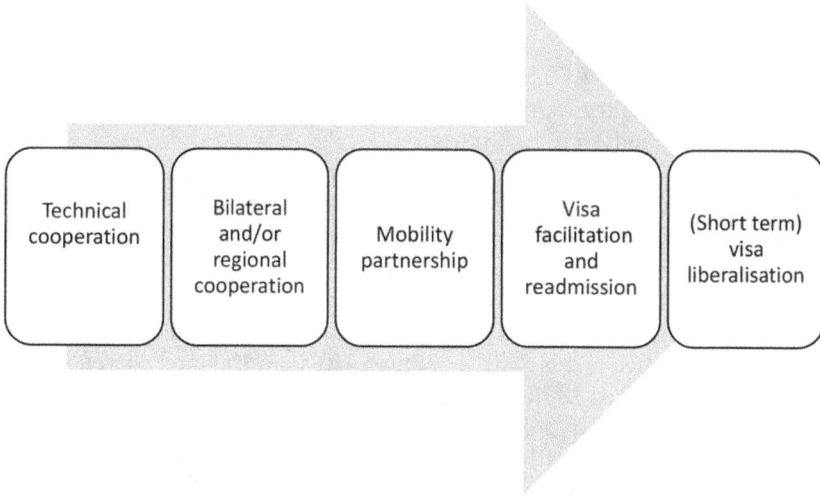

Figure 8.1 The advancement of the migration management project in Wider Europe

focused on human trafficking, the brain drain resulting from the exodus of skilled Belarusians (i.e. people working in the ICT sector) and the difficulties experienced by Belarusian citizens when applying for visas for EU countries. As Larissa Titarenko argues in this volume, migration seems to be a non-subject for the Belarusian authorities, although research has shown that migration, and especially emigration, represent crucial challenges for the country's leadership.

EU–Belarus relations are currently governed by the Conclusions of the Foreign Affairs Council (Council of the European Union 2012) as last set out in October 2012. These do not specify the EU's migration policy for Belarus but focus on overall political relations between the two actors. They state the importance that the EU attaches to Belarus and its citizens while voicing concern about Belarus's lack of respect for human rights, democracy and the rule of law. The ratification of an EU–Belarus Partnership and Cooperation Agreement was negotiated in 1995 but the process came to a halt in 1997 for the reasons evoked above. The official position of the EU is a commitment to a policy of critical engagement with Belarus through a technical dialogue and within the multilateral track of the Eastern Partnership initiative (European Commission 2013b). The EU has, for instance, offered to start negotiations on visa facilitation and readmission agreements but has received no response from the Belarusian authorities. Belarus is covered by the European Neighbourhood Policy, yet no action plan has been decided upon.

The EU's position on migration and Belarus can be found in the Country Strategy Paper 2007–2013 (European Commission 2006h), which declares that, although migration management is a policy sector that requires official participation and is therefore difficult to conduct under the present circumstances, it is possible to implement programmes that allow low-level contacts with officials of the Belarusian administration and ongoing contacts with the Belarusian population. Continuing cooperation would ensure increased information about the EU and its values in the country and reduce Belarus's role as a transit country for increasing (legal and illegal) migratory movements between Eastern and Western Europe.

EU-funded assistance and cooperation with Belarus involves nearly 100 million euros worth of projects, including regional and thematic initiatives, both ongoing and in preparation (Delegation of the European Union to the Republic of Belarus 2014). The EU is, for example, funding the activities of the European Humanities University in Vilnius, Lithuania, to enhance the possibilities of young Belarusians to seek education abroad. In the field of migration, assistance to border cooperation has been the most significant aid target in Belarus. Since 2001, the EU has allocated more than EUR80 million to various projects meant to deliver equipment, develop border infrastructure or offer training and policy advice. The main beneficiaries have been the State Border Committee and the State Customs Committee. Other projects, in the sphere of asylum and the prevention of human trafficking, have been smaller in size (Delegation of the European Union to the Republic of Belarus 2014).

Moldova and Ukraine – almost model students

Ukraine's and Moldova's relationship with the EU is of a very different nature. The EU has sought increasingly closer relations with both countries through gradual economic integration and deeper political cooperation and, regardless of intermittent turmoil, this has met with a mostly favourable response in the field of migration. Both countries have concluded Partnership and Cooperation Agreements with the European Union, which entered into force in 1998, and participated in negotiations about Association Agreements to replace the PCAs (European Commission 2013a and 2013c).

The EU–Republic of Moldova visa facilitation and readmission agreements entered into force in January 2008 and a wider Mobility Partnership was signed in June 2008. In June 2010 a dialogue was opened with the aim of examining conditions for visa-free travelling of Moldovan citizens to the EU as a long-term goal. Since 1991 the European Union has allocated more than EUR1 billion to Moldova, among them EUR21 million for the Support to Implementation of Visa Liberalisation Action Plan (Delegation of the European Union to Moldova 2014). Several other projects have been conducted to promote legal mobility between Moldova and the EU and to tackle the negative effects of migration. An example of the latter is the project coordinated by the Italian Ministry of Labour, Health and Social Policies that focuses on the negative effects of migration on minors and families that are left behind when Moldovans settle in the EU either temporarily or on more permanent basis.

For the citizens of Ukraine, the EU has offered to introduce a visa-free travel regime 'in due course', that is, after the conditions for 'well-managed and secure mobility', spelled out in the Association Agreement, will have been fulfilled. The list of priorities defined in the EU–Ukraine Association Agenda for 2011–2012 (Joint Committee at Senior Official's Level of EU–Ukraine Association 2011) included several migration-related initiatives. First, the parties have agreed on the need to develop a better legislative and institutional framework for Ukraine's migration management, particularly in view of fighting illegal migration, smuggling and the trafficking of human beings. They have also declared to pursue the operational phase of the visa dialogue, with the long-term perspective of establishing a visa-free regime between the EU and Ukraine on the basis of the EU–Ukraine Action Plan on visa liberalisation presented at the EU–Ukraine Summit of 22 November 2010 and after the successful implementation of the Ukrainian National Plan approved by the President of Ukraine in 2011. In addition, there are plans in place to move towards the implementation of both the visa facilitation and readmission agreements concluded between Ukraine and the EU. Since 1991, assistance provided by the European Community to Ukraine has amounted to over EUR2.5 billion for the funding for projects, including several initiatives related to migration and border management (Delegation of the European Union to Ukraine 2014).

EU, Azerbaijan and the challenge of an internally divided Caucasus

The countries of the South Caucasus have proceeded at a different pace towards closer integration with the European Union. Georgia has made the most progress, while the integration of Armenia and Azerbaijan has been slower. Azerbaijan is the most prosperous country in the region because of its oil and gas reserves. For decades Azerbaijan has been perceived as a country of mass emigration as in the 1990s a large number of Azerbaijanis migrated to other countries, mainly to the Russian Federation. There exist no exact data on migration but, according to different estimates, the number of labour migrants since the collapse of the Soviet Union has varied between 500–600,000 and one million (IOM 2008: 17) or even 1.3 million (World Bank 2011a: 25). In recent years, however, Azerbaijan has started to attract an increasing number of foreign citizens and stateless persons, partly because of its developing economy and partly because conflicts and instability in neighbouring regions have transformed Azerbaijan into a transit country for migrants.

According to official data, Azerbaijan has had a positive net migration rate since 2007 (IOM 2008). This seems to affect Azerbaijan's migration policy, which in recent years has focused on the issues of illegal immigration and border protection, although the role and worldwide influence of the Azeri diaspora has also been of major interest to the country's leadership (Rumyantsev and Sotkasiira forthcoming). The third aspect affecting Azerbaijan's migration situation is the armed conflict between Azerbaijan and Armenia over the territory of Nagorno-Karabakh, which has meant that up to 600,000 people were internally displaced in Azerbaijan as of the end of 2012 (Internal Displacement Monitoring Centre 2014).

The objectives of the EU policy on borders and migration in relation to Azerbaijan were first defined in the jointly agreed EU–Azerbaijan ENP Action Plan adopted in 2006, where they under the heading Cooperation in the Field of Justice, Freedom and Security (European Commission 2006g). The objectives are divided into three subcategories: cooperation on border management; migration issues; and the fight against organised crime, trafficking in human beings, drugs and money-laundering. More particularly, cooperation on migration issues includes the prevention and control of illegal migration, readmission and facilitation of the movement of persons and, finally, the further development of Azerbaijan's national asylum and protection system in line with international standards. Lifting the EU visa requirement for the citizens of Azerbaijan travelling to the EU is a long-term goal. Negotiations on the Mobility Partnership between Azerbaijan and the EU were finalised in Autumn 2013 and at the time the EU (European Commission 2013e) expected the Visa Facilitation and Readmission Agreements to enter into force in early 2014.

Since Azerbaijan's independence, the EU has funded grants worth over AZN500 million (roughly EUR450million) in support of the country's development. EU support is channelled in two main ways: either directly to Azerbaijani governmental bodies through the ENPI or to civil society organisations through Horizontal Thematic Programmes (European Commission 2012a). In addition to border development initiatives, the main migration-related targets have included work on internally displaced people, their rights and living-conditions and assistance to further the local integration of refugees and asylum seekers (Delegation of the European Union to Azerbaijan 2014).

Migration and security in Central Asia

Because of Tajikistan's geographic location, and particularly its long border with Afghanistan, security concerns have played a pivotal role in EU-induced cooperation, including the elaboration of migration policies. The civil war in 1992–1993 and the subsequent period of political instability, which lasted until 1997, produced forced migration, replaced in the early 2000s by mainly economic migration. The majority of migrants are young men, which has profound impacts on the situation and livelihoods of women and children, especially in rural areas (IOM Dushanbe 2009). As in Moldova and Ukraine, remittances have been crucial as one of the drivers of economic growth during the past several years, which explains, among other things, why Tajikistan's government has been perceiving emigration not only as a risk but as an asset. More recently, the government has introduced initiatives to support managed migration from the country.

The framework for cooperation between the EU and its Central Asian partners has been outlined in Partnership and Cooperation Agreements with each country and in a document entitled European Union and Central Asia:

Strategy for a New Partnership (Council of the European Union 2007). A Partnership and Cooperation Agreement (European Commission 2009b) between the EU and Tajikistan was signed in 2004 and entered into force in the beginning of 2010. It has three main components: political dialogue, cooperation and trade. The political dialogue includes cooperation on the prevention and control of illegal immigration as one of its primary objectives, alongside cooperation against terrorism, the proliferation of weapons of mass destruction and trafficking, including the drugs trade. Under the cooperation section, the Agreement also provides for commitments and cooperation on readmission, the control of illegal immigration and combating drugs and organised crime.

Although present in the bilateral agreements between the EU and Central Asian states, migration in Central Asia is considered by the EU as an issue that requires a regional approach (Council of the European Union 2007: 11). In the Central Asian context, EU documents emphasise the importance of fighting organised crime, focusing on illegal migration and the trafficking of human beings, preventing and countering drugs trafficking, improving the institutional capacity of law enforcement agencies and strengthening regional cooperation to combat transnational organised crime. The security perspective is dominant and often linked to the region's geographical location, notably shared borders with Afghanistan, Pakistan and Iran. The spread of radical Islam is a threat envisaged not only by the EU but by the government of Tajikistan and international actors. The centrality of security concerns does, however, not imply the complete absence of the management approach. The EU offers assistance to interested Central Asian States – both on the national and regional level – for managing migration 'in a more balanced manner' (Council of the European Union 2007: 25). This means, for example, setting up systems to match labour demand and supply in the region, facilitating the integration of legal migrants and providing international protection to asylum seekers, refugees and other vulnerable persons.

'The streets abroad are not paved with gold'

In conclusion, the diagram in Figure 8.2 shows how far each of the countries studied here has 'advanced' on the EU-envisaged path of migration management, which, in the light of policy documents and their practical outcomes, seems to end with the signing of visa facilitation and readmission agreements. The ultimate prize of a visa-free travel regime with the EU is, in principle, available to all ENP partners but conditioned by fulfilling the requirements set by the EU of establishing a *well-managed and secure system of mobility*. Unless there will be some unforeseen political developments, a visa-free travel regime appears therefore a distant possibility for the majority of countries in Wider Europe.

EU cooperation on migration with Belarus and Tajikistan is least developed, while that with Ukraine and Moldova has been more elaborate and ambitious,

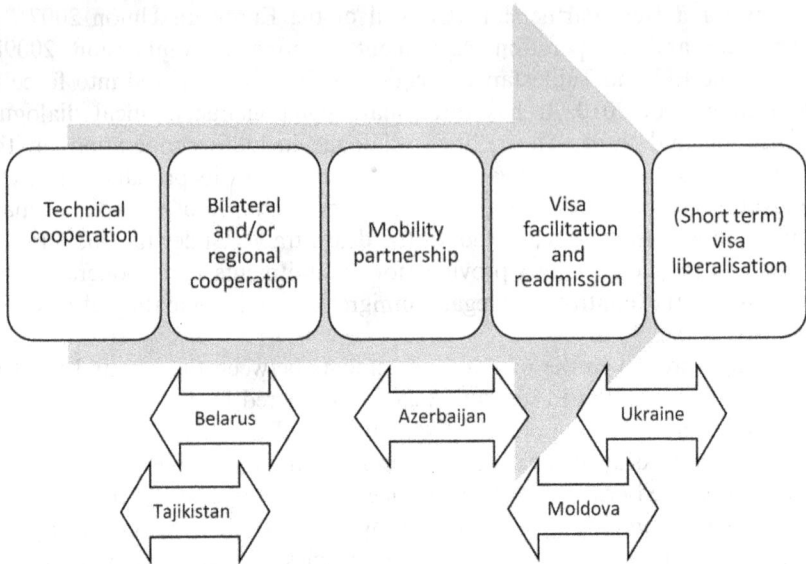

Figure 8.2 The case countries, migration and the EU

with Azerbaijan somewhere in the middle. This suggests a link between geographical proximity to the EU and the level of cooperation. But the case of Belarus serves as a reminder that broader relations between the EU and each of its eastern partners can be no less important (see Wunderlich 2012).

An examination of the EU's migration policy towards the various countries of Wider Europe reveals that instruments are available for conducting a more proactive policy in the sense of the migration management approach. In addition to measures to combat illegal migration, the Mobility Packs and other documents outline prospects for normalising migration, such as issuing free visas to certain categories of persons (students, researchers, business people etc.) or improving the dissemination of information on employment, education and training opportunities available in the EU. For the 'most advanced' countries, like Ukraine, specific documents, such as the National Plan on Implementation of the EU–Ukraine Action Plan on visa liberalisation and the subsequent progress reports, include lists of legislative changes and amendments to be adopted by Ukraine to benefit from visa-free travel regime for its citizens. Thus, it could be argued that one of the EU's accomplishments in the field of migration policy has been to offer to its neighbours a straight path towards achieving 'everything but institutions', as proposed by Romano Prodi in 2002 (Prodi 2002).

In reality, the development of integrated migration management has resulted in a phased process in which advances have been followed by set-backs and vice versa. More importantly, it seems that this process is largely based on the EU's understanding of how migration management should be implemented and not on a political dialogue where partners have equal standing. Cooperation on migration management has rather come across as a sort of benchmark test, in which the neighbours' migration processes and practices are compared to what the EU considers optimal. On the one hand, the analysed policy papers portray the EU as a centre of innovation surrounded by poorer and unstable countries whose citizens are ready to do just about everything to enter EU territory. On the other hand, there is a competing discourse of the EU as an ageing and fragile actor whose well-being largely hinges on imported care-providers, but who is not yet willing to accept this extensive dependence. Either way, the movement of people within Wider Europe is understood as a one-way operation dominated by the EU and its interests. For this reason, the security narrative, which depicts migration from the east as a risk that the EU has to somehow manage, has proven difficult to challenge.

Research conducted in the EU on the securitisation of migration tends, however, to overlook the fact that the countries in the EU's immediate neighbourhood, too, are prone to securitise migration. This applies both to immigration and the mobility of their own citizens. Thus, Azerbaijan shares with the EU an anxiety over the impact of accelerating immigration, while Moldova and Ukraine are examples of countries deeply concerned about the negative effects of large-scale outmigration on the social fabric and future economic development. Belarus, on the other hand, officially refuses to identify migration as an issue that needs political attention, while simultaneously allowing its governmental bodies to work with international partners and produce a discourse on the securitisation of emigration. In Tajikistan, a similar discourse prevails but the risks are not associated with migration to and from the countries in its immediate neighbourhood rather than cooperation with the EU.

During an earlier period, Azerbaijan's concerns about migration mostly focused on internally displaced persons – the result of its conflict with Armenia – and on the high numbers of emigrants leaving for Russia, mainly for economic reasons. Today, the country's leadership strongly promotes an image of Azerbaijan as a target country for immigrants (Rumyantsev and Sotkasiira forthcoming). Consequently, attention has been directed away from still prevailing economic disparities that force people to move, at first to urban areas, mainly Baku, and then abroad. Azerbaijan's migration policy is now being built on the need to secure the national borders and set quotas for immigrants who want to live in the capital or enter the labour market. Much as in the European Union, immigration in Azerbaijan is being portrayed in a contradictory light: the country's great attractiveness to foreigners is contrasted with the need to protect the rights of its citizens through policies that restrict immigration. Or in President Ilham Aliyev's words:

> The number of foreigners intending to visit the Republic of Azerbaijan will increase while Azerbaijan is developing. This can be considered as a positive factor for our country. However, in any case, we must prefer the

interests of our state, people, citizens, and this must be the priority
direction of our migration policy.

(Azerbaijan Republic State Migration Service 2012)

Belarus, on the other hand, officially refuses to acknowledge the challenges of
migration, other than by complaining about the EU's unfair visa policy. Yet,
the IOM actively works there in cooperation with state authorities and other
international organisations to distribute information about the dangers of
emigration. Campaigns, including the establishment of the hotline 'We don't
give bad advice', target people planning to work abroad and urge them not to
trust foreign employers. They are funded and implemented to create an
atmosphere of suspicion and mistrust among potential migrants (IOM 2012).
In Georgia, a similar campaign was launched in 2006 under the slogan 'The
streets abroad are not paved with gold', whose main purpose was to warn
people against migration-related criminal practices and the trafficking of people,
but also unrealistic expectations about foreign migration (IOM 2006). In fact, all
the countries studied here have seen such campaigns, although their messages have
generally been less stark.

In Ukraine and Moldova, outmigration is perceived as a threat to the social
order. Although citizens of both sexes are equally involved in foreign labour
migration, local discourses of risk and anxiety tend to be of a gendered nature.
Alongside human trafficking as a source of worry, the morality of female migrants
in particular forms part of the discursive landscape of migration (for Moldova, see
Keough 2004). Leyla Keough (2006), for example, has argued that, in Moldova,
much of the anxiety surrounding transnational labour is directed at migrant
mothers accused of abandoning their children and of splitting up families.
According to Keough (2006: 442), many international non-governmental organisations contribute to reinforce these concerns through campaigns that identify
orphaned children as the main targets of traffickers. These campaigns are
often co-financed by the EU and local governments. Thus, the EU, while
publicly declaring its commitment to a more holistic approach to migration, at
the same time works hand in hand with governments in Wider Europe to
demonise parties and actors involved in the process of migration.

Protecting the borders of the European Union

The stated principles of the EU's immigration policy are those of prosperity,
solidarity and security. In short, the EU emphasises the linkages between legal
immigration and its contribution to Wider Europe's socio-economic development. Illegal immigration, on the other hand, is perceived as a problem that has
to be tackled thoroughly. As far as solidarity is concerned, the EU highlights the
need for its members to share the financial burden caused by migration, to
help countries of origin and transit to manage migration and to collaborate
with non-EU countries on all aspects of migration issues. Keeping these policy
objectives in mind, the EU's attempts to manage migration cooperatively with

neighbours in Wider Europe has met with a certain success: discussions have been held on different levels, agreements have been signed and progress has been made, especially regarding the securitised areas of engagement within migration policy. All the EU's partners in Eastern Europe, the South Caucasus and Central Asia have, for example, shown interest in applying more effective border controls and taking part in border management programmes; co-financed campaigns targeting smuggling and human trafficking have been launched in all the countries studied here.

However, while greater mobility has been regularly associated with positive outcomes such as innovation, the exchange of ideas, more efficient labour markets and even democratisation, this has always been accompanied by references to the risks entailed by migration. Indeed, the idea of balancing the benefits and risks of migration is a cornerstone of the current discourse on migration, a situation unlikely to change in the near future. It is reflected in the European Council's policy documents on the future development of the ENP. The underlying attitude towards migration appears to be that 'you can have your cake and eat it, too'. Migration is at the same time to be encouraged, if it is legal and orderly, and curtailed, if it is not. Typical of this view is, for example, the Commission's argument that 'dealing firmly and effectively with irregular migration is a precondition for a credible migration and mobility policy' (European Commission 2011a: 9). In other words, the fluid movement of people across Europe's borders is perceived as being dependent on efficient border-controls and the successful coping with the manifold issues of border security. This perception of migration management is largely shared across Wider Europe.

Whereas Didier Bigo (2002) sees the very statehood of Western liberal states at stake in the current discourse on migration, an evaluation of the EU's migration policy towards countries of Wider Europe shows that similar concerns have been expressed in the EU's eastern neighbourhood. It is not difficult to understand why official Belarus has repeatedly refused to acknowledge the challenges of migration and the need for cooperation in this field or why Azerbaijan chooses to concentrate on immigration at the expense of tackling the causes of outmigration. Many countries in Wider Europe are either themselves prone to violent and armed conflicts or have neighbours that are only a step away from them, thus imperilling border areas. The recent developments in Ukraine are a case in point. In the absence of mutually agreed systems to govern migration and the movement of people across state borders, migration management risks being reduced to the management of national security.

In the current discourse of migration, the normalisation of movements across the borders of the EU is conditioned by political stability, the rule of law and democracy in the EU's neighbourhood. At the same time, it is perceived as leading to economic development and better mutual understanding, the exchange of ideas and the spreading of innovation, as well as opening ways to better tackle unemployment and deal with various social issues

(European Commission 2011c: 11). However, it appears that the notion that advances in the field of migration management are being conditioned by the well-functioning economy and state–society relations works against the stated goals of greater mobility and more intensive and numerous people-to-people contacts. If the benefits associated with the movement of people in and out of the EU are taken seriously, we need to ask whether it makes sense to understand migration management as a tool for prosperity and collaboration or whether it should not rather result from these very same qualities.

9 The new concept of migration policy of the Russian Federation

Revolution or re-evolution?

Sergei Riazantsev

Due to stable migration flows between the countries of the former Soviet Union, Russia is today the centre of one of the largest migration systems in Eurasia. Since 1991, over 20 million people living in the former Soviet republics have changed their place of residence and 90 per cent of them have resettled in neighbouring countries. During the period 1992–1997, Russia alone took in about 12 million immigrants from these countries, roughly a third of them were officially recruited as labour migrants. Overall, 92 per cent of the immigrants in Commonwealth of Independent States (CIS) countries are from other CIS countries and 72 per cent of emigrants have moved to another CIS country (Ivakhnyuk 2008: 5–10).

The emergence of this migration system can be explained by historical factors, notably a long common history within a single state and the great importance of the Russian language in the region. Russia's central role and higher attractiveness to migrants are due to its superior economic potential, the size of its labour market and the higher level of wages. Moreover, Russia shares a border with most CIS countries. Politically, it has shown a strong interest in strengthening the integration of CIS countries, with policy cooperation on immigration high on the agenda. Indeed, adverse qualitative and quantitative trends in its demographic evolution have created a strong demand for foreign labour that is likely to increase in time. Even today immigration does not entirely compensate the natural decline of Russia's population. If present trends are to continue Russia will have a population of only 112 million by 2050, making it the seventeenth-biggest country by population down from the current ninth position. It is also expected that the ageing of its population will not only lead to a shortage of labour but also affect other sectors, such as the military and education. Finally, the evolution of the Eurasian migration system and the probable emergence of new centres attractive for migrants, in Kazakhstan and the Ukraine in particular, may soon result in a diversification of migration flows within the post-Soviet space, where Russia will then face increasing competition for human resources. Under these conditions the development of a strategically calibrated national migration policy and regional integration policies aimed at creating a common labour market, as well as active cooperation on migration with countries exporting labour to

DOI: 10.4324/9781315858036-13

Russia have become a vital task for the Russian government (Ivakhnyuk 2008a: 12).

Although the Russian Federation's migration policy since the collapse of the Soviet Union has been undergoing several changes in response to varying migration flows, it has been pointed out that, in comparison to other countries, it has remained strongly informed by the notion that cross-border flows have to be strictly controlled (Iontzev and Ivakhnyuk 2012: 6; Ryazantsev and Horie 2011: 35). There exist indeed stringent rules for issuing visas. The procedures for registering one's residence and obtaining a work permit are complicated and bureaucratic, and it is difficult to obtain Russian citizenship. At the same time, citizens from many countries of the former Soviet Union benefit from a visa-free regime. The recent introduction of special work permits, so-called 'patents', have greatly facilitated the hiring of foreign workers by private households. It could therefore be argued that Russia's present migration policy is not hostile towards immigration. Rather, it does not produce the desired results.

The reasons for this lack of effectiveness are manifold. Until recently, Russia's migration policy was not based on a strategic concept. New laws and measures often contradicted earlier ones and policy-making appeared to follow the principle of 'one step forward, two steps back'. The resulting complexity of the legal rules, as well as their lack of responsiveness to economic demands means that migrants and employers are often ill-informed and forced to resort to one of the increasing number of intermediaries or even to corrupt practices. The regular channel to obtain a work permit, for example, is through the Federal Migration Service, which administers a quota system and delivers permits for a fee equivalent to USD100. Since the number of (possible) applicants far exceeds the quota, many migrant workers and employers acquire permits on the black market at ten times the cost from private companies who in turn pay off public officials. Until now, the authorities have been unwilling to reform the system, possibly because they do not want to deprive the participants in this trade of their income. Similar services are available for persons who wish to obtain Russian citizenship, a long and laborious procedure that can be cut short at additional cost through bribery or a marriage in name only. In addition to providing civil servants with a supplementary income illegal proceedings have also led to the exploitation of migrants by employers who deprive them of their labour rights and pay no social and pension contributions.

It has taken Russia's political leadership quite some time to realise that migration is an important component of the socio-economic and demographic development of the country. Consequently, the elaboration of a valid concept of migration management has been a slow process. The Concept of Regulation of Migration Processes in the Russian Federation,[1] a governmental decree from 1 March 2003, was frequently criticised for insufficiently responding to the country's needs, as well as being too restrictive and not doing enough for the integration of immigrants. In the late 2000s the Federal Migration

Service started drafting a new concept, which was presented to the general public during a two-year period before being approved by President Vladimir Putin in a presidential decree on 13 June 2012. The following is an attempt to show that, despite certain shortcomings, 'The Concept of State Migration Policy for the period up to 2025' represents a significant step forward by introducing several 'revolutionary' ideas that take much better into account Russia's socio-economic and demographic situation.

The first part of this chapter will give an overview of the present state of labour migration in the Russian Federation by focusing on the socio-demographic characteristics of migrants, their regional distribution and the role of undocumented, or illegal, migrants. It will be followed by an analytical reading of the recent State Migration Policy Concept, with an emphasis on the – at least within the Russian context – radically new ideas it contains. The final part will address the shortcomings of the Concept and point out some of the missing elements in Russia's present migration policy. The analysis is based on statistical data, expert opinion and a review of the scientific literature on migration and Russian migration policy.

Labour migration in the Russian Federation: characteristics and trends

Labour migration accounts for the largest share in the Russian Federation's migratory flows and also receives most attention in the media and political discussions. Although the overall share of foreign labour migrants has remained relatively small (between three and five per cent of the employed population), it has reached much higher proportions in certain sectors. Foreign workers are strongly present in occupations characterised by hard labour conditions and low wages, notably in construction, transport, agriculture, certain industries and employment by private households. In the construction sector, for example, migrants make up almost 19 per cent of the workforce and even more when it comes to heavy and temporary work. If undocumented (illegal) workers are included, this share can attain 50 to 60 per cent in some sectors. In agriculture, it is estimated to be roughly 40 per cent (Ryazantsev and Horie 2011: 14). It is then hardly surprising that the modern Russian economy has been said to be 'dependent on the migrant economy' and to be an 'economy that exploits migrant workers'. Konstantin Romodanovsky, the director of the Federal Migration Service, has estimated that migrant labour is responsible for eight per cent of Russia's GDP.[2]

While the Russian economy has been hit hard by the 2008 crisis and has seen a reduction in the number of legal migrants in 2009 and 2010, the demand for foreign workers has begun to rise once more since then. Moreover, in July 2010, the Russian authorities legalised the status of foreigners working for households by introducing so-called 'patents' for citizens from countries that do not have a visa-free regime with the Russian Federation. Official data from the Federal Migration Service show that over 950,000 such patents were granted during the second half of 2010 (see Table 9.1).

Table 9.1 Number of work permits and 'patents' issued in Russia, 1994–2010

Year	Number of work permits	Number of 'patents'
1994	129,000	–
1995	281,000	–
1996	292,000	–
1997	245,000	–
1998	242,000	–
1999	211,000	–
2000	213,000	–
2001	284,000	–
2002	360,000	–
2003	378,000	–
2004	460,000	–
2005	703,000	–
2006	1,014,000	–
2007	1,717,000	–
2008	2,426,000	–
2009	1,473,000	–
2010	1,641,000	951,000

Source: Federal Migration Service of the Russian Federation. Online. Available at: www.work.ua/ news/world/269/ (last accessed 10 July 2012).

According to Ekaterina Egorova, deputy director of the Federal Migration Service, some two million foreign workers received patents between mid-2010 and September 2012.[3]

The great majority (70 per cent) of officially employed labour migrants have a long-term contract with the companies that have hired them. Only five per cent work for unincorporated employers, that is mainly households, as nannies, gardeners, maintenance workers, construction workers, guards, servants etc., generally without any formal contract. Their true numbers are likely to be much higher (Ryazantsev *et al.* 2012: 3). Estimations of the number of undocumented migrants are hard to come by. Representatives of the Ministry of Internal Affairs have spoken of some ten million people and some politicians have even advanced the figure of 15 million workers (Ryazantsev 2007: 67). Both figures appear questionable as they are not based on solid scientific research. The 2002 census identified two million persons not registered with the Ministry of Internal Affairs, while the 2010 census indicated an additional million of unregistered individuals, possibly because of a significant increase of temporary labour migrants. The author's own calculations arrive at an estimate of five million persons (Ryazantsev 2007: 56). Most undocumented workers are probably citizens of other CIS countries who have the right to enter Russia without a visa and subsequently fail to register or to obtain a work permit. They generally stay in Russia for several years, although some periodically return to their home country.

Currently, foreign workers in Russia are from more than 120 different countries. The largest suppliers of foreign labour in 2010 were three countries in Central Asia: Uzbekistan, Tajikistan and Kyrgyzstan (see Table 9.2), followed by other CIS countries, including Ukraine, Moldova, Armenia and Azerbaijan. Significant numbers of people also arrive from China, Turkey, Vietnam and North Korea. After the procedure for registering and obtaining work permits was simplified for citizens of other CIS countries in January 2007, the share of officially employed labour from these countries rose to reach some 75 per cent. Similarly, since the introduction of patents (see above), the share of migrants from countries with no visa agreement who work for households and individuals exceeded 85 per cent in this economic sector.

There is a clear segmentation of the Russian labour market with regard to migrants' countries of origin. Studies have shown that Tajik migrants mainly work in the construction as well as housing sectors and for municipal public utilities. Those from Uzbekistan tend to concentrate in the construction, agricultural, housing and utilities sectors as well as in commerce. Migrant workers from Kyrgyzstan are strongly present in the housing sector, services, as well as transport and trade. The majority of Ukrainians are employed in the construction sector or in maintenance, but also in manufacturing and transport. Moldovans mostly work as builders and drivers, while Chinese and Vietnamese migrants predominate in trade, agriculture and the light industry. Turkish migrants predominantly work in the construction sector. By contrast, foreign top managers in the banking and insurance sectors, in commerce and manufacturing are mainly recruited from the United States, Japan and Europe.

Table 9.2 Migrant workers by country of origin and type of administrative permit, 2010–2011

Country of origin	Number of work permits	Number of 'patents'
Uzbekistan	512,000	478,000
Tajikistan	267,000	207,000
China	186,000	–
Ukraine	167,000	39,000
Kyrgyzstan	118,000	65,000
Moldova	72,000	39,000
Armenia	60,000	70,000
Vietnam	46,000	–
Turkey	46,000	–
Azerbaijan	4,040,000	–
North Korea	37,000	–
Other countries	423,000	6,000

Source: Federal Migration Service of the Russian Federation.

Nine out of ten labour migrants are men and four out of five of them are aged from 18 to 39. Demand is indeed especially strong for low-skilled workers in the construction and housing sectors, in agriculture, transportation and public utilities, where occupations frequently imply heavy work. In recent years, there has been a trend for migrants to be younger. Starting in 2007, labour migrants aged 18 to 29 began to prevail over those aged 30 to 39. In 2008, the younger group accounted for 37 per cent of migratory flows to Russia. There are indications that young people with a degree in secondary or higher education are increasingly involved in labour migration to Russia (Ryazantsev and Horie 2011: 30). However, many migrants have occupations that are not related to their educational level or to previous work experience and the Federal Migration Service does not collect data on professional or educational qualifications.

Geographically, the Central Federal District is the main centre of attraction for migrants; 47 per cent of the officially employed foreign workers are registered there. Within this region, the city of Moscow receives about a third of all migrant workers in the country and Moscow region about six per cent. Next comes the Urals Federal District, where one out of six labour migrants is employed, mainly in the oil industry and the construction sector of the Yamal-Nenetsky and Khanty-Mansiysky Autonomous Districts, which respectively occupy the second and third place. Another popular destination for migrant workers is the Far Eastern Federal District with a share of ten per cent, mostly composed of Chinese, North Koreans and Vietnamese employed in the construction sector, agriculture and forestry in the Primorsky and Khabarovsky Krays and the Amurskaya Oblast.

Overall, it is possible to identify five types of areas where labour migrants are concentrated in specific economic sectors (see Ryazantsev and Horie 2011: 18). The first, which is dominated by construction workers, includes, among others, the Smolensk, Yaroslavl, Rostov, Samara and Krasnodar regions, as well as the Moscow region and the city of Moscow, although in the latter two the occupational structure is much more diversified. All of them are economically dynamic regions that have been experiencing a construction boom, at least until the 2008 crisis. The second type, with a strong presence in the transport sector, includes the Kaliningrad and Kaluga regions, although migrants are employed as drivers in many other regions and their overall share in the transport sector has increased in recent years.[4] The third area is composed of most parts of Central Russia, the North-West, the Novosibirsk region and Kabardino-Balkaria, where migrants are predominantly employed in manufacturing and the transport sector. The fourth, with significant numbers of migrants employed in trade and the services sector, includes the Bryansk, Orel, Saratov, Penza and Stravropol regions and the Altai and Primorsky Krays of the Urals District. The fifth, finally, is composed of regions where migrants work in the agricultural and forestry sector, as labourers on collective and private farms, as tenants, as loggers or collecting forest products such as berries, mushrooms or grass. It includes Karelia, Kalmykia, the Novogorod,

Volgograd, Astrakhan, Kirov, Omsk and Amur regions, as well as the *krays* of Krasnoyarsk and Khabarovsk.

Labour migration is also the source of significant benefits for the countries of origin. In 2011, remittances sent from Russia, mainly to other CIS countries, amounted to USD15 billion. In Tajikistan, for example, remittances exceed 45 per cent of GDP, in Moldova 40 per cent and in Kyrgyzstan 35 per cent, mostly originating from the Russian Federation (Ryazantsev and Horie 2011: 87). Together with the accumulated savings that are reinvested, remittances help reduce balance of payments deficits, provide for the migrants' families and relatives, bring down the local unemployment rate and contribute to the easing of social tensions. They are also an important mechanism for the economic integration of the CIS states.

Revolutionary ideas in the new Concept of State Migration Policy

The new Concept of State Migration Policy of the Russian Federation for the Period to 2025 clearly contains several ideas that constitute a radical departure from earlier policy statements and will help Russia to regulate migration in a way that will better serve its national interests. Perhaps the most significant change is ideological in nature as it sees migration no longer only as a threat to the country but as a major development resource: 'Migration processes play an important role in the socio-economic and demographic development of the Russian Federation. Over the past two decades, net migration has to a large extent compensated the natural decline of the population' (President of the Russian Federation 2012: Article 6, Section II). Indeed, immigration currently offsets about 70 per cent of the natural decline and entirely does so in eleven regions. For the first time, the government recognises that the:

> Resettlement of migrants for permanent residence in Russia has become one of the sources of the population increase in the country as a whole and in the regions' and that 'the attraction of foreign workers in the priority groups of professional qualifications in accordance with the needs of the Russian economy is a necessity for its further advance.
> (President of the Russian Federation 2012: Paragraph 7, Section II)

Another first is the statement that the Russian Federation needs to promote internal migration and increase the geographical mobility of the Russian population, explaining that 'adverse trends are observed in internal migration' and that 'the population of the Russian Federation has a low geographical mobility (including at the local level) in comparison to other countries' (President of the Russian Federation 2012: Article 10, Section II). According to the 2002 census, 97 per cent of Russia's citizens continue to live in their place of birth and internal migration concerned only some two million people. Despite high unemployment numbers in many regions, most Russians are not ready or are unable to move to another part of the country, the main difficulty being the absence of an efficient housing market but also the lack of well-functioning labour exchanges and schemes to promote labour mobility.[5] Job vacancies are therefore often filled by illegally employed foreign workers, whose numbers are estimated at three to five million (President of the Russian Federation 2012: Paragraph 12, Section II). Proposals to promote the employment of Russian nationals and to increase economic productivity can be found in Paragraph 24, Section III.

For the first time too, the Concept raises the question of the integration of immigrants. Paragraph 17 of Section III in particular recognises that 'an important element of the state migration policy of the Russian Federation is to create proper conditions for the adaptation and integration of migrants'. This can be linked to the changing socio-demographic profile and ethnic origin of recently arriving permanent and temporary labour migrants (Osipov and Ryazantsev 2009: 57). The 1990s mainly saw ethnic Russians from the former Transcaucasian Republics and Central Asia returning to Russia, whereas in recent years the majority of immigrants applying for permanent residence are from CIS countries such as Kazakhstan, Uzbekistan and Tajikistan. The share of ethnic Russians is down from 74 per cent in 1995 to only 60 per cent in 2007. In public discourse, immigrants from Central Asia are perceived as having a poor command of the Russian language and little formal education. They also tend to increasingly come from rural areas or belong to vulnerable populations. Many are young. They are often perceived as being unfamiliar with life in a big city and are thought of as lacking even the basic social skills necessary to adapt to their new environment. At the same time, Russia does not have a sufficiently developed infrastructure dedicated to promote their integration through Russian-language courses, centres for counselling, community clubs and similar institutions (see Tkach and Brednikova in this volume).

Closely linked is the idea that the Russian education system does not focus enough on recruiting foreign students as a source of highly qualified and well-integrated labour (President of the Russian Federation 2012: Paragraph 16, Section III). Already the Concept of Demographic Policy of the Russian Federation until 2025 (President of the Russian Federation 2007) had declared the need to attract young foreigners for training and internships in view of allowing them to become Russian citizens after graduation. Similarly, the Concept of Long-Term Socio-Economic Development of Russia until 2020 (Ministry for Economic Development of the Russian Federation 2008) had among its targets an increase of up to five per cent of the share of foreign students in Russian universities and improved conditions of training for students from other CIS countries in educational institutions. While many Russian universities have made attempts to enter the international educational market, these have been isolated efforts that were not part of an integrated state policy and received no government funding. Measures that would favour the recruitment of foreign students and help to cope with the expected shortage of highly qualified professionals include a grants system, Russian-language courses in target countries, an appropriate information policy as well as scientific and educational exchange programmes. In 2011, Russia had enrolled only 90,000 foreign students, most of them from Kazakhstan, China, India, Ukraine, Vietnam and Uzbekistan. Students from other CIS countries often choose Russia because of their familiarity with the Russian language, similar systems of education and already existing family ties, although a growing number now prefer to train in Europe or the United States. Those from China, India and Vietnam usually come because of the lower costs but there, too, Russian universities have lost ground.[6]

Another truly revolutionary idea, at least within the Russian context, is to attract foreign entrepreneurs and investors by offering them permanent residence status or even citizenship. This proposal could be particularly beneficial for citizens of other CIS states, China and Vietnam. However, as no further details about the scheme have been published, it is not yet known what criteria will be applied (size and nature of the investment etc.) and whether it will be accompanied by other measures designed to improve the business climate, such as fiscal incentives. The scheme could be of particular importance for the economic development of the Far East and Siberia, two regions that have respectively lost one million and one and half million of their inhabitants between 1996 and 2008, and of the area surrounding Moscow region, which has suffered a net loss of 2.3 million people. Job opportunities have indeed favoured more dynamic regions such as Moscow and Moscow region (net gain of 1.9 million) and the North Caucasus (plus 1.1 million).

The new Concept has also reaffirmed the government's commitment to continue state support for programmes encouraging the return of Russian citizens living abroad and which go back to a presidential decree of 2006 (Federal Migration Service 2006: Article 24, Section III). Regional resettlement schemes, initially implemented in twelve regions, currently exist in 71.[7] But there is still room for further improvement, notably in housing and employment. Another preoccupation is the very uneven distribution of returnees over the Russian territory. Kaliningrad Oblast, for example, has attracted 54 per cent of them, thanks to a combination of factors including its geographical location, a favourable climate, its economic development and the quality of life as well as the governor's open-door policy.[8] By contrast, the regions of the Far East offered a new home to only five per cent. The programme, which has been extended for the period after 2012, is the only resettlement scheme receiving funding from the central government; the funding for housing, for instance, has been transferred to the regional governments, which often are not prepared to shoulder an additional financial burden if they are poor.

Finally, the Concept alludes to the demographic situation in Siberia and the Far East where it expects to achieve a migratory inflow by the end of the third phase, in 2026 (President of the Russian Federation 2012: Paragraph 32, Section VII). Given the present trends, this would require drastic measures. It is not yet clear what form these would take. Among the ideas mooted to boost socio-economic development and to stop outmigration in these eastern regions are temporary income-tax exemptions for individual entrepreneurs and owners of business start-ups; opportunities for long-term land leases to promote industrial and agricultural activities; federal funding to improve the housing situation for newcomers and the local population in the form of soft loans and grants, particularly in view of attracting and retaining students, young professionals and business people; salary increments depending on the length of residence; free travel for local residents to the European and other parts of Russia; and the stimulation of tourism.

Emigration: the missing element in Russia's migration policy

Unfortunately, the new Concept does not consider the problem of emigration, which is only referred to in one sentence about 'continuing emigration out-flows from the country' (President of the Russian Federation 2012: Paragraph 9 of Section II). Expatriates are mentioned casually in the context of the migration of returnees. However, more than 1.2 million citizens have left Russia for other countries since 1989. More importantly, many of them have received a higher education: this has been the case for one out of five persons moving to another CIS country, and the numbers are even higher for emigrants to non-CIS countries, such as the United States (35 per cent) and Israel (32 per cent). Indeed, after the collapse of the Soviet Union, a wave of scientists, doctors, teachers, computer programmers and other professionals left Russia in search of better working conditions and higher wages, mostly for Western countries. According to estimates advanced by the International Organisation for Migration, the technology sector in the United States employs more than 100,000 Russian specialists, and some 50,000 Russian programmers are working in Germany (Ryazantsev and Pismennaya 2013: 34). Scientists and other highly educated people from Russia probably form the world's largest scientific diaspora.

Numerous high-ranking government officials have repeatedly acknowledged that emigration adversely effects the socio-economic development of the Russian Federation, and in particular the scientific sector. Thus, Dmitry Livanov, the present Minister of Education and Science of the Russian Federation, has stated:

> From 1989 to 2004 some 25,000 scientists have left Russia and 30 million are working abroad on temporary contracts, among them the best and most prolific. Today the number of people employed in science is about 40 per cent of what it was in the 1990s.
>
> (Quoted in Ryazantsev and Pismennaya 2013: 34)

However, virtually nothing has been done to identify the causes of this emigration (the so-called push factors) or the circumstances under which it is taking place. There exists hardly any information on whether this migration will be temporary or permanent and under which conditions these emigrants

Table 9.3 Number of Russian emigrants to selected countries, 2008–2011

	Year			
	2008	*2009*	*2010*	*2011*
Greece	98	80	92	105
Sweden	157	102	128	136
Bulgaria	163	125	112	194
Australia	202	172	184	249
China	53	57	248	507
Canada	516	457	497	471
Finland	620	685	517	480
Israel	1,040	894	947	977
USA	1,722	1,440	1,461	1,422
Germany	4,916	4,115	3,725	3,815

Source: Rosstat (2013).

would be willing to return to the Russian Federation. Even precise numbers for this scientific diaspora and its characteristics are unavailable. Nor has there been, until recently, any government policy aimed at cooperating with this diaspora.

Only in recent years have the Russian authorities been taking steps to promote the return of Russian scientists working abroad. Thus, on 12 November 2009, the then Russian president Dmitry Medvedev announced the creation of the Skolkovo Innovation Centre near Moscow, a site intended to encourage scientific and technological development through high-technology clusters, promote technological start-ups, ensure the proper marketing of new technologies and even facilitate the employment of foreign nationals. It is yet too early to assess the results of this policy in terms of academic achievement or the numbers of Russian scientists attracted from abroad. However, critics have pointed out that the establishment of the centre, launched at costs unprecedented in recent Russian history, is likely to take place at the expense of existing institutions, such as the Russian Academy of Sciences and leading universities that continue to lack adequate funding for their activities. They have also raised serious doubts about the centre's capacity to live up to expectations that it could create *ex nihilo* new scientific schools and regretted that no plans exist at the Ministry of Education and Science to open a programme of state grants designed to promote the return of Russian scientists.

Recent scientific literature has interpreted the process of intensive migration by highly skilled professionals as part of a wider trend caused by globalisation and introduced the term 'brain circulation' to describe this phenomenon, a term which has increasingly been applied to the emigration of specialists from Russia. The notion of circulation suggests that this form of migration is temporary, because scientists and other highly qualified labour are thought to follow the movements of capital and participate in projects abroad for a limited period of time before returning to their country of origin. Thus, the British research foundation Open Economy has estimated that some 1.4 million citizens of the United Kingdom with a degree in higher education leave every year to work abroad, mostly in the United States, and that more than 800,000 people with such a degree do so from Germany (Ryazantsev and Pismennaya 2013: 34). Migration theories assume that migration from Western Europe to the United States is dominated by pull factors, less the perspective of higher wages than better working conditions – better equipment, better organisation, better funding and better prospects for a scientific career.

Is there evidence for the emigration of Russian scientists being part of this international 'brain circulation'? Obviously, the push factors appear to be stronger in this case and, more generally, in emigration from the CIS and developing countries. In Russia, scientists receive low pay and suffer from poor living conditions. The average monthly salary of a Russian scientist rarely exceeds USD1,000, compared to five to seven thousand in the United States, and a skilled Russian programmer working for a large foreign company, such as Alcatel, can earn as much as 100–120,000 dollars a year, worth 5.6 million roubles at home (Perminova 2004: 68). Research institutions in Russia are mostly underfunded, lack adequate facilities and equipment and at most receive funds for salaries and basic utilities. Funds for research proper have to be obtained elsewhere, often through highly bureaucratic procedures.

The numbers of highly qualified scientists and other experts desiring to leave Russia has remained very high. Thus, an estimated 200–250,000 programmers want to leave the country to work abroad; one out of ten scientists are looking for employment outside the country, 40 per cent of them already work at least partly for foreign foundations and other organisations and 20 per cent envisage temporary emigration. Only 30 per cent declare having no intention to emigrate (Perminova 2004: 68). Similarly, a recent survey, conducted by the Russian agency Romir in 2012, has shown that almost one third of Russia's urban residents stated that they would like to emigrate; this represents an increase of 12 per cent compared to another survey, carried out seven years earlier.[9]

Additionally, respondents who had declared their desire to leave the country were asked which country they would like to move to (detailed results are shown in Table 9.4). European countries were the most attractive, particularly

Table 9.4 'To which country do you want to emigrate?' (%)

	2005 survey	2012 survey
Other European countries	37	51
Australia or New Zealand	18	23
North America	18	23
Other countries	8	21

Source: Romir Research Holding (2012).

for younger respondents (35 to 44 years of age) who are not married and have a degree in secondary education. More generally, it is mostly the young educated and skilled part of the active population that is concerned by emigration. Roughly 87 per cent of Russian emigrants had a previous experience of migration, either within Russia or towards a foreign country. In a globalised world, it is the countries which offer the highest wages and the best working conditions that are winning the competition for the best minds, above all the United States, Australia, Canada, Japan and the countries of Western Europe, followed by China, Singapore and the Gulf countries. While in most developed countries, this migration is dominated by pull factors, in Russia push factors prevail, notably low wages and difficult academic working conditions, leading to a 'brain drain'. Russian science has not only been losing individual scientists and specialists but whole schools of thought and research teams, endangering the national future of disciplines, such as mathematics, physics and genetics. It must be feared that this trend has an irrevocable character.

Questions left open by Russia's new Concept of State Migration Policy

The new Concept of State Migration Policy can be considered a major achievement because it recognises for the first time the importance of migration for the present and future demographic, social and economic development of the Russian Federation. In addition to 'national security, maximum security, comfort and well-being of Russia's population', the document thus defines two other goals for the country's migration policy (President of the Russian Federation 2012: Paragraph 21 of Section III). These are the 'stabilisation and increase of the resident population' and the need for foreign labour to promote the Russian economy as well as the need for 'modernisation, the development of innovation and enhancing the competitiveness of its industries'. However, it could be said that these targets have their place in other concepts, namely of national security, demographic policy and economic development, and that the new Concept lacks in focus, because the main objective of migration policy should have been formulated more specifically as aimed at minimising emigration flows from the Russian Federation and promoting the immigration of economically relevant categories of persons for permanent residence, work and study, as well as encouraging internal migration by improving the conditions for residential and labour mobility. This should have been the starting point.

It is regretful that the Concept gives little detail on how to reduce the impact of push factors at work in outmigration, when the desire to emigrate is stronger than ever, especially outside the metropolitan regions and among the most qualified and dynamic Russians (professionals, academics, young people, businessmen and, more generally, the middle class). Of course, the problems faced by migrant workers in Russia and their integration have to be addressed but the Concept should have been more clear about how the government intends to redress the demographic and socio-economic situation of the country. Although the document repeatedly states the need to attract migrants and lists the main categories of desired migrants, it has little to say about where these are to come from, in what numbers and, most importantly, what their motivation would be. Similarly, it neglects the subject of internal migration as a means to promote social and economic development. Overall, it remains unclear on what grounds the various measures to be implemented have been selected.

Secondly, the new Concept, unfortunately, dedicates little space to existing problems related to migration statistics and their solution. Paragraph 26 of Section V modestly states the need to 'develop a system of statistical surveys based on administrative systems of registration and sample surveys'. Indeed, information on migration is presently only available in a fragmented form. Thus, Rosstat publishes data on the permanent residence of Russian citizens; the Federal Migration Service focuses on temporary labour migration of foreign nationals and the number of foreigners that are granted Russian citizenship while other institutions, such as the Ministry of the Interior, the Ministry of Education or the Border Service, produce statistics on yet other fields related to migration. Creating a single information system related to migration should therefore be a priority. As a first step in this direction, there needs to be established a working group composed of representatives of the various agencies dealing with migration as well as of scientists and other experts working in this field. Statistics on migration should also be more precise, published in time and made more accessible to academic researchers and other interested experts. More research needs to be done on the scope and trends of migration, including the reasons for migration. In the absence of these improvements, it is hard to see how the government and its various agencies will be able to effectively regulate and monitor migration and how they will be able to make recommendations that will ensure a more efficient migration policy. Moreover, the concerned agencies should also make efforts to better coordinate their decisions and the measures they implement.

Finally, there remains the question of the implementation of the Concept. There is at present no clear time frame for the required legislative changes, and it remains, of course, uncertain how the different policy statements will be practically implemented by new laws and other legal and administrative measures.

Notes

1   Readers unfamiliar with the Russian legal system should note that legislative acts are either 'concepts', which define general principles for regulations, or 'laws', which implement these principles by specifying concrete realisations of these principles.
2   Quoted in 'V svyazi s krizisom chislo trudovyh migrantov v Rossii umen'shilos' na 13%', *Work.ua*, 15 September 2009. Online. Available at: www.work.ua/news/world/269/ (last accessed 18 July 2012).

3 See Ekaterina Egorova's report on 'Labour Migration to Russia' presented at the international symposium 'Migration Bridges in Eurasia', held on 7 November 2012 at the Russian Academy of Sciences (Egorova 2012).

4 In the recent past, several city officials have voiced concern about passenger safety. On 1 January 2010, the Moscow government has forbidden commercial companies, but not state-owned companies, to employ foreign drivers of minibuses. Similarly, the former mayor of St Petersburg, V. Matviyenko, has stated the need for providing additional training to help foreign drivers better cope with heavy traffic in dense urban areas.

5 There were 6 million officially unemployed people in 2011. In sixteen regions, their number exceed 100,000 and in twenty-three 50,000. The Chechen Republic (300,000), Dagestan (250,000) and Ingushetia (130,000) suffer from particularly high unemployment rates. See Trud i zaniatost' v Rossii 2011, Moskva. *Federal'naia sluzhba gosudarstvennoi statistiki.* Online. Available at: www.gks.ru/bgd/regl/b11_36/IssWWW. exe/Stg/d1/01-51.htm (last accessed 20 August 2013).

6 This is confirmed by a data survey carried out in Vietnam among 300 Vietnamese from eight provinces who have worked or studied in Russia or the Soviet Union. A third of the parents wanted their children to study in the United States, 20 per cent in the United Kingdom, 18 per cent in Australia and 9 per cent in Japan. Already 32 per cent of the students study in Vietnam the language they expect to be trained in, namely English.

7 The 12 regions are Krasnoyarsky, Primorsky and Khabarovsky Krays, and the Amur, Irkutsk, Kaliningrad, Kaluga, Lipetsk, Novosibirsk, Tambov, Tver and Tyumen regions.

8 Kaliningrad's governor has declared that the region is ready to accept up to 300,000 persons.

9 See Romir press release 'Vse bol'she rossiyan zadumyvaiutsya ob emigratsii', 20 September 2012. Online. Available at: http://romir.ru/studies/390_1348084800/ (last accessed 15 August 2013). The sample was representative of the economically active urban population in Russia and included respondents from eight federal districts over 18 years of age living in cities with a population over 100,000.

10 The Republic of Belarus

Flows and tendencies in migration processes

Larissa Titarenko

Migration is not a recent phenomenon for Belarus. In earlier times it was the result of wars and changes in the political regime (Zlotnikau 2004: 25). In the more recent past, it has been a consequence of the break-up of the Soviet Union. Economic and political turmoil engendered numerous and strong migration flows within the post-Soviet space as well as towards countries beyond it. In the early 1990s, migration both from and to Belarus was thus part of the reconstitution of the region's social and political space. Since then, it has been sustained by ongoing integration processes in the post-Soviet space and beyond as well as by Belarus's unfavourable economic situation. The reasons for including Belarus in a discussion of regional stability in Eastern Europe are directly related to the country's geographical location – it borders three member states of the European Union – and its role as a transit country for migration towards EU countries, even though Belarus has been reluctant to cooperate with the EU within the framework of the Eastern Partnership and EU initiatives promoting migration management.

The aim of this chapter is to outline recent trends in migration from and to Belarus. The first section explains Belarus's duality with regard to two major 'zones of influence'. The next section will focus more specifically on migration to the Russian Federation and the European Union. This will be followed by an evaluation of the migration policies promoted by Belarus and the European Union in view of understanding how both respond to the challenges posed by these migration processes. The chapter will place the debate on migration in the general framework of EU–Belarus cooperation, European security and regional stability, and examine how factors external to migration come into play when defining the objectives of migration policies. The conclusion will review some of the consequences of the current policies for the Belarusian state and society and plead for a more realistic approach to migration policy by both Belarus and the European Union.

In view of the chapter's aims, it has been necessary to consult a variety of sources that present the official position of the Belarusian authorities, non-official assessments from Belarus and the EU's approach to Belarus-related issues of migration and regional stability.[1]

DOI: 10.4324/9781315858036-14

Migration processes in Belarus will be discussed within two contexts. The first is that of the Eastern Partnership (EaP), which assumes that cooperation between the EU and its eastern neighbours, as well as a common approach to regional stability, will result in mutual benefits for the partners involved – if non-EU countries are willing to accept so-called European values and bring their legislation into line with EU standards. As Belarus has so far refused to meet this precondition, its relations with the European Union have not followed this scenario. The EU views Belarus as lagging behind all other EaP members because of the weakness of external political linkages and slow adaptation to EU norms (Solonenko 2012). Neither party perceives the other as an equal partner (Klaskovskiĭ 2013b).

The second context is that of the Union State of Russia and Belarus. Since 1999, when the Union State was finally established, Belarus's foreign policy has been subordinated to that of the Union State; all important issues are discussed within the framework of 'the basic directions of migratory policy in territories of the state-participants of the Union of Belarus and Russia' (Government of Belarus 2005). Currently, Belarusian labour migrants in Russia do not need work permits, their employment is not regulated by the quota system and they enjoy the same rights as Russian citizens.[2]

The level of Russian–Belarusian cooperation increased when the Customs Union of Russia, Belarus and Kazakhstan came into force in mid-2010 and after the declaration announcing the creation of the Common Economic Space on 1 January 2012. Since then, migration and other issues have been subject to common regulations within the Customs Union.[3] When discussing Belarusian migration policy, one must therefore consider that the decisions adopted on the level of the Customs Union or the Union State of Russia and Belarus are binding on Belarus (Aleshina 2012: 62). Finally, the new Russian Concept for a State Migration Policy for the Period up to 2025, signed by President Putin on 18 July 2012, also stipulates greater facilities for Commonwealth of Independent States' (CIS) citizens to be employed in the Russian Federation.

Belarusian migration: between two poles of attraction

The two above-mentioned contexts explain why Belarus is situated at the intersection of two zones of influence, those of Russia and of the EU. This should imply that Belarus has to develop good relations with both neighbours, including on migration issues. In recent years, Belarus has been increasingly turning towards Russia, redefining its geopolitical and even cultural borders with the EU in a way that has reduced interrelations and cooperation with the latter. However, during the EaP Summit in Vilnius, in November 2013, the Belarusian government took a step towards the EU and agreed to launch negotiations over a visa facilitation and readmission agreement (Council of the European Union 2013). Before this event, during the period 2004–2013, both the EU and the Belarusian government set several preconditions that made negotiations impossible (e.g. the issue of progress in the respect of human rights in Belarus, put forward by the EU, and that of separate visa facilitation and readmission agreements, as envisaged by Belarus). After Belarus signed readmission agreements with two other Customs Union states in 2013, it expressed a desire to intensify negotiations with the EU (Korovenkova 2013b; Yeliseyev 2013b).

Looked at through the lens of regional security and migration management issues, this is an important event as Belarus is the only EaP member that has not yet signed such an agreement. At the same time, at the grassroots level, Belarusians are not less interested in contacts with the EU than Ukrainians. According to the Eurasian Development Bank Integration Barometer (2012–2013), the populations of both Ukraine and Belarus are more oriented towards the EU in the spheres of culture and economy than towards the CIS; this contrasts with a more pro-CIS orientation in the political sphere, which is more related to the institutional level, though the aggregated index for Ukraine is pro-EU, while for Belarus it is pro-CIS (Eurasian Development Bank 2012: 68 and 2013: 28). IISEPS (Independent Institute of Socio-Economic and Political Studies) surveys also confirm the ambiguity of geopolitical orientations among Belarusians: for several years almost one third of respondents have leant towards the EU, while a similar number of Belarusians have done so towards Russia (IISEPS 2013b). As Russia is pursuing a policy of post-Soviet integration, trying to retain the status of regional leader, it provides economic assistance to Belarus in the political context of further integration. As a result, Belarus is becoming more and more dependent on Russia – selling its industrial enterprises to Russian investors, hosting a Russian strategic military base on Belarusian territory and accepting Russian loans.[4]

Belarus is a borderland country and as such its geopolitical orientations are crucial in practice: they influence the foreign policy of the state and contribute to the situation of regional security and stability. Historically and culturally, the people of Belarus have a more positive attitude towards the EU and wish to be closer to its member countries; on the other hand, Belarus's economy is totally dependent on Russia. It is not a surprise that the foreign policy of the Belarusian state reflects this dependency.[5]

In the context of a weak opposition and immature political parties, the citizens of Belarus have to behave according to their geopolitical and economic realities: the visa-free and borders-free regimes within the Customs Union make it easy for Belarusians to move to Russia. This migration flow, although small in comparison to migration from Central Asia, strengthens Russia and helps stabilise the Belarusian regime through a lower unemployment rate and increasing remittances from Russia. In the long run the location between two strong geopolitical poles may push more qualified Belarusians to leave the country, resulting in an increasing labour shortage in Belarus as well as further economic dependency on Russia. Therefore, it does not seem impossible that Belarus may in the future become part of the Russian Federation, if there is the political will in Russia (Klaskovskiĭ 2013a).

According to official Belarusian migration statistics, immigration exceeds outmigration: net migration with other CIS countries has been positive since the turn of the millennium and that with non-CIS countries slightly positive since 2008 (Belstat 2013). Official discussions on migration issues in Belarus are rare and often superficial, and research in this field has been fragmentary and hampered by methodological errors. Zagorec and Zagorec (2011: 74), for example, have recently pointed out erroneous calculations in census statistics and shown that outmigration is a real problem for Belarus; in reality, the country has had a negative migratory balance since 1989. This is particularly true for Belarus's balance with the Russian Federation (Zagorec 2012: 97). However, these corrections are not reflected in the data presented on the Belarusian statistical office's (Belstat) official website.[6]

Belarus's official position on its relations with the European Union and on the Eastern Partnership can be found in the declarations made by President Lukashenko, who sees the EU as one vector of Belarusians interests that must be developed to balance the second vector, represented by the Russian Federation and the CIS. Various articles published in the media confirm a focus on security issues (BelaPAN 2012b; Korovenkova 2013a). Lukashenko has insisted that the EU has to take a step forward if it wants to continue cooperation with Belarus.[7] Indeed, in its relations with the EU, Belarus has lived through several crises that have found an echo in the national media (BelaPAN 2012b), resulting in the common description of the country's foreign policy as one of 'political isolation' (Yeliseyev 2012: 1). Thus, the agreement between Belarus and Poland on local cross-border movements has not entered into force, a failure attributed by the Belarusian Foreign Ministry to Poland's hostile attitude towards Belarus (Korsak 2013). Several independent experts have attempted to explain Belarus's contradictory foreign policy and made recommendations on how it could be improved (see Bosse and Korosteleva-Polglase 2009 and Lavenex 2008).

More specifically, Lukashenko has explained that migration to Russia is 'not a big problem' as both states are part of the Union State, although it has in fact increased during the recent deep economic crisis.[8] Overall, he considers migration policy an internal issue and has rejected any interference by the European Union. He has emphasised that the country will protect the stability of its borders and control migration on the basis of its own laws. Russian experts have, however, warned that Belarus's demographic decline is being aggravated by growing outmigration and could lead to political and social instability (e.g. Suzdal'tsev 2013).

In Belarus–EU relations, as in the relations of the EU with other EaP states, migration and border management play a large role (see Freyburg *et al.* 2011). The EU's approach to these relations has been to make the signing of a readmission agreement a condition for easing the present strict visa regime applying to Belarusian citizens (Yeliseyev 2012: 2). It prioritises the EU's security interests, whereas the Belarusian regime prefers to focus its efforts on ensuring secure borders in line with the financial support provided by the EU for this task (Korovenkova 2012). Only after the 2013 EaP Summit in Vilnius did both sides appear to reach an agreement on how to solve these contentious issues in the near future.

Migration in Belarus

According to the National Programme on the Demographic Security of the Republic of Belarus (Government of Belarus 2011), migration issues are closely connected to the employment situation, national security and demographic challenges. In addition to outmigration, Belarus is suffering from a declining birth rate and an ageing population, meaning that the demand for labour exceeds the supply, thus endangering economic growth. Like Russia, Belarus has experienced a significant demographic decline, which started in 1994 (Zagorec 2012: 94). In 2012 Belarus had a population of 9,465,000, down from 10,189,000 in 1990 – a net loss of 724,000 (Belstat 2012). At the same time, there is little justification for hope that the losses due to natural demographic factors and emigration will be compensated by attracting immigrants. Experts have calculated that even an annual positive net migratory balance of 50,000 would be insufficient to stabilise the country's population (Shakhot'ko 2009).

In the early 1990s, 75 per cent of Belarus's Jews left the country (Belstat 1999), mainly for the United States and Israel. During roughly the same period, thousands of ethnic Belarusians returned from other parts of the former Soviet Union, together with others, of various ethnic origins, fleeing violent conflicts. At the time, Belarus welcomed any former Soviet citizen who wished to apply for permanent residence. However, recent research (Zagorec and Zagorec 2011: 73) has revealed that Belarus had an overall negative migratory balance of 131,500 for the period 1989–2010 and a consistently negative balance since 1994. A characteristic feature of migration processes in the 2000s was, indeed, the gradual decrease of the positive net migration balance with other CIS countries, which reached insignificant values. An earlier fluctuating, but overall negative migratory balance with non-CIS countries finally turned positive in 2008, but net migration gains have remained very modest. Several surveys conducted to measure the population's emigration mood elicited positive responses from 10 to 15 per cent of respondents, a share not considered critical, but the percentage is double among those belonging to 'risk' categories, such as well-educated youth, young scholars and qualified specialists (Artyukhin, Dmitruk and Yevelkin 2008: 5; Zhakevich 2008: 88). According to another survey, 35 per cent of respondents expressed their desire for emigration, among them many people with a high level of human capital (BelaPAN 2013d), while an IISEPS survey from March 2013 reported that 34 per cent of respondents had worked abroad repeatedly and 15 per cent at least once (IISEPS 2013a).

According to experts who rely on data collection methods different from those employed by official bodies, recent negative economic trends have led to an increase in the number of labour migrants. While the official statistical office has registered 9,297 immigrants in 2011 and 8,378 in 2012 (Belstat 2012 and 2013), independent experts have indicated a steady growth of emigrants over the last years (Luchenok 2012; Yeliseyev 2013a). Since there exist no common statistics for the Union State of Russia–Belarus, Belarusian official data only reflect a small part of overall labour migration. Experts from the Eurasian Development Bank have produced estimates of 78,451 to 170,920 migrants (Eurasian Development Bank 2012: 16). Some Belarusian experts (e.g. Luchenok and Kolesnikova 2011) have arrived at similar results on the basis of data published by the World Bank (2012) and calculated that the remittances Belarusian migrants sent home in 2010 amounted to almost 2 per cent of the country's GDP, or 2.6 per cent of its gross external debt, and thus represented a significant contribution to the national economy. To sum up, the growth of labour emigration and the resulting cash flows can be considered typical features of contemporary migration in Belarus, just as in several other post-Soviet countries such as Armenia and Moldova.

Luchenok and Kolesnikova (2011) have shown that among those leaving Belarus, highly educated professionals account for a large share: doctors (12 per cent), engineers (10 per cent) and biologists (7 per cent). At the same time, almost 30 per cent of migrants from Belarus do not have any significant qualifications, their main motivation being higher wage-levels abroad. Belarus itself has been attracting only less skilled labour migrants from Moldova, Kyrgyzstan, Tajikistan and Ukraine. The brain drain from the country has been aggravated as a result of the currency crisis (2009–2011) and has become a prominent feature of current migration processes (Andreeva 2012).

Major countries of destination

Belarusian emigrants move in three directions: Russia, the EU and the United States, each destination linked to specific goals. Generally speaking, Belarusians leave for the United States to apply for permanent residence there, depart to EU countries because these offer better living standards and move to the Russian Federation simply because incomes are higher there (Shymanovich and Chubrik 2013: 7). In addition to earlier patterns of migration (relying on family networks and undertaken with the aim to obtain any, even unqualified, work abroad), new ones have appeared, such as the exodus of IT specialists from Belarus. Around 80 per cent of labour migrants work in four neighbouring countries: Russia, Poland, Ukraine and Lithuania (IISEPS 2013c), 60 per cent of them in Russia.

Russia as a major country of destination for Belarusian labour migrants

Most migrants leave Belarus for the countries of the former Soviet space, mainly in search of temporary employment, but also sometimes to take up permanent residence. Russia is the most attractive country in this respect. It is easy to find employment there and wages are higher. There are no legal restrictions, as Belarusians, thanks to the Union, need apply neither for a visa, nor for a work permit and can get registered easily. Moreover, both countries have a similar language and culture as well as a common history.

During the last decade, and especially in 2011–2013, Russia has become even more attractive because of decreasing incomes and living standards in Belarus. A recent trend has been observed according to which well-educated Belarusians (e.g. doctors, managers, scholars) move to Russia permanently. Extrapolating from current economic, political and migration processes, some scholars foresee that Russia will soon be the only major destination for Belarusian migrants (Ambrazhevich 2012: 44). Many labour migrants from Belarus are now working in the construction, agricultural and oil-industry sectors in Russia, staying there for periods ranging from several months to several years (Morgunova 2010: 110) and only returning home during holidays. This pattern benefits both Russia and Belarus: the former, because it helps to cope with labour shortages, and the latter, because it lowers the unemployment rate, improves the balance of payments through remittances and contributes to higher living standards, at least for migrants' families.

It is important to note that labour migration is attractive not only for young and well-educated people but also for Belarusians in their thirties and forties (IISEPS 2013b). Belarusians often leave the country to take up temporary employment in Russia if their professional qualifications are needed there. As a result, Belarus, with its state-dominated model of a rather egalitarian society, risks losing out to Russia with its market-oriented economy. Indeed, many well-qualified Belarusians would prefer more competitive working conditions with higher salaries in Russia to the country's unreformed economy that ensures only modest wages (BelTA 2011).

Not only are Belarusian labour migrants well-trained and familiar with the Russian language and culture, they also rarely move their families to Russia and therefore do not risk becoming a social burden on their employers or the local authorities at their place of residence. The Russian Federation in turn welcomes Belarusian workers and students as part of its policy of attracting Russian-speaking migrants from within the CIS.[9] For Belarus, this means the loss of skilled labour and a strong risk that these well-qualified workers and professionals will never return home. At the same time, the Russian Federation has consistently extended economic assistance to the Belarusian state in the form of access to cheap raw materials, without which the national economy would not have been able to survive. This has, however, created a dependence that discourages economic reforms and leaves few prospects for modernising the country and thus increasing the living standards of its citizens.

Most skilled migrants migrating to Russia come from Minsk, since this urbanised population is more attracted by good pay and a better quality of life. Young adults (18 to 30 years of age), and especially university graduates, are the ones most interested in emigration, whereas Belarusians with low incomes tend to rely more on national programmes of social welfare. Survey data have shown that the most able-bodied and professionally successful workers leave Belarus more often than less qualified people (Artyukhin, Dmitruk and Yevelkin 2008: 125).

Indeed, the educational level and professional qualification of migrants moving to Russia are higher than the average levels of Belarus's working population and immigrants. Some experts have calculated that 50 to 60 per cent of emigrants have completed or at least received some form of higher education, while almost 30 per cent of immigrants in Belarus are low-skilled workers (Luchenok and Kolesnikova 2011). IISEPS has conducted a survey in which young people were asked whether they thought it possible to have a successful career in contemporary Belarus. Only 46 per cent gave a positive answer, whereas 45 per cent answered in the negative and 9 per cent were uncertain (IISEPS 2012). Although academics overall rarely emigrate, it is the most productive young scholars who are leaving the country to pursue their studies or to accept temporary work contracts, often with the intention of not returning home (Andreeva 2012).

Thanks to the Common Economic Space in force since 2012, Belarusians can easily find legal employment in Russia and Kazakhstan, which along with Ukraine are the major migration target countries for Belarusians within the CIS. The Customs Union has led to a convergence of prices, with salaries in Belarus not keeping pace. High levels of inflation and a weak currency, together with legislation that promotes labour mobility within the Customs Union, are acting as incentives to leave for Russia temporarily or permanently. The Russian Federation has thus implemented a highly successful strategy for attracting labour from neighbouring countries.

The EU as a destination for migrants: specific features

Labour migration from Belarus to the European Union follows a well-known pattern of successive migratory waves. The most attractive destinations are the old member states, such as Germany (Artyukhin 2012; IISEPS 2008 and 2013b). However, these core countries are more open to citizens of other EU countries. As soon as these citizens leave their native states, people from non-EU neighbouring states are ready to replace those who have found a job in Germany, France or the United Kingdom. Belarus also fits this pattern, although the number of migrants moving to the EU is much smaller than those leaving for Russia. Officially, emigration to non-CIS states only amounts to 10–15 per cent of Belarus's migration flows. Belarusian migration to neighbouring EU countries has, thus, a regional character and is increasing. In 2011, the share of EU visas issued to Belarusian citizens (61 per cent) was higher than those issued to citizens from any other CIS country, including Russia (Yeliseyev 2012: 10), even if not all of them involved labour migration.

Poland has been the first destination for migrants. In 2011, almost every fifth visa (55,200 out of 299,300) issued by the Polish consulates in Belarus was a National Long-Stay Visa (Yeliseyev 2012: 9). This long-term visa is most often granted to those studying or working in Poland or who, for other reasons, have a residence permit (a so-called 'Polish Card'). Belarusians usually prefer Poland if they wish to obtain a long-term labour contract: over 90 per cent of all long-term visas issued by EU countries to Belarusians in 2011 came from Polish consulates. The reasons for this popularity are economic and cultural, as many Belarusians are able to understand Polish (a closely related language).

Generally, migrants to Poland can be divided into two categories. The first consists of well-educated professionals (e.g. university professors, athletic instructors and doctors), for whom there is a strong demand as they replace Polish professionals who have migrated further west. During the term of their employment, these Belarusians either reside permanently in Poland or regularly spend there one or two weeks per month, sometimes keeping their job in Belarus and using their employment in Poland as a source of additional income. The second category includes skilled workers with a work visa (e.g. lorry drivers[10]). They live in Poland for months but regularly visit their home in Belarus.

Lithuania is the second destination and also the second EU country issuing the greatest number of visas to Belarusians: 144,300 in 2011, 34 per cent of them multiple-entry visas (Yeliseyev 2012: 7). The most important category of migrants is composed of university professors and well-educated young scholars who have moved permanently to Vilnius or regularly visit the city if they are employed by the European Humanities University, a Belarusian university-in-exile. Hundreds of students from Belarus have taken up permanent residence in Vilnius or commute there every weekend to pursue their studies; after graduation, only half of them return to Belarus. Finally, some journalists and politicians of the opposition have moved their offices to Vilnius and commute regularly between the city and Belarus.

Germany occupies a particular place in the dreams of those Belarusians who think of leaving the country: it is the most desirable country for permanent relocation. According to two IISEPS surveys, 16 per cent out of a total of 45 per cent of Belarusians wishing to emigrate selected Germany as their preferred destination (March 2011), while two years later, in March 2013, 11 per cent out of a total of 40 per cent expressed the same desire (IISEPS 2013c). Official statistics indicate that 28 per cent of all Belarusians emigrating to a non-CIS country settled in Germany, followed by other EU countries (Italy, the Czech Republic) and non-EU countries (United States, Israel) (Belstat 2011: 43).

Female migration to the European Union along the lines of that practiced by Moldovan women for many years (see the chapter by Olga Davydova-Minguet *et al.* in this volume) is a more recent phenomenon. Over the last decade the number of women moving abroad has increased and almost every second emigrant to a non-CIS state is female (Belstat 2011: 43). The major destinations are Germany, Italy and Lithuania. In many cases women find employment in the services sector, while others move abroad to marry (Titarenko 2012: 52).

Regardless of the Blue Card programme and other opportunities for potential migrants, finding a job in an EU country is not easy, except for academic scholars and IT specialists who succeed in obtaining temporary contracts and thus manage to spend many years abroad. The ongoing financial and economic crisis in the EU has made migration even more difficult, although the above-mentioned professionals have been less affected by it. Experts do not expect an increase in labour migration to the EU even after the signing of a visa simplification agreement (Yeliseyev 2013b). For the time being, the number of Belarusians registered in the EU is several times lower than that for Moldovan or Ukrainian citizens. The impact of this migration is generally the same as that to Russia, although on a much reduced scale.

Belarus's migration policy and its relation to EU Neighbourhood policies

Statistical data show that immigrants in Belarus have lower average levels of education and professional qualifications than Belarusian citizens and tend to be older. It is therefore not surprising that the official migration policy of Belarus as stated, for example, in the National Programme on Demographic Security (Government of Belarus 2011), aims to attract higher-skilled labour in the long run to cope with demographic deficits and labour shortages that risk compromising the country's future economic and social development. Among the measures mooted are facilities for foreigners who have successfully completed their studies in Belarus to stay on and work in Belarus, as well as a plan to promote the return of Belarusian scientists from abroad in order to stimulate innovation, although financial support is rather limited compared to that offered in Russia (Artyukhin 2012; BelaPAN 2012a). Other measures envisaged to stimulate economic development include reforms of the labour market in view of changing the employment structure and increasing labour productivity. However, these are mostly blueprints that are unlikely to be implemented soon without market reforms.

Russia's similar policy to attract Russian-speaking migrants from other CIS countries, its Strategy 2020, seems to be much more efficient. In Belarus there are no special instruments for the integration of Russian migrants in Belarusian society, whereas Belarusian workers and students are welcome in Russia. Several Russian universities offer, for example, grants to students from Belarus.

The second focus of Belarus's migration policy is national security and in particular the control and regulation of unwanted migrants who often use Belarus as a transit country to enter the European Union. After finally signing the first three agreements on readmission in 2013, there is a realistic expectation to negotiate and sign a similar agreement with the EU.[11] While, in 2011, Belarusian authorities did not want to discuss readmission together with visa simplification issues, stressing that this only served the EU's interests (BelaPAN 2011), prospects for successful negotiations have improved since (Korovenkova 2013b). However, this does not mean that the Belarusian regime is ready to accept other EU policy interests (such as human rights) that were considered by the Union a precondition for further talks on readmission and visas. Indeed, the EU's policy of linkages and conditionality were among the key obstacles to successful negotiations as the Belarusian regime rejects any interference in this sphere.

Nor should Russia's role be forgotten in this context. As already explained above, Belarus has binding obligations as a member of the Union State. In addition, most third-country nationals that would be subject to a read-mission agreement with the EU enter Belarus from Russia. Only now, after readmission agreements have been signed, is there a legal basis for returning unwanted migrants to Russia. Obviously, Russia's influence in and ties with Belarus are much stronger than the EU's influence. Closer integration with the European Union is not an incentive as Belarus has shown little interest in it. To sum up, the impasse is due to 'the very limited leverage of the EU over the country' (Bosse and Korosteleva-Polglase 2009: 143; see also Scott's and Marin's contributions in this volume).

The EU policy of 'external governance' does not always result in the sub-ordination of the other state; it may even provoke rejection (Fedorov 2013). Building a new security system should involve all partners in a way that takes into account their interests, even if these do not coincide with those of a more powerful partner. The case of Belarus illustrates the failure of the EU's policy to impose its rules and values beyond its borders on a supposedly weaker neighbour. For the promotion of goals such as democratisation, 'a far deeper understanding of autocratic narratives is needed, associated with a much closer look at societal norms and values, as well as an individual country's geopolitical resources and strategies' (Korosteleva 2012: 37).

Earlier expectations that the European Neighbourhood Policy (ENP) could help establish a new form of regionalism and increase mutual interdependence of countries in this region have not materialised. In practical terms, there has been no promotion of regionalism in Belarus through the ENP, just as there has been no visible progress on migration issues and, although this is a shared concern, no significant financial contribution from the EU to ensure border security (see the contribution by Scott in this volume). On migration issues in particular, both the EU and Belarus have had their actions limited by each other, but still have tried to pursue their own interests without a willingness to compromise. A realistic model of EU–Belarus relations in this field ought to be based on the understanding of mutual interdependence and geopolitical interests within the existing geopolitical context. This might bring about a change in mutual attitudes, taking into account the interests of regional cooperation. As an assessment of the results of cooperation between the EU and other neighbouring countries shows (Freyburg *et al.* 2011: 1026), inter-dependence and different types of cooperation are good instruments to promote democracy and improve the relationship between states.

There is no consensus among EU officials on how to break the deadlock. EU representatives continue talks with Belarusian officials and intend to develop these contacts further (Council of the European Union 2013; see also BelaPAN 2013b). At the same time the EU does not forget about democratic values as preconditions for a real dialogue. Both parties need to make concessions to meet the challenge of reconceptualising the social–political space under new geopolitical conditions that currently are not favourable for the EU. It seems that the Arab Spring has proved that the EU's future can hardly be bright if it is surrounded by poor and undemocratic states. At present, Belarus is one of these. Fears have been expressed that:

> The collapse of the existing social protection could transform Belarus into (something that resembles) a Latin-American state of the 70s or 80s of the twentieth century. The development in such a scenario would lead to an increase in social stratification and to the transformation of the present system of government into a completely repressive regime.
>
> (Belarus Security Blog 2012: 1–2)

Recognition by the EU that its instruments of external governance do not work well in the case of Belarus might be the first step towards a reformulation of EU policies towards Belarus that should be based, as two scholars have stated, on 'feasible conditionality criteria, enhanced support for the population and pragmatic partnership' (Bosse and Korosteleva-Polglase 2009: 159). Of course, these are only general principles for improving EU–Belarus relations. But their application could also contribute to progress on migration issues and would open new horizons for cooperation in this field. Visa facilitation, for example, could create the necessary dynamics for increased mobility, such as the possibility of temporary labour contracts for migrants from CIS countries in the European Union. Belarus and the EU could also cooperate on offering financial support (reintegration grants) to qualified migrants who wish to return to Belarus. Increasing the level of EU investments in Belarus might help create new attractive jobs there, while Belarus could invest in the EU and encourage Belarusian migrants to participate in such ventures. These are just some examples of what could be done if the starting point for the EU–Belarus dialogue were common practical interests on which it is possible to build regional stability, safe borders and common migration policies. Building bridges is more productive than creating new divisions within Europe.

Conclusions

The aim of this chapter has been to outline recent developments in Belarusian migration processes through the political framing of borders and migration policies in the post-Soviet space. Usually, the discussion of these issues is based on the EU's approach to them and does not take into account the role of the Union State of Belarus and Russia and the Customs Union, a gap filled here.

It has been shown that the main features of migration processes in Belarus do not differ significantly from those in neighbouring post-Soviet countries.

However, the scale of migration is at present substantially limited by laws and regulations in Belarus and by the state of EU–Belarus relations. In addition, regional post-Soviet integration processes promoted by Russia have created favourable conditions for attracting new migrants from Belarus to Russia.

Russia is currently the major destination for Belarusian labour migrants, both qualified and unqualified. The flow of qualified Belarusian professionals to Russia has intensified as a result of the 2011 financial crisis in Belarus. In 2012, the Union State was reinforced by the creation of the Customs Union of Russia, Belarus and Kazakhstan, and a new law on migration in Russia has further simplified immigration procedures there. However, the number of migrants from Belarus is not the main issue. Keeping Belarus as a partner is important for Russia, since Russia is striving to regain its status as a regional integration centre (Suzdal'tsev 2013).

The groups most likely to migrate to the EU are university graduates, young scholars, IT specialists and qualified workers. However, it is border security that remains the most substantial driving force stimulating cooperation between Belarus and the EU, despite the lack of a legal framework for such cooperation and recurrent political disagreements. While the interest of the EU lies in securing its borders and promoting smooth mechanisms of readmission for third-country citizens entering its territory from Belarus, the establishment of such a mechanism is unlikely before a readmission agreement will have been signed between Russia and Belarus.

It is expected that Belarus will face increased outmigration in the coming years (Suzdal'tsev 2013). Thus, Belarusian migration policies will likely constrain emigration. Although a growth in immigration is a declared goal, there are no significant financial incentives to attract the targeted groups.

As far as visa issues are concerned, the potential flow of migrants from Belarus to the EU is limited by current visa procedures and the frozen ratification of a cooperation agreement. Recently the Belarusian regime has agreed to negotiate such agreements; however, it may take a couple of years before their signing and implementation. Even then, this agreement will not really simplify the visa regime for all Belarusians (Yeliseyev 2013b). Therefore, it might be helpful for the Belarusian civil society if the EU would create more instruments and strategies within the EaP that promote contacts with ordinary citizens and focus rather more on opportunities for people-to-people communication than on contacts with the Belarusian authorities.

Notes

1 More particularly, the chapter uses the following data: (a) official Belarusian statistics (although they appear to contain errors and diverge from those produced by the Russian Federation and the World Bank); (b) data published within the framework of various research projects in the fields of migration and EU–Belarus relations, conducted by independent analysts and research centres such as the Belarusian Institute for Strategic Studies (BISS), the IPM Research Centre of the Office for a Democratic Belarus in Brussels and the Independent Institute of Socio-Economic

and Political Studies (IISEPS), a think tank currently operating in Lithuania after its move from Belarus; (c) information published by two major Belarusian news agencies, including the state agency BelTA, that publishes official statements, and the privately run BelaPAN, where independent analysts and experts express their opinions. Both agencies share a website (www.naviny.by) whose contents have been carefully monitored over the past years to observe the dynamics of Belarus-related migration processes. (d) information published by Russian media, as well as by international and regional organisations, namely the World Bank and the Eurasian Development Bank (St Petersburg, Russia).

2 See the Russian–Belarusian agreement on providing equal rights for citizens on the territory of both states, signed in 1996. No official statistical data on the number of migrants or their profiles are available, which makes it difficult to assess the impact on the labour market and the Belarusian economy (Supronovich 2012: 12).

3 See, for example, the agreements on the legal status of migrant workers and their family members and on combating illegal migration, signed on 19 November 2010.

4 See 'Novosti: v 2014 godu v Belorussii budet razvernuta rossiyskaia voennaia baza'. Online. Available at: www.regnum.ru (last accessed 10 December 2013); and 'Putin: Rossiia predostavit Belorussii zaem do $2 milliardov v 2014 godu'. Online. Available at: http://itar-tass.com/ekonomika/857721 (last accessed 26 December 2013). See also Klaskovskiĭ (2013a).

5 'Rossiia i Belorussiia soglasovali ob'em postavok nefti na 2014 god'. Online. Available at: www.vedomosti.ru/politics/news/20589091 (last accessed 23 December 2014).

6 See http://belstat.gov.by/home/ru/indicators/population.php (last accessed 25 June 2013).

7 See his statements during a press conference held on 15 January 2013. Online. Available at: www.sb.by/post/142276 (last accessed 16 January 2013).

8 See note above.

9 See the Strategy 2020 programme and the new Concept of State Migration Policy.

10 Belarusian drivers are employed at lower wages by Polish companies to drive lorries from Poland to Belarus, Russia and Ukraine, because they usually speak both Polish and Russian and do not need a visa to enter these countries.

11 The first agreement was signed in March 2013 with Turkey (BelaPAN 2013c), followed by others with Kazakhstan and with the Russian Federation, signed respectively on 4 October and on 15 November 2013 (BelTA 2013).

11 What kind of choice?

Understanding migration in Tajikistan

Paul Fryer, Joni Virkkunen and
Furugzod Usmonov

During the two decades that have followed the collapse of the Soviet Union, the phenomenon of international labour migration by citizens of Central Asian states to the Russian Federation has been well documented and researched (see, among others, Handå Myhre 2012; Migration Policy Centre 2013). Governments in the region not only acknowledge and accept this migration but, arguably, even encourage it as a strategy to increase their citizens' incomes and, thus, ensure domestic social and political stability. Despite the economic benefits that remittances have brought to individuals and families, neither the concerned states nor local communities, however, have been able to take full advantage of them to effectively promote long-term economic development. The countries in question remain poorly developed and economically weak, and poverty-related social problems are still common.

This chapter will discuss migration as a choice. Despite often difficult working and living conditions in the Russian Federation and increasingly acknowledged social problems in families and local communities back home that accompany migration, millions of Central Asian citizens migrate to the Russian Federation every year. One might easily think of migration as the only choice open to labour migrants and their families who are trying to cope with poverty. Simultaneously, one might question to what extent the 'export of labour' (FIDH and Memorial 2011) has been a conscious choice made by states eager to develop migration into a branch of the national economy that provides them and their citizens with much-needed employment, additional income and stability. But to what extent can this migration really be attributed to decisions made by such actors as the labour migrants, their families or the sending states? In the following, the popularity of international labour migration, through both formal and informal channels, among Tajikistani[1] citizens will be discussed against the background of the country's socio-economic and political situation.

The research presented here will in particular highlight the situation in the northern Sughd province and the Ferghana Valley, which are characterised by very high rates of migration, a demographic explosion and a critical shortage of land for housing and agriculture. After a short general discussion of migration and of the history of Tajikistani migration, this chapter will study the role of

DOI: 10.4324/9781315858036-15

various formal and informal institutions involved in the process of migration and the choices that lead to it. Empirical research was conducted over a period of three years and included structured and semi-structured interviews with officials, experts, migrants and members of their families, as well as a small pilot questionnaire disseminated in Sughd by students of Tajikistan's National University.

Migration and the choice to migrate as a global phenomenon

While migration has existed throughout world history, it has perhaps been studied most during the latter part of the twentieth century, when it was often associated with the end of the Cold War, the acceleration of globalisation trends and notions of disappearing borders (Hoerder 2002). The reasons people migrate are manifold, and types of migrants are no less diverse. It is well known that migration can be either voluntary or forced, and the reasons for moving to another country may involve a number of different economic, job-related, family-oriented, educational and other personal motives (see, among others, Brettell and Hollifield 2007). Classical economic theory treats migration as a result of rational personal choices, where individuals are making decisions to move based upon various 'push' and 'pull' factors, such as unemployment, poverty and low wage-levels at home, on the one hand, and better employment opportunities abroad, higher income or the possibility to send money back home.

Understandings of the causes of migration that rely on models of rational choice often result in the assumption that individual migrants are able to exercise their own free will in making the decision to stay at home or to leave for work elsewhere. In Central Asia, where the majority of a largely rural population lives in extreme poverty on only a few euros a day (see World Bank 2014), migration appears to offer good opportunities to individuals and families in search of sources of additional and stable income. Russia's growing economy, its very dynamic labour market and its good educational environment make the country an extremely attractive destination for these migrants.

There are a great number of institutions – both formal and informal and at various levels (ranging from international organisations and national governments to private employment agencies and social organisations such as the family) – that may play a role in prompting and facilitating or, on the contrary, preventing migratory movements. Countries such as the United States, Switzerland, the United Kingdom and the Russian Federation have accepted huge numbers of labour migrants to fuel economic development while at the same time aiming to control and limit their numbers in reaction to political and public pressure. Whereas the European Union has regularly been criticised for strict migration and refugee policies turning it into 'Fortress Europe' (Amnesty International 2014), the Russian Federation teeters between an extremely liberal visa and migration policy for citizens of other former Soviet republics and increasing restrictions on migration since the rise of domestic nationalist and xenophobic sentiments.

In this international context, governments in countries whose economy heavily relies on remittances from migrant labourers abroad, have not remained passive bystanders. The Philippines and Mexico, for example, have implemented pro-active policies designed to support their citizens who work abroad (Calzado 2007; de Haas 2005). The Organisation for Security and Cooperation in Europe (OSCE), the International Organisation for Migration (IOM) and the International Labour Organisation (ILO) frequently refer to the Philippines as an example for 'best practices' in this field, because its government combines strict control over state and private employment agencies, compulsory information seminars for migrants and a strong network of officials responsible for labour questions posted to the country's diplomatic missions (Calzado 2007; FIDH and Memorial 2011). The Philippine government has, indeed, adopted a three-fold approach to labour migration, aimed at ensuring the welfare of the workers themselves, their families and society as a whole (Calzado 2007: 1). This includes licensing and regulating employment agencies, training would-be migrants in necessary skills, providing documentation, safeguarding family support and offering reintegration programmes to returnees. The country also engages with host countries on a bilateral basis to ensure legal migration through so-called 'migration partnerships', thus minimising risks to both migrants and hosts (Groff 2005). The rationale behind such policies is clear, as the link between migration and development is well-documented (Calzado 2007; de Haas 2005; Levitt and Nyberg-Sørensen 2004). Remittances form an important part of the national GDP for countries of origin, and it is in the latter's interest to guarantee a safe and positive migration experience abroad for their citizens.

Recently, Central Asian governments, including Tajikistan, have more particularly looked to the Philippines for a model of efficient migration management and profit maximisation for the home country. This entails increased multi- and bilateral cooperation on migration (ratification of ILO conventions, CIS-level agreements on labour migration and social protection for migrant workers and their families, combating illegal migration etc.) and changes in the domestic legislation to define the rights and responsibilities of labour migrants (see FIDH and Memorial 2011).

On a theoretical level, the new institutionalist approach developed by sociologists and political scientists offers keys to understand this situation by identifying the constitutive role of culturally legitimate models of organisation and action in societies or, more specifically, formal and informal institutions and the way that these interact in and influence society and individuals' actions and decisions (see, for example, Clemens and Cook 1999; Powell 2007). Institutions are often viewed as reliable and durable and, therefore, mostly unchallenged, as they are seen as safeguarding stability (Clemens and Cook 1999). Moreover, any actions or words by such institutions, whether formal or informal, affect the actions of individuals. This is related to the theory of rational choice but differs from it in that individuals are understood to act because they can conceive of no other action rather than from a belief in making the best choice. Here, it is argued that Tajikistani labour migrants take their cue from surrounding institutions and see migration to Russia as the only path ahead.

A brief outline of Tajik labour migration

Tajikistan has a large labour migrant community abroad, with Russia reportedly hosting 97 per cent of all migrants (Olimova 2013: 66). Most observers suggest that the initial push towards migration has its origins in the Tajikistani civil war, which between 1992 and 1997 killed some 100,000 people and displaced 1.2 million inhabitants. Russians, other minorities and the well-educated intelligentsia (medical doctors, industrial and construction engineers, and other professionals) were the first to leave the country (see, among others, Hohmann 2013).

This brutal conflict created thousands of political and other refugees and internally displaced persons, but even others not fearing for their lives made the decision to leave for better prospects elsewhere, mainly to Russia. This was recognised during the later peace negotiations, whose participants were well aware that the new government had to improve economic conditions at home if it wanted its citizens to return (Usmonov 2001: 42). However, this task was hampered by the previous destruction of the country's small-scale industry and of critical infrastructure as well as a ravaged public sector, resulting in an economic vulnerability that was beyond the post-war regime's capabilities and continues to be the cause of high unemployment and extremely low wage and income levels.

As the country returned to peace, the scope of migration increased rapidly in the face of extreme poverty and the lack of employment and other income-generating activities, and migration became a major feature of the normalisation process (Ryazantsev and Horie 2011). By the end of the 1990s the less-educated rural population, too, began to move to Russia, mainly to work in services, the construction industry and agriculture (Hohmann 2013: 159). Despite low salaries and bad working conditions, Russia has become a window of opportunity for migrants and their families in search of additional income and better prospects for the future.

Today, the socio-demographic profile of Tajikistani migrants is well-established (Florinskaya 2013; Olimova 2010, 2013; Olimova and Bosc 2003; Ryazantsev 2014). Approximately three out of four migrants come from rural areas, and 85 per cent of all migrants are male. About half of all migrants are, somewhat vaguely, classified as 'poor'. In recent years, female migration has been a growing phenomenon, though it should be noted that the social conservatism of Tajikistani society means that the majority of them are following husbands or other family members. Migration is largely seasonal: 73 per cent of migrant workers leave Tajikistan in Spring and return in late Autumn, when winter sets in, which reflects the nature of the activities that Tajik migrants engage in abroad. Over 50 per cent of Tajik migrants work in construction – a sector requiring largely unskilled workers, reflecting the nature of the migrant pool – while trade and agriculture account for most of the remaining employment. Younger age cohorts predominate: 46 per cent are under the age of 30, 31 per cent are aged 30 to 39, while 24 per cent are 40 years or older. These figures are hardly surprising in face of the high level of youth unemployment and reflect the need of many young men to earn money abroad in order to be able to marry (Olimova and Bosc 2003). In terms of skill and education levels, most Tajikistani labour migrants have started or completed their secondary education (65 per cent), while only 30 per cent have specific professional skills or have received higher education. More generally, Olimova (2010: 185) has noted a deterioration in Tajikistan's human capital levels, stressing that the 'falling quality of education is especially noticeable for groups such as rural residents, the poorer sectors and girls', and that this constitutes a major factor in migration processes.

Migration from the Central Asian states to the Russian Federation is a relatively recent phenomenon. In Soviet times, Tajikistanis and other Central Asians rarely migrated to other parts of the Union, despite attempts by the authorities to entice surplus labour from the region to areas with a high labour demand in the Russian heartland. However, migration has expanded rapidly, especially since the late 1990s, with some estimates suggesting that over one million Tajikistanis and similar numbers of Kyrgyzstanis and Uzbekistanis are working in Russia at any given time (Marat 2009).

In the case of Tajikistan, some harsh demographic facts explain the present situation. In the years since independence (1991–2010), the population of the country has increased by almost 35 per cent, growing at a rate of 1.79 per cent annually, thanks to a fertility rate of 2.8 children per woman. Over half the population is under the age of 24. As a result, the country's labour force has grown by more than 70 per cent since independence, an evolution not matched by local employment opportunities. The average annual growth of the working-age population (3.9 per cent) is seven times higher than that of the employment rate (0.56 per cent), although these official figures do not reflect the true situation in the country, where many more individuals see few prospects for employment at home and prefer to work abroad (Ashurov 2009; Indexmundi 2013).

In 2010, 1.2 million migrants were working in Russia 'officially', that is with a work permit, almost half of them from Central Asian states (see Table 11.1), though these figures do not tell the entire story. In fact, the majority of Central Asian migrants arrive in Russia thanks to informal personal networks, and this form of labour migration has been taking place largely outside the legal framework. Concretely, people make use of the visa-free regime that exists between Russia and other Commonwealth of Independent States (CIS) countries to enter the country, find employment and take up residence there, even though they could have legally obtained work and residence permits. In the currently very liberal and highly segmented Russian labour market, there is a strong demand for cheap foreign labour, and especially for unorganised

Table 11.1 Number of Central Asian migrants officially registered in Russia, 2010

	Number of migrants	Percentage of total migrant population
Uzbekistani	511,500	28
Tajikistani	268,600	15
Kyrgyzstani	117,700	5

Sources: Iontzev and Ivakhnyuk 2012: 10–11; Ryazantsev and Khorie 2011: 23–25.

labour migrants who lack the proper documentation. Tajik labour migrants in particular often engage in seasonal migration, leaving home in Spring to take up jobs in the construction or agricultural sectors and returning home in late Autumn when they are no longer needed (Kerr Chiovenda 2013). The true number of Central Asian labour migrants in Russia is therefore much higher than suggested by official figures and remains a source of continued speculation, where figures are regularly being manipulated by the authorities or public interest groups according to their needs. As Ryazantsev (2014: 22) has stated, a more accurate estimate of Tajikistani migrant workers in Russia would be 600,000 to 1 million, or 26 per cent of Tajikistan's economically active population.

Central Asian governments, while acknowledging that emigration is an issue in domestic politics, are unwilling to impose restrictions on it because their national economies depend on remittances and because they fear domestic instability, as they are unable to create sufficient employment opportunities at home. Ryazantsev (2014: 22) has estimated that remittances sent to Tajikistan amounted to USD2.1 million in 2010, a huge proportion of the country's GDP. Respondents to the above-mentioned questionnaire, administered in February 2011, often evoked seasonal labour migration to Russia as their main source of income, contributing some USD300–500 per month to the family budget. Despite being aware of the risks, Tajikistanis are not willing to stay at home where they face few economic prospects.

This raises a number of questions. Has migration to Russia become a 'natural choice' thanks to a familiarity with the Russian language, a shared Soviet history, and already existing strong networks in Russia? Or has the Tajikistani government actually made the choice to allow and even support migration as a form of industry that creates wealth for its citizens? Despite the fact that migration has numerous negative side effects on communities in Central Asia, such as a very high gender imbalance and various social problems, the ensuing employment and increase in family incomes have brought some level of social stability. Thus, the migration of less-educated young men, which became common in the early 2000s, has not only provided additional income but also relieved pressure on local labour markets, a potential source of dissatisfaction and social unrest. What follows is a discussion of different formal and informal institutions involved in migration and the way that they may have an impact in promoting or managing Tajikistani migration to Russia.

Formal channels and the choice of migration

With foreign labour migration playing such an important role in Tajikistani society since the end of the civil war, it is not surprising that the government has attempted to manage it through formal institutions, including state agencies, legislation and treaties with destination countries, with international organisations (IOM, ILO, EU etc.), banks and private employment agencies complementing state policies. Studying choice in migration against the background of formal institutions is a challenging enterprise. These organisations vary not only with regard to their – public or private – status but also according to their purpose, function and role. In this section, a brief outline of Tajikistan's formal institutions addressing migration is provided. This will be followed by a case study of the choices migrants face in this formal environment, where the focus will be on two employment agencies, one state-funded, the other private.

Despite indications that something needed to be done after the civil war, the state started to introduce legislation on migration only in 2000. This move was accompanied by the posting of Ministry of Labour representatives to five regions of the Russian Federation and the development of a network of employment agencies to help citizens find work abroad. The following year, the new Law on Migration was expanded to include regulation of foreign labour migration and this contributed to develop a migration policy that has ever since remained one of the state's priorities. In 2002 a state programme on foreign labour migration was adopted for the period 2003–2005, later followed by a second one for the years 2006–2009 (e.g. Ganguli 2009; Kuddosov 2010; Olimova 2013). Over the years, legislation has thus made it easier to send and receive remittances, in recognition of the importance these transfers have for migrants supporting their families back home.

After growing public concerns over problems experienced by migrants in Russia, the government was forced to act and, in 2004, signed a bilateral agreement with Russia with the aim of protecting labour migrants from violence, corruption and illegal business practices. In 2006, the responsibility for foreign labour migration was transferred from the Ministry of Labour to the Ministry of Internal Affairs, another indication that the state was paying increasing attention to the situation of its citizens working abroad. The Ministry of Internal Affairs began to assume a role in monitoring the activities of employment agencies involved in sending migrants abroad and, in 2010, discussions started to prepare a new law regulating private employment agencies. In 2011, the government moreover established an independent Migration Service to oversee its migration-related activities and, importantly, opened offices in Russia to act as contact points between state representatives and migrants.

The aim of these formal state initiatives was, as the well-known Tajik labour researcher Dzhamshed Kuddosov has noted, to create a legal framework that would facilitate the orderly and efficient organisation of foreign labour migration in response to the needs of the Russian labour market. This included the evaluation of migrants' professional qualifications and support for their training, as well as the regulation of employment agencies and organisations that acted as intermediaries between Russian employers and migrants. These efforts have, however, not gone uncriticised, because they were seen as insufficiently funded (Kuddosov 2010: 101–102). Others have questioned the qualifications of the appointed state authorities to organise 'civilised migration' (Ganguli 2009: 3).

Overall, the situation is unlikely to change in the near future, as both the government and the general public consider that any regulation should only make migration easier and less risky. There are, however critics, at home and abroad, who have suggested that the state, in spite of adopting regulatory measures, is actually encouraging migration, with negative effects on Tajikistani society (Interview with a politician from the opposition in Dushanbe, June 2010). More generally, the government has, over the last two decades, been criticised for not doing enough to prevent migration, or even addressing the issues that ensue from it. There have indeed been few job creation programmes, the education system is failing students, the social welfare system has remained weak, and corruption is still endemic.

These accusations have been strongly denied by representatives of the state. Moreover, in 2011, the government announced plans to create 250,000 new jobs to keep potential migrants in Tajikistan and has since claimed success, though critics have described these efforts as hollow and unrealistic in the country's current situation and as mere announcements to direct attention away from the state's failings (Atovulloev 2013; Khovar 2011; Salimov 2014).[2] Certainly, the official discourse has changed over the years, as the state has come to recognise problems related to migration and to acknowledge that proper and efficient management practices are required to keep migrants safe. But research conducted by the authors suggests that state institutions are, directly and indirectly, encouraging Tajikistanis to emigrate in search of work (see also Kerr Chiovenda 2013: 12–13; Ryazantsev 2014: 21). Indeed, it can be argued that the range of institutional measures adopted cannot but leave potential migrants under the impression that they have few other choices than working in the Russian Federation: licensing officially designated employment agencies, developing special educational and training programmes for migrants (such as Russian-language courses), providing migration-related services abroad in consulates and for the diaspora, the early adoption of a law that allows for dual Russian and Tajikistani citizenship and, more directly, the signing of bilateral agreements on labour migration, notably with Russia.

In February 2011, students of the Tajik National University in Dushanbe carried out a small survey in five border settlements in northern Sughd province. Its purpose was to gauge the influence of the nearby state borders on local social and economic life. Throughout the 41 semi-structured interviews conducted in either Tajik or Uzbek, inhabitants from the towns of Asht, Isfara, Istarafshan, Shaidon and Zafarobod consistently and strongly emphasised the lack of any support from the authorities to encourage people to remain and work in

Tajikistan, very much forcing them into labour migration. Respondents underlined the fact that it was not just the lack of local jobs but rather the range of employment opportunities and the better wages that attracted people to Russia. This has been confirmed by numerous other interviews as well as by statistical data showing that Tajikistan has the lowest average monthly salaries amongst the post-Soviet countries. By contrast, Russia has enjoyed strong economic growth and its GDP per capita has risen to USD14,037 in 2012, while Tajikistan's is only USD872 (World Bank 2013). In the early 2000s, many Tajikistanis were either unemployed or at most earned the local minimum wage of USD45 per month.

In addition to Russian migration policy, labour mobility between Central Asia and the Russian Federation has been the object of joint declarations by the Commonwealth of Independent States and is being regulated through various intergovernmental agreements, such as the 1992 Agreement on the Visa-Free Movement of Citizens of CIS Countries, the Guarantees of Rights to Citizens of CIS Member States in the Field of Retirement Benefits and the joint 2007 Tajik–Russian residence rights agreement for Tajik citizens in the Russian Federation (Ryazantsev 2014: 43–50). In addition, international organisations, such as the International Organisation for Migration (IOM), the International Labour Organisation (ILO), the United Nations Development Programme (UNDP), UN Women and the European Union, have made various contributions to certain fields of migration policy. They also have taken a very active role in assisting Central Asian states in developing, drafting and implementing policies of border and migration management, conflict prevention and management, community stabilisation, the prevention of trafficking and health.

The websites of any of the larger organisations active in Tajikistan (e.g. IOM and ILO) publish a multitude of studies that address workers' rights abroad or brochures and pamphlets that aim to educate international labour migrants and make them more aware of their situation. These organisations conduct studies and policy research, host conferences, seminars and round tables, fund studies and publications, campaigns and capacity-building training as well as set up various programmes in cooperation with foreign embassies and international organisations. However, ordinary citizens, and thus potential migrants, are hardly concerned by these 'high-level' activities and their message, that one might choose to stay at home, remains inaudible. Despite good intentions that inspire them and their great potential, these activities have been strongly criticised as inefficient.[3] The same applies to the EU's Global Approach to Migration and Mobility (GAMM) framework and its Regional Strategy Paper for Assistance in Central Asia.

According to Oleg Korneev (2013: 309, 317–318), the lack of a regionally initiated bottom-up approach constitutes a serious challenge for international 'governors of migration' who deal with migration processes that are multilateral, embedded and transregional. The various organisations are strongly competing with each other for donors and implementation partners, even though there is some policy co-ordination. Many critiques (e.g. Eisele 2012; Peyrouse 2014) argue that international organisations fail to take into account the complex nexus between migration and development and to make long-term commitments in the region. Most of their activities are based on short-term projects in capitals or regional centres, resulting in poor performance and frustration in other parts of the country where these initiatives are hardly known. Korneev (2013: 314) has critically commented that programmes such as the EU's Border Management Programme in Central Asia (BOMCA) appear to have significantly different goals from those proclaimed. In his view, the EU rather strives to broaden and strengthen its presence in the region than attempts to implement coherent and well-coordinated programmes with a real impact. Similarly, the United Nations Special Rapporteur on the human rights of migrants, François Crépeau, has recommended that the European Union move away from its discourse on security and border controls towards a concrete 'Migration and Mobility Partnership': 'A large majority of regional migration initiatives coming from the EU continue to be focused on issues of border control, and do not consider important issues such as the facilitation of regular migration channels' (OHCHR 2012).

With all those efforts being deployed by international organisations and state agencies to manage migration, do potential migrants make use of these formal channels? In Spring 2011, while government debated a new law on regulating private employment agencies, interviews were conducted with representatives of two such organisations to uncover their relationship with migrants. In Dushanbe a meeting at the local IOM offices offered some explanations why so few agencies were operational despite the state's support. One of the main reasons seems to be the legal uncertainty surrounding their work. Thus, agencies can be held responsible for migrants' behaviour once these arrive in Russia and potentially incur financial liabilities, especially if a migrant does not fulfil his or her contractual obligations with a Russian company or if a promised employment does not meet a migrant's expectations. These intermediaries are therefore strong advocates of a stable legal framework for their activities.

At one such agency, the Youth Labour Exchange operated by the Ministry of Youth, Sports and Tourism, the director explained how Tajikistani youth were recruited for various jobs in different countries and that it was the responsibility of his organisation to ensure that potential migrants were properly prepared for their future employment in order to maintain credibility with foreign partners. However, overall demand for fully documented workers far outstripped supply, forcing the majority of Tajikistani labour migrants to enter Russia illegally. The Exchange charges a service fee of USD300 but, according to its director, clients arrive 'because it is a state organisation and you can ask about it; legally, you can ask to be compensated for any unfulfilled promises' (Interview in Dushanbe, May 2011). It is thus likely that migrants sometimes prefer the services of an official employment agency because it offers more security or, as Marthe Handå Myhre (2012: 69) has noted, to avoid long queues or various bureaucratic hassles.

In reality, only a few Tajikistani migrants resort to the services of an official agency. The director of the Youth Labour Exchange admitted that only some 300 to 400 workers had been placed during the past year. While he also claimed that he would be able to send more candidates to Russia if these had better qualifications, officials at the IOM reported that the agencies' services were simply too expensive for most would-be migrants. The overall costs for full documentation prior to departure and upon arrival in Russia can indeed amount to several thousand roubles. Why then not rather find work illegally and avoid all these fees and bureaucratic hurdles? Other problems have been pointed out. An ILO report thus states that Tajikistani youths, faced with the choice of obtaining a degree in higher education locally or emigrating to work in Russia, 'choose low-skilled work abroad, when in their homeland the options for adequate employment for educated and skilled people are limited, where even a certified specialist is in a worse situation in his homeland in comparison to being employed in low-skilled labour abroad' (ILO 2010: 68).

While most Tajikistanis appear to avoid formal channels when seeking employment in Russia, there are some exceptions to this rule. One private employment agency in Dushanbe, specialised in educational migration to the United States, was said by its director to successfully attract a clientele because of the benefits it offered to those going through formal channels (Interviews in Dushanbe, 2010 and 2011). The highly specialised agency offered English-language tutoring, provided help with the visa application and prepared candidates for the interviews at the embassy. It thus acted as a sort of gatekeeper which, at high costs to the candidates and their families, promised alluring long-term job prospects in the United States. By nature, its clientele comes from a privileged urban elite able to afford the agency's fees for their children. It must be emphasised here that only five per cent of all labour migrants come from the capital (Olimova and Bosc 2003: 33). However, family support is also a key factor in facilitating the migration of other migrants, and the role of the family and other social institutions for migration will be examined more closely in the next section.

Informal channels and choices

The Soviet legacy left Central Asian societies in disarray – norms changed, idealised family structures based on a 'traditional past' stressed extended and hierarchical units. This section looks at the role of two informal structures of Central Asian societies – *avlod* (patriarchal extended family) and *mahalla* (informal neighbourhood structure) in migration. Based on secondary literature on these informal structures and interviews conducted in Khujand (Tajikistan), Isfana (Kyrgyzstan) and amongst Tajik labour migrants and non-governmental organisations in Moscow and St Petersburg (Russia), this section discusses how these traditional social and community structures may perform as governors of migration. It can be argued that these institutions of traditional societies may appear relevant for migration choice that, thus, goes beyond an individual's perceived rational choice.

Despite seventy years of Sovietisation, Tajikistan remains a conservative society based on local Islamic traditions, said to have retained a strong 'patriarchal' character and where social relations still tend to be organised along strong hierarchical principles – features that are generally associated with an idealised past. Two of its key social institutions are the *avlod*, a term of Arabic origin often translated as 'extended patriarchal family', and the *mahalla*, a neighbourhood community or network. By definition, an *avlod* encompasses all living and deceased descendants in the male line of an ancestor who is traced back for some seven generations; its living members form the core of an extended family that is considered one of the major pillars of Tajik society (Abdullaev and Akbarzadeh 2010). The *avlod* has thus also been described as a 'patriarchal community of blood relatives who have a common ancestor and common interests, and in many cases shared property and means of production and consolidated or coordinated household budgets' (Nourzhanov and Bleuer 2013: 77; see also Olimova and Bosc 2003: 56). Ideally, the eldest active member of an *avlod* concentrates most of the power in his hands, and children are instilled with a strong sense of filial duty. According to Nourzhanov and Bleuer (2013: 78), the head of such a family has control over all major expenditures, determines the internal division of labour and decides over the future of junior members; even grown-up sons cannot claim complete economic independence, by virtue of belonging to this higher-order kinship group. Zharkevich (2010) considers the *avlod* system to be still one of the main organisational structures of Tajik society; based on kin ties and patronage networks, the *avlod* controls access to various resources, notably economic assets and political posts. It also assists its members in obtaining housing or employment, provides them with marriage partners and, to some extent, serves as a channel for political influence (Dar 2013).

Closely related to the *avlod*, the *mahalla* is an urban neighbourhood whose resident families, most of them related by kin and marriage ties, form an informal network. Its organisation resembles that of a clan-based village, with its self-administrative organ (the *mahalla* committee), its gathering place – usually a mosque or a teahouse (*chaikhona*) – and its collectively organised neighbourhood events (Nourzhanov and Bleuer 2013: 80). *Mahalla* committees generally consist of a few respected local elders, spiritual leaders and wealthy merchants who meet regularly to discuss and solve various neighbourhood issues related to local infrastructure and development, promote local values, sanction the behaviour of members and organise communal life-cycle rituals such as weddings and funerals. A *mahalla* is sometimes said to control all aspects of its members' life, especially in rural areas where it is often considered almost an extension of an *avlod*: 'The forty-year-old passes (socially important information) from the mosque to his twenty-year-old son and his one-year old grandson' (Poliakov quoted in Nourzhanov and Bleuer 2013: 81–82). The institution of the *mahalla* has survived Soviet collectivisation and deportations, and remains a socially relevant entity in contemporary post-Soviet Central Asian societies. Unlike in neighbouring Uzbekistan, it has, however, no official administrative status in Tajikistan and should be seen as a form of self-organisation with control and regulatory functions for a community.

Given the above, it seems likely that the choice in favour of labour migration goes well beyond an individual's rational choice and that traditional social institutions play a certain, if not a key role. Indeed, as John Heathershaw (2009: 169) has noted, migrants generally receive strong support from relatives, who finance their journey, provide them with accommodation and a first job (see also Olimova and Bosc 2003: 58–61). He suggests that the *avlod* system exists in both local and translocal spaces and that decisions concerning migration are often taken by whole families or family heads, who send one or several sons abroad for work. In other words, migrants' choices are socially constituted within an extended family according to a member's income-generating potential.

An empirical study conducted by the authors through interviews in Khujand (Tajikistan), Isfana (Kyrgyzstan) and amongst Tajik labour migrants and NGO members in Moscow and St Petersburg confirms this hypothesis. The elderly head of a family and of the Usun-Soi *mahalla* in Isfana, close to the border with Kyrgyzstan, described the role of the family for migrants from his neighbourhood in the following terms:

> You know, the family takes the decision, the parents decide. The young men need to get a passport and master Russian, only then can they go to work in Russia. Sometimes families discuss the family decision with me. If there are no problems and everything is good, then the young man can leave. The eldest son must migrate to work and live in another country.
>
> (Interview in Isfana, June 2012)

As about 68 per cent of Tajikistanis declare that they feel belonging to an *avlod*, with minor social and regional disparities (Olimova and Bosc 2003: 56; see also Collins 2009: 70; ILO and IOM 2009: 4), one can say that these traditional power structures and kinship relations continue to play a crucial role in contemporary Tajikistani migration. Migrants, thus, consist mainly of 'fathers' and 'sons', household members who carry the economic responsibility for the rest of the family (Hohmann 2013: 159).

The importance of family networks was also apparent in answers to the above-mentioned questionnaire: a majority of the 41 correspondents from Tajik–Uzbek border villages noted that employment in Russia was arranged through their family and friends, and only six said that they had found a job via a private employment agency. As activists from the St Petersburg NGO Memorial, based on their work with Tajikistani labour migrant families, emphasised, fathers view efforts to facilitate the departure of their sons to Russia as part of their parental responsibility, even if it means these young people are dropping out of school (Interview in St Petersburg, October 2012).

In Central Asian societies, much influence is held by community elders, as well as by the local religious leader, or *molla*. [4] Families are expected not only to uphold the values of the community but also to contribute, financially or in kind, to its upkeep and development. Amongst both ethnic Tajiks and Uzbeks, this generally takes place at the level of the *mahalla*.

Although *mahallas* are not concerned directly by migration, their very nature – a very tight network of families and neighbours with clear financial responsibilities for neighbourhood development – means that their members sometimes exercise social pressure on families of migrants to make donations. Ongoing research in collaboration with Sergei Ryazantsev and Norio Horie on the relationship between *mahallas* and labour migrants in Russia has shown that the latter make significant financial contributions to *mahalla* development through remittances sent to their families back home with the express purpose of helping the community.[5]

The preliminary results of the study are, however, rather contradictory: while interviewees have declared that they consider financial support to their community of origin necessary and thus contribute to the funding of water and road infrastructure projects and the construction of mosques, schools or hospitals, investments to set up new businesses or aimed at the long-term development of a neighbourhood are rare. As one informant from the Panshanbe *mahalla* in the northern Tajik city of Khujand explained: 'All think first of their own families, and that's why no one helps (the *mahalla*)' (Interview in Khujand, November 2011). Indeed, remittances, which are estimated to account for up to 46 to 49 per cent of Tajikistan's GDP (Olimova 2013: 66; see also FIDH and Memorial 2011: 23), are primarily used to pay for items of daily consumption, family construction projects and the organisation of life-cycle ceremonies such as weddings. The opinion quoted above may, however, have overstated its case and reflect the young age or social position of the interviewee or, less likely, should be seen as an indicator of the modernisation traditional social practices are undergoing in a globalising *mahalla*.

In general, *mahallas* are viewed positively by their residents, even though social pressure is sometimes being brought upon members to meet unspoken expectations and to provide resources for the common good, thus contributing to stimulate migratory flows towards Russian regions that experience labour shortages. A community leader of the Usun-Soi *mahalla* has well described this mechanism:

> For events, we always collect money. But the parents of the migrants contribute money, instead of their children. If there is a wedding in the village, so the parents of the migrants bring and contribute. ... Even if the contribution is small, the family will be happy to get the contribution of neighbours. But in the envelope with money, we give the list of those families who have made the contribution. Everything should be transparent and the list informs the amount of contribution. Otherwise someone can contribute 500 soms but others can contribute 1000 soms.
>
> (Interview in Isfana, June 2012)

Conclusion

In transitional Central Asia, migration is generally perceived as still the only choice for many people, who seem to ignore the many risks entailed but argue that options to stay at home are unavailable to them – a fact underlined in responses to the questionnaire administered in northern Tajikistan. Further evidence from the studies conducted suggests that support for migration from official and social institutions exercises real or imagined pressure on individuals who then feel that they have no other choice but to leave the country and work abroad. Formal institutions, such as employment agencies, may not directly affect decisions related to migration, but there can be no doubt that the state's legislative efforts, for example, have created a climate in which the encouragement of labour migration is perceived as official policy. Indeed, the state itself appears to see emigration as the only possible outlet, given the risk of economic instability and political unrest under conditions characterised by poor governance. Emigration offers one way to escape from, among other things, abuses linked to corruption and other malpractices. An individual's choice to migrate or not is also being constrained by social institutions to which s/he belongs by virtue of birth, such as the family and the *avlod*, whose other members exercise considerable influence on migration-related decisions, and by the local community (*mahalla*) through more indirect social pressure. In this sense, these institutions reinforce a pattern that favours labour migration.

Under these circumstances, there is a danger for Tajikistani society that migration becomes normalised and so embedded in it that its members will be unable to grasp new opportunities closer to home if ever these should become available. Rapid population growth combined with very few employment opportunities, as well as continued easy access to the Russian labour market through a visa-free regime, makes the Russian Federation with its labour shortages very attractive, especially when salaries there can be as much as five times higher than comparable ones at home. Nor is it a secret that the present regime sees the current extensive migration as a key mechanism to release political pressure that is threatening its very existence. 'Labour exports' are thus part of a larger strategic issue that, at the same time, makes the Tajik government entirely dependent on the migration and labour market policies of the Russian Federation. This vulnerability should not be overlooked, and neither the Tajik state nor the international community should neglect the promotion of education and business activities or long-term development policies as an alternative to labour migration, while also addressing more general issues of corruption. If these capacity-building measures were taken, then such 'pull' institutions would counter the 'push' institutions that currently dominate Tajikistan. The EU in particular would be wise to focus its attention on supporting such endeavours instead of solely funding 'migrant-friendly' programmes that are perceived as encouraging the country's youth to move abroad, thus depriving Tajikistan of its greatest resource. The international community, by supporting the Tajik government's policy of labour migration, ignores the enduring weakness of the Tajik state, which continues to lack the stability so desired by Brussels and, more generally, the outside world.

Notes

1 The population of Tajikistan is largely comprised of Persian-speaking ethnic Tajiks (80 per cent), followed by a Turkic-speaking Uzbek minority (15 per cent) and other smaller groups, including Russians and Kyrgyz (Indexmundi 2013). Here the term 'Tajikistani' is used to describe any citizen of the country, and 'Tajik' to refer to the ethnic group.
2 See also 'Prezident Tadzhikistana obeshchaet sozdat' v strane 250 tysiach rabochikh mest', *Vesti*, 20 November 2011, Online. Available at: www.vesti.ru/doc.html?id= 646477 (last accessed 18 July 2014).
3 For a good overview of Central Asian critiques of EU and international policies in the region, see Peyrouse (2014) and Giffen, Earle and Buxton (2005: 10–11).
4 Contemporary Tajik society has been and is, of course, being affected by modernisation processes, and traditional norms, values and social institutions are being challenged in this context, especially as the result of the massive mobility of young people.
5 This research is in its early stages and its results have not yet been published, except in presentations by Horie (e.g. at the Fifth East Asian Conference for Slavic and Eurasian Studies in Osaka, Japan, on 10 August 2013).

Part Four

Migration and the everyday

12 Labour migration and the contradictory logic of integration in Russia

Olga Tkach and Olga Brednikova

Labour migration from the Commonwealth of Independent States (CIS) countries, particularly from Central Asia, to Russia is now widespread. It affects the majority of Russian regions, with migrants being mainly employed as unskilled labour across many sectors of the economy (Ryazantsev and Horie 2010: 5, 22–23). The need of the Russian economy for foreign labour is today recognised at the level of national policy.[1] At the same time migration has come to be seen as an urgent and pressing social problem by a variety of agents in a number of fields – political, social and academic – and has become a topic of public debate, triggering comment and action from the media. In this context 'integration' has over the last couple of years become the predominant term used by politicians, journalists and academics to discuss issues of labour migration and migration policies, displacing previously common notions such as assimilation and adaptation. Serving as an umbrella concept, integration not only describes the problems encountered by migrants (in terms of a lack of integration) but also offers a strategy, a positive programme for solving them. The concept is also universal in the sense that it circulates between the academic and political discourse.

This chapter focuses on the integration of migrants from CIS countries coming to Russia under a visa-free regime to work as low-skilled workers[2] and on the agents involved in the process of their integration, namely administrative officials, employers and members of the civil society (both migrants and members of the host community), with emphasis being placed on the national and local level. It is based on recent empirical research carried out by the authors at the Centre for Independent Social Research within the framework of the project Labour Migrants in Petersburg: Identifying Problems and Developing Recommendations,[3] which investigated social problems of migrants in St Petersburg with regard to their regularisation and interaction with state institutions, employment and working conditions, housing and medical care. The research included interviews with migrant workers, their employers and officials dealing with migrants, as well as desk research and regular monitoring through the consultation of relevant official documents and numerous media and online publications.

It is important to remark that the phenomenon of labour immigration in Russia is undergoing rapid changes. Almost every week new government

DOI: 10.4324/9781315858036-17

projects, institutions and civic initiatives are being set up and new regulations are being introduced. The present chapter will only offer a snapshot of the current situation (in late 2012 and early 2013), mainly relying on experiences made in St Petersburg, one of Russia's cities particularly attractive for labour migrants. It will begin by introducing some concepts related to the integration of migrants in the European context, identifying different levels and types of integration and analysing the contradictions typical of European immigration policies. The second part will then examine Russia's current immigration policy and outline the specifics of the 'turn to integration' in this policy field. The third part will investigate the contribution of a range of governmental and non-governmental agents to the integration of migrants on the local level, using the example of St Petersburg. In conclusion the authors will compare European and Russian tendencies in terms of the integration of immigrants and highlight the distinctive characteristics of the Russian situation.

Integration as a political and analytical category

Immigration is one of the most vigorous sources of cultural diversity in contemporary societies, which brings up the idea of a required mechanism that would facilitate social cohesion and stability and prevent tensions and cultural misunderstandings. Global social thought of the twentieth century has come up with two major alternative approaches to immigration as a source of cultural diversity: assimilation and integration. The assimilationist approach presumes that if immigrants 'want to be accepted as full and equal citizens, they should assimilate into the national culture, exchange their inherited or imported identity for one derived from their new country and undergo a kind of cultural rebirth' (Parekh 2008: 83). Unlike assimilationists, whose views have recently been recognised as 'unjust, unrealistic and illiberal', integrationists 'appreciate that immigrants might wish to, and indeed have a right to, retain parts of their cultural identity, and that integration could and should be "thin"', limited mainly to society's 'common institutions' (Parekh 2008: 86).

Russian scholarly debates refer to two types of relationships between adaptation and assimilation (Mukomel' 2013: 695). The first one performs as a continuum or path that immigrants should follow when they arrive in their country of destination. The chain 'adaptation – integration – assimilation' presumes that they gradually adjust to a new society with a follow-up incorporation into it and transformation into local citizens. Russian debates maintain the same logic of switching from assimilation to integration, which is linked to the re-evaluation of a primordial approach to culture and the acceptance of multiple and contextual identities. Therefore, the second approach sees integration as a two-way process, which involves both immigrants and a receiving society. They both are expected to adjust to each other to achieve a certain degree of integration.

The integration of immigrants is a multi-layered phenomenon as well as a complex concept which refers to the discourse on the role of migrants in the host society. As a concept it is contextual, that is discursively framed in national models, and politically biased through its use as an instrument in politics. Nowadays integration is an issue of high priority for policymakers in European societies (Joppke 2007b: 245). According to Goodman (2010: 769) it is even one of the most pressing policy and social challenges that liberal nation-states currently face. Although integration is a practical category taken from the world of politics, scholars use it to analyse various aspects, conditions and levels of integration even though its applicability as an analytical category is highly debatable (Joppke and Morawska 2003: 4). The following is an attempt to outline general tendencies in the scholarly and practical uses of integration through an overview of studies of integration policies in European states with particular emphasis on aspects that offer a useful analytical perspective applicable to the Russian situation.

Above all, integration policy is seen as a mechanism for producing and maintaining the boundaries of the liberal nation-state in terms of welfare and valued statehood (Koopmans 2010: 21; Pajnik 2007: 851). First, researchers have indicated a neoliberal turn in both welfare and integration policies as well as a turn, or return, to assimilation across Western Europe (Jørgensen 2012: 249). Despite differences across welfare states (Koopmans 2010: 8–9), scholars have advanced that overall welfare has become a deficit public good, and integration policies are now being formulated with the aim to limit migrants' access to it. Integration is being framed as providing access to the welfare state and full social benefits rather than achieving it through the welfare system (Jørgensen 2012: 251). The neoliberal economic project also presumes that the focus on socio-economic integration shifts the burden to individual immigrants, who become responsible for their integration (Jørgensen 2012). Second, much of the literature on immigrants distinguishes a trend from difference-friendly multiculturalism towards universalistic assimilation in integration policies (Joppke 2007b: 243; Nagel and Staeheli 2008: 415–416). Formulated and coordinated primarily on the national level, these policies are more concerned with abstract discussions about national values and their protection and for this reason are rather symbolic than concrete tools of integration (Jørgensen 2012: 252). Although institutions dealing with migration and integration vary across EU countries, they all share a mind-set that stresses the need to preserve the foundations and values of the nation-state (Pajnik 2007: 850–851). Processes of integration and naturalisation re-enact a nation's ideologically approved origins (Pajnik 2007: 862), and integration promotes an image of the host country as a homogeneous entity (Pajnik 2007: 853). This usually takes the form of civic integration policies (targeted selection, language acquisition, integration courses and various systems of assessment) that are being used as techniques of integration. Valenta and Strabac (2011: 667) define this approach as state-sponsored obligatory integration. On the one hand, migrants are required to assimilate through naturalisation, on the other hand, they are kept 'at a distance in a kind of a postcolonial isolation' (Pajnik 2007: 856). Much like everyone else, immigrants are always excluded and included at the same time: excluded as whole individuals and included as sectoral players or agents with specific assets and habitual dispositions in specific fields or systems (Joppke and Morawska 2003: 3; see also Pajnik 2007: 850).

Studies on policy-making in the field of immigration and integration point to the contradictory logic of this policy on the local, city or municipal level. This can be explained as a gap between discourse and practice, as an unsuccessful transfer of nationally formulated policies to the local level or as an outcome of diverging political rationalities on the local and national level (Jørgensen 2012: 245). Indeed, scholars usually pay great attention to the relationship between these two levels, to the question whether there is competition or congruence and to the extent that local approaches are independent from the national one. Jørgensen (2012: 268), for example, concludes that while the national political rationale and institutional logic are characterised by a tough and restrictive approach to integration, motivated by neoliberal ideology, local approaches are based on a rationale and logic of pragmatism and on the management of cultural diversity. Local integration policies, unlike national ones, are perceived as more sensitive towards the diversity of migrants and their demands (Jørgensen 2012: 257; see also Pajnik 2007: 855). Local governments work with people rather than ideas. In addition, civil society is more influential on the local level (Jørgensen 2012: 260).

Researchers also distinguish between various components of integration, which can be political (civic engagement, citizenship, national membership), economic (employment) or social and cultural. On the practical level, they emphasise concrete spheres or domains of integration, such as welfare, language acquisition, housing, job training and job placement for newcomers, health care, education, culture and leisure (e.g. Joppke and Morawska 2003; Koopmans 2010; Pajnik 2007). Particular attention has been paid to the political background and techniques of civic integration (Joppke 2007a, 2007b). To promote civic skills and to increase the commitment to national values, governments have defined a series of requirements ('civic hardware'), including integration contracts, classes, tests and ceremonies (Goodman 2010: 754). Civic integration of this kind implies two objectives that Goodman defines as the performance of incorporation (integration courses, mandatory tests and a top-down policy of homogenising acculturation) and state membership, related to concrete legal statuses and rights (Goodman 2010: 755 and 768). It has thus been suggested that integration has become a solution to presumed failures of border controls, functioning as a device for the selection of migrants, a disciplinary mechanism and a process of certification for those deemed to be worthy of 'the privilege of citizenship', instead of a by-product of citizenship, non-discriminatory treatment and investment in human capital (Kostakopoulou 2010: 843–844).

Studies of European integration policies thus point to the key role of a dialectic of inclusion and exclusion in the mechanisms of integration. As the following analysis will show, the ambivalence or contradictory nature of migration policies is also highly relevant for the Russian situation.

The 'turn to integration' in national migration policy: contradictory trends

Since the collapse of the Soviet Union, Russia has experienced a number of migratory waves, each of them triggering changes in the national immigration policy of Russia and its CIS neighbours. As Vladimir Mukomel' (2005: 11–43) has shown, migration caused by ethnic conflicts on post-Soviet territory has gradually given way to economic migration resulting from the social and economic development in Russia and other CIS countries. Correspondingly, policies targeted at refugees and forced migrants or aimed at the repatriation of compatriots have become of peripheral interest while those touching on the status of foreign citizens working on the territory of the Russian Federation have taken on greater social significance. Monitoring and controlling labour migration (and combating illegal immigration) have become central policy objectives. At the same time, rigid regulations and ineffective institutions have often made it difficult for immigrants to obtain a legal status and led to informal or even criminal practices that have forced the majority of labour migrants into a shadow labour market.[4] The year 2007 saw, however, major changes that inaugurated a new era in Russia's immigration policy.[5] The rules of entry to Russia and those regulating the duration of stay for foreign citizens were simplified and regularisation procedures (registration, work and residence permits) became more accessible for migrants. In July 2010, an amendment to the Federal Law 'On the Legal Status of Foreign Citizens in the Russian Federation' authorised labour migrants to work for households as domestic help or doing construction and repair work. This licence, better known as 'patent', has enjoyed considerable popularity with migrants, as it was easier to obtain and renew than an ordinary work permit. On the whole, the principal objective of immigration policy in Russia since the collapse of the Soviet Union has been concerned with the registration, legalisation and control of labour migration and the identification of undocumented or, in Russian political rhetoric, illegal migrants while questions pertaining to the integration of immigrants were ignored. Indeed, most of the labour migrants arriving in Russia in the 1990s and early 2000s spoke Russian, found accommodation and work on their own and coped themselves with safety problems in Russian cities. The authors' studies have shown that they did not regard Russia as a foreign country and often had social ties that were a legacy from the Soviet period (Brednikova and Tkach 2010: 51–57).

In recent years a 'turn to integration' has taken place in Russia's immigration policy. The first sign of this was Vladimir Putin's pre-election article 'Russia: The National Question', published on 23 January 2012 in the *Nezavisimaya Gazeta*. One of its sections, entitled 'Problems of immigration and our integration project', contains a number of reflections comprising a political programme for the integration of migrants in Russia, here understood rather in the sense of assimilation. Eighteen months later, on 13 June 2012, Putin, who had been re-elected president, signed into law the Concept of State Migration Policy in the Russian Federation, which discussed in more detail questions of adaptation and integration. This text can be considered a milestone in contemporary immigration policy. For the first time Russia's need for labour migration was officially acknowledged and along with it the need to perfect immigration policy: 'For the realisation of the positive potential from migration processes, the whole system of their regulation in the Russian Federation requires modernisation'.[6] Currently, Russia, like many European countries, is experiencing serious demographic challenges because of falling birth rates, an ageing population and a decline in the share of the working-age population. As a result, promoting the adaptation and integration of immigrants, as well as the development of constructive relations between them and the host society, has now been declared one of the tasks of immigration policy. The 'Concept' thus supports the trend towards a liberalisation of immigration policy, making it easier to obtain a permit or status or to apply for family reunification. The basic aim is to create agreeable and comfortable conditions for new migrants through various measures such as the 'development of infrastructure in the sphere of labour migration on the basis of a collaboration between state, private and commercial organisations'; 'ensuring access of foreign citizens and members of their family to social, medical and educational facilities corresponding to their legal status'; and the 'creation of programmes supporting constructive collaboration between immigrants and the host society'.[7]

However, although both the 'Concept' itself, which has a recommendatory character, and the legal initiatives resulting from it rhetorically declare the importance of integrating migrants, they have in fact created practical barriers to these goals, as integration is given equal priority to the preservation of the values and discourses of the host nation-state. Whereas the socio-economic contribution of labour migrants to the development of the Russian society is acknowledged as significant, immigrants nevertheless are not regarded as enjoying full rights in the labour market. The state's declared goal is 'the organised acquisition of foreign workers'. This recommendation found expression in the organisation of so-called centres of preparation for labour migrants on the basis of bilateral agreements, implemented in Russia by a department of the Federal Migration Service. Currently, a number of centres have been opened in Tajikistan and Kyrgyzstan (soon to be followed by others in Armenia and Uzbekistan) that are linked to employment agencies in Russia. The idea behind this initiative is – linguistic, professional and legal – 'integration from abroad' in order to facilitate later integration into Russian reality. The procedures have been designed to prepare labour migrants for specific employments in specific places. The status and effectiveness of these centres is not yet clear and requires research. In the authors' opinion, the initiative reduces the migrant to a *Gastarbeiter*, that is, somebody tied to a specific workplace and profession, with few options for competing in the open labour market and changing employers, a state of affairs less conducive to integration. Opportunities for migrants in the open labour market are similarly restricted by the quota system introduced in 2006, whereby the federal centre severely limits the annual number of work permits for each region. This measure not only makes immigrants more vulnerable but also hurts some employers, especially small and medium-sized enterprises, mostly neglected in favour of large companies. Despite criticism, including from inside the state administration, that this contradicts the idea of economic development, the quota system has not been abolished.

Access to health services has been another issue. Whereas Russian citizens benefit from free universal health care, employers will only be authorised to hire foreign citizens who have acquired a mandatory health insurance policy (Nikolaeva 2013), an idea first promoted by the Minister of Labour of the Russian Federation in early 2013. Since health care is already financed through taxes this places an additional burden on migrants.

On the cultural level, the 'Concept' opposes an assumedly homogenous Russian society with its 'cultural and historical traditions and local customs' to immigrants who might display 'inappropriate, aggressive, provocative and disrespectful behaviour'.[8] The rhetoric of political leaders thus creates and reproduces a normalised version of the ethnic and cultural otherness of migrants. Integration is here understood as the 'civilising' of migrants, i.e. through their acquaintance with Russian high culture, namely literature, history and the Russian language. It is reduced to a form of civic integration at the heart of which is the obligation of immigrants to acquire new cultural skills in order to confirm their right to remain and live in Russia:

> It is important that immigrants can adapt normally to our society. Yes, it is a basic requirement that people wanting to live and work in Russia should make our culture and language their own. Starting next year, it will be obligatory to pass an examination on Russian language, history and literature, the history of the Russian state and law in order to receive or extend immigrant status. Our state, just like other civilised countries, is ready to elaborate corresponding courses of instruction and to provide them to immigrants.[9]

Federal Law No. 185 of 12 November 2012 ('On Amendments in Article 13.1 of the Federal Law "On the Legal Position of Foreign Citizens in the Russian Federation" and Article 27.2 of the Federal Law "On Education"'), entered into force on 1 December 2012, has made it mandatory for foreign citizens arriving in the Russian Federation without requiring a visa to have at least a basic knowledge of Russian if they apply for a permit to work in the retail, housing and services sectors or in public utilities. Documentary proof takes the form of a certificate delivered after the applicant has successfully passed a language test. Neither the test nor preparatory language courses are provided free of charge.

Thus, the 'turn to integration' in Russia's current immigration policy is characterised by inherent contradictions. The state acknowledges its economic and demographic need for labour migrants and its responsibility for their integration into the life of the host society. At the same time, the programmes and ideas proposed for integration keep immigrants at a distance from this society and its resources. Preserving the *ethnos* of the nation-state remains the prevailing idea of integration policy in Russia. The tasks of integration, which are essentially anti-repressive, have been assigned to the Federal Migration Service and the police, whose basic modus operandi has been honed for other tasks. Both agencies are to a large degree responsible for monitoring and controlling immigration flows and combating illegal immigration. At present, neither the legislation nor the various institutions seem to be ready for systematic progress in the sphere of integration.

Immigrant integration on the local level: the case of St Petersburg

The governmental approach to integration

The contemporary political structure of the Russian Federation is organised according to the principle of the 'power vertical', which entails the strict ideological and economic dependence of local executive power from the federal centre and subordination to its decisions. Despite the insufficient development of an integration policy on the federal level, local officials are trying to bring their work into line with the Concept of State Migration Policy, although the latter does not have the status of a law but only expresses general principles and recommendations. It is argued here that the contradictions of the national integration policy in the sphere of immigration are reproduced to a greater or lesser degree on the level of the Russian regions, in this case of St Petersburg.

St Petersburg, Russia's second-largest city, is attracting an increasing number of labour migrants from other CIS countries that share a visa-free regime with the Russian Federation. In 2011 the Federal Migration Service in St Petersburg and the surrounding Leningrad region issued 186,033 work permits, mostly for low-skilled immigrants from Uzbekistan, Tajikistan and Ukraine.[10] There exists indeed a strong demand for this kind of workers in the local labour market. In addition to industry and agriculture, migrants are currently employed in the construction and street retail sectors, as street sweepers, cleaners, waiters, all-purpose helpers and porters in shopping malls, in public transport and as child minders and carers for the elderly. Having received work permits and registered, they become part of everyday life in the megalopolis. However, the 'turn to integration' in immigration policy has meant that labour migrants will now have to apply separately for work and residence permits.

In St Petersburg, there is currently no single specialised official body responsible for questions of integration. While the Federal Migration Service, in 2010, has created a department for cooperation and integration which is meant to develop a strategy for the integration of foreign citizens into Russian society and coordinate local initiatives and programmes in this field, its main administrative task since 1992 has been the monitoring and control of foreigners on the territory of the Russian Federation, and in particular the combating of illegal immigration (Gladarev and Tsinman 2011: 509). This still remains a priority, even after the promotion of integration has become part of its remit. As a rule, the responsibility for integration is spread between different city committees (executive bodies) such as those responsible for external communications, labour and employment, health, social policy, housing and education. These and other committees draw up and implement programmes for the employment of migrants and for the monitoring of their working conditions, health insurance and social security, accommodation and language instruction. However, experts generally acknowledge that in practice the intended measures have not yet reached a sufficient scale and have been hampered by organisational problems, lack of finance and existing legal rules. Frequently, initiatives get stuck at the planning stage or are implemented in a selective and fragmentary manner – in a few city districts, during a short-term campaign or the tenure of a particular official. Thus, in 2012, all districts of Petersburg set up official Russian-language courses for migrants but these were closed down after a year or so, partly because there was no demand for them and partly because they had not been properly planned, lacked funds and employed questionable teaching methods. In the authors' view, this and other failures can be attributed to officials who know little about the way a migrant's everyday life is organised and who are therefore incapable of developing effective mechanisms and techniques to facilitate integration. Furthermore, interviews conducted with officials have shown that their actions are often based on stereotypical preconceptions, in which migrants are often seen as disrupting the social order, as potential agents of criminal behaviour and epidemics or as competitors for jobs. On the other hand, there have been a number of local initiatives implemented successfully over several years. In the following, two of these will be examined more closely, particularly in view of how they reflect the dialectics of inclusion and exclusion of migrants. The first is concerned with housing, the second with cultural activities.

Research conducted by the authors has shown the diversity of housing among migrants, who often face great difficulty in finding decent accommodation in St Petersburg. Some occupy rent-subsidised rooms at their place of work, others rent beds for the night or rooms in crowded communal apartments and still others live in evacuated houses or squats (Brednikova *et al.* 2012). Since the Spring of 2011, low-skilled migrant workers living in St Petersburg or the Leningrad region have obtained the right to rent accommodation in hostels converted from former factory dormitories and other types of housing. The programme is being implemented by the city administration and housing committee with the support of the Federal Migration Service (FMS) with the aim of solving the residential problems of labour migrants. Currently 11 such objects are operating and another 89 are planned to open up by 2018. They offer labour migrants accommodation that is relatively cheap (EUR90–110 per month), safe and comfortable. The workers' hostels have dormitories with three to eight beds and offer the shared use of a kitchen, bathrooms, laundry facilities, safe boxes and other amenities.

Each resident has a bed, cupboard and shelf; a resident cleaner and janitor look after the premises.

Never before had the city government regarded social housing as a solution, since finding accommodation was previously left to the migrants themselves. The project therefore bears witness to the interest of local authorities in improving the living conditions of labour migrants and, more generally, their quality of life. However, according to the authors' observations, workers' dormitories as a physical space and an arena of interaction of migrants with local authorities have been designed in a way that prevents the migrant from acting as an autonomous subject enjoying the same rights as citizens. Firstly, the administration concludes a rental agreement not with individual migrants but only with their employers who thus take decisions on behalf of their workers.[11] This institutionalises the employers' responsibility for their employees beyond the working hours: when incidents such as breakages or a breach of regulations occur the hostel's administration informs the employer and may demand compensation. There is also a tendency to house migrants close to their work to save travelling time and to allow employers to control their workers more effectively – partly for this reason, corridors in these hostels are under CCTV surveillance. An expert from the St Petersburg housing committee explicitly advanced this argument for local employees in the housing and utilities sector: '(Labour migrants) must live close to the houses, backyards and refuse collection points where they work.' Migrants are thus seen exclusively as a source of labour.

Secondly, such hostels have an operating regime that is oriented towards an everyday control of residents, their movements and behaviour. A hostel is a type of housing designed for the collective accommodation of migrants, where men and women are housed separately and families are not allowed to live together. Migrants are not awarded full rights to their dwelling place: they can only enter or leave at specific times (each occupant has an electronic key), the courtyard for leisure (and smoking) is fenced off from the street, and residents are not allowed to invite guests or decorate the personal space of their rooms. Such a regime is informed by the notion of *Gastarbeiter*, that is, somebody who is not supposed to have other interests except earning money. Residents effectively find themselves in the position of minors who are forced to ask permission from the hostel's administration if their plans differ from the building's working regime.

This suggests that a workers' hostel, originally aimed at integrating migrants, works more like a company with a binding universal schedule of operation and little space for privacy even outside working hours. The concept of the workers' hostel aims to make the city safe from migrants and migrants safe from the city. It reproduces the fears and prejudices that hinder integration rather than developing it effectively.

The second long-term and much better-known integration project in St Petersburg relates to the cultural sphere. In 2006 the Tolerance programme was launched with the aim of 'confirming the values of civic solidarity, securing harmonious coexistence and constructive interaction of all ethnic and confessional groups present in the city, the prevention of all forms of xenophobia, the formation of effective mechanisms of social integration and cultural adaptation of migrants'.[12] The programme is being run by the committee for external relations as part of a process of mutual adaptation of migrants and the host society and of their interaction on the basis of mutual respect and social equality. The local authorities who initiated and implemented the programme were obviously willing to take on responsibilities for creating a general atmosphere of tolerance in a social context characterised by a significant level of xenophobia.

However, the Tolerance programme has been conceived in a way that tends to homogenise migrants, assigning them to specific ethnic diasporas and associations or communities based on their national culture of origin. The goals promoted by these state-supported organisations are often very remote from the interests and problems of most labour migrants arriving in Petersburg to earn money. An important aim of the programme has been the organisation of festivals and other cultural events where representatives of the diaspora acquaint Petersburgers with their national music and dances, cuisine and handicrafts, therefore leading to a 'folklorisation of migrants' (Pajnik 2007: 860). However friendly and interested such a relationship to the ethnic other may be, it also tends to keep migrants at a distance from other members of the local society. Indeed, migrants are generally regarded as culturally unsuited for life in a Russian city and incapable of respecting imagined 'traditional Russian values'. For this reason, migrants are thought to need teachers or mentors who will help them to become familiar with 'Petersburg rules of everyday behaviour'. An example of this attitude is offered by the so-called *Labour Migrant's Manual*, the first publication of this kind in the history of post-Soviet migration, which was published in St Petersburg in 2012 in Russian, Uzbek, Tajik and Kyrgyz.[13] The brochure is of interest both discursively and visually. Labour migrants arriving in St Petersburg are represented by their working tools – a mason's trowel, a decorator's brush and scraper or a street sweeper's broom – while members of the host society appear as human individuals: a police officer, a city guide, a doctor and a teacher, a visual presentation that triggered a public debate calling into question the very effectiveness of the Tolerance programme.[14] One of the chapters, entitled 'Useful Advice', admonishes migrants to follow cultural rules as practiced in Russia's 'cultural capital'. For instance, migrants should not 'everywhere and always wear traditional national dress, since it attracts attention that is not always necessary'; 'not continually wear tracksuits, especially together with outdoor street shoes (tracksuits are used for sports)'; 'not go out into the street wearing a house robe'; 'not crouch, instead of standing, when in public places'; 'not cook food on balconies, in courtyards or in the street'.[15] These and other recommendations mark off the migrant as a priori uncivilised, uncultured and lacking social competence, as an ethnic other whose behavioural skills are so foreign to the local community that he requires help in understanding basic rules of public and private life.

The analysis of the work of local authorities shows that together with the opportunities they offer to migrants they also place restrictions on the lives of migrants. In particular, the institutional mechanisms of integration mean that migrants do not enjoy full access to welfare; they are monitored and isolated from the 'local' population, and labelled as ethnic and cultural others. Official initiatives for integration that are inspired by the idea of controlling migrants create the reverse effect: integration can cut off migrants from the 'local' population, and their access to social institutions is not always free. Moreover, as research conducted by the authors shows, state agencies often try to avoid direct contact.

Employers and ethnic organisations as substitutes for state-led integration

While the government has initiated the project of integration and provided an institutional and legal framework for the process, the administration frequently has shown little interest in interacting directly with migrants, rather delegating some functions to intermediaries, notably employers and diaspora or ethnic organisations.

Currently employers are, for example, held responsible for the regularisation of migrants: companies are required to apply for quotas, obtain work permits for the migrants they employ and monitor their legal status in Russia. In addition, they must provide some social support for migrant workers, in particular solving issues of registration and accommodation as well as ensuring that they are covered by a health insurance policy. Employers thus almost bear full responsibility for their foreign employees and the Federal Migration Service's task is reduced to control employers' actions in this regard.[16]

Certainly, this kind of support for migrant workers, who face long and complicated bureaucratic procedures, has many advantages, especially where big companies have significant resources, for instance to build a dormitory or to hire staff who look exclusively after the migrants' paperwork. Other employers, however, are more likely to break the law and operate in a 'shadow' market. The policy obviously creates obstacles for small businesses where migrant labour is most in demand. By forcing employers to shoulder large responsibilities for their foreign employees, it also tends to transform otherwise formal labour relations into a system of mutual moral obligations. Thus, the majority of migrants interviewed in the authors' study refer to their employers as a 'master' and describe them in moral categories ('good'/'bad', 'kind'/'evil', 'generous'/ 'greedy' etc.). Among its consequences are abusive practices. Migrants are more likely to be exploited, for example through unpaid overtime or work at the home of the employer, while employers have reported small fraud or theft by migrants.

Today, in St Petersburg, there are many ethnic or, as they refer to themselves, 'national' organisations (Uzbek, Tajik, Azeri etc.). Despite their apparent differences, they all perform in fact similar functions, namely the promotion of a specific ethnic, or national, culture and practical support for compatriots. The local government sees these organisations as representatives of an 'ethnic culture' and usually invites their leaders to attend the various meetings organised by the executive branch responsible for dealing with migrants' issues. In St Petersburg, these organisations were involved in the Tolerance programme described above. But their role has been limited to provide samples of 'ethnic high culture' to the exclusion of everyday culture. Thus, these organisations participate in the construction and reproduction of an innocent, loyal and ethnic other that reinforces boundaries between the host society and migrants. In addition, they focus on supporting compatriots, in general by helping them to accomplish paperwork or to find a job or dwelling place. Most of these services have to be paid for, which means that the organisations actually operate as market intermediaries, even though they have the status of non-profit organisations. For these reasons it is argued here that both employers and ethnic organisations, who act as intermediaries of the state, in fact reproduce the same contradictory logic of inclusion and exclusion of migrants in regard to the host society as the state. Indeed, the migrants' relations with their employer effectively closes them off from society, and the cultural boundaries erected and emphasised through ethnic organisations reinforce this pattern. In a way this is hardly surprising since the state has expressly mandated these actors to implement its policy of integration, based on this very logic.

Grassroots initiatives of integration: networks and civic activities

Integration is not only a top-down process. Migrants' networks of support and solidarity have been important and effective tools of integration. Recent years have also seen the emergence of several grass-roots initiatives that comprise both migrants and members of the host society. Civil society should therefore be seen as another agent of integration.

Unlike ordinary local citizens, migrants have a smaller set of competencies in the new location, limited social ties and fewer sources of information. Social networks that include migrants and citizens have therefore become extremely important for social integration. New communication technologies, such as mobile phones and the internet, have greatly expanded the range and effectiveness of such networks. According to the authors' research, the main function of these networks is the transmission of information about jobs, housing and various sources of help. However, networks of this kind are not always a panacea for migrants. Some are too small and isolated to be efficient. Moreover, the nature of the relations between members, which are thought to be based on mutual moral obligations and therefore on trust, have led to numerous cases of betrayal and abuse.

The authors' study has shown a slowly increasing rejection of attempts to achieve integration only through social networks. One of the indicators of this process is the emergence of alternative agents of integration, notably grass-roots initiatives from within civil society. Furthermore, migrants have become more aware of legal recourses to solve their problems and to withdraw from shady transactions, a development linked to an increasingly important legal framework, the duration of migration and the more recent public debate about the rights of migrant workers. They no longer hesitate to approach non-governmental organisations, such as The Anti-Discrimination Centre (ADC) 'Memorial' or the Saint Petersburg International Cooperation Centre of the Red Cross. They also try to protect their labour rights more publicly. In October 2012, for instance; 50 Tajiks working as street sweepers in St Petersburg joined a trade union and went on strike to claim unpaid wages.[17]

One of the grassroots initiatives promoting integration is the Children of St Petersburg project, started in Spring 2012 by local citizens who act as volunteers to teach Russian to children of immigrant workers.[18] Its main objective is to facilitate the adaptation of children to their new life and to prepare them for school. In addition to language classes, teachers provide other services such as sightseeing trips, excursions and accompanied theatre visits.

Members of the civil society and mechanisms of immigrant integration operate independently from the state and are not engaged in politics. As a result, they are able to fill gaps in the state's policy. However, such civic initiatives are sporadic and mostly lack the necessary resources and personnel or the planning capacity required to successfully complete their task.

Conclusions

Immigration policies in Russia and the EU countries share a view of migrants as residents that lack certain competences and have to prove loyalty upon entering the national territory and afterwards remain under various forms of control that ensure that they are rendered harmless. This is the logic of state management of migration and the Russian case is not unique here. Moreover, both in Russia and in the European Union, national migration policies are based on a logic that simultaneously includes and excludes migrants. This does not mean that the state has two different policies, one providing migrants with opportunities for integration and another that is depriving them of such opportunities. It is rather that these opportunities (institutions) themselves inherently entail barriers that hinder and restrict a migrant's integration into everyday life.

However, in contrast to many European countries, integration is a recent problem for the Russian state. After two decades of combating illegal migration the state is now promoting integration, thereby acknowledging the importance of labour migration for the economic and social life of Russian society. Until now, the turn to integration has been mainly rhetorical, as many policy proposals have not yet been transposed into laws and most institutions designed to be responsible for integration have not yet been established. This chapter has provided only a snapshot of the current situation and it is clear that the creation of such institutions will take some time and that the evaluation of the social effects produced by the turn to integration will require further research.

In the sphere of integration, the state acts as a monopolist, and attempts to involve other agents in the process have not been very successful, because the state has either imposed responsibilities on these agents while subjecting them to strict controls (notably in the case of employers) or ignored or even rejected their initiatives (as in the case of civil society organisations). Contrary to what has happened within the European Union where these initiatives have been supported by the state, the situation in Russia is characterised by the state's attempts to bring them under control or to block them. This can be explained by the weakness of civil society in Russia and by the key role that national security plays in the state's migration policies.

The current policy towards migrants produces a specific type of integration that could be called 'fragmented' (Portes and Zhou 1993, quoted in Bolt, Özüekren and Phillips 2010: 182). First, the process of integration has a dialectical relationship with exclusion and control. Thus, a migrant living in a workers' hostel can be said to have become integrated in terms of housing, but at the same time the surveillance regime to which he is being subjected there effectively isolates him from the neighbourhood. Similarly, a migrant, despite steady employment and regular earnings, might find himself completely dependent on his employer who, having made investments to ensure the migrant's integration, then proceeds to exploit him. Second, the present politics of integration and institutionalisation are not sensitive to different scenarios and biographical situations that shape a migrant's everyday life, because they proceed from the assumption that there exist homogeneous categories of labour migrants and act on it. Third, integration is fragmented because migrants are integrated to varying degrees in different spheres of life. Thus, the state's policy has defined as its priorities for integration the legalisation of migrants and their acquisition of Russian-language skills but neglects such fundamental issues as medical and social insurance, which are left to the personal responsibility of the migrants themselves. Other integration agents demonstrate the same contradictory logic. Their lack of resources only allows them to develop sporadic and isolated integration projects which do not offer the multifaceted assistance needed by migrants to become successfully integrated into the host society.[19]

Integration is not only a political project of the state but the result of daily efforts accomplished by migrants. Some migrants regard themselves as being completely integrated even when they have no contacts with state institutions or long-term relations with locals. More, as Joppke and Morawska (2003: 3–4) put it, 'the non-integrated immigrant is a structural impossibility, because from the day she sets foot in the new society, she is always already "integrated" and engaged in certain fields and systems, be it the (in)formal economy, residential area, family or ethnic group'. Integration cannot be certified, it is an ongoing process to which the state should contribute by providing the necessary assistance and not by playing the role of a gendarme.

Notes

1 See the press release of the Federal Migration Service on the Concept of State Migration Policy of the Russian Federation for the period up to 2025. Online. Available at: www.fms.gouv.ru/upload/iblock/07c/kgmp.pdf (last accessed 20 August 2013).
2 Some of the ideas presented in this chapter equally apply to high-skilled migrants, whose stay in Russia is subject to other, more liberal laws and regulations.
3 The study was completed in 2011 and implemented as part of the project Complex Action on Protection of Migrants' Rights of the Saint Petersburg International Cooperation Centre of the Red Cross (funded by FP7, No. 2010/256–106). The authors would like to thank the project 'Homes, Phones and Development. Longing and Transnationality Through New Technologies at the Central Asian–Russian and the Thai-Burmese Borders', funded by the Academy of Finland, for financial and institutional support during work on this chapter, as well as the project EUBORDERSCAPES for financing the translation and copy-editing of parts of the chapter. They would also like to thank Graham Stack for his help with translating and copy-editing.
4 Labour migration during this period was mainly regulated by the Federal Law No. 115 'On the Legal Position of Foreign Citizens in the Russian Federation' (21 June 2002) and the Presidential Decree No. 2146 'Attracting and Employing Foreign Workers in the Russian Federation' (16 December 1993), amended on 5 October 2002 (No. 1129).
5 The framework of these changes was laid down by the Federal Laws No. 109 'On Monitoring Migration of Foreign Citizens and Stateless Individuals in the Russian Federation' (18 July 2006) and No. 110 'On Supplementing and Amending the Federal Law "On the Legal Position of Foreign Citizens in the Russian Federation"' (18 July 2006).
6 See note 1 (authors' translation).
7 See note 1 (authors' translation).
8 Vladimir Putin 'Rossiia: natsional'nyi vopros', *Nezavisimaia Gazeta*, 23 January 2012; authors' translation. Online. Available at: www.ng.ru/politics/2012-01-23/1_national.html (last accessed 15 July 2013).
9 See note 8 (authors' translation).
10 See 'FMS raskryla, skol'ko v Peterburge ofitsial'nyh gastarbaiterov', *Delovoe. Tv*, 31 January 2012. Online. Available at: http://delovoe.tv/event/UFMS_ne_znaet_skol_ko_n/ (last accessed 15 July 2013).
11 For more detailed information, see the website of the Committee for the Management of Municipal Property at: http://gosfondspb.ru/bronirovanie/zhilishhnyj-fond-komm ercheskogo-ispolzovaniya/dohodnye-doma/.
12 See the official website of the programme at: http://spbterance:ru/. In 2011 a new version of the programme was launched under the title 'Programme for the Harmonisation of Intercultural, Interethnic and Interconfessional Relations: The Nurturing of an Atmosphere of Tolerance in St Petersburg; 2011–2015'.
13 'Spravochnik trudovogo migranta', published in 2011 by the regional association View to the Future. Online. Available at: http://spbtolerance.ru/wp-content/uploa ds/2012/09/vostok-zapad-rus.pdf (last accessed 15 August 2013).
14 It should be noted that the manual was only made available through the programme's website, but has been authored by the regional association A View on the Future, with support from the FMS of St Petersburg and the Leningrad region. At the time (2012), representatives of St Petersburg's city administration acknowledged that the programme's implementation had not lived up to its expectations. In 2013, a complementary programme, entitled 'Migration', was initiated with the aim to 'provide measures to develop mechanisms for attracting qualified workers

and specialised programmes for short- and long-term labour migration, thus increasing the geographic mobility of the population within the North-Western federal region and the adaptation of migrants' ('Problemy trudovoi migratsii – delo vesh i kazhdogo'. Online. Available at: http://sbptolerance.ru/archives/10416).

15 'Spravochnik trudovogo migranta', pp. 38–39 (see also note 13).

16 If St Petersburg NGOs active in the field of human rights have at least rhetorically, and often actively, defended the issue of migrants' rights, they have so far neglected the rights of employers, a topic usually approached with a presumption of guilt.

17 See www.regnum:ru/news/polit/1579498.html (last accessed 31 January 2013).

18 For more details, see the association's website at: http://detipeterburga.ru.

19 Since this chapter was written in Spring 2013, the situation described here has undergone major changes for the worse. It now appears that the civic initiatives and even governmental programmes designed to further the integration of labour migrants no longer form part of the mainstream attitude towards migrants and constitute rather an exception against a background of growing xenophobia which is either ignored or, in some cases, even promoted by the state authorities in public debates and through legislative initiatives. Since late July and early August 2013, one can observe an obvious retreat towards combating 'illegal' migrants as the key mechanism of migration management, just as in the 1990s and early 2000s. This recent trend can be attributed to a general political and public climate, which includes bursts of nationalism and xenophobia actively promoted by the legislative and executive authorities both on the federal and local level. This has created favourable conditions for strengthening the position of radical nationalist groups and reinforcing the activism of extremist groups and conservative or patriotic communities and institutes, such as the 'Cossacks' and the Russian Orthodox Church. So-called 'illegal' migrants have become a convenient target of these groups which have declared them 'internal enemies'. The drive to fight illegal migration was triggered by a brawl at the Matveevsky market in Moscow on 27 July 2014 between the police and relatives of a rape suspect, Magomed Magomedov. One police officer was hospitalised with a fractured skull as a result of the fight. A series of raids organised by groups of activists and violent attacks on places where migrants work and live (market places, cafes, construction sites) ended with the detention of undocumented migrants. By and large, the police took the side of the extremists, even though their actions were illegal. A detention camp was set up almost immediately in Moscow. The shortage of detention facilities forced the Moscow police to open a temporary tented camp for several hundred immigrants, most of them Vietnamese, although nationals of Egypt, Syria and Afghanistan were also detained. The massive deportation without delay of migrants who received almost no legal support and which sometimes separated children from their parents, as well as other abuses of human rights, can be considered as evidence that migration management in the Russian Federation still has not adopted a long-term perspective with the aim to further the integration of labour migrants. Finally, the Federal Migration Service has drafted a bill to set up 83 new detention centres for illegal immigrants across the country.

13 Colonial imagination on a postcolonial periphery

Educational migration in Azerbaijan and the construction of an elite of expectations

Sergey Rumyantsev

From the late nineteenth century until the disintegration of the Soviet Union, Moscow and St Petersburg were the main centres of attraction for young Azerbaijanis. Throughout that period, and especially after the Second World War, thousands of natives from the republic seized the opportunity to receive higher education in the most prestigious universities of the Soviet Union, among them the incumbent Azerbaijani president, Ilham Aliyev, who graduated from the Moscow State University of International Relations (Andrianov and Miralamov 2007: 27–29 and 33–40).

In the aftermath of the Soviet Union's collapse, these leading higher educational institutions had to compete with US, British, German and French universities and noticeably lost their attractiveness. Studying in the West, that is, in the United States or in one of the EU countries, now appears more prestigious for many reasons. First, this is due to the perception of Azerbaijan's educational system as being in a state of permanent crisis because of insufficient state funding and high levels of corruption. Second, studying in the West generally means mastering a European language, most often English. It also considerably increases one's chances of finding a prestigious job with a major transnational company or an international organisation or foundation in Baku or elsewhere. Members of the political-bureaucratic elite of present-day Azerbaijan thus prefer to send their children to top universities in Europe or the United States. Ilham Aliyev's daughters, for example, have both studied at universities in Switzerland and the United Kingdom.[1] These recent shifts in preferences represent, however, only a minor change in a long-term trend that started in the last third of the nineteenth century. As part of this trend, Azerbaijan's political and cultural elites have recurrently expected various benefits from a process of Europeanisation that distances them from a backward East and orients them towards a modern West, thus allowing them to bring the light of modernisation to their home country.

This article focuses on Azerbaijanis who have received their higher education in EU countries or the United States during the post-Soviet period or are currently studying in European and North American universities. The main argument which will be outlined in this chapter is that over the past century and a half, representatives of the Western-educated Azerbaijani elite have

DOI: 10.4324/9781315858036-18

internalised a colonial discourse. In a slight paraphrase of Edward Said's (2003: 19) famous insight, it is claimed that Azerbaijani intellectuals who received their education in St Petersburg, Moscow or at European or North-American universities have contributed to maintaining the West's intellectual authority over the East. In other words, while aiming for Western education, these Azerbaijanis have actively participated in the construction of a discourse about Azerbaijan as part of a backward or developing East.

More precisely, the chapter examines if the post-Soviet Azerbaijani authorities reproduce and maintain or, on the contrary, contest the colonialist and essentialist view and discourses of an East–West division in the context of a national education policy that encourages young Azerbaijani citizens to study abroad, and especially in the European Union and the United States. In addition, it will examine the opinions of students and young professionals who have studied or are studying abroad and ask if they object to or reproduce this civilisational divide and these discourses.

The analysis presented here and its conclusions will be mainly based on participant observation, a biographical approach and critical discourse analysis as set out by Norman Fairclough (2010), for which a large variety of sources have been used, such as news articles, official documents, speeches by and inter-views with public figures and officials of different rank. From the numerous interviews conducted with Azerbaijani students and former students in Baku, St Petersburg, Paris, Berlin, Leipzig and Cologne, 20 have been selected for the present purpose. The interviews took place between 2007 and 2012 within the framework of different research projects. Fourteen of the interviewees, aged between 20 and 50 years, were male and six female, all of them born in Azerbaijan to parents who had both received a higher education. Six of them have been interviewed several times during this period to observe changes in their life scenarios and living experiences during their stay abroad. Initial contacts were established by visiting various events organised by Azerbaijani embassies or diaspora organisations and by snowball sampling. The discourse analysis has thus focused on a significant corpus of narratives that represent the official policy of sending young Azerbaijanis abroad for studies and include biographical presentations of 'successful' Azerbaijani intellectuals who have studied abroad to the extent that they contain views on how and if the Azerbaijani state and society should be modernised.

The chapter will start by outlining briefly how the receiving countries per-ceive the role of Azerbaijani students and other (potential) immigrants. This will be followed by an examination of how Azerbaijan's political elite defines the objectives and the significance of state programmes intended to promote educational migration and seeks to use it, including in cases where students do not return home. The analysis will then move on to present educational migration interpreted through the eyes of students and young professionals, many of whom receive grants from international organisations and are therefore less likely to submit to the influence exercised by the Azerbaijani authorities. Overall, the case of educational migration will be used to discuss if, in the context of contemporary modernisation discourses internalised by Western-educated intellectuals, it is still possible to uphold an Orientalist view of Azerbaijan that emphasises stark contrasts with the West. This discussion will be linked to the current regime's expectations to modernise the country through a Westernised elite.

Educational migration: its history and context

The habit of Azerbaijani intellectuals to talk about Azerbaijan and Azerbaijanis (i.e. a territory and an imagined community[2]) as objects in need of a degree of modernisation or Europeanisation has old roots. In fact, this debate dates back to the second half of the nineteenth century and the early twentieth century.[3] The first known ideologist of Turkish nationalism, Ali bey Huseynzade (1864–1940), who came from the territory of present-day Azerbaijan, is the author of the slogan 'Turkisation, Islamisation, Europeanisation'. Its meaning has been explained by a well-known contemporary Azerbaijani historian, who has popularised the legacy of the first-generation nationalist intellectuals, as follows: 'With this slogan he (i.e. Ali bey Huseynzade) defined the main direction of the Turkic nations' development – we need to keep up with the times and to adapt to the modern European civilisation based on our ethnic Turkic roots and not forgetting about our belonging to the Islamic world' (Balaev 2009: 21). In 1911, the slogan was borrowed by the founders of the Musavat (or Equality) Party, the most popular among Azerbaijani Turks at the beginning of the last century.

It was the Russian Empire that introduced European-style education in the region where the Azerbaijani Republic was subsequently established. Imperial governors and scholars of the Orient considered the lands of the Caucasus (as well as part of Siberia, the Far East and, of course, Central Asia) as the eastern imperial periphery. According to Austin Jersild (2002: 9) the region was considered to consist of imperial 'exotic borderlands and peoples'. Accordingly, many members of local elites were convinced of the inferiority of their culture compared to the European one (Tolz 2011: 111–134). At the turn of the twentieth century, an educated elite, which was modern for the time, started to take shape among Azerbaijanis. During that period, a European education became for the first time the main criterion to identify members of this elite. These were mainly recruited among Azerbaijani Turks wealthy enough to study in St Petersburg, Moscow or one of the European capitals. They wanted to modernise the patriarchal daily routine of Azerbaijani Turks and made early attempts to create a national discourse. The members of this elite were also the first to internalise the colonial discourse. In the context of ideas about a backward East propagated at these distant universities, modernisation meant above all Europeanisation (see Altstadt 1992; Auch 2004; Baberowski 2003; Shaffer 2002: 28–31; Swietochowski 1985: 14–27), although there existed also a group of intellectuals who were oriented towards Persia and did not share these goals and expectations. Many members of that generation had to leave Azerbaijan after Sovietisation had started in April 1920 or, later, fell victim to the terror that unfolded after the late 1920s. Others joined the new elite created by Sovietisation.

The new Soviet elite, shaped by the nationality policy and its promotion of an indigenous elite,[4] had more time and resources to modernise Azerbaijan. Despite their rather pompous anti-colonial rhetoric, the Bolsheviks quickly learnt their lesson from the earlier colonial discourse. According to Terry Martin (2001: 125) this was not at all surprising. Martin claims that in fact 'nothing better illustrates the way in which the Affirmative Action Empire (i.e. the Soviet Union) preserved imperial categories, while reversing their policy implications, than the maintenance and systematisation of colonialism's east/west dichotomy'. In this context Azerbaijan remained an integral part of the backward East, despite its new status as an outpost of socialism in the East and a success story of Soviet anti-colonial policy.

By the 1960s, or in some versions the early 1980s, representatives of the elite apparently started to believe that Azerbaijan had become almost modern, that is European – or at least its capital, the city of Baku. During that period and until the collapse of the Soviet Union, the republic's authorities actively took advantage of the opportunity for young people to study outside Azerbaijan. Thus, Heydar Aliyev,[5] speaking at the Founding Assembly of the All-Russian Azeri Congress (AAC) on 22 June 2000, stated:

> When I worked as one of Azerbaijan's leaders in the 1970s ... and up until the end of 1982 ... then I sometimes even administratively made sure that ... our young people, youth, went to other republics of the Soviet Union to receive an education. Back then, we did not have opportunities other than the Soviet Union, that is within the Soviet Union. ... From 1970 on, I set myself the task to send many Azeris outside Azerbaijan, primarily to Russia, primarily to Moscow, Leningrad, and other major centres for higher education, centres for science, centres for culture. ... In the beginning they issued a quota of one hundred (students) and, already in 1978–79, I managed to bring it up to eight hundred. This was such an important cause for me that with all my other responsibilities, which, maybe, were considered to be the most important ones for the republic's leader, I attended to this.[6]

Many of those who, as a result of this policy, studied at the Soviet Union's leading universities still recall how Heydar Aliyev in person saw them off.

> Heydar Aliyev personally sent me to study in St Petersburg. He person-ally hugged me, kissed me, gave me a briefcase and forty roubles and said: "Go, son, you will come back and put the mind of the people right." That was in eighty-one. Not only me, there were about twenty people.
>
> (Azer, male, 52 years, Baku, January 2009)

However, in the post-Soviet period, Azerbaijani social scientists and intellectuals began to perceive the Soviet nationality policy as colonialist. Thus, the already quoted historian Balaev, a proponent of modernisation theory, believes that the 'natural' process of Europeanisation was rudely interrupted by the intervention of the Bolsheviks in 1920 (see Balaev 2012). Accordingly, the new Musavat Party, which was established between 1989 and 1992, is presented by its founding fathers as a restoration. The idea of a succession has been reaffirmed by the adoption of the state flag in 1992, which was the same tricolour as the one chosen in 1918. According to the historian, philosopher and academician Afrand Dashdamirov, its colours are 'the symbolical embodiment' of the slogan quoted above. The idea of modernisation as Europeanisation is still very much present among the Western-oriented nationalists of the post-Soviet period. Thus, the main official ideologue of the regime, Ramiz Mehdiyev, head of the presidential administration but also a philosopher and academician, in an article on the country's strategy for the future, reflects on how post-Soviet Azerbaijan should be modernised, that is what could be usefully adopted from the Western model.[7]

Today, the authorities continue to send young people abroad with the same goal of modernising and Europeanising Azerbaijan. The government has, for instance, adopted an ambitious plan for the period 2007–2015 to implement programmes promoting education in EU countries.[8] In addition, the authorities generally do not interfere when Azerbaijanis want to complete an internship abroad for a period from two months to two years, and even longer. Moreover, they often keep open the positions these interns occupy in state institutions (universities, research institutes of the National Academy of Sciences etc.). Indeed, the government declares its wish to promote the development of such ties. As a result, a new generation of highly educated people are now continuing the tradition of modernising and Europeanising Azerbaijan.

State, political authorities and educational migration

It is suggested here that this educated elite is best described as an 'elite of expectations', including – and this is important – from the perspective of the major political actors outside Azerbaijan. As shown above, ideas of nationalism and modernisation entered the region together with the formation of the insignificantly small elite that had studied in Europe (Shaffer 2002: 28–31; Swietochowski 1985: 14–27). In a paraphrase of Partha Chatterjee (1995: 9), it is possible to say that nationalist and modernist thought in Azerbaijan is 'an export from Europe, like the printing press, radio and television'. For Azerbaijani intellectuals who experienced educational migration in the last third of the nineteenth and the early twentieth century, modernisation primarily implied the construction of an Azerbaijani nation (Baberowski 2003: 44–57 and 142–183). They were hoping to lead the imaginary community they were in the process of building along the same path of modernisation that Western

Europe's nations had followed (see Gellner 1983: 19–38; Hobsbawm 2002: 101–130). At the turn of the twentieth century, the representatives of an educated elite were expected to conduct the modernisation policy of the Russian empire. With the Bolsheviks' arrival in the region, plans to reorganise society became far more ambitious. Now modernisation or, as Anatoli' Vishnevski' (1998: 6) has put it, 'the great social mutation' implied not only nation-building but also efforts to overtake and surpass the West in terms of development. The Bolsheviks hoped that they would become the instruments of the regime's "conservative modernisation" in the "Soviet East"'.

In Western countries that today receive students from Azerbaijan (and elsewhere), these are often seen as promising young adults who, after the completion of their studies or their training, will either continue to stay on and become available to the national labour market (or that of another Western country) or return home and be expected to operate a certain transfer of Western values, primarily linked to the principles of the market economy, a democratic state and the respect of human rights. Their education and life experience in democratic countries is thought to make them an ideal conduit for policies that promote a similar kind of system for Azerbaijan, thus transforming them into agents of the host country's soft power.[9] At the same time, they are still considered part of the Muslim world or the wider East, which would make their actions even more effective. A symbolic indicator of this attitude were, for example, entirely unfounded expectations that the Arab Spring could be exported to Azerbaijan.

The current Azerbaijani regime and its political opposition pursue a greater variety of goals in their actions. Several opposition parties declare in their manifestos their adherence to the political and economic – but not cultural – values of Western democratic regimes and express their hope that these could be transferred to Azerbaijan with the help of Western-educated returnees, although it is almost impossible to find them among the leadership of these parties. By contrast, the Azerbaijani government, which many experts have described as authoritarian (Abbasov 2011: 108; Guliev 2011: 83–90; Ottaway 2003: 51–70), has different expectations from educational migration. Since the collapse of the Soviet Union and especially in the 2000s, it has very actively promoted a policy designed to create diaspora networks of students and graduate expatriates with close ties to the regime in the hope that they would accomplish more or less specific tasks set by the government.[10] If local news reports are to be believed, this seems to have led at times to somewhat unrealistic expectations, as in the following statement reportedly made by Qulu Novruzov, Deputy Minister for Education:

> Thanks to Azerbaijani students, very strong diaspora networks are forming in several countries. ... The Deputy Minister expressed his confidence that the number of diaspora networks will rise and Azerbaijani students will be more represented in the state structures of the countries they are studying in.[11]

More modest objectives probably include the defence of the regime's record, notably its claims of having successfully created a modern economic and political system, and advertising the country's tourist attractions. It was apparently hoped that those willing to participate in this scheme would speak the same language as officials in the European Union and the United States, thus helping maintain in power the present regime. Of interest in the present context is that these official representations of Azerbaijan depict it at the same time as a Muslim country that has remained part of a mythical East, 'a place of romance, exotic beings, haunting memories and landscapes, remarkable experience' (Said 2003: 1). The combination of these features has also given rise to the metaphor of Azerbaijan as a bridge between East and West, with the implication that the country has been borrowing what is best from both worlds or civilisations. Azerbaijan is here seen as a space in which the East and the West somehow organically coexist and interweave. Thus, the republic's capital, Baku, is said to be Eastern but with a 'European charm'. In this way, Azerbaijan is still being presented in the very terms of the colonial discourse.

A backward East or another civilisation?

The main content of this tradition can be conveyed by a brief and at the same time instructive observation made by one of the informants interviewed, Nizami,[12] an Azerbaijani man aged 43 who emigrated to the United States in 2008. The first step towards his emigration was a job with a US-based international humanitarian organisation. He first visited the United States in 2002–2003 to continue his studies. Under the terms of his contract, he was supposed to return to Azerbaijan after completing his course but in order to be able to go back to the United States Nizami continued to work for the same organisation in Afghanistan. When he was asked during a second interview with him in Baku, in 2009, to reflect on the differences between the countries where he had lived and worked, Nizami answered:

> It's the same as travelling by means of a time machine. I have been to absolutely different worlds. It's sometimes hard to believe that conditions people live in can be so different. Afghanistan compared to the States is like the sixteenth century. Nothing has changed ever since they got stuck in the past. However, Azerbaijan compared to Afghanistan is certainly a more advanced country. Azerbaijan compared to the USA, that's the eighteenth or nineteenth century.
>
> (Baku, September 2009)

Many current or former international students think in similar ways. For them Azerbaijan is part of a backward East. Others see the country as being closer to the developed world because it has succeeded in implementing various modernisation programmes, a view more in line with the Azerbaijani regime's official discourse. Still others go even further in their self-identification by distancing themselves from their Azerbaijani identity: 'I am not an Azerbaijani scholar, I am a representative of the Moscow school.' (interview with Mikael, 49, in Baku in March 2010). – 'We received special training. I represent the Petersburg school of Oriental Studies. That is the most progressive school that no other compares to.' (Interview with Arifa, a woman aged 42 years, in St Petersburg in April 2008) – 'It's impossible to receive a good modern education in Azerbaijan. Any specialist who has obtained his diploma in the UK or the USA is a cut above someone who graduated from a university in Baku. There is no real base and conditions to study. And more, there is corruption, too' (Interview with Faiq, a man of 32 years, in Berlin in July 2011).

However, several interviewees operate an inversion of the scale of values. To them, Azerbaijan is 'another civilisation', different from the Western one and which lives by its own more 'correct' rules. In this discourse, references to medieval history can serve as a resource to glorify this civilisation: 'Culture, sciences, civilisation – this all came to Europe from the East. They owe it all to us!' (Interview with Albufaz, a man born in 1976, in Baku in November 2010). Moreover, Azerbaijan is thought to compare favourably with the West in that relationships there are 'warmer' and more 'humane', even though this may come at a certain price:

> It is very hard to adapt to others' morals. You go outside and everything around you is alien. Everything is in German. German is spoken around you. All signboards are in German. Everything is in German! And relationships between people are completely different and people themselves are different. ... Family means nothing to them. Girls have sex when they are only teenagers. They have dozens of partners and hence infertility and various illnesses. I have two gay neighbours. They are men over 50 now – they live together. I am raising a son. When he asks me (about these neighbours), what will I tell him?
>
> (Interview with Rahim, male, 34, in Cologne, November 2008)

> I associate mainly with immigrants from the former Soviet Union, although I can freely communicate with the Germans. I thoroughly learned their mentality over the years. ... I can joke like them and I understand their jokes. But basically they are completely different people. ... Though if they were not such people, they probably would not have created such a thriving economy. This is the price of progress, a good life, and a developed economy.
>
> (Interview with Azer, male, 48, in Leipzig, October 2011)

Students abroad and back home

As the examples quoted above show, discourses about Azerbaijan that apprehend its specificities in terms of an East–West division should also be understood within a biographical context, such as (the desire for) a successful career or difficulties to adapt to a foreign life style. In fact, most students interviewed abroad declare that they do not wish to return home. A typical example for this attitude is Natavan, a 32-year-old Azeri woman. Eager to leave Azerbaijan, she first visited the United States for a couple of weeks to attend a conference. Subsequently, she won a competition that allowed her to study there. Although the terms of her contract stipulated a return to Azerbaijan after two years, she managed to stay on and continues to do so after a failed attempt to find employment in Greece, which would have brought her closer to her family in Baku:

> I went, together with friends from the States, to Athens because in Europe it's easiest to settle down in Greece. ... I stayed in the USA. Not because I had to, but because I think that there is no better place to live. In the States I have many friends and have never had a problem with a job. I even lived a good life on my scholarship. I bought a car and we travelled around the States when we were students. We went to a festival in New Orleans, to Las Vegas. I wanted to move to Athens to work, just in order to be close to Baku. My mom was staying in Azerbaijan. I should tell you that it's not that bad in Athens either. But I failed to find a job there and went back to the States. I do not regret this. Now I have my own house. I have a cooler car and have a good job. I am only dreaming about US citizenship and that's all! Live and enjoy your life. The way you want. It is more peaceful here. Free. You don't have to think about what other people think. You don't have to feel defective just because you are 32 and you are not married yet. And prospects for development are huge. You can find a job, with any salary you want.
>
> (Interview conducted in Baku, September 2010)

The very liberating aspects of a Western lifestyle invoked by Natavan are reinterpreted in a second, much less common scenario provided by Farid, a young man who, at the age of 18, left Azerbaijan to study in the United States and later the United Kingdom before returning home. Farid considers his attitude towards the West as conservative. In his view, Western life, although more modern, is not just different but cannot suit Azerbaijanis. Along with others, he considers it 'unacceptable' and argues that the Azerbaijani life style should not be destroyed or transformed but rather be preserved. Interestingly, while he does not mention other reasons for his return home than his attachment to his family and his own rejection of the Western life style, he still expresses the wish to continue his studies abroad or to work there:

> I would certainly like to go there to study once again. Or to work. But I would not like to live there. To me, motherland is not just a word. Perhaps, my approach to life is somewhat conservative. Society itself, their attitude to each other, all that is alien to me. They are sort of more individualised. Everyone is by himself. But here, I have my family, my parents. This is

very important to me. There, family life is in decline, both in Europe and America. I have actually never thought about making a choice – to leave or to stay. One needs to live in his motherland. Yes, not everything is fine in our country. But this is not a reason to emigrate. ... But to say the truth, out of the nineteen people who went under a programme from Azerbaijan to study, only me and another three guys did not particularly like America. This is all the skilful policy of soft power. To impose their lifestyle on us. Everyone else got Americanised very quickly.

(Interview conducted in Baku, November 2010)

For Farid, return home also means a return to the past, although his feelings are not free of ambiguity. Returning home can indeed be more difficult than leaving home. Or as Stefansson (2004: 8) notes: 'Because of the mismatch between the imagined and experienced homecoming, coming home can be more difficult and emotionally destabilising than leaving home and settling in a new part of the world.'

Conclusion

For a century and a half, Azerbaijani Turks have been going abroad to receive a better education, the most attractive centres being the former imperial metropolises (St Petersburg and Moscow), European capitals and, more recently and increasingly, universities in the United States. Thus, there exists a long tradition of discussing Azerbaijan's state of affairs from the perspective of Azerbaijanis who have been educated abroad. This educational experience not only enables those who have made it to see their homeland through the lens of another way of life but also pushes them to construct an imaginary necessary choice about the country's future: either to become modern and part of an imaginary of a Western world or to remain a no less imaginary backward East, generally with an inevitable answer in favour of the first.

It would certainly be a mistake to consider the Azerbaijani students in Europe and elsewhere as forming a homogeneous group. Although similar experiences abroad often lead to similar forms of self-identification, expressed, for example, in the boundary erected between those who hold a diploma from a European or North American university and those who have studied at home, biographical scenarios can strongly vary, depending especially on whether the stay abroad is considered a success or a failure. However, the most important criterion for describing this group, along with self-identification, seems to be the involvement of its members in the construction, or reproduction, of a colonial discourse about Azerbaijan as part of an East that requires modernisation. As Terry Martin (2001: 125) has noted: 'Today, when Edward Said has turned "orientalism" into a universally recognised term ... nothing seems to us more characteristic of colonialism than the division of mankind into the arbitrary, essentialised and hierarchical categories of east and west.' Voluntarily or not, many members of the Azerbaijani elite have acquired imperial or

Western ideological values and discourses during their education. According to John McLeod (2007: 5), whose thinking is also influenced by Said (2003), 'the very language we use may well be complicit in perpetuating forms of knowledge which support a colonialist vision of the world'. This supports the main argument of this chapter: although Azerbaijan has become an independent state in post-Soviet times, the language used by its intellectuals to (self-)describe their country has remained largely colonial.

Since the start of the post-Soviet period, the West has remained the main model for comparison and self-evaluation. In some regards, the discourse that contrasts East and West has become even more influential, as will be shown in the following paragraphs, which will focus on various aspects of educational migration from Azerbaijan to Western countries.

The best-known and most influential nationalists of the early twentieth century have pleaded the need to build a modern imagined community ('Europeanisation' and 'Turkisation') with obligatory reverence to the preservation of local specificities ('Islamisation'). They have, thus, made the nationalist ideas they had studied at European universities politically relevant for Azerbaijan, before passing the baton to the national Bolsheviks[13] who even more actively and purposefully attempted to transform the country into the first modern outpost of socialism in the East. In post-Soviet times, this has led to the emergence of the myth of a golden age of Azerbaijani nationalism, with the latter in the role of an avant-garde in the East.

Being first meant a striking success for the imaginary Europeanisation of Azerbaijan, the myth was seen as proof of Azerbaijanis' ability to learn how to be modern, because Western education, in addition to instilling the belief that the native imaginary community is backward and Eastern, also teaches how to overcome this state by internalising the colonial discourse. The signs of modernity are multiple: putting on a European costume, shaving off a beard and moustache, removing a woman's veil, learning English or French, building universities, writing an opera … Only when all this has been achieved, once modern operas and ballets (i.e. in the European spirit) will have been composed and staged, will it be possible to also love the traditional-minded folks, to make a careful study of folklore, for ethnographers to search for 'national origins' and, finally, to fabricate formalised versions of the local folklore that now appear exotic: professionals start performing folk dances and a formerly ordinary costume becomes a festive and expensive decoration.[14]

Towards the end of the Soviet era, all stages of Europeanisation appeared to have been accomplished. Then much of the progress made was suddenly swept away with the disintegration of the Soviet Union. Once more, Azerbaijan seemed to be located on an imperial periphery and the colonial discourse, although in a much transformed form, again proved to be in great demand. Despite the golden era of pre-Soviet nationalism, previous attempts at modernising the country were now thought to have largely failed because they had not taken into account the local context. Today, too, politicians in Western liberal democracies place their hopes in a young Azerbaijani elite to modernise the country, notably by bringing democracy to it. It is by now clear, that earlier expectations have turned out to be, if not completely futile, then at least grossly overstated.

Has anything changed in the post-Soviet period? Of course, the socio-political and cultural context is markedly different from those of earlier periods. However, the current situation can also be seen as the direct continuation of earlier traditions of internalising the colonial discourse. Most contemporary Western-educated intellectuals speak and think in terms that are characteristic of it and its perhaps most permanent feature, the boundaries drawn between a Western-educated elite and a people living in the past, has remained as strong as ever.

Notes

1 The elder daughter, Leyla Alieva, also studied at the same Moscow State Institute of International Relations in 2006–2008 (Andrianov and Miralamov 2007: 331, 383). See also the official websites of the President of Azerbaijan at: www.president. az/president/biography/; and of LeylaAlieva at: www.leyla-aliyeva.az/en/biografiya/ (last accessed 10 July 2013).
2 See Anderson (1998: 5–7).
3 See the following newspaper article on the anniversary of the independence of the Azerbaijani Democratic Republic by Naila Bagirov 'AK', '95 godovshchina so dnia provozglashenia Azerbaidzhanskoi Demokraticheskoi Respubliki', *azeri.ru*, no date. Online. Available at: www.azeri.ru/az/history/adr90/ (last accessed 25 June 2013).
4 For more details on the Soviet nationality policy and its promotion of indigenous elites, see: (Baberowski 2003: 316–348; Hirsch 2005: 145–186; Martin 2001: 1–28; Slezkine 1994; Suny 1993: 84–126).
5 Former First Secretary of the central committee of the Azerbaijani communist party and former president of post-Soviet Azerbaijan (1993–2003).
6 See the newspaper article published in Bakinskiy Rabochiy, on 28 June 2000.
7 'Opredelaya strategiyu budushego: kurs na modernizatsiyu', *1news.az*, 10 January 2008. Online. Available at: www.1news.az/articles.php?item_id=20080110113244532&sec_id=6 (last accessed 21 June 2013).
8 According to the Azerbaijani Ministry for Education, about 5,000 students are to study in EU countries, the United States, Japan and other countries under the State Programme on Education of Azerbaijani Youth in Foreign Countries for the period 2007–2015. Online. Available at: www.edu.gov.az/view.php?lang=ru&menu=256 (last accessed 3 July 2013).
9 Soft power 'uses a different type of currency (not force, not money) to engender co-operation – an attraction to shared values and the justness and duty of contributing to the achievement of those values. … (It) can rest on the attractiveness of one's culture and values' (Nye 2004: 7). For a critical analysis of conceptions of soft power, see Fergusson (2005).
10 The criteria employed in academic discussions or by leading scholars in this field (see Cohen 1996: 515; Safran 1991: 83–84; Sheffer 2003: 9–10) are not always relevant in the case of social networks and ethnic organisations of Azerbaijani emigrants. The most constructive approach in this context has been proposed by Brubaker (2005: 13) who notes that 'it may be more fruitful, and certainly more precise, to speak of diasporic stances, projects, claims, idioms, practices, and so on'. These networks seem to be rather good examples of transnational ties and spaces.

(On transnationalism see Schiller *et al.* 1992: ix; and Schiller and Cağlar 2008: 47). More importantly in this case, 'this term focuses on people and groups and does not necessarily refer to official bodies' (Ben-Rafael and Sternberg 2009: 1). Transnational networks and families (Bryceson and Vuorela 2002: 3) of migrants from Azerbaijan often play a wider role than that prescribed by the official political project of diaspora-building.

11 See 'Blagodaria azerbaidjanskim studentam v riade stran formiruitsa ochen silnie diasporskie seti', *AzerTAdj*, 23 August 2012. Online. Available at: www.azerbaijan. az/portal/newsru.html?action=GetFullNews&ldid=2005–07–26&ltid=21:42:12& ndid=2012–08–23&nid=7 (last accessed 8 February 2013).

12 The names of all informants have been changed for the sake of preserving their anonymity.

13 According to Brandenberger, national Bolshevism (Nationalkommunismus) refers to 'the phenomenon of nationalist sympathies within the party hierarchy, eroding prospects for world revolution, and the Stalinist elite's revision of Marxist principles' (Brandenberger 2002: 1). On national Bolsheviks in Azerbaijan see (Baberowski 2003: 223–312).

14 Soviet nationality policy has been described as 'strictly assimilationist' and aimed at the 'erosion of ethnicity' (Mammadli 2011: 180; 2008: 61). The ethnographic approach focuses on reinventing Azeri 'real' and 'almost lost' ethnic and folk traditions. The post-Soviet period has seen the publication of major ethnographic works in the classic imperial tradition that offer descriptions of Azeri and some native (korenii) ethnic groups, their folk or ethnic dresses, cuisine, housing etc. (see Abbasov 1998; Bunyadov 2007; Cavadov 2000; Cavadov 2004).

14 Gendered migration from Moldova and Ukraine to the EU

Who cares?

Olga Davydova-Minguet, Valeriu Mosneaga and Oleksii Pozniak

> On women's day, an international soccer match Spain vs. Italy took place in a Moldovan village. Men whose wives work in Spain played against those whose wives work in Italy.

The joke above was told to a group of academic scholars during a recent visit to Moldova. Migration is indeed a widespread phenomenon in both Moldova and Ukraine, a fact reflected in the humour of these countries. During the visit it seemed that all locals were somehow on the point of leaving the country. When people met, their relatives and friends were either discussing the possibility of migrating or were about to do so. The only queue in Chisinau was the line in front of the National Archive where people obtain documents to prove their ancestry from that part of Moldova which had belonged to Romania before the Second World War and thus can claim Romanian citizenship. This in turn allows them to work in a country of the European Union. The Moldovan countryside was full of unfinished spacious houses owned by labour migrants who were working abroad to earn the money necessary for completing the building.

One of the most frequently discussed topics in everyday conversations, but also in assessments produced by experts and in the scientific literature, is female migration and its numerous and varied consequences, such as social orphanhood, divorce, the trafficking of women and children, changes in gender roles and the traditional model of the family, remittances, economic assistance to families left behind and the loss of the country's demographic potential. This chapter investigates certain aspects of female migration from Moldova and Ukraine and, more particularly, relates them to the structural organisation of care in EU countries that are the targets of this migration. The aim is to highlight how female migration, its volume and directions, is interconnected with policies of social care, especially in target countries.

To contextualise this phenomenon the chapter starts by analysing recent migration trends in Moldova and Ukraine and by outlining some of their local impacts. It will then discuss female migration in relation to the care policies of EU countries. Since Italy is one of the most popular destinations for female migrants from Moldova and Ukraine, it will be used here as an

DOI: 10.4324/9781315858036-19

example for countries with a familialistic care model, that is where care is mainly provided by the family but nowadays often by female migrants in the employ of the family. In concluding, this care model will be assessed as to its sustainability and stability. From an analytical point of view, welfare policies of receiving countries are here considered as a structure that enables and encourages particular forms of labour migration from the EU's Eastern Neighbourhood.

Labour migration from Moldova and Ukraine

International labour migration started to flourish in Moldova during the second half of the 1990s and is today the far most predominant form of migration. It is also one of the most pressing issues facing the country. According to estimates published by the media, between 340,000 and one million Moldavans are working abroad (Moraru, Mosneaga and Rusnac 2012: 27) and the World Bank has claimed that over 700,000 people, that is almost half of the country's working population, are involved in labour migration (World Bank 2011b: 60).

The Republic of Moldova is located at the junction of the European (mainly EU) and the post-Soviet (Commonwealth of Independent States (CIS)) migration systems. Among the CIS countries, Russia, and in particular Moscow and the Moscow region, appear to be the major destinations for Moldovan migrants. Within the European Union, Italy is the core destination. Thus, a majority of Moldovan labour migrants reside in Russia (58.2 per cent), followed by Italy (19 per cent), Portugal (5 per cent), Spain, Greece, the Czech Republic, France, Germany, Ireland, Cyprus, Romania, Turkey, Israel and Ukraine (Lucke, Mahmoud and Steinmayr 2009).

Overall, migrants tend to concentrate in big cities. Almost three quarters of them live in ten cities: Moscow, Rome, St Petersburg, Paris, Lisbon, Padua, Milan, Istanbul, Odessa and Tyumen (Lucke, Mahmoud and Pinger 2007: 26). Secondly, there exists a gender division: some countries, such as Russia, Ukraine, France, the Czech Republic and Portugal are more popular destinations for men, while women predominantly move to Italy, Turkey, Spain and Greece. Contrary to public perception, the economic crisis starting in 2008 did not result in a large-scale reversion of these trends. Monitoring conducted through the sociological survey CBS AXA in 2008–2009 indicates that Moldavians continue to dream of migration and are still willing to work abroad. In times of crisis, these aspirations thus rather seem to receive a new impulse (IOM 2009).

Ukraine is one of the largest suppliers of labour to Europe and international labour migration is a mass phenomenon there, too. Much as in Moldova, labour migration flows began during the recession of the transitional period because employment opportunities in the official domestic labour market were scarce. They increased throughout the 1990s, as wages in the registered economic sector remained low and the unemployment rate and involuntary part-time employment rose, leading to the spread of poverty and high economic inequality. When the economy started to recover in 2000, the job situation and living standards improved. The unemployment and underemployment rates dropped significantly, the amount of unpaid salaries decreased rapidly and durable consumer goods became once more available. However, most indicators for Ukraine's social and economic development remain far below European standards, notably wage levels. There are therefore many reasons for Ukrainians to seek work abroad.

According to the State Employment Office, 85,000 Ukrainian citizens worked abroad in 2011 and almost 87,000 in 2012. Information about Ukrainian citizens officially working abroad is provided by private bureaus, agencies and various organisations that offer services related to employment outside Ukraine. Obviously, the number of workers who are placed in jobs through official channels does not reflect the real importance of labour migration from Ukraine. The monitoring currently carried out by the State Employment Office of Ukraine produces mostly data on sailors, which explains the significant share of men (93.8 per cent in 2012) in its figures for officially registered labour migrants.

In mid-2008 the Ukrainian Centre of Social Reforms (UCSR) and the State Committee of Statistics of Ukraine (SSCU) conducted the first large-scale survey on labour migration based on a household sample (UCSR and SSCU 2009). It will hereafter be referred to as the Labour Migration Survey. Four years later, a second nationwide survey, also based on a household sample, was carried out by the Ptoukha Institute for Demography and Social Research and the State Statistics Service of Ukraine but its results have not yet been published at the time of writing.

According to the Labour Migration Survey, 1.5 million Ukrainian residents were working abroad between early 2005 and 1 June 2008 and almost 1.3 million travelled abroad with the aim of finding employment between early 2007 and 1 January 2008 (UCSR and SSCU 2009). In total, labour migrants make up 5.1 per cent of Ukraine's working-age population, and those who migrated during the last 18 months of the period covered account for 4.4 per cent. Similar figures have been obtained through other methods employed during the survey, such as interviews with the heads of local councils or their deputies, asked to assess the impact of labour migration in their township or village, and with residents of rural areas (UCSR and SSCU 2009), as well as through another survey collecting demographic and health data (Ukrainian Centre for Social Reforms (UCSR), State Statistics Committee (SSC) of Ukraine, Ministry of Health (MofH) of Ukraine and Macro International Inc. 2008).

The main countries of destination for Ukrainian labour migrants are the Russian Federation (48 per cent), Italy (13 per cent), the Czech Republic (12 per cent), Poland (8 per cent), Hungary, Spain and Portugal. Almost all destinations are CIS or EU countries. The majority of labour migrants are male (two out of three in 2008). However, notable differences between the sexes can be observed for certain destination countries. Thus, whereas 61 per cent of the Ukrainian labour migrants in Italy are women, Hungary, the Czech

Republic and especially Russia mostly attract male migrants from Ukraine (the female share there is respectively 28, 30 and 19 per cent).

Another particularity are the regional variations. The ratio of labour migrants to the total working-age population ranges from practically zero, in some northern, central and southern regions, to almost 30 per cent in the Zakarpatska region, in southwestern Ukraine. Globally the ratio decreases from west to east, despite a slight increase in the Luhansk region in the southeast of the country. Lower ratios can also be observed for large multifunctional cities and their hinterland, namely the capital Kiev and the regions surrounding it.

In short, the major factors that define labour migration rates from Ukraine's regions appear to be:

- geographical proximity to Ukraine's state borders, especially with EU countries, that is areas from which it is easier and less expensive to migrate to another country;
- specific mental traits – residents of the western regions, for example, are widely known as being less paternalistic in outlook and more self-reliant when confronted with urgent problems and are therefore more likely to resort to labour migration in times of economic need;
- residence in or near a large multifunctional city that often offers more attractive employment opportunities than a foreign country;
- the overall level of a region's development – outmigration flows are stronger in little-developed regions such as that of Luhansk, which suffers not only from its marginal location but also from a consistently low level of human development.

In addition, the direction of migration flows is influenced by historical as well as mental and ethnical ties that link the inhabitants of certain Ukrainian regions to those of foreign countries (Pozniak 2009). The main destination countries for labour migrants from the Zakarpatska region are the Czech Republic, Hungary and Slovakia and for those from the Chernivtsi region, Italy. Poland attracts numerous migrants from other western regions, while the Russian Federation is the main destination for people from central, eastern and southern Ukraine. Almost all Ukrainian labour migrants in Hungary are from the Zakarpatska region and three out of four in Poland are from five regions in western Ukraine.

Migrants in neighbouring countries (Russia, Poland, Czech Republic, Hungary) usually stay there repeatedly for short periods, while migrants to southern Europe tend to remain for a longer period. Only about a third of the Ukrainians working abroad have residence and work permits, the others are undocumented migrants or partially fulfil the legal requirements. Those with an official status were most likely to work in the Czech Republic, Spain or Portugal, while the largest portion of migrants with no official status live in Poland and Italy. The majority of migrants are employed, but one out of six is self-employed or an employer, mostly in a neighbouring country, and especially in Hungary (Ptoukha Institute for Demography and Social Studies of National Academy of Science of Ukraine (IDSS) 2010).

Gendered migration: the well-being of migrants and their families

Studies from Moldova (Poalelungi 2010) offer useful information on the social and demographic profile of citizens involved in international labour migration. Most migrants are young adults: over 70 per cent of them are under 40 and almost 40 per cent are under 30 years of age; the average age is 35 years. Those aged 25 to 34 account for the largest part of migration flows (33.9 per cent) and most of them are male (63.6 per cent). Three out of four migrants (75.6 per cent) have completed their secondary education or had a professional education, but often occupy unskilled jobs abroad that are more accessible to foreigners.

Women account for up to a fourth of Moldovan labour migrants (Vaculovschi *et al.* 2010). Male labour migrants are employed in construction, the transport sector, industry and agriculture. The vast majority (51 per cent) of Moldavians work in construction. Female migrants are employed in industry and commerce, care for the elderly, sick and children, work as domestic help or provide sexual services. Most labour migrants do not work in the field for which they have been trained. This is especially the case in Western European countries. By contrast, migrants are more likely to find employment related to their training or earlier work experience in Russia, notably in the construction sector, agriculture, industry, trade, services and the transport sector.

Professionals (teachers, engineers, doctors etc.), too, are involved in international labour migration. As one survey has shown, a quarter of all migrants from Moldova are individuals with a secondary or professional education (respectively 25.5 per cent and 25.6 per cent in 2010). Their main motivation for seeking temporary or permanent residence abroad is the lack of attractive and well-paid jobs in Moldova. In addition, the majority of young Moldavians studying in Russia, Romania and Western European countries do not return home after completing their education. Thus, Moldova is also becoming a supplier of skilled labour at the expense of its own development (Moraru 2011: 66).

Studies from Ukraine provide a similar, sometimes more differentiated picture. Thus, male migrants from Ukraine are engaged mainly in construction, but as Table 14.1 shows, they predominantly do domestic work in Italy, while in Poland they are mainly employed in agriculture.

Female labour migrants from Ukraine are mainly working in the domestic sphere (as in Portugal, Spain and, especially, Italy), in trade (mainly in the Russian Federation and Hungary) and the construction sector (in Hungary, Portugal, the Czech Republic and the Russian Federation). In Poland, agriculture is the main sector where they are employed (see Table 14.2).

International labour migration has distinctive effects on Moldovan and Ukrainian society. Especially in Moldova, labour migration is so omnipresent

Table 14.1 Ukrainian male labour migrants by country of destination and type of economic activity in the host country (in %), 2007–2008

	Czech Republic	Hungary	Italy	Poland	Portugal	Russian Federation	Spain	Other countries	All countries
Agriculture	7.5	5.4	9.6	43.0	2.6	3.6	48.0	13.3	8.4
Industry	6.2	12.5	3.3	3.1	1.4	5.7	0.0	8.5	5.7
Construction	82.1	49.1	33.8	37.7	64.1	78.3	52.0	34.2	67.6
Wholesale and retail trade	0.5	33.0	0.0	8.9	2.9	3.9	0.0	9.4	4.8
Hotels and restaurants	2.1	0.0	0.0	0.0	3.3	0.8	0.0	0.9	0.9
Transport	0.0	0.0	2.1	0.0	12.4	4.2	0.0	13.8	3.9
Domestic work	1.0	0.0	43.8	7.3	13.3	1.2	0.0	15.8	6.4
Other	0.7	0.0	7.4	0.0	0.0	2.1	0.0	4.1	2.2
Total	100.0	100.0	100.0	100.0	100.0	100.0	100.0	100.0	100.0

Source: Ukrainian Centre for Social Reforms (UCSR) and State Statistics Committee (SSCU) (2009).

Table 14.2 Ukrainian female labour migrants by country of destination and type of economic activity in the host country (in %), 2007–2008

	Czech Republic	Hungary	Italy	Poland	Portugal	Russian Federation	Spain	Other countries	All countries
Agriculture	5.5	0.0	4.0	56.9	3.7	0.5	17.1	2.9	8.5
Industry	16.3	24.8	0.4	0.0	0.0	5.6	0.0	6.1	5.1
Construction	44.9	51.1	2.9	2.7	48.8	30.2	19.9	11.6	19.8
Wholesale and retail trade	5.9	20.3	2.1	15.3	0.0	35.4	7.2	10.2	14.6
Hotels and restaurants	16.5	0.0	10.8	0.0	3.3	1.3	27.6	3.0	6.8
Transport	0.0	0.0	0.0	0.0	0.0	0.4	0.0	5.0	0.9
Domestic work	9.4	0.0	75.7	21.6	44.1	17.5	28.3	34.1	36.1
Other	1.3	3.8	4.1	3.5	0.0	9.0	0.0	27.1	8.3
Total	100.0	100.0	100.0	100.0	100.0	100.0	100.0	100.0	100.0

Source: Ukrainian Centre for Social Reforms (UCSR) and State Statistics Committee (SSCU) (2009).

that it affects all parts of the country and permeates every sphere of public and private life. The impacts on rural areas and their socio-demographic situation are particularly acute as the exodus there is more intense than in urban areas. In 2010, 70.9 per cent of those who left the country came from rural areas. In many cases, few men of working-age remain in the villages, just as in times of war. In other villages, particularly in the south, there are virtually no women of working-age left, so that during weddings men often dance with each other (Moraru, Mosneaga and Rusnac 2012: 58). Labour migration also alters the patriarchal model of the family. While families materially benefit from labour migration, emotional ties suffer from the prolonged absence of a family member (Moraru, Mosneaga and Rusnac 2012). Many of the predominantly young migrants end up becoming permanent residents in their host country and will take their children with them. This process has actually started to gain momentum in the early 2000s. In 2011 alone, some 28,000 children left the country with their parents to take up permanent residence abroad.[1] This aggravates Moldova's demographic decline.

The main positive effect of migration are the money transfers from migrants that are conducted through both official and unofficial channels. Remittances have been increasing almost every year. Their value has reached USD1.45 billion in 2012, only slightly less than in 2008, when they amounted to USD1.66 billion (National Bank of Moldova 2013).

Remittances are mostly spent on private consumption. Only 16.8 per cent of respondents in a survey declared their intention to save money in order to start a business and only some 10 per cent of former migrants said they had done so (Moraru, Mosneaga and Rusnac 2012: 55). Remittances are invested mainly in agriculture, transport, the retail and entertainment sector as well as real estate. Some money is also spent on community development, as people remain attached to the locality where they were born or have lived before leaving. Every ninth labour migrant thus financially assists a parish, sports club or other local institutions but the geographic distribution of this assistance is very uneven and rarely of great significance.

The growing cash flows from abroad have profoundly transformed Moldovan society. In addition to reinforcing negative demographic trends (a declining birth rate and an ageing population), they have led to unsustainable levels in the country's balance of payments (many imports are financed by remittances) and an appreciation of the currency that reduces its international competitiveness. Equally important are the social consequences. Family life has been strongly affected by the increasing number of social orphans (i.e. children left behind by their migrant parents) and by changing gender roles, which also have an impact on the wider community and the whole country. At the cost of destroying social networks, migration has worked towards reducing poverty in recent years. Accordingly, migration is now being re-evaluated and questions have been raised whether the present model of socio-economic development relying on migration is sustainable. The remittance economy also has negative impacts on the migrants themselves, as many of them accept low living standards abroad to send money back home to their relatives, saving on expenses for health care and food and endangering their personal safety, which has resulted in numerous deaths, occupational injuries and growing numbers of ill-health and, more generally, in a lower 'threshold of health' (Moraru, Mosneaga and Rusnac 2012: 60).

Another migration-related risk in both Moldova and Ukraine is that of becoming a victim of trafficking in human beings. At least 22,000 citizens of Ukraine are estimated to live in conditions of slavery abroad (Ball and Hampton 2009). The Ukrainian government has therefore launched several initiatives to combat this form of trafficking, which have met with some success in recent years. During the period 2002–2012, the Ministry of Internal Affairs has registered 3,200 criminal cases and 776 prosecution cases related to the trafficking in human beings. Despite this, Ukrainians have remained largely unaware of the risks involved. According to data from the Ukraine 2007 Health and Demography Survey (UCSR *et al.* 2008), 48 per cent of the respondents had never heard of cases of human trafficking, 51 per cent were unable to estimate their personal risk of becoming a victim and 56 per cent declared that they did not know whether the risk of trafficking had increased or decreased over the last three years. Respondents from rural areas and those with little education and low incomes were particularly ill-informed.

According to the International Organisation for Migration, more than 9,000 victims of trafficking received some form of assistance during the years 2000 to 2012; their annual number had been growing until 2007 and only stabilised in 2008. Until 2007 the overwhelming majority (more than 80 per cent) of victims were women. Since then the gender ratio has slowly reverted with 76 per cent of female victims given assistance in 2007, 64 per cent in 2010, 57 per cent in 2011 and 44 per cent in 2012. Between 2010 and 2012, 24.4 per cent were victims of sexual exploitation (mostly women) and 68.2 per cent of labour exploitation (mostly men), some of the latter being forced to become beggars.

Welfare, care and migration

The majority of female migrants from Moldova and Ukraine have been heading for Southern Europe, namely Italy, Spain, Greece and Portugal. In addition to the cultural proximity of countries where Latin languages are spoken, other factors, linked to the transformation of the social structure in these countries, have contributed to make them attractive for migrants from (Wider) Eastern Europe, such as increasing female employment, growing individualisation and related changes in the family structure (Bettio, Simonazzi and Villa 2006: 271; van Hooren 2011: 42–47). Labour migration can thus not only be explained by the economic and post-socialist transformations that have been taking place in the EU's Eastern Neighbourhood. Obviously, there are also other push factors at work. As elsewhere in the former Soviet Union, female employment rates were high in Moldova and

Ukraine. When the demand for female labour decreased in post-Soviet times, women have often sought to utilise their gendered qualifications, notably for motherly care, by searching employment abroad. With changing family structures, older women in their fifties, for example, are no longer needed to care for their grandchildren and therefore become free to provide care abroad (Solari 2011). The subject requires, however, more research to investigate its numerous causes and effects and their interconnectedness and mutually reinforcing character.

The most interesting approach to female labour migration relates it to different welfare regimes in the receiving countries. Their classification is based on the analysis of how social services are produced by and allocated between different care providers, such as the state, the market, non-profit organisations and families. In its most classical expression, a typology is derived from notions of class stratification and decommodification (Bonoli, George and Taylor-Goodby 2000: 8–28). Building on Esping-Andersen's classification, feminist critique and the notion of a defamilialisation of care, van Hooren (2011: 29) divides European welfare regimes into three ideal-types: a liberal, a familialistic and a social-democratic care regime. In the first, care is being provided predominantly by the market or, if the state retains responsibility for care, is being outsourced to private agencies on the basis of means and needs testing. In the second, families are required by law to take care of their dependents, which puts the family at the heart of care. Publicly provided care is subject to strict means and needs tests and only available if families are unable or fail to carry out their responsibilities, although they may receive cash benefits for organising care or, alternatively, contract out services to the third sector. Familialism can be explicit, when families receive cash benefits, or implicit, when no subsidies are available for families acting as care providers. In the third regime, services of care are a universal entitlement based on needs testing alone. Most services are thus being provided by the state, which leads to the defamilialisation of care. In practice, national models of care usually rely on a combination of the various regimes, which depends, for example, on the categories of persons that need care. Arrangements for child care may therefore differ from those made for the care of the elderly. Moreover, in recent years, the diversity of arrangements has increased even within countries, since all European countries have liberalised their economies and attempted to cut social expenditure. Nonetheless, these ideal-types offer a useful hermeneutic tool that allows a better understanding of the main features of each particular welfare system.

Closely related to this is the notion of a care culture, that is the national and regional discourses on what constitutes good care, reflected in individual preferences of how to care for children or the elderly and how people in need wish to be cared for. In some ways, care cultures appear to be connected with the predominant institutionalised care regimes at certain historical moments (see, for example, Zdravomyslova (2009). In the present context, it is interesting that several scholars (Bettio and Plantenga 2004; Bettio,

Simonazzi and Villa 2006; van Hooren 2011) have stressed that familialistic care regimes in particular significantly depend on care being provided by migrants.

Migrants in familialistic care regimes

Thus, in Mediterranean countries, such as Greece, Spain and Italy, the organisation of care is being delegated almost exclusively to the family, resulting in a system where the care culture and institutionalised care arrangements seem to mutually reinforce each other. Families who employ a migrant to look after their elderly relatives, for example, do so because it is considered a moral (and legal) duty for children to arrange care for their elderly parents and not so much because they themselves particularly favour such an arrangement. In Italy, the law obliges spouses, children, parents, siblings, as well as close in-laws (sons-in-law, daughters-in-law and parents-in-law) to provide care for a relative in need, as there exists no comprehensive system of social welfare on the state level that would guarantee to all citizens a minimum standard of care. The strong familialism of this care regime is here implicit, since the state does not provide any support to the family that acts as a care provider, except in cases where the family's resources are deemed insufficient. The state only performs a subsidiary role and care provided by it is considered a last resort. As a result, there are now large variations in the quality and extent of care services offered by various commercial and third-sector organisations, such as volunteer organisations linked to the Catholic Church (van Hooren 2011: 42–43).

A nationwide survey conducted in 2001 has shown that long-term needs are predominantly met by the family and friends (83.1 per cent), followed by private care providers (9.7 per cent) or a combination of the two (2.1 per cent), and that public services (sometimes in collaboration with other providers) cater for the remaining cases (Bettio and Plantenga 2004: 78). At the same, Italy has one the highest old-age dependency rates, that is the proportion of people aged over 65 to the working-age population, in Europe and the rate is increasing (Bettio, Simonazzi and Villa 2006: 273). Family care is thus structurally prescribed and culturally embedded in Italian society, while the public and commercial sectors have remained underdeveloped.

In some cases, families receive, however, cash benefits. With regard to care for the elderly, there are two kinds of transfer payments. The Attendance Allowance, administered by the state, is meant for elderly people with severe disabilities who are in need of constant care for everyday activities. Its allocation is not means-tested and there is no control over how the money is being spent. In 2011, the basic allowance amounted to EUR 487.39 but payments could reach up to EUR 807.35 in cases of blindness. The proportion of beneficiaries to the population aged over 65 has increased from 5 per cent in the early 1990s to 9.5 per cent in the late 2000s. In 2008, almost a quarter (24 per cent) of persons aged over 80 had received the allowance. The Local Care Allowance, granted by regional and municipal authorities, is means- and needs-tested but can be freely spent. In 2006–2007, monthly payments ranged from EUR 300 to 500 per person, but only 0.5 per cent of the elderly received the allowance (Gagliardi et al. 2012: 95–96). It is in part these payments that allow families with limited financial resources to employ migrants for care.

Francesca Bettio and her co-authors (2006) describe the situation in Italy as a 'migrant in the family' care model. Together with the ever growing work burden shouldered by an ever decreasing number of native 'natural' carers (women in their forties or fifties), monetary transfers enhance the 'care drain' from Eastern and Central European countries. In the 1970s and 1980s, female migrants in Italy mostly came from former colonies; they were employed by well-off urban families and had long-term plans to stay. Today's migratory flows from Eastern Europe, which started in the mid-1990s, are more hetero-geneous. Female labour migrants are generally middle-aged, well-educated, married and have children. They usually enter the host country with a tourist visa, work in a family for three or four months, long enough to earn money for some particular project at home (e.g. construction work on the house, children's education etc.), return home for several months and then restart working for the same family. This rotational form of temporary migration enables women to work abroad while maintaining family responsibilities at home. It also means that several women are sharing the same job abroad, a typical feature for employment in private households. The women work as live-ins, have long working hours and the relationship with their employer can be characterised as one of servant to master. Being intensively involved in the care of disabled people, migrant women have few possibilities to socialise or to find a better job in the Italian labour market, and even less to fully participate in the Italian society. There are, of course, deviations from this very common working pattern of the *badanti* (Bettio, Simonazzi and Villa 2006). Women sometimes find it impossible to return home, because they cannot finance the journey for example, and the migration then ceases to be rotational, with nefarious consequences for their own family life.

The earnings of care workers vary but on average are comparable to female wages for a manual job in the Italian industrial sector. In addition, almost all of them can go into savings when the employer provides for board and lodging. The average salary of the *badanti* has been estimated at EUR 879, that is, roughly 15 times as much as the average female worker earns in Moldova. Generally, the unregulated nature of care work tends to reduce the costs of care for the employer. In cases where the carer resides with the family, the hourly wage can be less than three euros, even though the official rate quoted by a local cooperative of carers is roughly eight or nine euros (Bettio, Simonazzi and Villa 2006: 281). There are therefore no incentives for the Italian authorities to develop local care services, as both families and the government are satisfied with the present situation, the former because they benefit from flexible, respectful and cheap care services and the latter because social expenditure by the state remains low.

It is difficult to estimate the number of immigrants employed by households, as there are many informal arrangements and no controls by the authorities. According to a survey quoted by Bettio, Simonazzi and Villa (2006: 279), migrant workers usually enter the country as tourists or students and not all of them regularise their status later on, although the possibility exists. It has been estimated that for every regularised worker there are 2.5 undocumented ones (Bettio, Simonazzi and Villa 2006). Another estimate gives the same numbers for formally and informally employed migrants (van Hooren 2011: 49–54). Gagliardi *et al.* (2012: 97) advance the number of 1.5 million individual care providers, 72 per cent of them immigrants. Finally, Lamura and Nies (2009) have estimated that some 700,000 immigrants in Italy were employed as domestic workers in 2007, accounting for 90 per cent of all domestic help. Seventy-one per cent of workers also lived with their employers and, among the remaining, 23 per cent were working during the day and 6 per cent during the night. In any case, the notable increase of migrant workers caring for elderly dependents has been the most striking change in the Italian care sector over the last two decades.

Legal factors, too have contributed to this change. Italian immigration policy, for example, can be characterised as being open towards care workers but restrictive towards other forms of migration. Among its typical features are large-scale regularisations of undocumented migrants already living in the country, thanks to which several hundred thousand people have received work and residence permits in 2002 and 2009. The Bossi–Fini Act of 2002 has introduced yearly quotas for immigrants and quotas for work permits have been set regularly since 2005. Romanians and Bulgarians are free to work as domestic workers and assistants (van Hooren 2011: 62). Already in 2002, migrants from countries with the largest share of female migrants, such as Romania, Ukraine, Ecuador, Poland and Moldova, benefitted more than others from the regularisation, a clear signal that care workers are the immigrants most in demand (Bettio, Simonazzi and Villa 2006: 280).

Extensive regularisations in particular have helped perpetuate the influx of new migrants and made care work even cheaper. While they have offered more protection to regularised care workers, by guaranteeing, for example, maternity leaves, they have made their employment more expensive, thereby creating an even stronger demand for unregulated labour and rising expectations in countries of origin. According to one estimate from the mid-2000s, more than half of the immigrants in Spain had no official status, more than one third in Portugal and nine out of ten in Greece (Bettio, Simonazzi and Villa 2006: 276). The development of the 'migrant in the family' care model has also been favoured by a large 'grey economy' that easily accommodates new immigrants, as citizens do not compete for jobs in this market which they consider unattractive. This is to say that the growing informal employment market does not result from the inflows of unauthorised migrants, but that the demand for cheap or, in other words, unregulated labour is a precondition for massive immigration inflows (Bettio, Simonazzi and Villa 2006: 275; Solari 2011; van Hooren 2011: 62).

The combination of all these factors has resulted in a new welfare mix where care is being organised differently. Families still retain their responsibility for providing care but the role of women involved in care in particular has been profoundly altered. Female family members now act as organisers and coordinators of care work and have become official or informal employers. If paramedical aid is required for example, a trained medical nurse, usually a local, intervenes on a temporary basis or aid will be provided by a medical or nursing facility. The most time-consuming and labour-intensive work, that is long-term care, is, however, accomplished by a migrant who often lives with the family. Care services have thus led to segregation along the lines of ethnic origin and social class and increased inequality among women, while maintaining traditional familialism. As Bettio and her co-authors (2006: 282) write, 'a complex segmentation of the market along gender and ethnic lines has thus arisen from an abundant supply of cheap labour combined with a limited supply of specialised public services'. It can be assumed that this kind of organisation of care also alters the gender contract of a society (Solari 2011; Zdravomyslova, Rotkirch and Temkina 2009).

Conclusion

The 'migrant in the family' care model corresponds to the familialistic care culture and its structural organisation. It is perceived as flexible, personalised and inexpensive by both the families involved and the state. The main question mark concerns its sustainability. Will this arrangement of care survive a diminishing supply of cheap female labour once the economies of Eastern Europe will have further developed? The viability of the system is also called into question by its tendency to slow down and interfere with the development of local care institutions. In the long run, it may not be possible to rely on a welfare system that continuously produces inequality on the basis of gender, ethnicity, citizenship and social class (e.g. Bettio, Simonazzi and Villa 2006; van Hooren 2011). Moreover, it is questionable whether this can be reconciled with the demand for more flexible services and a more flexible labour force needed to provide good-quality care. Even in countries with a predominantly social-democratic welfare model, the public sector has been shrinking in recent years. Care services have been outsourced to the market to better cope with this demand for flexibility (Bonoli, George and Taylor-Goodby 2000).

It is striking that within the European Union the ethical sustainability of this model is usually being discussed in terms of the target countries – how their welfare systems are being negatively affected by this development, while the debate in the two Eastern European countries studied here has focused on the care deficit caused by female outmigration. Despite the remittances they receive from migrants, neither the Moldovan nor the Ukrainian society, both largely involved in international labour migration, seem capable of sustainable development under these circumstances. Their situation should therefore be taken into account in discussions on the EU level.

International labour migration has both positive and negative effects in these countries. It relieves tensions on the national labour market, improves the economic situation of migrants' households and may even contribute to a better understanding of the values and standards promoted by the European Union. However, its nefarious consequences are equally numerous and the migrants' largely unprotected status in their host country remains an ongoing concern. Too many still become victims of abuse by employers and various intermediaries and face inhuman living and working conditions.

One of the outcomes of this strongly asymmetrical solution to the care deficit in the 'old' European countries has been the development of inequality. Some experts interviewed during field trips have expressed their hope that returning labour migrants would eventually help bring European values to Ukraine and Moldova. But in the face of the working and living conditions that female migrants from these two countries have to put up with in Italy, it could be asked which values these migrants are supposed to bring back. The organisation of care there confines migrants to private households and virtually isolates them from any form of participation in the host society. They are working long hours for minimal pay, often outside any legal framework, and are completely dependent on their employer. In this perspective, the European Union appears to have assumed the role of the head of a patriarchal family. Western Europe, and its southern part in particular, is being cared for and served by women from the EU's eastern neighbours. This conveys a particular shade of meaning to policies of the European Union designed to promote gender equality in Moldova and Ukraine.

Fiona Williams (2008, 2011), who has extensively written about the interrelations of migration and social and labour policies in contemporary Europe, is convinced that in designing future politics and policies we should be aware of the transnational economy of care and aim at global justice and the transnational political ethics of care. The migration of female care providers takes place in the context of unequal geopolitical interdependence. For the care sector this means that a 'care drain', caused by the migration of unskilled care providers, occurs simultaneously with the movement of highly trained health care professionals. Both deprive poorer countries of skills and sources for the provision of care. This requires the development of an ethical code for the recruitment of care providers, preferably on the EU level. The second aspect of the global political economy of care is the transnational dynamics of care commitments of those who have to leave behind them dependents. Transnational care takes place in many ways (remittances, phone calls and other communication through the internet, visits home etc.) and this care is as valuable as the paid one that migrant workers provide in the richer host countries. In commercial care, the movement of international capital should be acknowledged. Williams (2008: 12) also points to the transnational influence on care discourses and policies (e.g. the spread of paternity leave) and the transnational development of social movements, NGOs and grassroots campaigns. This transnational economy of care can and should be assessed through the political ethics of care as a method and a normative framework. Williams (2008: 12) insists on the following starting points when thinking about care: interdependence of individuals rather than their autonomy, sensitivity to context, responsiveness as the ability to perceive others on their own terms, and sensitivity to the consequences of choices. In other words: what are the material and social outcomes of such actions? Transnational and ethical approaches should be taken into account when aiming at (gender) equality, stability and sustainability for all societies involved in the processes of international migration.

Note

1 V. Lutenco, Counsellor of the Prime Minister of the Republic of Moldova, during a round table of the TV programme 'Fabrica', *PUBLICA TV*, 15 September 2012.

15 Contemporary Ukrainian migration to EU countries

Trends and challenges

Ihor Markov

This chapter will attempt to show that the future of external migration, as well as the evolution of its meaning, will be determined above all by a transformation of social mobility spaces. It will be argued that the development of social networks by Ukrainian migrants has taken place independently from the underlying causes of migration, notably high unemployment and low wage-levels at home, which have contributed to the mass exodus of labour migrants in the 1990s and still remain in force. The flows of new migrants and the migration systems of which they are part form a mobility space that exists in parallel to others constituted in the host and sending societies and states. The focus here will be on changes in the mobility spaces of three generations of Ukrainian labour migrants who have moved to EU countries over the last two decades. However, these changes have a wider impact on Ukrainian society and are likely to give rise to future patterns of social behaviour and life strategies adopted by Ukrainian citizens.

The following discussion is based on the findings of a comprehensive study of migration processes that have seen Ukrainians move to EU countries and the Russian Federation, undertaken between 2006 and 2011 by a research team of which the author is a member (see Ivankova-Stetsiuk 2010, 2012; Markov 2009; Markov *et al.* 2009a and 2009b). This research focused attention on and evaluated host country immigration policies with regard to Ukrainian citizens. In addition to interviews with experts (members of various representative migration bodies), government officials, employers, church representatives, trade union officials, representatives of NGOs and members of self-organised bodies of Ukrainian migrants), monitoring was carried out on legislative changes and legal trends in the host countries as well as on publications by Ukrainian media on migrations issues. This component also included the analysis of statistical data on migration and the consultation of migration studies from seven EU countries.

The study was designed to capture as many aspects as possible of contemporary Ukrainian migration, including the motivation for emigration, the practical modalities of moving to another country, living and working conditions abroad, the development of social networks and relations with employers, the authorities, citizens and migrants of other countries in the host country,

DOI: 10.4324/9781315858036-20

migrants' ties with their homeland, changes in life strategies and personal outlook, and migration policies of Ukraine and the host countries. Empirical research, which combined quantitative and qualitative methods, took place in the seven EU countries that are the major destinations for migrants from Ukraine, namely Italy, Greece, Spain, Portugal, Ireland, Poland and the Czech Republic.

One major objective of the study was to identify determinants of Ukrainian migrant workers' behaviour patterns. Ethnographic fieldwork was used to collect data on the daily activities of labour migrants to investigate cultural aspects of their life (norms and values, traditions, specific patterns of social behaviour and communication etc.). Group interviews in particular were conducted in cities with a heavy concentration of Ukrainian migrants, namely Naples and Bologna (Italy), Murcia and Barcelona (Spain), Lisbon (Portugal), Warsaw (Poland) and Prague (Czech Republic), to apprehend mobility features of specific categories of migrants: those who arrived earlier in their host country and have settled there permanently (permanent migration); those who have arrived more recently and are still actively looking for work (primary dynamic migration); and those who continue to move across countries and regions in search of better living and working conditions (secondary dynamic migration).[1]

A second objective of this research was to describe features of self-determination of Ukrainian labour migrants within the migration space. Here, some ninety life stories were collected through in-depth semi-structured interviews with migrants contacted through snowball sampling or with the help of various organisations to which these migrants belong or whose activities focus on migration issues (religious communities, NGOs etc.).

The research documented below indicates that Ukrainian migrant workers have developed strategies that enable them to efficiently react to changing conditions within national labour markets and legal environments abroad. This has resulted in new migration patterns, such as circular migration, and new forms of mobility that take place within new transnational spaces. Unfortunately, rather than interpreting such migration systems as a possible means to develop regional ties and co-operation between the EU and Ukraine, EU members states have applied ever more restrictive migration policies. Such policies not only contribute to illegal and thus often exploitative working situations but also erect new borders between European societies.

Properties and trends of Ukrainian migration processes

Ukraine is today one of the five largest suppliers of migrant labour in the world and a main transit country for migration flows from East to West (World Bank 2011a). The fourth and most recent wave of Ukrainian external migration has its origins in the early 1990s when the disintegration of the Soviet Union led to increased freedom of movement for Ukrainians, including across borders, and the effects of the gradual transition towards a market economy in post-independent Ukraine (and elsewhere) acted as a push factor for external migration. Ukrainian external migration also happened under the conditions of an accelerated globalisation of social relations and is part of wider global migratory movements of people from the South to the North and from the East to the West (Vyshnevs'kyi 2005: 2–3).

Research carried out by the author and his colleagues has defined the major features of the most recent migration wave that distinguish it from earlier ones during the twentieth century. In the first place, the current wave is the most widespread, covering dozens of countries on several continents with most migrants having moved in equal proportions to the European Union or the Russian Federation (Libanova 2009; Malynovska 2011: 5; Markov 2009: 69). Ukrainian experts have unanimously pointed out the lack of reliable statistical data about the number of citizens who have left post-independent Ukraine to work abroad and still remain there. However, estimates based on various methodologies indicate a number that ranges from 1.5 to 5 million people (Malynovska 2011: 4–5; Markov 2009: 7–8 and 59; Pozniak 2012). In addition to traditional destination countries in Central and Eastern Europe (mainly Poland, the Czech Republic and Hungary), recent migration flows are now increasingly targeted at Southern Europe (mainly Portugal, Italy and Spain) and Ireland. Other countries of Western Europe, primarily Germany, France and the United Kingdom, are among the most popular destinations of would-be emigrants but strict immigration laws offer only scarce opportunities there. An exception to this rule are labour migrants who move there from another EU country (ETNAS 2008: 545) and students who, once they have completed their studies there, become permanent residents.

A second characteristic of contemporary migration patterns is that external migration affects all major age-groups of the economically active population, low-skilled and high-skilled Ukrainians, the little-educated and the well-educated, even if employment in the host country is temporary and precarious or consists of a menial job (Markov 2009: 62–63). However, sociological studies, surveys and official statistical data from the host countries have shown that migrants predominantly have received a higher or specialised secondary education. Indeed, there has been a growing demand for skilled labour with academic or vocational qualifications in EU countries, which has also led to the exodus of thousands of highly qualified professionals from Ukraine who often work abroad on the basis of temporary contracts.

It has also been possible to ascertain that Ukrainian immigrants, as those from other countries, have often worked and stayed in their host countries for extended periods without the necessary papers. Thus, according to one survey, based on a sample of households in Ukraine, only one out of three immigrants had a written labour contract (Libanova 2009: 37). Even so, four Ukrainian immigrants in five end up by having a legal residence and employment status (Briazgunova 2013). It is also important to point out that women account for a larger share among immigrants in EU countries than men. Although two Ukrainian labour migrants out of three are men (Pozniak 2012: 3), women are far more numerous in Italy (82 per cent), Poland (67 per cent) – the two countries with the highest share of Ukrainian immigrants, – and Greece (70 per cent). It should be noted that this high female participation is characteristic of the present wave of migration (Markov 2009: 60–61).

Ukrainian migration to EU countries is characterised by a gradual transition of migration patterns: 'shuttle' migration to neighbouring countries (in the context of seasonal work) has increasingly been replaced by extended stays in Greece, Italy, Spain and Portugal and, beyond, by transnational migration. During the earlier stage, migrants often went abroad for additional income to finance particular projects (repayment of personal debt, tuition fees for children, buying accommodation etc.). The more recent practice implies the necessity to care for the material needs of family members left behind (ETNAS 2008: 575a). Over time, many migrants who take up permanent residence in the host country prefer their family members to join them. At the same time, Ukrainian labour migrants are highly mobile within their host country but also easily cross borders to settle wherever salaries are higher and working conditions better (ETNAS 2008: 575a). Thus, many Ukrainians moved from Poland to the Czech Republic because of better opportunities for legal employment there, after the new EU member states of Central and Eastern Europe, where there is a strong demand for technically skilled labour, joined the Schengen convention. Similarly, the construction boom ahead of the 2012 Summer Olympic Games attracted many migrants affected by the economic crisis in their host country to London (Markov 2009: 71). The highest concentration of Ukrainians can be found in metropolitan areas, such as Madrid, Rome, Milan, Lisbon, Athens and Moscow.

An important aspect of Ukrainian migration is the emergence of widely distributed social networks that serve multiple purposes, such as offering transport facilities to and from Ukraine, sending remittances home, conveying information about the situation of local labour markets and opportunities to obtain accommodation, and providing legal advice on how to obtain the necessary documents for regularisation, family reunification and migration-related subjects. In Rome, Naples, Bologna, Barcelona, Madrid and other cities with a strong Ukrainian community, migrants turn up once a week at fixed meeting-places, often where buses and minibuses from Ukraine arrive, to meet fresh migrants, receive letters and parcels from home or send them off, or obtain Ukrainian newspapers and magazines. Over 60 per cent of remittances, for example, are sent home through a personal friend, a relative or a courier (e.g. a driver), the rest being conveyed through official channels, such as banks or postal services (Briazgunova 2013). This practice has hardly changed since 2008, when the first national survey on labour migration, based on a household sample, was carried out (Libanova 2009: 37).

The series of surveys of which it is part has also shown that more than three Ukrainians in four seek jobs abroad by contacting relatives, friends and acquaintances, while the rest are relying on direct contacts with employers, private agencies or other individual intermediaries (Briazgunova 2013). Well-organised networks have contributed to the great flexibility with which

Ukrainian migrants react to changing conditions in labour markets, particularly in times of crisis. Recent Ukrainian migration appears to be largely self-regulated. The emergence and development of such networks have created a common space that links Ukraine and the host countries and within which takes place an intensive exchange of information, goods, money and even people.

Recent data show that the desire to emigrate remains strong in Ukraine, especially among the younger generation, because of the systemic crisis which has led to the rise of unemployment and falling wages in real terms. A poll conducted in November 2012 by the Russian online recruitment company HeadHunter, which promotes the development of businesses in the Commonwealth of Independent States countries and the Baltic states, has asked the site's users in Ukraine about their intentions to leave Ukraine and work abroad.[2] More than five thousand respondents (48 per cent of them young professionals who have received or completed higher education, with an average age of 30) reported serious intentions to do so, 43 per cent admitted the possibility and only 4 per cent did not plan to leave Ukraine. The modest popular destinations were European countries (63 per cent), North America (42 per cent) and Australia (20 per cent), mainly because of the high level of education and the availability of scholarships. Among the main reasons identified were the lack of prospects for themselves and their families (72 per cent), low pay (44 per cent), missing conditions for professional self-realisation (41 per cent), the unstable political situation (34 per cent), the possibility of obtaining a regular, even menial job abroad (33 per cent) and the facility to start a business (14 per cent). Most respondents declared that it is better to emigrate when young. Interestingly, the recent financial and economic crises have not resulted in a significant reversal of migratory flows along the migration corridors that link a host country to Ukraine. A majority of the few who returned home are unlikely to stay there. If anything, the last years have shown that strong and multiple migration movements will remain a permanent feature, regardless of the state of the world economy (Markov 2011).

In recent years, the number of Ukrainian immigrants has grown primarily because of family reunification, as young people have left to study abroad and stayed on in their host country. Germany is the most popular destination for students and, according to the latest household survey on migration (Briazgunova 2013), also attracts most of the labour migrants who are graduates (90 per cent), followed by Hungary and Spain (both 19 per cent).

Ukrainian migrants, an ethnic group on the move

It is interesting to contrast the attitudes of recent Ukrainian labour migrants in EU countries with those who have moved from a new member state in Central Europe, Poland for example, to an old member state. The latter generally see themselves as mobile persons who are responding to economic opportunities rather than as emigrants who have left their home for good to settle abroad and, consequently, often entertain few contacts with fellow immigrants and citizens of their host country. As S. Toruńczyk-Ruiz from the Center for Migration Research in Warsaw has shown for Polish labour migrants in the Netherlands, the identity of these migrants reveals a relation between immigrants and citizens of the host country that refers to a single space of political communication in which immigrants have their 'locus', although within the 'coordinate system' of Western society (Toruńczyk-Ruiz 2008: 76). It is argued here that this feeling of 'locus', that is of belonging, in this case, to Polish society is enhanced and explains the observed detachment from fellow immigrants and local citizens.

Ukrainian migrants, by contrast, view themselves as being part of a sustainable space of coexistence, because they 'seek where it is good' to live and work. They often feel that they are left to themselves, as the Ukrainian state does not protect them abroad nor offers any support when they attempt to obtain a full legal status in their host country, often after a long period living in a legally precarious situation. This sentiment of 'abandonment', evoked by numerous migrants interviewed, also extends to the reasons for their emigration, since the Ukrainian 'state didn't create a corresponding number of jobs and, most importantly, (ensure) decent wages'. Ukrainian migrants feel culturally akin to EU citizens, yet believe that they belong to 'another world'. Unlike citizens of their host country, they are not part of the political space and, even more, not of any political space.

Migrants with a 'locus' use their social networks to facilitate migration processes but not to create their 'own locality' in the host country. They consider migration a temporary phase of their life and retain membership in their society of origin, as shown above for the Polish migrants. By contrast, the effective interpersonal networks created by Ukrainian (and other) migrants represent more established livelihoods, structures of coexistence shaped by traditional ethnic forms. Returning home is rather a dream that helps these migrants get used to their emigrant life during its earlier stages. The ties to the home country are embodied in ethnic immigrant communities where social–cultural forms are recreated through self-organisation, characteristic of traditional diasporas (cultural, educational, students' or women's associations, religious communities, publications etc.), to form a sustainable space of coexistence. The Ukrainian state hardly intervenes in this process; its support is mostly declarative, if it does not react negatively.

Generally, Ukrainian migrants of the fourth wave, despite feelings of cultural affinity with their host society that favour rapid integration, remain strongly attached to their home country: they maintain regular and intense contacts with their family and relatives back home, are aware of the country's political and economic situation and show interest in cultural events. Like their compatriots at home, they follow national political events by reading the Ukrainian press and watching Ukrainian television channels. Their plans are linked to projects at home (buying a house or flat, paying for the education of children left behind etc.). Whenever possible, they travel to Ukraine, generally at least two or three times during the year (ETNAS 2006: 545a). In the host country, interpersonal networks that primarily include compatriots but also employers, officials of migration services, members of NGOs, friends and fellow immigrants form their space of communication in most cases. Some migrants have made the decision to settle permanently. They form communities, establish a family or take out a mortgage, as observed in Italy, Greece, Spain and Portugal. Overall, there is increasing evidence of a determination to meet personal needs and to realise oneself in the host country, contrary to an earlier period (from the 1990s to the mid-2000s), when the focus was on saving and satisfying the needs of family members back home. This has also contributed to a better acceptance of Ukrainian migrants in the host country, notably in southern Europe and Ireland (Markov 2009: 65–66).

Ongoing migration processes reproduce some of the traditional meanings of migration (moving from one country to another) and its socio-cultural forms, as found in older Ukrainian diasporas. But they can be better understood as taking place in a transnational space comprised of the country of origin, countries of transit and host countries, where assimilation into the host society is no longer a major goal. Movement within this space is favoured and facilitated by social networks that allow migrants to quickly react to changing conditions and thus facilitate and favour movement within this space. Even those migrants who have decided to stay in their host country or who have returned home generally remain part of it. The latter, for example, perceive themselves as a separate social group within Ukrainian society.

Transforming space mobility or three generations of fourth-wave Ukrainian migrants

One indicator of the existence of such a transnational space and its information network can be found in data that relate to the motives for emigration. The two main reasons for Ukrainian international labour migration are low income (or wage) levels and high unemployment rates in Ukraine (Detz 2008: 33). This has been confirmed by numerous interviews conducted with Ukrainians at home and abroad. Interestingly, the respective importance of these two factors has changed over the last years, as the series of household surveys on labour migration has shown. Wage levels have become by far the most important argument advanced by respondents (79 per cent) while the high unemployment rate is now a distant second with 11 per cent (Briazgunova 2013). This suggests that Ukrainians are today much better informed about wages in different countries, very likely because the transnational networks described above, together with modern communication technologies, act as disseminators of information that was formerly much less accessible. At the same time, these networks also supply information about employment opportunities abroad and even contribute to their creation, as Elena Tiuriukanova has advanced. In her view, labour migrants, because of growing labour shortages, form their own 'employment niches' that 'gradually deepen and expand and may no longer be filled by the national labour force, even when there are no shortages, and ... emerging migrant networks then pull in the main stream of foreign workers' (Tiuriukanova 2010: 13).

The importance of this transnational space becomes even more obvious when the fourth wave of Ukrainian migrants is compared to previous ones. Emigration during the earlier waves of the late nineteenth and the twentieth century took people from one socio-cultural space to another, with the distance between the two often being perceived as a temporal one, too – Ukraine appeared to belong to a different historical era. Thus, a migrant's communication was in synchrony with his environment in the host society but had a diachronic character in his ties with people back home, as letters exchanged, for example, had little bearing on his life in the host country because they referred to a different time frame. Migrants during the early part of the twentieth century, thus, left Ukraine for good, because they did not have access to land or a job, started a new life abroad, together with their family or by creating one through marriage with a compatriot, and often became part of a diaspora that cherished Ukrainian customs, traditions and rituals and was an integral part of the host society and its cultural landscape. Recent migration patterns have retained some of these features. Social and cultural diaspora-like forms of self-organisation are still being reproduced (Markov 2009: 82–83) and the family is still of central importance, as efforts to provide for its material needs show. But recent migrants more often leave their family in Ukraine and more frequently return home between periods of temporary employment abroad or try to reconcile their new life abroad with family obligations at home, as interviews with female migrants who left for Greece or Italy in the early 1990s show. In their case, a woman's life is no longer largely confined to the family but can be seen as characterised by attempts of self-realisation within the new environment of their host society while maintaining a commitment to the family. More generally, modern communication technologies in particular have reduced distances in time and space, as well as cultural distance, to the point of almost abolishing them.

However, recent migration processes are not homogeneous. The results of the individual in-depth interviews and the group interviews conducted with Ukrainian migrants in seven EU countries suggest that the dynamics of the fourth wave of Ukrainian emigration can best be understood in terms of three generations. The members of these generations not only belong to different age-groups but also have a distinct attachment to the socio-cultural environment of their countries of origin and residence that illustrates the transition from territorial migration – from one place to another – to transnational and, beyond, to geographically decentred migration.

The first generation is composed of now older labour migrants in their fifties who left Ukraine some seven to ten years ago with the intention to improve the economic situation of their family and then return home. Although this return has been postponed, they are likely to eventually rejoin their family and thus become an addition to life in Ukraine.

The second generation is comprised of men and women who are between 35 and 50 years old. Some of them have left their family back home, others have been rejoined by it but still help parents and other relatives living in Ukraine. Their projects often include buying a home in Ukraine or providing for the education of children left behind. But they live in-between, not entirely integrated into their host country, because they continue to believe that they will return home some day, yet increasingly become disconnected from life in Ukraine as ties become looser and rarer. Several Ukrainian women in Italy, thus, complained that their children in Ukraine often treat them as a 'cash machine'. After returning to Ukraine and spending some time there, these women frequently leave for Italy once more. This has led to horizontal circular migration patterns.

The third generation is composed of young adults, mostly in their twenties, who are highly mobile. Often comparatively well-educated, they easily master the language (in the literal and figurative sense) of their host country or countries or, if they have grown up as migrants' children, easily move between two or more worlds, since they either have benefitted from education in Ukraine provided by their parents or have first-hand experience of life in a host country. Even if they have to start out life abroad by accepting physically demanding low-skilled jobs, their previously acquired qualifications allow them to successfully seize opportunities that offer better perspectives, such as a professional career. Their life takes place in a transnational, or supranational, space within which they are always searching for the place that holds the best prospects for employment, a high salary and social security and is punctuated by visits to their home country and regular and intensive exchanges of information.

Conclusion

Over the past two decades Ukrainian labour migrants have formed a migration system that enables them to efficiently react to changing conditions in national labour markets and legal regulations for immigrants in (potential) host countries. This has resulted in new migration patterns, such as circular migration, and new forms of mobility that take place within a transnational space composed of the countries of origin, transit and destination. Emigration no longer means being cut off from life in Ukraine, as contacts are maintained through more or less regular and extended visits and through modern communication technologies that have considerably reduced the distance that separates migrants from their country of origin. While some earlier features of migration have been retained, the most recent migrants seek self-realisation by combining ways of life at home and abroad or by moving to whichever country or city offers the best living and working conditions.

However, the borders between Ukraine and the European Union and within the latter have remained in place. For host countries, these new forms of migration mean a flexible supply of labour in sectors that are increasingly in demand of cheap and flexible labour, such as the care sector in southern

Europe (see the chapter by Olga Davydova et al. in this volume) or the construction sector in the United Kingdom, as described above, and the Ukrainian migration system can be partly seen as a response to these new conditions. EU migration policies and those of individual EU countries have, in some cases, taken into account this new environment by providing a legal framework for it (e.g. work permits for seasonal employment in agriculture or green cards for IT specialists) but more often have erected barriers to the free movement of Ukrainians to EU countries. Undocumented labour migrants, for example, find it difficult to visit their home country because they are afraid of not being able to return to their host country. National policies within the EU widely differ, ranging from strict immigration rules in Germany, a popular destination of Ukrainian would-be emigrants, to the tolerance of large numbers of undocumented labour migrants, as in Poland or Italy and Spain, where repeated large-scale regularisations have attempted to create more secure working and living conditions for migrants and, unsuccessfully, to stabilise migration flows. These differences have contributed to reinforce the observed migration patterns, as labour migrants are willing, or forced, to move from one host country within the EU to another (see the Polish–Czech example above), always in the hope of improving their situation. Perhaps, legislators on the EU and national levels should make an effort of better coordinating national migration regimes and think about making them more flexible, in their own interest but also to effectively implement values that the European Union is promoting in its Eastern Neighbourhood, such as the free movement of people.

Notes

1 Of particular interest in this context was a group interview in Prague during which permanent migrants, who arrived in the early 1990s and formed a diaspora, met others who continue to return home on a regular basis.
2 See 'Ukrainskie spetsialisty chotat rabotat za granitsej. Rezultaty oprosa, provedjonnogo mezdunarodnym kadrovym portalom www.hh.ua v nojabre 2012 goda', *HeadHunter*, no date. Online. Available at: http://hh.ua/article.xml?articleId=13006 (last accessed 10 April 2013).

Concluding observations

The European Union, partnership and neighbourhoods

Ilkka Liikanen, James W. Scott and Tiina Sotkasiira

One of the principal messages conveyed by the contributions to this volume is that 'Eastern Neighbourhood', in geographical terms, implies more than proximity: it is an area of gravitation, mobility, migration and interaction that reflects Soviet-era ties and economic relations but also new East–West orientations. In a positive reading, the Neighbourhood could be a space of possibility both for regional cooperation and for intercultural encounters, especially if understood in a more long-term perspective that takes into consideration the vicissitudes of EU–Russia relations and other geopolitical contexts. Furthermore, neither Neighbourhood nor Eastern Partnership can be understood from an EU-centric vantage point alone. This would limit understandings of Neighbourhood to a mere policy framework based on a normative and positivist reading of global politics. Neighbourhood rather includes both the EU and the partners – it is not by definition or of necessity about spheres of influence and external or extra-territorial borderlands. Neighbourhood exists at the nexus between geopolitical practices, economic interaction and cultural communication so that these various realms become closely linked and difficult to separate.

The concept of Neighbourhood as something geopolitical is part of the rethinking of the European Union's general societal impact within the setting of post-Cold War reconfigurations of interstate relations. Neighbourhood is also a concept that is more generally associated with the emergence of the EU as a political actor on the world scene and that reflects recognition of growing interdependencies between the EU and neighbouring states. The idea of neighbourhood as a 'special relationship ... founded on the values of the Union' is enshrined in Article 8(1) of the Treaty on European Union. However, despite this eurocentric mission statement the difference between Neighbourhood as originally defined by the EU and the realist concept of 'spheres of influence' is precisely that of possibility. Spheres of influence are unambiguously linked to state interests and projections of power that entail some form of territorial control or domination. Here we are reminded of geopolitical discourses that have sought to demarcate 'Europe' from 'Eurasia' and vice versa through an emphasis of difference and diverging historical paths (see, for example, Nartov 2004; Sengupta 2009). Neighbourhood, on the other hand, has the potential

DOI: 10.4324/9781315858036-21

to open up new spaces for interaction. In the joint consultation paper on the renewal of the European Neighbourhood policy (ENP) (European Commission 2015), the EU's ambitious goals of regional cooperation through partnership signal sustained commitment to a new style of international relations. In its most positive understanding, the renewed ENP could emerge as a concrete reflection of New Regionalism (see Farrell, Hettne and van Langenhove 2005; Söderbaum 2013; Söderbaum and Shaw 2003) where, despite different local interests, cooperation spaces are jointly created and based on common concerns.

In general terms, the EU's regional cooperation agenda attempts to strike a balance between different political roles of promoting development, peace, human rights and stability in the immediate neighbourhood and in the post-Soviet space. However, there is no inevitability to the emergence of an alternative Neighbourhood scenario. On the one hand, the Neighbourhood cooperation policies that the EU has been actively pursuing since 2003 involve a complex mix of traditional realism with idealist notions of mutual interdependence. From its beginnings the ENP/Eastern Partnership policy complex has been regarded as a source of mixed messages: it is often perceived as paternalistic, inflexible and insensitive to local concerns. On the other hand, this space of possibility is also challenged by hard geopolitical realities; the crisis that erupted in 2014 over Russia's annexation of the Crimea and incursions into eastern Ukraine has added a new and politically charged layer of complexity to questions regarding the future of Neighbourhood relations. Indeed, the implications of Eastern partners' closer association with the EU, including the development of EU–Russia relations, are as yet uncertain.

The second principal message of this book is that if the EU's ambitions to promote democratic transition as well as social and economic development are to succeed, a greater degree of engagement with post-Soviet societies is necessary. Ukraine, Moldova and Belarus, among others, live with the challenges of rapid change, tackling in very specific ways the problems of so-called triple transition: marketisation, democratisation and unfinished state- and nation-building. With its cross-border cooperation programmes the EU has resolutely promoted economic and democratic reforms in countries of the ex-Soviet Union. However, the third dimension of 'triple transition' has been more controversial and there has been a lack of understanding of nation-building processes within EU policies. In the present geopolitical context, nationalism and nation-building in post-Soviet states are often viewed as antithetical to ideas of shared Europeanness. This predisposition is not always helpful in developing regional cooperation policies as it promotes simplified models of the relationship between democracy and nationalism (see Calhoun 2010; Schöpflin 2000; Smith 2009). Shared Europeanness and European values have, for example, frequently been offered as an alternative to national identification and the strengthening of national political communities. As a result, the EU has promoted western liberal economic and social institutions with little concern for their potential to mobilise people and to strengthen political community and citizen engagement. In this sense, EU policies have also been problematic in part because post-Soviet nation-building is often interpreted as producing security risks and being associated with the exacerbation of ethnonational and linguistic tensions. This has had consequences for strengthening trust between the EU and neighbouring countries. There is an obvious need for a more nuanced view on the problems of the triple transition which does not address democratisation and nation-building simply in terms of convergence to Western liberal models.

The reconfiguration of borders and boundaries in the post-Soviet context, border management and cross-border cooperation, together with migration issues, have all been focal areas of the research documented in this book. Recently, they have become matters of high domestic and international politics, engaging the attention of international organisations, states and communities of states, including the European Union. In the present situation, border management and cross-border cooperation are considered as vital instruments for managing these and other security risks. However, the focus on border regimes is only one aspect of the EU's relations with its regional neighbours. From a security standpoint, post-Soviet states, particularly those with sizeable numbers of Russian-speaking citizens, are seen as weak and unconsolidated and thus subject to Russian influence. As is well known, borders in the post-Soviet space are mostly new constructions based on short or weak traditions of international agreements. Similarly, national institutions and modern civic ties are in many cases mainly products of the Soviet era. To a large degree, it is Soviet-era institutional and discursive practices – and not earlier ethnic cultural traditions – that form the strongest bases for the formation of the new nation-states. The problem is that these structures are often autocratic or corrupt and, as long as they remain unreformed, they provide extremely weak foundations for solidarity and trust. Forced nationalisation is, however, a poor answer to this problem. Ethnic mobilisation played a crucial role in challenging Soviet power structures. It has, however, proved to be problematic as a basis for post-Soviet nation-building.

In situations where nations are to a great extent built on Soviet-time traditions and ethnic tensions are not just products of geopolitical pressures, cooperation requires specifically tailored approaches. On the one hand, it is important to ensure that cooperation programmes do not support old, corrupt power structures. On the other hand, it is vital to remember that forced modernisation of the Soviet type has produced civic ties that may form functioning platforms for building modern nations and democratic political communities. In this respect, a focus on regional or local levels and support to grassroots-level civic engagement can bring solutions that are not tied to pre-given ethnic classifications.

It has been suggested above that Neighbourhood signifies more than proximity and should be seen not in terms of normative 'spheres of influence' but rather as possible spaces of broader cooperation. As the EU forges ahead with Deep and Comprehensive Free Trade Agreements (DCFTA), multilateral cooperation platforms, mobility partnerships and security cooperation, the importance of greater social involvement needs to be emphasised. Social development and regional stability are mutually reinforcing rather that mutually exclusive. ENP and Eastern Partnership (EaP) could thus become powerful tools to address: social issues (ranging from poverty, health and vocational training to the promotion of entrepreneurial skills), cultural cooperation (such as education and research) and regional inequalities through targeted investments rather than temporary aid mechanisms. In effect, this would involve incorporating principles of European Cohesion into ENP and EaP policies (see Lepesant 2014).

As this book was being written and compiled, the basic geopolitical context was rapidly changing and several assumptions that had informed the EU's Neighbourhood Policy as well as the partnership with Russia were fundamentally questioned. What we thus propose in this concluding chapter is a brief 'stock-taking' of the Eastern Partnership (and more generally ENP) and some thoughts on how regional cooperation can be improved. This involves a perspective that eschews geopolitics of grand gestures and visionary pathos and instead champions more pragmatic approaches.

Eastern Partnership and its challenges – geopolitical and geo-economic contexts

Inaugurated in 2009 during the Czech EU presidency, the EaP is in itself a logical consequence of the EU's push for a more central geopolitical role in the post-Soviet space. Since 2009, the Eastern Partnership has been bolstered by Association Agreements with Ukraine and Moldova, as well as Armenia and Georgia, and the prospects of a Deep and Comprehensive Free Trade Area. The EU's regional cooperation agenda also seeks to promote democracy and good governance, energy security, public sector reform and environmental protection. In effect, the EaP is a security, stability and development package that aims to increase the EU's overall influence in these countries. The EaP has also held out the promise of easier travel to the EU through a gradual process of visa liberalisation, accompanied by measures to tackle illegal immigration.

Perceptions of the EU's attempts at partnership in the region paint a mixed picture, and there is an obvious need to consider how the EaP affects the setting. On the positive side, the EU's initiatives are praised in the sense that they have established a new platform for political, technical and social cooperation that has assisted in institutional capacity-building and social modernisation. The EU has also facilitated important investments in technical infrastructure and the training of public servants in more effective administration techniques. In addition, the EU has to a limited extent helped develop policy areas (migration, health, justice, economy) in neighbouring states, for example by promoting social welfare agendas in the post-Soviet context.[1] More generally, the EU's role is also seen as positive in that it offers alternative models of social and cultural development. It has also provided capacity-building for private and civic organisations. However, as several contributions to this volume indicate, the EU's positive impact is tarnished by a failure to deliver on many of its promises. To begin with, there is the sense that EaP, as part of the overall ENP framework, unwisely attempted to bypass Russia, thus heightening regional tensions and eliciting Russian disapproval and distrust. Since 2009, there was also a move from developing shared areas of opportunity towards more traditional bilateral relations with 'Eastern' neighbours (e.g. the Finnish Wider Europe Initiative). Other problematic aspects along these lines will be elaborated below. These include: perceptions of EU unilateralism, the issue of 'common values' as an ideational basis for regional cooperation, and a lack of support for reciprocal forms of cross-border cooperation.

Perceptions of EU unilateralism

One main criticism that has emerged from most interviews and background research is that perceptions of a top-down and unilaterally imposed EU cooperation model are not conducive to more open working partnerships. The EU has been seen to be somewhat blind to the social sensibilities and developmental needs of neighbouring states and more intent on imposing its security-focused agenda (e.g. border controls, migration and crime management). This shortcoming weakens the EU's claims to be a 'credible force for good' and limits the overall positive effects of the ENP/EaP. The principle of joint ownership of ENP/EaP policy agendas, which initially motivated neighbouring states to participate, is often seen to have been replaced by the language of 'mutual commitments' that more strictly correspond to the EU's security interests. Within this context, the issue of the EU's restrictive (Schengen) visa regime is critical and affects perceptions of the EU in a profound way. The visa issue also reveals tensions in neighbourhood relationships as it openly exposes EU mistrust of the institutions and polices of neighbouring states, such as the ability to issue legitimate travel documents and carry out reliable passport controls and border checks.

Ultimately, this can also translate into an EU mistrust of the citizens of neighbouring states. Despite the abundance of cheap opportunities for travel, the EU discourages Moldovans, Ukrainians, Belarusians and others from applying for visas by imposing strict bureaucratic procedures and creating financial obstacles. This reinforces a perception of 'Fortress Europe' in the minds of ordinary citizens. In addition, the visa regime is seen as creating a travelling elite with the resources to obtain multiple-entry and long-term visas; this discriminates against younger and less well-off citizens of neighbouring states.[2]

EU policies such as the EaP are thus seen to offer too little to neighbours in order to be taken fully seriously. In other words: the latter keep 'giving' in to EU demands without receiving commensurate recognition or reward, such as prospects for candidacy or the lifting of visa and mobility restrictions. In interviews carried out before the Ukrainian crisis citizens of Ukraine and Moldova in particular saw themselves forced to accept an inherently asymmetric relationship with the EU and this has evidently resulted in a reduced level of genuine local engagement. Hence, commitments by Moldova, Ukraine and other states are often of a proclamatory and symbolic nature. This, when read as lack of confidence in building genuine multilateral-architecture international relations, frustrates the EU's cooperation agendas, hindering real progress in the promotion of partnership and integration.[3]

'Common values' as an arena of political and social contestation

How do local actors perceive the idea of 'common European values'? How do they perceive the EU as a transformative agent in post-Soviet contexts? Our interviews were conducted before the 2014–15 crisis but at that time almost all recognised the need for a basic set of principles that facilitates positive interaction and a sense of joint purpose. Europe is also perceived as a success story in terms of social development and welfare, which is not only a distinguishing and thus differentiating feature but also a bridge between EU-Europe and neighbouring states. However, the idea that democracy and respect for human rights are somehow specific to the EU is clearly rejected. The notion of European values reproduces stereotypic understandings of Western and Eastern models of civil society and politics that lead to policy recommendations ill-suited to post-Soviet realities. On the level of building external relations the demand for opting for European values is easily read as making an ideological choice between East and West imposed from above – a setting that especially the Ukrainian interviewees explicitly rejected.

Our research indicates that the EU's ambitious value-laden agenda can be understood to partly alienate potential partners in neighbouring states in that it suggests different categories of 'Europeanness' based on the degree of local convergence to proclaimed EU standards (Christou and Croft 2012; Franke *et al.* 2010; Raik 2011; Wisniewski 2013). Civil society actors in Belarus, Moldova and Ukraine have been among the most vocal in this regard – they take umbrage with the idea that there might be an EU 'moral hegemony'. In the specific case of Belarus, the concept of European values has in fact led to a general rejection of much of the ENP agenda; here, the political regime insists on stability and economic development rather than convergence to international norms as societal priorities. This particular situation is, of course, difficult for the EU to navigate – although our interviewees have suggested that a less pointedly political strategy on the part of the EU might have enhanced the ENP's effectiveness.

However, these criticisms of EU policy practises do not mean that civil society actors are uncritical of their own governments. There are obvious tensions within Moldova, Ukraine and Belarus in particular, where political liberalisation is contested by different groups and often hampered by political elites. Indeed, several actors have decried what they see as a lack of substantive political commitment of the EU to supporting citizens' movements and rights in neighbouring states. And yet civil society actors understand basic rights, the rule of law, social solidarity etc. to be much more general in nature; these do not in themselves constitute a unique European identity or sense of purpose. EU-Europeanness in their view is mainly seen in terms of specific attitudes towards efficient governance, the value of work (e.g. reliability!) and related issues.[4]

Support of cross-border cooperation

When the ENPI was introduced as the financial instrument for EU neighbourhood policies, it replaced many previous support mechanisms for local and regional cross-border cooperation. Since then EU engagement in compensating programmes with the neighbouring states has often been considered altogether insufficient. In this view, the clear shift towards a more structured foreign policy dialogue between centres of power in the EU and neighbouring states constitutes a major policy error as long as it takes place at the expense of cross-border cooperation (CBC) in terms of promoting local and regional development. Material support for CBC is indeed meagre in comparison to other priorities and lacks effective focus. In addition, there is a neglect of civil society as a CBC actor despite rhetorical claims to the contrary.

Competing rationales of EU policies

In this regard, there is a need to analyse the changes in and possible alternatives available to redirecting EU Neighbourhood policies. Our joint research has identified four phases in the development of EU CBC policies that can serve as bases for this analysis: 1) an apolitical vision of CBC as a means of cohesion and regional development policies typical of the first INTERREG programmes; 2) CBC as a tool of pre-integration and enlargement with ideological Europeanising features characteristic of the last INTERREG period; 3) visions of the EU as a new kind of international actor which included new spatial imaginaries of neighbourhood as a shared area of action and opportunity; and 4) consolidation of the political union and its external relations that have been discussed in more classical terms of foreign policies and geopolitics.

In the context of the Ukrainian crises a more pronounced policy choice concerns developing EU policies either in terms of active support for attempts at building the role of the EU as a new kind of international actor or opting for a return to a more classical type of common foreign policy that promotes EU interests. The worst option is that the EU sticks to sovereignty-challenging rhetoric while engaging in policies that juxtapose this with hard geopolitical policy goals. Introducing sovereignty-challenging practices to the neighbours through unilateral conditionality while enhancing EU sovereignty in full can hardly create trust in EU policies.

Towards pragmatic understandings of Neighbourhood and Partnership

The EU's ENP and Eastern Partnership strategies appear to suffer from their own ambitions and assumptions. One of the more problematic assumptions is that the EU can directly influence developments in neighbouring states. There is no doubt that the EU has had transformational impacts on the societies of the former Soviet Union and has, in its own way, contributed to more open and empowered societies. However, this normative power does not automatically provide the EU with the power to elicit institutional 'convergence' given the differences in state–society relations that exist between EU member states and their eastern neighbours.

Asymmetry in political clout and financial resources are accompanied by asymmetries of geopolitical interests. The eastern neighbours – at least Georgia, Moldova and Ukraine – have embarked on regional cooperation with the EU both as a sort of development platform and as a prospect for future membership. In both cases, the results have been rather disappointing for the neighbours given the EU's reluctance to discuss membership and the strong security focus (borders, migration, drug-trafficking, passport security etc) of its cooperation agendas (Habets 2014). The security cooperation imperative penetrates the highest and most sensitive levels of government in neighbouring countries while the EU is seen to offer relatively modest assistance and slow progress in opening its borders in return. Based on the information we have gathered in this volume, policy-makers in Brussels might be well advised to scale down partnership goals in order to achieve a more symmetric working relationship with the EU's eastern neighbours.

One major policy consideration that emerges from this is the need for a locally balanced, rather than a fully fledged foreign policy as advocated by the EU in its Eastern Partnership Programme. The strength of this initiative has, evidently, been the promotion of concrete development tasks and practical cooperation instead of ideological assertions and the marketing of pre-given Western models. Further elaboration of the Eastern Partnership needs to be conceptualised both in terms of the vision of the EU as a new kind of international actor and as a policy frame for practical cooperation. In the best of cases it can be used for seeking a balance between competing security and cooperation agendas. The Ukrainian crisis has been read in many quarters as a return to Cold War geopolitics. One perspective for the EaP programme is to keep an open mind for alternative policy options that go beyond the immediate crisis situation.

A particular danger of strict conditionality combined with highly ambitious cooperation agendas is the possible, if unintended, exacerbation of East–West divisions and a counterproductive forcing of neighbours into exclusionary choices of cooperation partners. Avoiding situations like this implies adjusting and sharpening cooperation agendas – based on pragmatic rather than maximalist cooperation strategies, with a greater emphasis on 'soft' areas of cooperation. More generally, the EU should also learn to work with and encourage gradual – if often slow and frustrating – institutional change. What could be strengthened, for example, is dialogue and targeted cooperation initiatives on social matters and social policies (e.g. poverty reduction, employment) as well a greater cooperation in the area of regional development.

Such cooperation would reduce counterproductive political antagonisms generated by conflicts of interest while maintaining the EU's positive influence. A more symmetric relationship along these lines could also contribute to meeting legitimate popular expectations of the EU in non-EU European societies. Similarly, it would be helpful to take contextual – i.e. historical and geographical – situations into greater consideration. This could in the longer run include a more sensitive treatment of Belarus', Moldova's and Ukraine's geopolitical positions between the EU and the Russian Federation. At the same time, and in recognising the foreign policy constraints of these countries, the EU could build on a flexible notion of partnership in which any step towards integration with the EU would be considered within the context of current crises of EU–Russia relations. EaP policy approaches would be viable as long as they correspond to the democratically expressed will of these countries but at the same time do not compromise long-term perspectives for stabilising relations with Russia. More recent EaP strategy documents of the European Commission (2012c: 2) might signal a shift in this direction by way of an 'approximation to EU standards through dialogue and exchange of best practice'. The development of four multilateral partnership platforms that includes person-to-person contacts could be a further step in this direction.

A third point to be made here is that the EaP should be exploited more effectively as a platform for transnational cooperation and development. In order to achieve stability and conditions for democratic development, certain issues such as migration must be seen in a greater regional and international context. Migration has to be approached in terms of a long-term focus on the causes and consequences of increasing migration, rather than merely in terms of border security and the policing of individuals. EU platforms for regional cooperation can also improve the level of policy dialogue between post-Soviet neighbours, especially if they go hand in hand with a greater degree of inclusion of civil society actors (see below).

The 'more-for-more principle'

The joint communication issued in May 2011 under the title 'A New Response to a Changing Neighbourhood' (and delivered by the High Representative of the Union for Foreign Affairs and Security Policy and the European Commission) expressed the objective of the European Union to provide greater support to those partners who have made progress in their democratic reforms and institution-building. While this more-for-more principle can be expected to have some benefits, its overall effect remains doubtful. Cooperation on migration policy, for example, has encountered most difficulties in countries like Azerbaijan and Belarus that have recurrently been pointed out by the EU for lagging behind in democracy, rule of law and transparency in government. For the regimes in these countries it has been more important to portray a positive image of their situation, and the image of masses of citizens eagerly waiting to leave the country does not square with these aspirations.

If EU funds are to be distributed according to a country's democratic or economic performance, then this approach ought to be accompanied by an evaluation of its impacts. Who will actually benefit from increased funding? Which groups among the population will suffer most from local reluctance to invest in cooperation with the European Union? More importantly, if there are reasons to suspect that a target country is not committed to democratic reforms, should financial support, instead of being scaled down, not rather be redirected towards those domestic actors who have already proved their reliability and whose activities are more likely to produce positive outcomes in the field of human rights, including the right to development and decent work? There is also a risk that the EU's credibility with actors committed to its principles of cooperation will suffer if they attribute diminishing funds to constraints resulting from the present financial crisis rather than to well-founded claims about insufficient democratic performance in a target country.

Cross-border cooperation and social engagement

Finally, cross-border cooperation, both between the EU and its neighbours and between these neighbours themselves, should enjoy much greater policy significance within the ENP and EaP contexts. While the ENPI-CBC programme has provided support for local and regional cooperation between the EU and neighbouring states, the relative importance of the programme within the overall ENP framework has been marginal. It would be a mistake to neglect local and regional cross-border cooperation on the EU's external borders, especially if the objective to avoid new divisions within Europe is to be taken seriously. The clearest long-term contribution of cross-border cooperation to social modernisation in post-Soviet states has been that of reframing social and welfare issues. Furthermore, considerable potential exists for horizontal, non-hierarchical institutional learning that involves motivated sectors of the population and strengthens their social impact locally and regionally (Scott and Laine 2012).

Almost all of the contributors to this volume suggest that the EU has been missing important opportunities to develop neighbourhood partnerships by neglecting the role of civil society. Working with and through civil society actors helps promote new forms of policy learning outside formal institutionalised policy channels by creating a pragmatic rather than normative environment of transnational communication and exchange. New support structures could promote collaborative forms of policy formulation and delivery based on partnerships involving the state, the private sector, foundations as well as civil society at large. One possible strategy would be to promote international networks between actors in the public, private and non-profit sector. These could, for example, provide assistance to emerging and future social entrepreneurs through a variety of means, such as: support in project development, securing grants (including the provision of guarantees), assistance in the acquisition and provision of loans and investment capital, as well as training and informational backing. At the same time, such support could not only reduce one-sided grant dependency but establish a greater rapport between CSOs and local governments. Helping to create a critical mass of CSO 'infrastructure' would, in addition, serve local communities and groups to deal more effectively with changing economic and social conditions as well as adapt to shifts in public policy that target social and welfare issues.

With the evolution of the European Neighbourhood Policy framework and the EaP, a crucial future question remains as to how to adapt the regional perspectives of EU external relations to existing institutional models and how to bring local and regional actors in Ukraine, Belarus and Moldova into the implementation and targeting of new policy instruments. In this setting, it also remains to be seen to what extent cross-border cooperation can be further elaborated as an arena of adjusting regional, national and supranational interests, policy frames and instruments. Furthermore, if regional development partnerships between the EU and non-EU states are to be taken seriously, such partnerships require policy thinking that goes beyond traditional, i.e. territorialised, forms of cooperation policy and accommodates the relational and networked nature of cooperation.

Notes

1 See, for example, Scott and Laine (2012).
2 One important change has taken place: in July 2009, a regulation on local border traffic went into effect which allows for passport-free travel within designated 30–50 km border zones.
3 See, for example, Stegniy (2012).
4 Many activists from civil society organisations have benefitted from training and education opportunities through EU-sponsored projects. This has led to the absorption of institutional rhetoric that reflects an emphasis on effective and efficient problem-solving.

Bibliography

Primary sources

Amnesty International (2014) *The Human Cost of Fortress Europe: Human Rights Violations against Migrants and Refugees at Europe's Borders*, Report No. EUR 05/001/2014. Online. Available at: www.amnesty.org/en/library/asset/EUR05/001/2014/en/48cb6136-cefc-4fd0-96cd-cd43b46eb5a8/eur050012014en.pdf (last accessed 31 July 2014).

Azerbaijan Republic State Migration Service (2012) 'Statement by the President of the Republic of Azerbaijan His Excellency Mr. Ilham Aliyev'. Online. Available at: www.migration.gov.az/index.php?section=000&subsection=000&lang=en (last accessed 16 August 2012).

BelaPAN (2011) 'Minsku predlagayut nachat' peregovory ob uproshchenii vizovogo rezhima s Litvoi'. Online. Available at: http://naviny.by/rubrics/politic/2011/12/22 (last accessed 15 December 2012).

BelaPAN (2012a) 'Belarusi poka ne udalos' ostanovit' utechku mozgov'. Online. Available at: http://naviny.by/rubrics/society/2012/05/03 (last accessed 3 May 2012).

BelaPAN (2012b) 'Minsku predlagayut nachat' peregovory ob uproshchenii vizovogo rezhima s Litvoi'. Online. Available at: http://naviny.by/rubrics/politic/2011/12/22 (last accessed 15 December 2012).

BelaPAN (2013a) 'Evrosoiuz gotov nachat' peregovory po oblegcheniiu vizovogo rezhima s Belarus'iu'. Online. Available at: http://naviny.by/rubrics/eu/2013/02/18 (last accessed 18 February 2013).

BelaPAN (2013b) 'Doklad eurodeputata Paletskisa po Belarusi pomozet aktivizirovat' dialog s Brusselem, schitaiut v MIDe'. Online. Available at: http://naviny.by/rubrics/eu/ 2013/03/19/ic_news (last accessed 19 March 2013).

BelaPAN (2013c) 'Belarus' i Turtsiia podpisali soglasheniia o bezvizovykh poezdkakh grazhdan'. Online. Available at: http://naviny.by/rubrics/tourism/2013/03/29 (last accessed 29 March 2013).

BelaPAN (2013d) 'Opros: boleie 35% zhitelei Belarusi hotiat uiehat' za rubezh'. Online. Available at: http://naviny.by/rubrics/society/2013/11/01/ic_news_116_427533 (last accessed 4 January 2013).

Belarus Security Blog (2012) *Analytical Report 2012*, Minsk: BISS. Online. Available at: www.bsblog.info (last accessed 15 January 2013).

Belstat (1999) 'Perepis' naselenia Respubliki Belarus' 1999 goda. Natsional'nyi sostav naselenia Respubliki Belarus'. Online. Available at: http://belstat.gov.by/homep/ru/perepic/p5.php (last accessed 22 June 2013).

Belstat (2011) *Osnovnye itogi migratsii naseleniia Respubliki Belarus*, Minsk: Belstat.

Belstat (2012) 'Demographicheskaia situatsia'. Online. Available at: http://belstat.gov. by/homep/ru/indicators/doclad/2012_12 (last accessed 5 January 2013).

Belstat (2013) 'Novosti'. Online. Available at: http://belstat.gov.by/homep/ru/indica tors/pressrel/demographics.php (last accessed 30 December 2013).

BelTA (2011) 'Pravitel'stvo obespokoeno utechkoy kvalifitsirovannykh kadrov za gran-itsu'. Online. Available at: http://naviny.by/rubrics/society/2011/11/04 (last accessed 29 December 2012).

BelTA (2013) 'Belarus' i Rossiia podpisali soglashenie o readmissii'. Online. Available at: www.belta.by/ru/all_news (last accessed 18 November 2013).

Border Monitoring Project Ukraine (2010) *Access to Protection Denied. Report. Refoulement of Refugees and Minors on the Eastern Borders of the EU – The Case of Hungary, Slovakia and Ukraine.* Online. Available at: http://bordermonitor ing-ukraine.eu/files/2010/11/refoulement-report.pdf (last accessed 15 October 2010).

Commission of the European Communities (1990) *Technical Fiche for INTERREG I*, Brussels: EU Directorate General for Regional Policy.

Council of the European Union (2000) Council Regulation of 29 December 1999 Concerning the Provision of Assistance to the Partner States in Eastern Europe and Central Asia. EC, Euratom 99/2000.

Council of the European Union (2002) Copenhagen European Council 12 and 13 December 2002. Presidency Conclusions. POLGEN 8415917/02.

Council of the European Union (2003) *A Secure Europe in a Better World. European Security Strategy, 12.12.* Online. Available at: www.consilium.europa.eu/uedocs/cm sUpload/78367.pdf (last accessed 1 June 2012).

Council of the European Union (2007) *The European Union and Central Asia: Strat-egy for a New Partnership.* Online. Available at: www.eeas.europa.eu/central_asia/ docs/2010_strategy_eu_centralasia_en.pdf (last accessed 2 June 2013).

Council of the European Union (2009) J*oint Declaration of the Prague Eastern Part-nership Summit*, Prague, 7 May. Online. Available at: http://ec.europa.eu/europeaid/ where/neighbourhood/eastern_partnership/documents/prague_summit_declaration_ en.pdf (last accessed 3 August 2013).

Council of the European Union (2012) 'Council Conclusions on Belarus', *3191st Foreign Affairs Council meeting in Luxembourg*, 15 October. Online. Available at: www.con silium.europa.eu/uedocs/cms_data/docs/pressdata/EN/foraff/132836.pdf (last accessed 2 January 2013).

Council of the European Union (2013) 'Joint Declaration of the Eastern Partnership Summit, Vilnius, 28–29 November 2013'. Online. Available at: www.consilium. europa.eu/press (last accessed 10 December 2013).

Delegation of the European Union to Azerbaijan (2014) 'List of Projects'. Online. Available at: http://eeas.europa.eu/delegations/azerbaijan/projects/list_of_projects/ 229711_en.htm (last accessed 6 January 2014).

Delegation of the European Union to Moldova (2014) *EU Assistance to Moldova.* Online. Available at: http://eeas.europa.eu/delegations/moldova/projects/overview/ index_en.htm (last accessed 6 January 2014).

Delegation of the European Union to the Republic of Belarus (2014) 'Project Over-view'. Online. Available at: http://eeas.europa.eu/delegations/belarus/projects/over view/index_en.htm (last accessed 6 January 2014); and 'EU Activities in Belarus'. Online. Available at: http://eeas.europa.eu/delegations/belarus/documents/eu_activ ities_in_belarus_11_2012.pdf (last accessed 6 January 2014).

Delegation of the European Union to the Republic of Tajikistan (2012) 'EU Supports Border Delimitation in the Fergana Valley', 27 February. Online. Available at: http:// eeas.europa.eu/delegations/tajikistan/press_corner/all_news/news/2012/20120227_en. htm (last accessed 11 February 2015).

Delegation of the European Union to Ukraine (2010) 'List of the EU–Ukraine Association Agenda Priorities for 2010'. Online. Available at: http://ec.europa.eu/ delegations/ukraine/eu_ukraine/political_relations/association_agenda/association_ agenda_en.htm (last accessed 15 January 2011).

Delegation of the European Union to Ukraine (2014) 'EU Financial Co-operation with Ukraine'. Online. Available at: http://eeas.europa.eu/delegations/ukraine/eu_ ukraine/tech_financial_cooperation/index_en.htm (last accessed 6 January 2014).

Eastern Partnership Panel on Migration and Asylum (2007) 'Ukraine and Hungary Organizes "Small Cross-border Movement"', 10 December. Online. Available at: http://eapmigrationpanel.org/page16611.html (last accessed 19 August 2013).

Eastern Partnership Panel on Migration and Asylum (2009) 'Ukraine–Poland Small Cross-border Movement Agreement', 24 July. Online. Available at: http://eapmigra tionpanel.org/page25392.html (last accessed 19 August 2013).

EEAS (2014) *European External Action Service. Strategy Papers*. Online. Available at: http://eeas.europa.eu/enp/documents/strategy-papers/index_en.htm (last accessed 2 January 2014).

ETNAS (Archive of the Ethnology Institute of the National Academy of Sciences of Ukraine) (2006–2011) Fund 'Field Materials'. F.I. – Description 2. – 545a, 575a, 591a, 614.

Eurasian Development Bank (2012) 'Labour Migration in the CES: Economic Effects and Legal-Institutional Consequences of Labour Migration Agreements'. Online. Available at: www.eabr.org/general//upload/docs/CCI/migration_report_new.pdf (last accessed 22 June 2013).

Eurasian Development Bank (2013) *Eurasian Integration Yearbook 2013*. Online. Available at: www.eabr.org/e/research/publications/IntegrationYearbook/Integratio nYearbook2013/index.php?id_4=387 (last accessed 21 December 2014).

European Commission (2001a) Communication from the Commission to the Member States of 7 May, 'Interregional Cooperation' 1188 Final.

European Commission (2001b) *A Guide to Bringing INTERREG and TACIS Funding Together*, Luxembourg: Office for Official Publications of the European Communities.

European Commission (2002) *Brochure. Structural Policies and European Territory. Cooperation without Frontiers*, Luxembourg: Office for Official Publications of the European Communities.

European Commission (2003) *Communication from the Commission to the Council and the European Parliament: Wider Europe – Neighbourhood: A New Framework for Relations with our Eastern and Southern Neighbours*, COM (2003) 104 Final.

European Commission (2004a) *Communication from the Commission to the Member States of 2 September 2004 Laying Down Guidelines for a Community Initiative Concerning Trans-European Cooperation Intended to Encourage Harmonious and Balanced Development of the European Territory INTERREG III*, Official Journal of the European Union, 10 September. COM (2004) C 226/02.

European Commission (2004b) *INTERREG in 2004*. Online. Available at: http://ec. europa.eu/regional_policy/archive/interreg3/new/doc/interreg2004_en.pdf (last accessed 3 August 2013).

European Commission (2004c) *Proposal for a Regulation of the European Parliament and of the Council. Laying Down General Provisions Establishing a European Neighbourhood and Partnership Instrument.* COM (2004) 628.

European Commission (2004d) *Communication from the Commission, Building Our Common Future. Policy Challenges and Budgetary Means of the Enlarged Union 2007–2013.* COM (2004) 101.

European Commission (2004e) *Communication from the Commission, European Neighbourhood Policy. Strategy Paper.* COM (2004) 373 final.

European Commission (2005) 'EU Border Assistance Mission to the Republic of Moldova and Ukraine'. Online. Available at: http://ec.europa.eu/world/enp/pdf/country/enpi_csp_ukraine_en.pdf (last accessed 17 January 2011).

European Commission (2006a) *European Neighbourhood and Partnership Instrument. Cross-Border Cooperation. Strategy Paper 2007–2013, Indicative Programme 2007–2013,* Brussels: Commission of the European Communities.

European Commission (2006b) 'European Neighbourhood and Partnership Instrument. Ukraine. Country Strategy Paper 2007–2013'. Online. Available at: http://ec.europa.ec/world/enp/pdf/country/enpi_csp_ukraine_en.pdf (last accessed 17 January 2011).

European Commission (2006c) 'European Neighbourhood and Partnership Instrument. Ukraine. National Indicative Programme 2007–2010'. Online. Available at: http://ec.europa.eu/world/enp/pdf/country/enpi_nip_ukraine_en.pdf (last accessed 17 January 2011).

European Commission (2006d) *Communication from the Commission to the European Parliament and the Council – Thematic Programme for the Cooperation with Third Countries in the Areas of Migration and Asylum.* Online. Available at: http://eur-lex.europa.eu/lexuriserv/lexuriserv.do?uri=com:2006:0026:fin:en:pdf (last accessed 6 August 2013).

European Commission (2006e) *Communication from the Commission to the Council and the European Parliament on Strengthening the European Neighbourhood Policy.* Online. Available at: http://eeas.europa.eu/enp/pdf/pdf/com06_726_en.pdf (last accessed 2 August 2013).

European Commission (2006f) *Communication from the Commission to the Council and the European Parliament – 'The Global Approach to Migration One Year On: Towards a Comprehensive European Migration Policy'.* Online. Available at: http://eur-lex.europa.eu/LexUriServ/LexUriServ.do?uri=CELEX:52006DC0735:EN:NOT (last accessed 2 January 2013).

European Commission (2006g) 'EU–Azerbaijan ENP Action Plan'. Online. Available at: http://ec.europa.eu/world/enp/pdf/action_plans/azerbaijan_enp_ap_final_en.pdf (last accessed 2 January 2013).

European Commission (2006h) 'European Neighbourhood and Partnership Instrument. Belarus Country Strategy Paper 2007–2013 and National Indicative Programme 2007–2011'. Online. Available at: http://ec.europa.eu/world/enp/pdf/country/enpi_csp_nip_belarus_en.pdf (last accessed 2 January 2013).

European Commission (2009a) 'Commission Staff Working Document. Implementation of the European Neighbourhood Policy in 2008. Progress Report: Ukraine', Brussels, 23 April. Online. Available at: http://ec.europa.eu/world/enp/pdf/progress2009/sec09_515_en.pdf (last accessed 25 January 2011).

European Commission (2009b) *Partnership and Cooperation Agreement Establishing a Partnership between the European Communities and their Member States, of the One Part, and the Republic of Tajikistan, of the Other Part,* L 350, 29/12/2009, p. 3.

Online. Available at: http://ec.europa.eu/world/agreements/downloadFile.do?full Text=yes&treatyTransId=12861 (last accessed 12 January 2014).

European Commission (2011a) 'Communication on Migration', *Communication from the Commission to the European Parliament, the Council, the Economic and Social Committee and the Committee of the Regions Communication on Migration Communication from the Commission to the European Parliament, the Council, the Economic and Social Committee and the Committee of the Regions.* Online. Available at: http:// eur-lex.europa.eu/legal-content/EN/TXT/HTML/?uri=CELEX:52011DC0248&from= EN (last accessed 20 March 2015).

European Commission (2011b) 'The Global Approach to Migration and Mobility Brussels', *Final Communication from the Commission to the European Parliament, the Council, the European Economic and Social Committee and the Committee of the Regions.* Online. Available at: http://eur-lex.europa.eu/LexUriServ/LexUriServ.do? uri=COM:2011:0743:FIN:EN:PDF (last accessed 2 January 2013).

European Commission (2011c) 'A New Response to a Changing Neighbourhood: A Review of European Neighbourhood Policy', *Joint Communication by the High Representative of the Union for Foreign Affairs and Security Policy and the European Commission.* Online. Available at: http://ec.europa.eu/world/enp/pdf/com_11_303_ en.pdf (last accessed 6 January 2014).

European Commission (2012a) *EuropeAid. European Union Funding to Civil Society in Azerbaijan.* Online. Available at: http://eeas.europa.eu/delegations/azerbaijan/docum ents/press_releases/2010-grants-brochure-final_en.pdf (last accessed 6 January 2014).

European Commission (2012b) 'Migration and Asylum Thematic Programme'. Online. Available at: http://ec.europa.eu/europeaid/how/finance/dci/migration_en.htm (last accessed 2 January 2013).

European Commission (2012c) *Joint Staff Working Document. Eastern Partnership Roadmap 2012–2013: the Multilateral Dimension.* SWD (2012) 108 Final.

European Commission (2013a) 'European Commission Completes Steps for Signature of Association Agreement with Ukraine'. Online. Available at: http://ec.europa.eu/ commission_2010-2014/fule/headlines/news/2013/05/20130515_en.htm (last accessed 2 June 2013).

European Commission (2013b) 'ENP Package – Belarus'. Online. Available at: http:// europa.eu/rapid/press-release_MEMO-13-244_en.htm (last accessed 2 June 2013).

European Commission (2013c) 'EU–Moldova Association Agreement'. Online. Available at: http://eeas.europa.eu/moldova/assoagreement/index_en.htm (last accessed 2 June 2013).

European Commission (2013d) 'Migration, Asylum and Borders'. Online. Available at: http://ec.europa.eu/dgs/home-affairs/financing/fundings/migration-asylum-borders/ index_en.htm (last accessed 2 June 2013).

European Commission (2013e) 'Mobility Partnership Signed between the EU and Azerbaijan'. Online. Available at: http://europa.eu/rapid/press-release_IP-13-1215_ en.htm (last accessed 6 January 2014).

European Commission (2015) *Joint Consultation Paper. Towards a New European Neighbourhood Policy.* JOIN (2015) 6 Final.

European Commission and High Representative of the European Union for Foreign Affairs and Security Policy (2012) 'Eastern Partnership Roadmap 2012–2013: the Multilateral Dimension'. SWD (2012) 108 Final. Online. Available at: http://ec. europa.eu/world/enp/docs/2012_enp_pack/e_pship_multilateral_en.pdf (last accessed 17 October 2013).

European Communities (1990) *Technical Fiche on INTERREG I.* Online. Available at: www.interact-eu.net/downloads/2463/Technical_Fiche_on_INTERREG_I_-_European_Commission.pdf (last accessed 3 August 2013).

European Parliament (2007) *European Parliament Resolution of 15 November 2007, Strengthening the European Neighbourhood Policy.* Online. Available at: www.europarl.europa.eu/sides/getDoc.do?pubRef=-//EP//TEXT+TA+P6-TA-2007-0538+0+DOC+XML+V0//EN (last accessed 2 October 2015).

Federal Migration Service (2006) *Gosudarstvennaya Programma sodeystviya dobro-volnomu pereseleniyu sootechestvennikov v Rossiyu na 2006–2012 gody* [The 2006–2012 State Programme on Providing Support for Voluntary Resettlement of Compatriots to the Russian Federation]. Online (in Russian only). Available at: www.fms.gov.ru/pro grams/list.php (last access 15 August 2013).

FIDH and Memorial (2011) 'Tajikistan: Exporting the Work Force – at What Price? Tajik Migrant Workers Need Increased Protection'. Online. Available at: www.fidh. org/IMG/pdf/taj_report-2.pdf (last accessed 24 February 2014).

Finnish Foreign Ministry (2011) *Implementation of EU External Border Cooperation after 2012, Particularly on Borders with the Russian Federation*, Helsinki: Foreign Ministry.

FRONTEX (2008) *EU External Borders Agency Report with Evidence, 5 March*, London: House of Lords. Online. Available at: www.publications.parliament.uk/pa/ld200708/ldselect/ldeucom/60/60.pdf (last accessed 21 January 2011).

Gosstatizdat (1926) *Vsesoiuznaia Perepesi Naselenia*, Vol. 4, Moscow: Gosstatizdat.

Government of Belarus (2005) 'Osnovnye napravleniia migratsionnoy politiki na ter-ritorii gosudarstv – uchastnikov Dogovora o sozdanii Soiuznogo gosudarstva', *Postanovlenie Soveta Ministrov Soiuznogo gosudarstva*, no. 23 ot 29 oktiabria goda. Online. Available at: www.soyuz.by/ru (last accessed 15 December 2012).

Government of Belarus (2011) 'Natsional'naia programma demograficheskoi bezo-pasnosti Respubliki Belarus' na 2011-2015'. Online. Available at: http://pravo.by (last accessed 5 April 2012).

IISEPS (2008) 'Veterdal'nikh stranstviy'. Online. Available at: www.iiseps.org/analitica/264 (last accessed 1 December 2012).

IISEPS (2012) 'Novosti'. Online. Available at: www.iiseps.org (last accessed 24 June 2012).

IISEPS (2013a) 'Novosti'. Online. Available at: www.iiseps.org (last accessed 14 December 2013).

IISEPS (2013b) '*Portret belorusskogo gastarbaĭtera*'. Online. Available at: www.iiseps. org/analytica/537 (last accessed 15 December 2013).

IISEPS (2013c) 'Okhota k peremene mest'. Online, Available at: www.iiseps.org/ana litica/560 (last accessed 17 December 2013).

ILO (2010) 'Migration and Development in Tajikistan – Emigration, Return and Diaspora'. Online. Available at: www.ilo.org/public/english/region/eurpro/moscow/info/publ/migration_development_report_taj.pdf (last accessed 25 February 2014).

ILO and IOM (2009) 'Labour Migration and the Emergence of Private Employment Agencies in Tajikistan: A Review of Current Law and Practice'. Online. Available at: www.ilo.org/sapfl/Informationresources/ILOPublications/WCMS_120534/lang–en/index.htm (last accessed 22 February 2014).

Indexmundi (2013) 'Tajikistan Demographics Profile 2013'. Online. Available at: www.indexmundi.com/tajikistan/demographics_profile.html (last accessed 24 February 2014).

Internal Displacement Monitoring Centre (2014) 'Azerbaijan: After Some 20 Years, IDPs Still Face Barriers to Self-reliance'. Online. Available at: www.internal-displa cement.org/countries/azerbaijan (last accessed 6 January 2014).

IOM (2005) 'International Agenda for Migration Management'. Online. Available at: http://publications.iom.int/bookstore/free/IAMM.pdf (last accessed 2 June 2013).

IOM (2006) 'Educating Georgia's Potential Migrants'. Online. Available at: www.iom. ge/index.php?releases&education (last accessed 6 March 2014).

IOM (2008) *Migration in the Republic of Azerbaijan: A Country Profile*, IOM, International Organization for Migration.

IOM (2009) *Socio-Economic Impact of the Economic Crisis on Migration and Remittances in Moldova: First Indicators – Spring 2009*. Online. Available at: www.migratie.md/files/ elfinder/documents/110_2009_06_02_socio_economic_impact_eng.pdf (last accessed 10 February 2013).

IOM (2012) *Goriachaia liniia. Plohogo ne posovetuet*. Online. Available at: http://iom. by/en/2012/12/03/hot-line-russian (last accessed 6 March 2014).

IOM Dushanbe (2009) *Abandoned Wives of Tajik Labor Migrants*, IOM Study on the Socio-economic Characteristics of Abandoned Wives of Tajik Labor Migrants and Their Survival Capabilities. Online. Available at: www.iom.tj/pubs/abandoned_wives_ English.pdf (last accessed 2 January 2013).

Joint Committee at Senior Official's Level of EU–Ukraine Association (2011) 'List of the EU–Ukraine Association Agenda Priorities for 2011–2012'. Online. Available at: http://eeas.europa.eu/ukraine/docs/2011_12_eu_ukraine_priorities_en.pdf (last accessed 2 January 2013).

Khovar – Natsional'noe Informatsionnoe Agentstvo Tadzhikistana (2011) 'Vystuplenie Prezidenta Respubliki Tadzhikistan na rasshirennom zasedanii pravitel'stva strany', *Khovar*. Online. Available at: http://khovar.tj/rus/speeches/31485-vystuplenie-prezi denta-respubliki-tadzhikistan-na-rasshirennom-zasedanii-pravitelstva-strany.html (last accessed 18 July 2014).

Legea privind aprobarea concepţiei politicii naţionale a Republicii Moldova nr. 546-XV din 19.12.2003. Online. Available at: www.lex.justice.md/md/312846/ (last accessed 12 November 2010).

'Legea privind Declaraţia de Independenţă a Republicii Moldova' [Law on the Declaration of the Independence of the Republic of Moldova], in *Legi şi Hotărîri adoptate la Sesiunea a şasea a Parlamentului Republicii Moldova de legislatura a douăsprezecea*, 691-XII, 27 August 1991, Vol. 2. Chişinău: Cartea Moldovenească.

Memorandum ob osnavah normalizatzii otnoshenii mezhdu Respublikoi Moldova in Pridnestroviem. Online. Available at: www.olvia.idknet.com/memorandum.htm (last accessed on 23 May 2008).

Migration Policy Centre (2013) 'Russia: Migration Profile'. Online. Available at: www.migrationpolicycentre.eu/docs/migration_profiles/Russia.pdf (last accessed 25 February 2014).

Ministry for Economic Development of the Russian Federation (2008) *Concept of Long-term Socio-Economic Development of the Russian Federation for the Period Up to the Year 2020*. Online (in Russian only). Available at: www.economy.gov.ru/wps/ wcm/myconnect/economylib/mert/resources/3879cd804ab8615ab426fc4234375027/kdr_ 171108.doc (last accessed 18 November 2015).

Ministry for Foreign Affairs of Finland (2009) *Wider Europe Initiative – Framework Programme for Finland's Development Policy – Implementation Plan for 2009–2013*, Helsinki: Ministry of Foreign Affairs.

Ministry for Foreign Affairs of Finland (2011) *Implementation of EU External Border Cooperation after 2013, Particularly on Borders with the Russian Federation*, Helsinki: Ministry for Foreign Affairs-Unit for Regional Cooperation.

Ministry for Foreign Affairs of Finland (2012) *Guidelines for Finland's Policy on the Eastern Partners of the EU and on Central Asia*, Helsinki: Ministry for Foreign Affairs.

Ministry of Foreign Affairs of Romania (1991) 'Relaţiile politico-diplomatice moldo-române', 27 August. Online. Available at: www.mae.ro (last accessed 4 December 2010).

National Bank of Moldova (2013) *Transferuri de mijloace băneşti din străinătate effectuate în favoarea persoanelor fizice (rezidente şi nerezidente) prin băncile din Republica Moldova, decontări nete. Dinamica anuala*. Online. Available at: www.bnm.md/md/external_operations_via_banc_system (last accessed 2 June 2013).

OHCHR (2012) 'UN Expert Urges the EU to See Beyond Security and Border Control in its Migration Partnership with Tunisia', 12 June, Press release. Online. Available at: www.ohchr.org/en/NewsEvents/Pages/DisplayNews.aspx?NewsID=12232&LangID=E (last accessed 30 July 2014).

President of the Russian Federation (2007) *Executive Order #1351 of October 09, 2007, Approval of the Concept of the Demographic Policy of the Russian Federation to the Year 2025*. Online. Available at: http://document.kremlin.ru/doc.asp?ID= 041941 (last accessed 9 August 2013).

President of the Russian Federation (2012) *The Concept of the State Migration Policy of the Russian Federation for the Period to 2025*. Online. Available at: http://cis-legislation.com/document.fwx?rgn=52502 (last accessed 10 November 2015).

Prodi, R. (2002) 'A Wider Europe – A Proximity Policy as the Key to Stability'. Speech to the Peace, Security and Stability International Dialogue and the Role of the EU, Sixth ECSA-World Conference. Brussels, 5–6 December.

Ptoukha Institute for Demography and Social Studies of National Academy of Science of Ukraine (IDSS) (2010) *Naselennya Ukrayiny. Trudova emigratsiya v Ukrayini*, Kiev: Ptoukha Institute for Demography and Social Studies of National Academy of Science of Ukraine.

Republica Moldova (1991) *Parlamentul Lege Nr. 691, din 27.08.1991, privind Declaraţia de independenţă a Republicii Moldova*, Chişinău: Republica Moldova.

Republica Moldova (2002) 'Tratat intre Republica Moldova si Ucraina cu privire la frontiera de stat din 18.08.1999', *Tratate internationale*, 29: 434.

Rosstat (2013) *Chislennost' i migratsia naselenia Rossiiskoi Federatsii v 2010, 2011, 2012, 2013 godakh Rosstat*. Online. Available at: www.gks.ru/bgd/regl/b13_107/IssWWW.exe/Stg/%3Cextid%3E/%3Cstoragepath%3E:|tab2–06–12.xls (last accessed 20 August 2013).

Statement by European Commissioner for External Relations and European Neighbourhood Policy, Benita Ferrero-Waldner, on the Eastern Partnership (2009). Online. Available at: www.enpi-info.eu/library/content/eastern-partnership-ambitious-project-21st-century-european foreign-policy (last accessed 3 August 2013).

Tratat intre Republica Moldova si Ucraina cu privire la frontiera de stat [Republic of Moldova–Ukraine], 18 August 1999. Online. Available at: www.undp.md/border/Tratat_RM-Ucaina_frontiera_de_stat.html (last accessed 11 January 2011).

Ukrainian Centre for Social Reforms (UCSR) and State Statistics Committee (SSCU) (2009) *Ukrainian External Labour Migration*, Kiev: Ukrainian Centre for Social Reforms and State Statistics Committee.

Ukrainian Centre for Social Reforms (UCSR), State Statistics Committee (SSC) of Ukraine, Ministry of Health (MofH) of Ukraine and Macro International Inc. (2008) *Health and Demographic Survey of Ukraine in 2007*, Calverton, MD: UCSR and Macro International.

Urząd Statystyczny we Wrocławiu (2007) *Euroregiony na granicach Polski 2007*, Wrocław: Urząd Statystyczny we Wrocławiu. Online. Available at: http://wroclaw.stat. gov.pl/euroregiony-na-granicach-polski-2007-202/?pdf=1 (last accessed 10 November 2015).

Verhovnogo Soveta SSSR (1940) *Sed'maja Sessij,a 1–7 avgusta 1940. Stenograficeskii octet*, Moscow: Verhovnogo Soveta.

World Bank (2011a) *World Bank Migration and Remittances Factbook*, Washington, DC: World Bank.

World Bank (2011b) *Moldova – After the Global Crisis: Promoting Competitiveness and Shared Growth*. Online. Available at: https://openknowledge.worldbank.org/ha ndle/10986/2805 (last accessed 27 December 2014).

World Bank (2012) 'Migration and Remittances Data, Estimates of Migrant Stocks'. Online. Available at: http://econ.worldbank.org/WBSITE/EXTERNAL/EXTDEC/ EXTDECPROSPECTS/0,,contentMDK:22803131~pagePK:64165401~piPK:64165 026~theSitePK:476883,00.html (last accessed 4 February 2013).

World Bank (2013) 'Featured Indicators. GDP Per Capita (Current US$)'. Online. Available at: http://data.worldbank.org/indicator/NY.GDP.PCAP.CD/countries (last accessed 17 August 2013).

World Bank (2014) 'Regional Dashboard: Europe and Central Asia – Poverty'. Online. Available at: http://povertydata.worldbank.org/poverty/region/ECA (last accessed 20 February 2014).

Secondary sources

Aalto, P. (2006) *European Union and the Making of a Wider Northern Europe*, London and New York: Routledge.

Abbasov, A. (1998) *Azerbaijidjantsi: Istoriko-Ethnographicheski' Ocherk*, Baku: Elm.

Abbasov, S. (2011) 'Achievements and Missed Opportunities', in *South Caucasus: 20 Years of Independence*, Berlin: Friedrich-Ebert-Stiftung, 108–122.

Abdullaev, K. and S. Akbarzadeh (2010) *Historical Dictionary of Tajikistan*, Lanham, MD: The Scarecrow Press.

Adams, T.D., M. Emerson, L.D. Mee, and M. Vahl (2002) *Europe's Black Sea Dimension*, Brussels and Athens: Centre for European Policy Studies and International Center for Black Sea Studies.

Agnew, J. (2009) *Globalisation and Sovereignty*, New York: Rowman and Littlefield.

Ahror, K. (2012) 'Landmines Still a Threat on Tajik–Uzbek Border', *Institute of War and Peace Reporting – IWPR Radio*, 12 September. Online. Available at: www.ecoi. net/local_link/226951/334712_en.html (last accessed 12 February 2015).

Akiner, S. (1997) 'Melting Pot, Salad Bowl – Cauldron? Manipulation and Mobiliza-tion of Ethnic and Religious Identities in Central Asia', *Ethnic and Racial Studies*, 20(2): 362–398.

Aleshina, V. (2012) 'Edinaya ekonomicheskaya doktrina Edinogo ekonomicheskogo prostranstva', *Belaruskaya Dumka*, 10: 61–68.

Allina-Pisano, J. (2009) 'From Iron Curtain to Golden Curtain: Remaking Identity in the European Union Borderlands', *East European Politics and Societies*, 23(2): 266–290.

Altstadt, A. (1992) *The Azerbaijani Turks: Power and Identity under Russian Rule*, Stanford, CA: Hoover Institution Press.

Ambrazhevich, A. (2012) 'Suchasnyia migratsyinyia pratsesy u svetse I Respublitsy Belarus', *Vestsi Natsyianal'nai akademii navuk Belarusi, ser. Human. Navuk*, 1: 40–46.

Anderson, B. (1998) *Imagined Communities: Reflections on the Origin and Spread of Nationalism*, London and New York: Verso.

Anderson, J. (ed.) (2007) *Geopolitics of European Union Enlargement: the Fortress Empire*, London: Routledge.

Andreeva, E. (2012) 'Iz Belaruski utekli I mozgi I ruki'. Online. Available at: http://na viny.by/rubrics/economic/2012/09/19 (last accessed 9 September 2012).

Andrianov, V. and G. Miralamov (2007) *Ilham Aliyev*, Moscow: Molodaia Gvardia.

Arango, J. and P. Martin (2005) 'Best Practices to Manage Migration: Morocco–Spain', *International Migration Review*, 39(1): 258–269.

Arendt, H. (1958) *The Human Condition*, Chicago, IL: University of Chicago Press.

Arnason, J.P. (2006a) 'Europe's Eastern Borders: Historical and Comparative Reflections', *Australian Slavonic & East European Studies*, 20(1–2): 117–138.

Arnason, J.P. (2006b) 'Historians in Search of Borders – Mapping the European East', *H-Soz-u-Kult*, 31 May. Online. Available at: http://hsozkult.geschichte.hu-berlin.de/forum/2006-05-004 (last accessed 3 August 2013).

Artyukhin, M. (2012) 'Monitoring razvitiia kadrovogo potentsiala nauki i intellek-tual'noi migratsii v Respublike Belarus'. Online. Available at: http://socio.bas-net.by (last accessed 12 June 2012).

Artyukhin, M., P. Dmitruk and G. Yevelkin (2008) *Migratsiia naseleniia Respubliki Belarus'*, Minsk: Belaruskaya Navuka.

Ashurov, S. (2009) *Voprosy trudovoi migratsii i zaniatosti v sovremennom Tadzhikistane*, Dushanbe: Irfon.

Atovulloev, F. (2013) 'Migrant – zolotoi "telets" Tadzhikistana', *TsentrAziia*, 26 December. Online. Available at: www.centrasia.ru/newsA.php?st=1388005140 (last accessed 18 July 2014).

Auch, E.-M. (2004) *Muslim, Untertan, Bürger: Identitätswandel in gesellschaftlichen Transformationsprozessen der muslimischen Ostprovinzen Südkaukasiens*, Wiesbaden: Reichert.

Averre, D. (2011) 'Competing Rationalities: Russia, the EU and the "Shared Neigh-bourhood"', in J. Gower and G. Timmins (eds) *The European Union, Russia and the Shared Neighbourhood*, London and New York: Routledge.

Baberowski, J. (2003) *Der Feind ist überall: Stalinismus im Kaukasus*, Munich: Deutsche Verlags-Anstalt.

Bachmann, V. and J.D. Sidaway (2009) 'Zivilmacht Europa: A Critical Geopolitics of the European Union as a Global Power', *Transactions Institute of British Geographers*, 34(1): 94–109.

Balaev, A. (2009) *Mamed Emin Rasulzadeh (1884–1955)*, Moscow: Flinta.

Balaev, A. (2012) *Azerbaijanskaya Natsiya: Osnovniye Etapi Stanovleniya na Rubeje XIX–XX Vekov*, Moscow: TeRu.

Ball, D. and R. Hampton (2009) *Estimating the Extent of Human Trafficking from Ukraine*. Final Report Commissioned by the International Organization for Migra-tion, with Financial Support from the United States Agency for International Development (USAID, IOM). Online. Available at: http://digitalcommons.unl.edu/cgi/viewcontent.cgi?article=1025&context=humtraffconf (last accessed 13 November 2015).

Barbé, E. and E. Johannson-Nogués (2008) 'The EU as a Modest "Force for Good": The European Neighbourhood Policy', *International Affairs*, 84(1): 81–96.

Barbé, E., O. Costa, A. Herranz, E. Johansson-Nogués, M. Natorski and M.A. Sabiote (2009) 'Drawing the Neighbours Closer... to What? Explaining Emerging Patterns of Policy Convergence between the EU and its Neighbours', *Cooperation and Conflict*, 44(4): 378–399.

Barrington, L.W. and E.S. Herron (2004) 'One Ukraine or Many? Regionalism in Ukraine and its Political Consequences', *Nationalities Papers*, 32(1): 53–86.

Bassin, M. (1991) 'Russia between Europe and Asia: The Ideological Construction of Geographical Space', *Slavic Review*, 50(1): 1–17.

Batt, J. (2003) 'The EU's New Borderlands', Working Paper. London: Center for European Reform. Online. Available at: www.cer.org.uk/pdf/wp483_borderlands_ba tt.pdf (last accessed 17 January 2011).

Ben-Rafael, E. and Y. Sternberg (2009) 'Debating Transnationalism', in E. Ben-Rafael and Y. Sternberg (eds) *Transnationalism: Diasporas and the Advent of a New (Dis)Order*, Leiden: Brill.

Berg, E. and P. Ehin (2006) 'What Kind of Border Regime? Towards a Differentiated and Uneven Border Strategy', *Cooperation and Conflict*, 41(1): 53–71.

Berger, S. (2009) 'History and Forms of Collective Identity in Europe: Why Europe Cannot and Should Not be Built on History', in L. Rorato and A. Saunders (eds) *The Essence and the Margin. National Identities and Collective Memories in Contemporary European Culture*, Amsterdam and New York: Rodopi.

Bettio, F. and J. Plantenga (2004) 'Comparing Care Regimes in Europe', *Feminist Economics*, 10(1): 85–113.

Bettio, F., A. Simonazzi and P. Villa (2006) 'Change in Care Regimes and Female Migration: The "Care Drain" in the Mediterranean', *Journal of European Social Policy*, 16(3): 271–285.

Bialasiewicz, L. (ed.) (2012) *Europe in the World. EU Geopolitics and the Making of European Space*, Farnham and Burlington, VT: Ashgate.

Bialasiewicz, L., S. Elden and J. Painter (2005) 'The Constitution of EU Territory', *Comparative European Politics*, 3(3): 333–363.

Bideleux, R. and I. Jeffries (1998) *A History of Eastern Europe: Crisis and Change*, New York: Routledge.

Bigo, D. (2002) 'Security and Immigration: Toward a Critique of the Governmentality of Unease', *Alternatives*, 27: 63–92.

Boian, V. (2009) 'Relaţiile Republicii Moldova cu Ucraina', in V. Chirila, (ed.) *Evoluţia politicii externe a Republicii Moldova*, Chişinău: Cartidact.

Bojcun, M. (2005) 'The European Union's Perspectives on the Ukrainian–Russian Border', *Eurozine*, 12 January. Online. Available at: www.eurozine.com/pdf/2005-01-12-bojcun-en.pdf (last accessed 15 September 2010).

Bolt, G., S. Özüekren and D. Phillips (2010) 'Linking Integration and Residential Segregation', *Journal of Ethnic and Migration Studies*, 36(2): 169–186.

Bonoli, G., V. George and P. Taylor-Gooby (2000) *European Welfare Futures. Towards A Theory of Retrenchment*, Cambridge: Polity Press.

Boonstra, J. and M. Denison (2011) 'Is the EU–Central Asia Strategy Running Out of Steam?', *EUCAM Policy Brief*, No. 17. Online. Available at: www.eucentralasia.eu/uploads/tx_icticontent/Policy_Brief_17.pdf (last accessed 11 February 2015).

Borren, M. (2008) 'Arendtian Politics of In/Visibility', *Ethical Perspectives*, 15(2): 213–237.

Bosse, G. (2008) 'Justifying the European Neighbourhood Policy Based on "Shared Values": Can Rhetoric Match Reality?', in L. Delcour and E. Tulmets (eds) *Pioneer Europe? Testing EU Foreign Policy in the Neighbourhood*, Baden-Baden: Nomos.

Bosse, G. and E. Korosteleva-Polglase (2009) 'Changing Belarus? The Limits of EU Governance in Eastern Europe and the Promise of Partnership', *Cooperation and Conflict*, 44(2): 143–165.

Boswell, C. and A. Geddes (2011) *Migration and Mobility in the European Union*, Basingstoke and New York: Palgrave Macmillan.

Brandenberger, D. (2002) *National Bolshevism: Stalinist Mass Culture and the Formation of Modern Russian National Identity, 1931–1956*, Cambridge, MA: Harvard University Press.

Brednikova, O. and O. Tkach (2010) 'Reshaping Living Space: Concepts of Home Represented by Women Migrants Working in St. Petersburg', in C. Gdancec (ed.) *Cultural Diversity in Russian Cities. The Urban Landscape in the Post-Soviet Era*, Oxford and New York: Berghahn Books.

Brednikova, O. *et al.* (2012) *Trudovye migranty v Sankt-Peterburge: vyiavlenie problem i vyrabotka rekomendatsii. Rezul'taty issledovaniia*, St Petersburg.

Brettell, C. and J. Hollifield (2007) 'Migration Theory: Talking Across Disciplines', in C.B. Brettell and J.F. Hollifield (eds) *Migration Theory: Talking Across Disciplines*, New York and London: Routledge, 1–26.

Briazgunova, O. (2013). 'Pro doliu ukrains'kyh zarobitchan rozpovidaiut' cyfry'. Online. Available at: http://kvpu.org.ua/uk/news/6/2275/pro-dolyu-ukrainskikh-zarobi tchan-rozpovidayut-cifri (last accessed 29 May 2013).

Browning, C.S. and P. Joenniemi (2008) 'Geostrategies of the European Neighbourhood Policy', *European Journal of International Relations*, 14(3): 519–551.

Brubaker, R. (2005) 'The "Diaspora" Diaspora', *Ethnic and Racial Studies*, 28(1): 1–19.

Brubaker, R. (2011) 'Nationalizing States Revisited: Projects and Processes of Nationalization in Post-Soviet States', *Ethnic and Racial Studies*, 34(11): 1785–1814.

Bryceson, D. and U. Vuorela. (2002) 'Transnational Families in the Twenty-first Century', in D. Bryceson and V. Ulla (eds) *The Transnational Family: New European Frontiers and Global Networks*, Oxford: Berg.

Bunyadov, T. (ed.) (2007) *Azərbaycan etnoqrafiyası. Üç cilddə*, Vol. 1–3, Baku: Sherq-Qerb.

Buzalka, J. and V. Benč (2007) *EU Border Monitoring: Slovak–Ukrainian Border Vyšné Nemecké/Uzhgorod and Veľké Slemence/Mali Selmenci*. Report, November, Bratislava and Prešov, Slovakia: Research Center of the Slovak Foreign Policy Association. Online. Available at: www.infolizer.com/sf6p1aa1sk/Eu-border-monitor ing-slovak- ukrainian-border.html (last accessed 15 October 2010).

Calhoun, C. (2007) *Nations Matter: Culture, History and the Cosmopolitan Dream*, London: Routledge.

Calhoun, C. (2010) 'Nationalism and the Cultures of Democracy', in P. Kivisto (ed.) *Social Theory: Roots and Branches*, New York: Oxford University Press, 424–433.

Calzado, R. (2007) 'Labour Migration and Development Goals: The Philippine Experience', Paper presented at the International Dialogue on Migration, 8 October, Geneva. Online. Available at: www.iom.int/jahia/webdav/shared/shared/mainsite/m icrosites/IDM/workshops/global_labour_mobility_0809102007/presentations/paper_ca lzado.pdf (last accessed 17 August 2013).

Cavadov, Q. (2000) *Azərbaycanın Azsaylı Xalqları və Milli Azlıqları*, Baku: Elm.

Cavadov, Q. (2004) *Talışlar. Tarixi-Etnoqrafik Tədqiqat*, Baku: Elm.

Ceccorulli, M. (2010) 'Security and Migration: The Development of the Eastern Dimension', *European Security*, 19(3): 491–510.

Chatterjee, P. (1995) *Nationalist Thought and the Colonial World: A Derivative Discourse?* Minneapolis, MN: University of Minnesota Press.

Chirila, V. (2009) 'Relaţiile Republicii Moldova cu România', in V. Chirila (ed.) *Evoluţia politicii externe a Republicii Moldova*, Chişinău: Cartidact.

Christiansen, T., K. Jorgensen and A. Wiener (2001) 'Introduction', in T. Christiansen and A. Wiener (eds) (2001) *The Social Construction of Europe*, London, New York and Thousand Oaks, CA: Sage.

Christou, G. (2010) 'European Union Security Logics to the East: The European Neighbourhood Policy and the Eastern Partnership', *European Security*, 19(3): 413–430.

Christou, G. and S. Croft (eds) (2012) *European Security Governance*, London: Routledge.

Cioranescu, G., G. Filiti, M. Korne *et al.* (1967) *Aspects des relations russo-roumaines: retrospectives et orientations*, Paris: Minard.

Clemens, E. and J. Cook (1999) 'Politics and Institutionalism: Explaining Durability and Change', *Annual Review of Sociology*, 25: 441–466.

Cohen, R. (1996) 'Diasporas and the Nation-state: From Victims to Challengers', *International Affairs*, 72(3): 507–520.

Collins, K. (2009) *Clan Politics and Regime Transition in Central Asia*, Cambridge: Cambridge University Press.

Coulibaly, S. (2012) 'Shifting Comparative Advantages in Tajikistan: Implications for Growth Strategy', *The World Bank Policy Research Working Paper*, No. 6125. Online. Available at: http://www-wds.worldbank.org/servlet/WDSContentServer/WDSP/IB/2012/07/11/000158349_20120711105205/Rendered/PDF/WPS6125.pdf (last accessed 11 February 2015).

Dar, F. (2013) 'The Role of NGOs in Independent Tajikistan', *The International Journal of Not-for-Profit Law*, Vol. 15. International Centre for Not-for-Profit Law. Online. Available at: www.icnl.org/research/journal/vol15iss1/art_3.htm (last accessed 22 February 2014).

Darbouche, H. (2008) 'Decoding Algeria's ENP Policy: Differentiation by Other Means?', *Mediterranean Politics*, 13(3): 371–389.

Davies, N. (1996) *Europe: A History*, New York: Harper Collins.

Delcour, L. and E. Korosteleva-Polglase (2009) 'Changing Belarus? The Limits of EU Governance in Eastern Europe and the Promise of Partnership', *Cooperation and Conflict*, 44: 143–165.

Demytrie, R. (2010) 'Tajikistan Looks to Solve Energy Crisis with Huge Dam', *BBC News*, 23 March. Online. Available at: http://news.bbc.co.uk/2/hi/asia-pacific/8580171.stm (last accessed 11 February 2015).

Detz, B. (2008) 'Die Ukraine im europäischen Migrationssytem', *Aus Politik und Zeitgeschichte*, 58(35–36): 33–38. Online. Available at: www.econbiz.de/literatur-und-faktensuche/detailed-view/doc/die-ukraine-im-europ%C3%A4ischen-migrations system-dietz-barbara/10003744830/ (last accessed 22 August 2013).

Egorova, E. (2012) 'Labour Migration to Russia', Report presented at the international symposium 'Migration Bridges in Eurasia', 7 November, Russian Academy of Sciences.

Eisele, K. (2012) 'Reinforcing Migrants' Rights? The EU's Migration and Development Policy under Review', *Global Justice: Theory Practice Rhetoric*, 5: 31–46. Online.

Available at: www.theglobaljusticenetwork.org/wp-content/uploads/3_GJN5_Eisele.pdf (last accessed 31 July 2014).

Erkut, G. and S. Mitchell (2007) *The Black Sea: Past, Present and Future*, London: British Institute at Ankara.

Fairclough, N. (2010) *Critical Discourse Analysis: The Critical Study of Language*, Edinburgh: Pearson Education Limited.

Farrell, M., B. Hettne and L. van Langenhove (eds) (2005) *The Global Politics of Regionalism. Theory and Practice*, London: Pluto Press.

Fedorov, A. (2013) 'Minsk predlagaet Evrope partnerstvo po sobstvennym pravilam'. Online. Available at: http://naviny.by/rubrics/eu/2013/02/23/ic_articles_627_180935 (last accessed 23 February 2013).

Fergusson, N. (2005) *Colossus: The Rise and Fall of the American Empire*, London: Penguin Books.

Filippova, O. (2010) 'Granitsa i Pogranich'e v kontekste politik identichnosti', *Metodologia, teoriya ta praktyka sociologichnogo analisu suchasnogo suspilstva*, 1: 394–401.

Florinskaya, Y. (2013) 'The Scale of Labour Migration to Russia', *Russian International Affairs Council*, 13 September 2013, Online. Available at: http://russia ncouncil.ru/en/inner/?id_4=2343#top (last accessed 18 July 2014).

Follis, K.S. (2012) *Building Fortress Europe, The Polish–Ukrainian Frontier*, Philadelphia, PA: University of Pennsylvania Press.

Forsberg, T. (2011) 'Normative Power Europe, Once Again: A Conceptual Analysis of an Ideal Type', *JCMS: Journal of Common Market Studies*, 49(6): 1183–1204.

Franke, A., A. Gawrich, I. Melnykovska and R. Schweickert (2010) 'The European Union's Relations with Ukraine and Azerbaijan', *Post-Soviet Affairs*, 26(2): 149–183.

Freyburg, T., S. Lavenex, F. Schimmelfennig, T. Skripka and A. Wetzel (2011) 'Democracy Promotion Through Functional Cooperation? The Case of the European Neighbourhood Policy', *Democratization*, 18(4): 1026–1054.

Friedman, J. (2001) 'History, Political Identity and Myth', *Cultural Anthropology*, 7(2): 194–210.

Fritsch, M. (2009) 'European Territorialization and the Eastern Neighbourhood: Spatial Development Co-operation between the EU and Russia', *European Journal of Spatial Development*, No. 35. Online. Available at: www.nordregio.se/Global/EJSD/Refereed%20articles/refereed35.pdf (last accessed 17 October 2013).

Fruntaşu, I. (2002) *O istorie etnopolitică a Basarabiei. 1812–2002*, Chişinău: Cartier.

Fryer, P., E. Nasritdinov and E. Satybaldieva (2014) 'Moving Towards the Brink? Migration in the Kyrgyz Republic', *Central Asian Affairs*, 1(2): 171–198.

Furman, D. (2006) 'Live History. A Silent Cold War', *Russian in Global Affairs*, 2. Online. Available at: http://eng.globalaffairs.ru/number/n_6573 (last accessed 13 August 2013).

Gagliardi, C., M. Di Rosa, M.G. Melchiorre, L. Spazzfumo and F. Marcellini (2012) 'Italy and the Ageing Society: Overview of Demographic Trends and Formal/Informal Resources for the Care of Older People', in J.A. Jaworski (ed.) *Advances in Sociology Research*, Vol. 13, Hauppauge, NY: Nova Science Publishers, Inc., 85–104.

Gallina, N. (2011) 'Ukraine: Nation-Building Revisited – The Ukrainian Presidents and Their Understanding of Identity Politics', *Political Sphere*, 15. Online. Available at: http://ssrn.com/abstract=1876652 (last accessed 13 May 2013).

Ganguli, I. (2009) 'Tajik Labour Migration to Russia: Is Tajikistan at a Crossroads?', *Irex Scholar Research Brief.* Online. Available at: http://irex.org/sites/default/files/Ina_Gangulil.pdf (last accessed 25 February 2014).

Garnett, S.W. (1997) *Keystone in the Arch. Ukraine in the Emerging Security Environment of Central and Eastern Europe*, Washington, DC: Carnegie Endowment.

Gawrich, A., I. Melnykovska and R. Schweickert (2010) 'Neighbourhood Europeanization Through ENP: The Case of Ukraine', *JCMS: Journal of Common Market Studies*, 48: 1209–1235.

Geiger, M. and A. Pécoud (2010) 'The Politics of International Migration Management', in M. Geiger and A. Pécoud (eds) *The Politics of International Migration Management*, Basingstoke: Palgrave Macmillan.

Geiger, M. and A. Pécoud (2012) 'The Politics of International Migration Management', in M. Geiger and A. Pécoud (eds) *The Politics of International Migration Management Migration, Minorities and Citizenship*, Basingstoke and New York: Palgrave Macmillan.

Gellner, E. (1983) *Nations and Nationalism*, Ithaca, NY: Cornell University Press.

Giffen, J., L. Earle and C. Buxton (2005) *The Development of Civil Society in Central Asia*, Oxford: INTRAC. Online. Available at: http://r4d.dfid.gov.uk/pdf/outputs/urbanisation/r7649-report.pdf (last accessed 31 July 2014).

Gladarev, B. and Zh. Tsinman (2011) 'Povysilas' li "migratsionnaia privlekatel'nost'" Rossii? Analiz vzaimodeistviia sotrudnikov militsii i FMS s migrantami posle izmenenii migratsionnogo zakonodatel'stva', in V. Voronkov, B. Gladarev and L. Sagitova (eds) *Militsiia i etnicheskie migranty: praktiki vzaimodeistviia*, St Petersburg: Aleteiia.

Goodman, S. (2010) 'Integration Requirements for Integration's Sake? Identifying, Categorising and Comparing Civic Integration Policies', *Journal of Ethnic and Migration Studies*, 36(5): 753–772.

Gower, J. and G. Timmins (2011) *The European Union, Russia and the Shared Neighbourhood*, London: Routledge.

Groff, A. (2005) 'Migration Partnerships: New Tools in the International Migration Debate', *Global Migration Perspectives*, 21. Online. Available at: www.gcim.org/gmp/Global%20Migration%20Perspectives%20No%2021.pdf (last accessed 17 August 2013).

Guiraudon, V. and G. Lahav (2000) 'A Reappraisal of the State Sovereignty Debate: The Case of Migration Control', *Comparative Political Studies*, 33(2): 163–195.

Guliev, Z. (2011) *Azerbaijan Posle Geidara Aliyeva*, Moscow: Regnum.

Haas, H. de (2005) 'International Migration, Remittances and Development: Myths and Fact', *Global Migration Perspectives*, 30. Online. Available at: www.gcim.org/attachements/GMP%20No%2030.pdf (last accessed 17 August 2013).

Habets, I. (2014) 'Alternative Prospects for Eastern Partnership Countries', *European View*, 13(1): 125–132.

Hajda, L.A. (ed.) (1998) *Ukraine in the World. Studies in the International Relations and Security Structure of a Newly Independent State*, Cambridge, MA: Ukrainian Research Institute, Harvard University.

Halenko, O. (2004) 'Poshuky Krymu v mynulomu ta siohodenni Ukrainy', *Krytyka*, 12: 26–33.

Hammer, D. (1997) 'Hannah Arendt, Identity and the Politics of Visibility', *Contemporary Politics*, 3(4): 321–339.

Handå Myhre, M. (2012) *Labour Migration from Central Asia to Russia: State Management of Migration*, unpublished thesis, University of Oslo. Online. Available at: www.duo.uio.no/bitstream/handle/10852/33968/MasteroppgavexxMyhre.pdf? sequence=1 (last accessed 25 February 2014).

Haukkala, H. (2008a) 'The Russian Challenge to EU Normative Power. The Case of European Neighbourhood Policy', *The International Spectator*, 43(2): 35–47.

Haukkala, H. (2008b) 'Russian Reactions to the European Neighbourhood Policy', *Problems of Post-Communism*, 55(5): 28–39.

Haukkala, H. (2009) 'Lost in Translation? Why the EU Has Failed to Influence Russia's Development', *Europe–Asia Studies*, 61(10): 1757–1775.

Haukkala, H. (2010) *The EU–Russia Strategic Partnership. The Limits of Post-Sovereignty in International Relations*, London: Routledge.

Haydukiewicz, L. (2011) 'Historical and Geographic Regionalization versus Electoral Geography', *Procedia: Social and Behavioral Sciences*, (19): 104–106.

Heathershaw, J. (2009) *Post-Conflict Tajikistan: The Politics of Peacebuilding and the Emergence of Legitimate Order*, Central Asian Studies Series, London and New York: Routledge.

Hirsch, F. (2005) *Empire of Nations: Ethnographic Knowledge and the Making of the Soviet Union*, Ithaca, NY and London: Cornell University Press.

Hiscock, D. and M. Paasiaro (2011) 'Looking Back to Look Forward: Learning the Lessons of Conflict Prevention in Ferghana Valley', *Saferworld Report*, May. Online. Available at: www.saferworld.org.uk/resources/view-resource/567-looking-ba ck-to-look-forward (last accessed 10 November 2015).

Hnatiuk, O. (2005) *Proshchannia z Imperieju: Ukrains'ki dyskusii pro identychnist'*, Kiev: Krytyka.

Hobsbawm, E. (2002) *Nations and Nationalism since 1780: Programme, Myth, Reality*, Cambridge: Cambridge University Press.

Hoerder, D. (2002) *Cultures in Contact. World Migrations in the Second Millennium*, Durham, NC: Duke University Press.

Hohmann, S. (2013) 'Socio-Economic Migrations and Health Issues Resulting from the Tajik Civil War', in M. Laruelle (ed.) *Migration and Social Upheaval as the Face of Globalization in Central Asia*, Leiden: Brill.

Hooren, F. van (2011) 'Caring Migrants in European Welfare Regimes: The Policies and Practice of Migrant Labour Filling the Gaps in Social Care', Florence: European University Institute. Online. Available at: http://cadmus.eui.eu/bitstream/handle/ 1814/17735/2011_VanHooren.pdf?sequence=2 (last accessed 15 June 2013).

Hrytsak, Y. (2004a) 'On Sails and Gails, and Ships Sailing in Various Directions: Post-Soviet Ukraine', *Ab Imperio*, 1: 229–254.

Hrytsak, Y. (2004b; 2nd edn 2011) *Strasti za natcionalizmom. Istorytchni esei*, Kiev: Krytyka.

Hughes, J. and G. Sasse (eds) (2002) *Ethnicity and Territory in the Former Soviet Union: Regions in Conflict*, London: Frank Cass.

Huntington, S.P. (1997) *The Clash of Civilizations and the Remaking of World Order*, New York: Touchstone Rockefeller Center.

Huysmans, J. (2000) 'The European Union and the Securitization of Migration', *JCMS: Journal of Common Market Studies*, 38(5): 751–777.

Huysmans, J. (2006) *The Politics of Insecurity: Fear, Migration and Asylum in the EU*, London: Routledge.

Iontzev, V. and I. Ivakhnyuk (2012) *Analytical Report of the Project on the Theme: 'The Role of International Labor Migration for the Economic Development of Russia'*, CARIM-East RR 2012/28, Robert Schuman Centre for Advanced Studies,

San Domenico di Fiesole (FI), Florence: European University Institute. Online. Available at: www.carim-east.eu/media/CARIM-East-2012-RU-28.pdf (last accessed 10 July 2012).

Ishchenko, V. (2011) 'Fighting Fences vs Fighting Monuments: Politics of Memory and Protest Mobilization in Ukraine', *Debatte: Journal of Contemporary Central and Eastern Europe*, 19(1–2): 369–395.

Ivakhnyuk, I. (2008) 'The Formation and Functioning of the Eurasian Migration System', Abstract of the doctoral thesis for the degree of doctor of economic sciences, Specialty 08.00.05 – Economy and management of a national economy (Economy Population and Demography), Moscow: Moscow State University.

Ivankova-Stetsiuk, O. (2010) 'Osnovni rysy ukrains'koi trudovoi migratsii', in R. Kis' (ed.) *Trudova migratsiia iak instrument internatsionalizatsii*, Lviv: Drukars'ki kunshty.

Ivankova-Stetsiuk, O. (2012) *Tserkva u prostori migratsii: etnosotsial'ni resursy ta sotsiointegratyvnyi potentsial religiinykh spil'not ukraiintsiv*, Lviv: Artos.

Jacoby, V. (2013) 'If Only it Was Only Water... the Strained Relationship between Tajikistan and Uzbekistan', *Central Asia Policy Brief*, 9. Online. Available at: http://centralasiaprogram.org/publications/central-asia-policy-forum/ (last accessed 11 February 2015).

Jamoat Resource Centre of Vorukh (2011) *Potential for Peace and Threats of Conflict: Development Analysis of Cross-Border Communities in Isfara District of the Republic of Tajikistan (Vorukh, Chorkhuh, Surkh, Shurab) and Batken District of the Kyrgyz Republic (Ak-Sai, Ak-Tatyr, and Samarkandek)*. Report. Online. Available at: www.undp.tj/files/Report%20in%20English(2).pdf (last accessed 11 February 2015).

Jersild, A. (2002) *Orientalism and Empire: North Caucasus Mountain Peoples and the Georgian Frontier, 1845–1917*, Montreal: McGill-Queen's University Press.

Joenniemi, P. (2008) 'Re-negotiating Europe's Identity. The European Neighbourhood Policy as a Form of Differentiation', *Journal of Borderlands Studies*, 3(23): 83–94.

Jones, A. and J.R.A. Clark (2008) 'Europeanization and Discourse-Building: The European Commission, European Narratives and the European Neighbourhood Policy', *Geopolitics*, 13(3): 1–27.

Joppke, C. (2007a) 'Beyond National Models: Civic Integration Policies for Immigrants in Western Europe', *West European Politics*, 30(1): 1–22.

Joppke, C. (2007b) 'Transformation of Immigrant Integration: Civic Integration and Antidiscrimination in the Netherlands, France, and Germany', *World Politics*, 59(2): 243–273.

Joppke, C. and E. Morawska (2003) 'Integrating Immigrants in Liberal Nation-States: Policies and Practices', in J. Christian and E. Morawska (eds) *Towards Assimilation and Citizenship: Immigrants in Liberal Nation-States*, Basingstoke and New York: Palgrave Macmillan.

Jørgensen, M. (2012) 'The Diverging Logics of Integration Policy Making at National and City Level', *International Migration Review*, 46(1): 244–278.

Juraev, S. (2012) 'Central Asia's Cold War? Water and Politics in Uzbek-Tajik Relations', *PONARS Eurasia PolicyMemo*, 217. Online. Available at: www.ponarseurasia.org/sites/default/files/policy-memos-pdf/pepm_217_Juraev_Sept2012_0.pdf (last accessed 11 February 2015).

Kabirova, S. *et al.* (eds) (2011) *Tadzhikskii aliuminii: vchera, sevodnia, zavtra*, Dushanbe: TALCO.

Kaganskii, V. (2001) *Kul'turnyj landshaft i Sovetskoe obitaemoe prostranstvo*, Moscow: NLO.

Kaiser, R. (1995) *The Geography of Nationalism in Russia and the USSR*, Princeton, NJ: Princeton University Press.

Kappeler, A. (2009) 'The Politics of History in Contemporary Ukraine: Russia, Poland, Austria, and Europe', in J. Besters-Dilger (ed.) *Ukraine on its Way to Europe: Interim Results of the Orange Revolution*, Frankfurt am Main, Berlin and Bern: Peter Lang.

Keough, J.L. (2004) 'Driven Women: Reconceptualizing Women in Traffic Through the Case of Gagauz Mobile Domestics', *Focaal*, 43: 14–26.

Keough, J.L. (2006) 'Globalizing "Postsocialism": Mobile Mothers and Neoliberalism on the Margins of Europe', *Anthropological Quarterly*, 79(3): 431–461.

Kerr Chiovenda, M. (2013) 'Tajik Labour Migration to Russia: Tajik Responses to Migrant Vulnerability and Russian State Policies', *The Eurasia Studies Society Journal*, 2(1). Online. Available at: http://eurasiahistory.files.wordpress.com/2012/10/m elissa-kerr-chiovenda-tess-eurasia-journal-vol-2-no-1-february-2013.pdf (last accessed 24 February 2014).

Khobta, S. (2010) 'Vostochnyi uchastok ukrainsko-rossiyiskoi granitsy: osobennosti vospriyatia granitsy i perspektivy demarkatsii', *Metodologia, teoriya ta praktyka sociologichnogo analisu suchasnogo suspilstva*, 1: 412–416.

Klaskovskiĭ, A. (2013a) '*Poka Evropa budet zhdat' Belarus'*, *Moskva eë s"est bez soli'*. Online. Available at: http://naviny.by/rubrics/eu/2013/11/27/ic_articles_627_183775 (last accessed 20 December 2013).

Klaskovskiĭ, A. (2013b) '*V Vil'niuse Makeĭ sygral vizovoĭ kartoĭ'*. Online. Available at: http://naviny.by/rubrics/eu/2013/11/29/ic_articles_627_183812 (last accessed 10 December 2013).

Klinke, I. (2012) 'Postmodern Geopolitics? The European Union Eyes Russia', *Europe–Asia Studies*, 64(5): 929–947.

Klitsounova, E. (2008) 'Promoting Human Rights in Russia by Supporting NGOs: How to Improve EU Strategies', CEPS Working Paper Document, No. 287, April 2008. Online. Available at: http://aei.pitt.edu/9376/9376.pdf (last accessed 18 October 2013).

Knight, D. (1982) 'Identity and Territory: Geographical Perspectives on Nationalism and Regionalism', *Annals of the Association of American Geographers*, 72(4): 514–531.

Kochenov, D. (2008) *EU Enlargement and the Failure of Conditionality: Pre-accession Conditionality in the Fields of Democracy and the Rule of Law*, The Hague: Kluwer Law International.

Kochenov, D. (2009) 'The Eastern Partnership, the Union for the Mediterranean and the Remaining Need to do Something with the ENP', CRCEES Working Paper Series, Glasgow: Centre for Russian Central and East European Studies.

Kohut, Z.E. (2001) *History as a Battleground: Russian–Ukrainian Relations and Historical Consciousness in Contemporary Ukraine*, Saskatoon: Heritage Press.

Kononov, I. (2010) 'Granitsa mezhdu Ukrainoi i Rossiei: vzgliad s rossiskoi storony', *Metodologia, teoriya ta praktyka sociologichnogo analisu suchasnogo suspilstva*, 1: 402–411.

Koopmans, R. (2010) 'Trade-Offs between Equality and Difference: Immigrant Integration, Multiculturalism and the Welfare State in Cross-National Perspective', *Journal of Ethnic and Migration Studies*, 36(1): 1–26.

Korneev, O. (2013) 'EU Migration Governance in Central Asia: Everybody's Business – Nobody's Business?' *European Journal of Migration and Law*, 15(3): 301–318.

Korosteleva, E. (2012) 'The Eastern Partnership Initiative: A New Opportunity for the Neighbours?', in E. Korosteleva (ed.) *Eastern Partnership: A New Opportunity for the Neighbours*, Abingdon: Routledge.

Korostelina, K.V. (2013): 'Mapping National Identity Narratives in Ukraine,' *Nationalities Papers*, 41(2): 293–295.

Korovenkova, T. (2012) 'Evrope nuzhen belorusskiĭ shchit, no ne nuzhna belorusskaia dubinka'. Online. Available at: http://naviny.by/rubrics/eu/2012/12/16 (last accessed 17 December 2012).

Korovenkova, T. (2013a) 'Belarus – Evrosoiuz'. Online. Available at: http://belapan.com/archive/2013/03/19 (last accessed 19 March 2013).

Korovenkova, T. (2013b) '*Belarusian–Russian Readmission Agreement Will Facilitate Belarus-EU Visa Talks, Deputy Foreign Minister Rybakow Says*'. Online. Available at: http://en.belapan.by/archive/2013/11/22/en_20261122m/ (last accessed 10 December 2013).

Korsak, A. (2013) 'MID: u Pol'shi zhestkaia antibelorusskaia positsiia'. Online. Available at: http://naviny.by/rubrics/politic/2013/03/21 (last accessed 21 March 2013).

Kostadinova, V. (2009) 'The Commission, ENP and Construction of Borders', *Geopolitics*, 14(2): 235–255.

Kostakopoulou, D. (2010) 'Matters of Control: Integration Tests, Naturalisation Reform and Probationary Citizenship in the United Kingdom', *Journal of Ethnic and Migration Studies*, 36(5): 829–846.

Kotskaya, J. (2006) 'Transpamezhnaya palityka ES na uskhodnikh mezhakh: Euroregion "Nioman"', *Wider Europe Review*, 4. Online. Available at: http://review.w-europe.org/9/2.html (last accessed 11 August 2013).

Kozhevnikov, R. (2012) 'Uzbekistan Resumes Gas Supplies to Tajikistan', *Reuters*, 16 April. Online. Available at: www.reuters.com/article/2012/04/16/tajikistan-gas-idUS L6E8FG3YL20120416 (last accessed 11 February 2015).

Kuddosov, D. (2010) *Obzor rynka truda v Tadzhikistane*. Online. Available at: www.labour.tj/files/Final%20Report%20LM_%20TJ_rus.pdf (last accessed 25 February 2014).

Kuras, I.F. and V.F. Soldatenko (2001) *Sobornytctvo i regionalism v Ukrains'komu derzhavotvorenni (1917–1920)*, Kiev: Ukrainian Academy of Sciences Press.

Kuus, M. (2004) 'Europe's Eastern Expansion and the Reinscription of Otherness in East-Central Europe', *Progress in Human Geography*, 28(4): 472–489.

Kuus, M. (2007) *Geopolitics Reframed: Security and Identity in Europe's Eastern Enlargement*, New York: Palgrave Macmillan.

Kuzio, T. (2000) 'Nationalism in Ukraine: Towards a New Framework', *Politics*, 20(2): 77–86.

Kuzio, T. (2001) 'Historiography and National Identity Among the Eastern Slavs: Toward a New Framework', *National identities*, 3(2): 110–133.

Kuzio, T. (2002a) 'History, Memory and Nation Building in the Post-Soviet Colonial Space', *Nationalities Papers*, 30(2): 241–264.

Kuzio, T. (2002b) 'The Myth of the Civic State: A Critical Survey of Hans Kohn's Framework for Understanding Nationalism', *Ethnic and Racial Studies*, 25(1): 20–39.

Lacroix, J. and K. Nicolaïdis (eds) (2011) *European Stories: Intellectual Debates on Europe in National Contexts*, Oxford: Oxford University Press.

Laine, J. and A. Demidov (2012) 'Civil Society Organisations as Drivers of Cross-border Interaction: On Whose Terms, for Which Purpose?' in H. Eskelinen,

I. Liikanen and J. Scott (eds) *The EU–Russia Borderland: New Contexts for Regional Cooperation*, London and New York: Routledge.

Lamura, G. and H. Nies (2009) 'Developments in Carer Research', Paper presented at the *Eurocarers Autumn Seminar* on 16 November in Brussels.

Landsberg-Uczciwek, M. and T. Zan (2003) 'Bug Surveys: An Initiation of Transboundary Cooperation', in F. Bernardini, M. Landsberg Uczciwek, S. Haunia, M. Adriaanse and R.E. Enderlein (eds) *Proceedings of the International Conference on Sustainable Management of Transboundary Waters in Europe, 21–24 April 2002*, Miedzyzdroje, Poland, Szczecin: International Water Assessment Center. Online. Available at: www.iwacportal.org/File/downloads/landsberg_zan_2003.pdf (last accessed 11 August 2013).

Laruelle, M. (2008) *Russian Eurasianism: An Ideology of the Steppe*, Washington, DC: Woodrow Wilson Press.

Lavenex, S. (2008) 'A Governance Perspective on the European Neighbourhood Policy: Integration Beyond Conditionality?' *Journal of European Public Policy*, 15: 938–955.

Lavenex, S. (2011) 'Concentric Circles of Flexible European Integration: A Typology of EU External Governance Relations', *Comparative European Politics*, 9: 372–393.

Lavenex, S. and F. Schimmelfennig (2011) 'EU Democracy Promotion in the Neighbourhood: From Leverage to Governance?' *Democratization*, 18: 885–909.

Lavenex, S. and E.M. Uçarer (2004) 'The External Dimension of Europeanisation: The Case of Immigration Policies', *Cooperation and Conflict*, 39(4): 417–443.

Lazarev, A. (1974) *Moldavskaia Sovetskaia Gosudarstvennost' i Bessarabskii Vopros*, Chişinău: Cartea Moldovenească.

Lepesant, G. (2014) 'The EU and Its Eastern Neighbourhood: Policy Transfer in the Area of Regional Policy', *Regions*, 296(3): 19–21.

Levitt, P. and N. Nyberg-Sørensen (2004) 'The Transnational Turn in Migration Studies', *Global Migration Perspectives*, 6. Online. Available at: www.gcim.org/gmp/Global%20Migration%20Perspectives%20No%206.pdf (last accessed 17 August 2013).

Levy, A. (2012) 'The European Border Assistance Mission EUBAM and the Remote-Control Border: Managing Moldova', in L. Bialasiewicz (ed.) *Europe in the World. EU Geopolitics and the Making of European Space*, Farnham: Ashgate.

Libanova, E. (ed.) (2009) *Zovnishnia trudova migracija naselennia Ukrainy*, Kiev: DP Informatsijno-Analitychne Ahenstvo.

Liikanen, I. (2013) 'EU Common Foreign Policies and CBC in a Wider Europe', in A. Ergun and H. Isaxanli (eds) *Security and Cross-Border Cooperation in the EU, the Black Sea Region and Southern Caucasus*, Amsterdam: IOS Press.

Liikanen, I. and P. Virtanen (2006) 'The New Neighbourhood: A Constitution for Cross-border Cooperation?', in J. Scott (ed.) *EU Enlargement, Region Building and Shifting Borders of Inclusion and Exclusion*, Aldershot: Ashgate.

Luchenok, A. (2012) 'Belorusskie migrant v 2010 godu peredali na rodinu bole milliarda dollarov'. Online. Available at: http://luchenok.blogspot.com/search/label (last accessed 15 October 2012).

Luchenok, A. and I. Kolesnikova (2011) 'Vliianie migratsionnykh potokov na sotsial'no-ekonomitseskiepokazateli Belarusi'. Online. Available at: http://luchenok.blogspot.com/2011/09 (last accessed 5 August 2012).

Lucke, M., T.O. Mahmoud and L. Pinger (2007) *Patterns and Trends of Migration and Remittances in Moldova*, Chişinău: IOM.

Lucke, M., T.O. Mahmoud and A. Steinmayr (2009) *Labor Migration and Remittances in Moldova: Is it Boom Over?* Chişinău: IOM.

Lysiak-Rudnytsky, I. (1987) *Essays in Modern Ukrainian History*, Edmonton: CIUS Press.

McLeod, J. (2007) 'Introduction', in J. McLeod (ed.) *The Routledge Companion to Postcolonial Studies*, London: Routledge.

Malynovska, O. (2011) *Trudova migratsia: sotsialni naslidky ta shliakhy rehuluvannia. Analitychna dopovid*, Kiev: National Institute for Strategic Studies. Online. Available at: www.niss.gov.ua/content/articles/files/Malin_migraziya-dace3.pdf (last accessed 10 April 2013).

Mammadli, A. (2008) *Sovremenie Etnokulturnie Protsesi v Azerbaijane: Osnovnie Tendentsii i Perspektivi*, Baku: Khazar University.

Mammadli, A. (2011) 'Soviet Era Anthropology by Azerbaijani Scholars', in F. Mühlfried and S. Sokolovskiy (eds) *Exploring the Edge of Empire: Soviet Era Anthropology in the Caucasus and Central Asia*, Berlin: Lit.

Manners, I. (2002) 'Normative Power Europe: A Contradiction in Terms?', *Journal of Common Market Studies*, 40(2): 235–258.

Marat, E. (2009) 'Labor Migration in Central Asia: Implications of the Global Economic Crisis', *Silk Road Paper*, May. Washington, DC: Central Asia-Caucasus Institute and the Silk Road Studies Program, Johns Hopkins University.

Marat, E. (2013) 'Russia: Migration Profile'. Online. Available at: www.migrationpoli cycentre.eu/docs/migration_profiles/Russia.pdf (last accessed 25 February 2014).

Marciacq, F. (2012) 'The Political Geographies of Europeanisation: Mapping the Contested Conceptions of Europeanisation', *Journal of Contemporary European Research*, 8(1): 57–74.

Marin, A. (2006) 'Integration without Joining? Neighbourhood Relations at the Finnish–Russian Border', *DIIS Working Paper*, No. 14, Danish Institute of International Studies. Online Available at: www.diis.dk/files/Publications/WP2006/WP2006-14.pdf (last accessed 23 October 2013).

Marin, A. (2011a) 'From Breach to Bridge: The Augustów Canal, an Ecotourism Destination Across the EU's Border with Belarus', *Articulo – Journal of Urban Research*, 6. Online. Available at: http://articulo.revues.org/1705#text (last accessed 11 August 2013).

Marin, A. (2011b) 'Saving What Can Be: What the Eastern Partnership Could (Still) Bring to Belarus', *Eastern Partnership Review*, 3. Online. Available at: www.eceap. eu.eu/ul/EaP_3__artikkel.pdf (last accessed 12 August 2013).

Marin, A. (2013) 'La forêt primaire de Bélovej, un patrimoine transfrontalier', *Regard sur l'Est*, 15 November. Online. Available at: www.regard-est.com/home/breve_con tenu.php?id=1392 (last accessed 12 August 2013).

Marin, A. and L. Titarenko (2011) 'Les Bélarusses victimes du rideau Schengen', *Regard sur l'Est*, 15 November. Online. Available at: www.regard-est.com/home/ breve_contenu.php?id=1251 (last accessed 12 August 2013).

Markov, I. (2009) 'Arbeitsmigration aus der Ukraine in die Europäische Union', Arbeitsbericht. Online. Available at: www.heimatgarten.de/index.php?article_id= 43&clang=0 (last accessed 17 November 2011).

Markov, I. (2011) 'Features of Social Communications of Ukrainian Immigrants in EU'. Online. Available at: www.uef.fi/c/document_library/get_file?uuid=d0131449-20e9-4f94-b3c6-8d3eebfce212&groupId=208747&p_l_id=2000673 (last accessed 10 April 2013).

Markov, I., Y. Boyko, O. Ivankova-Stetsyuk, H. Seleshchuk *et al.* (eds) (2009a) *Na Rozdorizzi. Analitychni materially kompleksnoho doslidzennia protsesiv ukrainskoji trudovoji mihratsii (Krainy Evropejskoho Sojuzu ta Rosijska Federatsija)*, Lviv.

Markov, I., O. Ivankova-Stetsiuk and H. Seleshchuk (2009b). *Ukrainian Labour Migration in Europe. Findings of the Complex Research of Ukrainian Labour Immigration Processes*, Lviv: Caritas Ukraine.

Martin, P., M. Abella and E. Midgley (2004) 'Best Practices to Manage Migration: The Philippines', *International Migration Review*, 38(4): 1544–1559.

Martin, T. (2001) *The Affirmative Action Empire: Nations and Nationalism in the Soviet Union, 1923–1939*, Ithaca, NY: Cornell University Press.

Martinez, O. (1994) 'The Dynamics of Border Interaction', in C. Schofield (ed.) *Global Boundaries. World Boundaries*, London: Routledge.

Megoran, N. (2004) 'The Critical Geopolitics of the Uzbekistan-Kyrgyzstan Ferghana Valley Boundary Dispute, 1999–2000', *Political Geography*, 23(6): 731–764.

Megoran, N. (2006) 'For Ethnography in Political Geography: Experiencing and Re-imagining Ferghana Valley Boundary Closures', *Political Geography*. 25(6): 622–640.

Megoran, N. (2012) 'Rethinking the Study of International Boundaries: A Biography of the Kyrgyzstan–Uzbekistan Boundary', *Annals of the Association of American Geographers*, 102(X): 1–18.

Melnykovska, I., R. Schweickert and T. Kostiuchenko (2011) 'Balancing National Uncertainty and Foreign Orientation: Identity Building and the Role of Political Parties in Post-Orange Ukraine', *Europe–Asia Studies*, 63(6): 1055–1072.

Melyantsou, D. and V. Silitski (2008) 'How to Lower Schengen Visa Fees for Belarusians', Belarusian Institute for Strategic Studies Policy Paper, 1 June. Online. Available at: http://pdc.ceu.hu/archive/00003818/04/PDC_feature_lower_schengen_visa_fees_for_belarusians.pdf (last accessed 12 August 2013).

Mezhevich, N. (2009) *Prigranichnoe sotrudnichestvo i praktika dejatelnosti evroregionov na Severo-Zapade Rossii i v Respublike Belarus*, St Petersburg: Levsha.

Michnik, A., I. Grudzińska-Gross and R.S. Czarny (2011) *In Search of Lost Meaning: The New Eastern Europe*, Berkeley, CA: University of California Press.

Mitriaeva, S. (2007) 'Peredmova. Round Table Pidgotovka Novych Chleniv ES – Krain-Susidiv – do Vstupu v Schengen i Vyklyki dlia Ukrainy', Ukraine, 27 February. Online. Available at: http://old.niss.gov.ua/book/ec/content/01.htm (last accessed 15 November 2010).

Moraru, V. (ed.) (2011) *Brain drain: cazul Republicii Moldova*, Chişinău: Sirius.

Moraru, V., V. Mosneaga and G. Rusnac (2012) *Mayatnik migratsii*, Chişinău: Sirius.

Morgunova, A. (2010) '"Zaniatost" v Belarusi: politika I povsednevnost', *Vestnik obshchestvennogo mneniia*, 4(106): 98–115.

Morris, L. (1997) 'A Cluster of Contradictions: The Politics of Migration in the European Union', *Sociology*, 31(2): 241–259.

Motyl, A. (1992) (ed.) *The Post-Soviet Nations: Perspectives on the Demise of the USSR*, New York: Colombia University Press.

Mrinska, O. (2006). 'The Impact of EU Enlargement on the External and Internal Borders of the New Neighbours: The Case of Ukraine', in J.W. Scott (ed.) *EU Enlargement, Region Building and Shifting Borders of Inclusion and Exclusion*, Farnharm and Burlington, VT: Ashgate.

Mukomel', V. (2005) *Migratsionniia politika Rossii: postsovetskie konteksty*, Moscow, Institute of Sociology RAS: Dipol'&T.

Mukomel', V. (2013) 'Adoptaciya i integratciya migrantov v Rossii', in I. Ivanov (ed.) *Migraciya v Rossii 2000–2013, Hrestomatiya v 3 tomah. T.1, chast' 2*, Moscow: Speckniga.

Myrzabekova, A., I. Sikorskaya and A. Khaldarov (2013) 'Kyrgyzstan Enclave in Turmoil', IWPR – RCA, 693, 11 January. Online. Available at: http://iwpr.net/report-news/kyrgyzstan-enclave-turmoil (last accessed 11 February 2015).

Nagel, C.R. and L.A. Staeheli (2008) 'Integration and the Negotiation of "Here" and "There": The Case of British Arab Activists', *Social and Cultural Geography*, 9(4): 415–430.

Nartov, N.A. (2004) *Geopolitika*, Moscow: Edinstvo.

Neumann, I. (1996) *Russia and the Idea of Europe: A Study in Identity and International Relations*, London: Routledge.

Newman, D. (2003) 'On Border and Power: A Theoretical Framework', *Journal of Borderland Studies*, 18(1): 13–25.

Nielsen, K., E. Berg and G. Roll (2009) 'Undiscovered Avenues? Estonian Civil Society Organizations as Agents of Europeanisation', *TRAMES*, 13(3): 248–264.

Niemann, A. and T. de Wekker (2010) 'Normative Power Europe? EU Relations with Moldova', *European Integration Online Papers* (EioP), 14, Article 14. Online. Available at: http://eiop.or.at/eiop/index.php/eiop/article/view/2010_014a (last accessed 20 October 2013).

Nikolaeva, D. (2013) 'Migrantam vypisyvaiut meditsinskii polis', *Kommersant*, 18 January. Online. Available at: www.kommersant.ru/doc/2106854 (last accessed 15 July 2013).

Nourzhanov, K. and C. Bleuer (2013) *Tajikistan: A Political and Social History*, Australian National University, Canberra: ANU E Press.

Nye, J.S. (2004) *Soft Power: The Means to Success in World Politics*, New York: Public Affairs.

O'Loughlin, J. and P.F. Talbot (2005) 'Where in the World is Russia? Geopolitical Perceptions and Preferences of Ordinary Russians', *Eurasian Geography and Economics*, 46(1): 23–50.

O'Tuatheil, G. and S. Dalby (1998) 'Rethinking Geopolitics: Towards a Critical Geo-politics', in G. Ó'Tuatheil and S. Dalby (eds) *Rethinking Geopolitics*, London and New York: Routledge.

Olimova, S. (2010) 'The Impact of Labour Migration on Human Capital: The Case of Tajikistan', *Revue européenne des migrations internationales*, 26(3). Online. Available at: http://remi.revues.org/5239?lang=en#tocto2n1 (last accessed 18 July 2014).

Olimova, S. (2013) 'To Stay or Not to Stay: The Global Economic Crisis and Return Migration to Tajikistan', in M. Laruelle (ed.) *Migration and Social Upheaval as the Face of Globalization in Central Asia*, Leiden: Brill, 65–85.

Olimova, S. and I. Bosc (2003) *Labour Migration from Tajikistan*, Dushanbe: International Organization for Migration (IOM). Online. Available at: http://publications.iom.int/bookstore/free/Labour_Migration_Tajikistan.pdf (last accessed 23 February 2014).

Omelianuk, I. (2005) 'Best Practices to Manage Migration: China', *International Migration Review*, 43(5): 189–206.

Osipian, A.L. and A.L. Osipian (2012) 'Electoral Resource, 2004–2010: Regional Diversity and Divided Memories in Ukraine: Contested Past as Electoral Resource, 2004–2010', *East European Politics and Societies*, 26: 616–642.

Osipov, G.V. and S.V. Ryazantsev (2009) *Atlas of Russia's Demographic Development*, Moscow: Economic Education.

Ottaway, M. (2003) *Democracy Challenged: the Rise of Semi-Authoritarianism*, Washington, DC: Carnegie Endowment International Peace.

Pajnik, M. (2007) 'Integration Policies in Migration between Nationalising States and Transnational Citizenship, with Reference to the Slovenian Case', *Journal of Ethnic and Migration Studies*, 33(5): 849–865.

Parekh, B. (2008) *A New Politics of Identity. Political Principles for an Independent World*, Basingstoke and New York: Palgrave Macmillan.

Parker, N. (2008) 'A Theoretical Introduction: Spaces, Centers and Margins', in N. Parker (ed.) *The Geopolitics of European Identity: Centers, Boundaries and Margins*, New York: Palgrave Macmillan.

Pavliuk, O. (1999) 'The Ukrainian–Polish Strategic Partnership and Central European Geopolitics', in K. Spillmann, A. Wenger and D. Muller (eds) *Between Russia and the West: Foreign and Security Policy of Independent Ukraine*, Studies in Contemporary History and Security Policy, Vol. 2, Bern: Peter Lang.

Pazdnyak, V. (2006) 'Evropa regionov, evropejskaya politika sosedstva i Belarus: v poiskakh "dorozhnoy karty"', *Wider Europe Review*, 3: 18–25. Abridged English version. Available Online. Available at: http://pdc.ceu.hu/archive/00003032/ (last accessed 12 August 2013).

Pentland, Ch. (2008) 'Ukraine and the European Neighbourhood Policy', in J. De Bardeleben (ed.) *The Boundaries of EU Enlargement. Finding a Place for Neighbours*, Basingstoke and New York: Palgrave Macmillan.

Perminova, E. (2004) 'Market Grimace on the Face of the Russian Science', *Moscow, GDP*, 3, July: 34–35.

Peyrouse, S. (2009) 'The Central Asian Power Grid in Danger?', *CACI Analyst*, 12 September. Online. Available at: http://old.cacianalyst.org/?q=node/5232 (last accessed 11 February 2015).

Peyrouse, S. (ed.) (2014) 'How Does Central Asia View the EU?', *EUCAM Working Paper*, No. 18, June. Online. Available at: www.eucentralasia.eu/fileadmin/user_upload/PDF/Working_Papers/EUCAM-WP18-How-does-Central-Asia-view-the-EU-1.pdf (last accessed 31 July 2014).

Pipes, R. (1964) *The Formation of the Soviet Union*, Cambridge, MA: Harvard University Press.

Platonov, A. (2010) 'Vtorichnyi rynok prodazhi aktsii Roguna: ocherednaia obdiralovka po Rakhmonovski', *TJKNEWS.COM*, 2 December. Online. Available at: http://tjknews.com/?p=3998 (last accessed 11 February 2015).

Plokhy, S. (2007) *Ukraine's Quest for Europe: Borders, Cultures, Identities*, Mohyla Lecture Publication, Homeland series No. 4, Saskatoon: Heritage.

Plokhy, S. (2011) 'The "New Eastern Europe": What to Do with the Histories of Ukraine, Belarus, and Moldova?', *East European Politics and Societies*, 25: 763–769.

Poalelungi, O. (2010) 'Aspecte ale securitatii sociale a lucratorilor migranti din Republica Moldova: intre prezent si viitor', *Revista de filozofie, sociologie si stiinte politice*, 3: 122–129.

Popescu, G. (2008) 'The Conflicting Logics of Cross-border Reterritorialization: Geopolitics of Euroregions in Eastern Europe', *Political Geography*, 27: 418–438.

Popławski, T. (2010) 'Belarus-Poland', in Institute for International Sociology of Gorizia (ed.) *ISIG Swot Analysis and Planning for Cross-Border Co-operation in Central European Countries*, Institute of International Sociology of Gorizia (ISIG), report prepared for the Council of Europe. Online. Available at: www.coe.int/t/dgap/

localdemocracy/areas_of_work/transfrontier_cooperation/SWOT_Central_Europe_
Final.pdf (last accessed 12 August 2013).

Portes, A. and M. Zhou (1993) 'The New Second Generation: Segmented Assimilation
and its Variants', *Annals of the American Academy of Political and Social Science*,
530: 74–96.

Portnov, A. (2009) *Suchasna Ukraina u prostori mizhnarodnykh intelektualnykh
dyskussii mizh 'Tsentralnoiu Yevropoiu' ta 'Ruskim mirom'*, Kiev: RNBO.

Portnov, A. (2010) 'Historical Legacies and Politics of History in Ukraine. Intro-
ductory Remarks', in H. Best and A. Wenninger (eds) *Landmark 1989: Central and
Eastern European Societies Twenty Years After the System Change*, Berlin: LIT
Verlag Münster.

Powell, W. (2007) 'The New Institutionalism', *The International Encyclopedia of
Organization Studies*, London: Sage Publications.

Pozniak, O. (2009) 'Trudova emigratsiya v Ukrayini yak chynnyk rozvytku rynku
pratsi', in O. Vlasyuk (ed.) *Ukrayina v Yevropeyskiy ta Yevraziyskiy migratsiynykh
systemakh: regionalni aspekty'*, Kiev: Stylos.

Pozniak, O. (2012) *Socialni naslidky evrointrehratsii Ukrainy. Mizhnarodna migratsia*,
Kiev: Friedrich-Ebert-Stiftung. Online. Available at: http://library.fes.de/pdf-files/
bueros/ukraine/09446.pdf (last accessed 17 March 2013).

Prozorov, S. (2006) *Understanding Conflict Between Russia and the EU: The Limits of
Integration*, New York: Palgrave Macmillan.

Prozorov, S. (2007) 'The Narratives of Exclusion and Self-Exclusion in the Russian
Conflict Discourse on EU–Russia Relations', *Political Geography*, 26(3): 309–329.

Putnam, H. (2004) *Ethics without Ontology*, Cambridge, MA: Harvard University
Press.

Radchuk, T. (2011) 'Contested Neighbourhood, or How to Reconcile the Differences',
The Journal of Communist Studies and Transition Politics, 27(1): 22–49.

Rahimov, M. and G. Urazaeva (2005) *Central Asian Nations & Border Issues*, Conflict
Studies Centre (05/10), Defence Academy of the United Kingdom. Online. Available
at: www.da.mod.uk/Research-Publications/category/69/central-asian-nations-border-
issues-0510-7674 (last accessed 11 February 2015).

Raik, K. (2011) 'Between Conditionality and Engagement: Revisiting the EU's
Democracy Promotion in the Eastern Neighbourhood', Briefing Paper, No. 80,
Helsinki: Finnish Institute of International Affairs.

Reeves, M. (2005) 'Locating Danger: Konfliktologiia and the Search for Fixity in the
Ferghana Valley Borderlands', *Central Asia Survey*, 24(1): 67–81.

Reeves, M. (2009) 'Materialising State Space: "Creeping Migration" and Territorial
Integrity in Southern Kyrgyzstan', *Europe–Asia Studies*, 61(7): 1277–1313.

Reeves, M. (2014) *Border Work: Spatial Lives of the State in Rural Central Asia*,
Ithaca, NY and London: Cornell University Press.

Repida, A.V. (1977) *Formarea RSS Moldoveneşti*, Chişinău: Cartea Moldovenească.

Riabchuk, M. (2007a) 'Has the Second Rzecz Pospolita Expanded to the Borders
of the First RP in the Contemporary Ukraine?', *Nationalities Affairs=Sprawy
Narodowosciowe*, 31: 29–37.

Riabchuk, M. (2007b) 'Ambiguous "Borderland": Ukrainian Identity on the Crossroads of West and East'. Online. Available at: www.omp.org.pl/stareomp/riabchuk.
php (last accessed 23 June 2013).

Roll, G. (2001) 'Implementation of Policies for the Management of Transboundary
Waters on the Eastern European Border in a Perspective of the "New" EU Water

Policy', in G. Bucken-Knapp and M. Schack (eds) *Borders Matter: Transboundary Regions in Contemporary Europe*, Aabenraa: Danish Institute of Border Region Studies.

Romir Research Holding (2012) 'More and More Russians Ponder Emigration'. Online. Available at: http://romir.ru/studies/396_1348084800/ (last accessed 18 November 2015).

Rosière, S. and R. Jones (2012) 'Teichopolitics: Reconsidering Globalization Through the Role of Walls and Fences', *Geopolitics*, 17(1): 217–234.

Rumyantsev, S. and T. Sotkasiira (forthcoming) 'Azerbaijan, the EU and Migration Policy: Looking at the Bigger Picture', in M. Palonkorpi (ed.) *Final Report of Security and Development Research within the Wider Europe Initiative Security Cluster*, Helsinki: Aleksanteri Institute.

Ryazantsev, S. (2014) 'Russia and Kazakhstan in Eurasian Migration System: Development Trends, Socio-Economic Consequences of Migration and Approaches to Regulation' (with the contribution of O. Korneev), in A. Di Bartolomeo, S. Makaryan and A. Weinar (eds) *Regional Migration Report: Russia and Central Asia*, Florence: Migration Policy Centre, European University Institute. Online. Available at: www.migrationpolicycentre.eu/migration-report (last accessed 30 July 2014).

Ryazantsev, S. (2007) *Labor Migration in the CIS and the Baltic States: Trends, the Impact of the Regulation*, Moscow: Formula prava.

Ryazantsev, S. and N. Horie (2010) *Trudovaia migratsiia v litsah: rabochiie-migranty iz stran Tsentral'noi Azii v Moskovskom regione*, Moscow: 'Economic Education'.

Ryazantsev, S. and N. Horie (2011) *Stimulation of Labor Migration from Central Asia to Russia. Economic and Sociological Research*, Moscow: Scientific World.

Ryazantsev, S. and E. Pismennaya (2013) 'Emigratsiya uchënyh iz Rossii: "tsirkulyatsiya" ili "utechka" umov', *Sociological Research*, 4: 24–34.

Ryazantsev, S., I. Gorshkova, S. Akramov and F. Akramov (2012) *The Practice of Using Patents for Labour Activity by Foreign Citizens – Migrant Workers in the Russian Federation (The Results of the Study)*, Moscow: International Organization for Migration.

Safarov, S. and Sh. Rizoev (2010) 'Sotrudnichestvo s Kyrgyzskoi Respublikoi v ramkakh natsional'nykh interesov Respubliki Tadzhikistan', in N. Kerim (eds) *Kyrgyzstan-Tadzhikistan: kurs na ukreplenie partnerstva v kontekste regional'nykh sviazei*, Bishkek: Obshchestvennyi fond Turdakuna Usubalieva. Online. Available at: http://library.fes.de/pdf-files/bueros/bischkek/08172.pdf (last accessed 11 February 2015).

Safran, W. (1991) 'Diasporas in Modern Societies: Myths of Homeland and Return', *Diaspora*, 1(1): 83–99.

Said, E. W. (2003) *Orientalism*, London: Penguin Books.

Salimov, O. (2014) 'Tajikistan Ratifies Agreement with Russia on Tajik Labour Migrants', *The Central Asia-Caucasus Analyst*, 19 February. Online. Available at: www.cacianalyst.org/publications/field-reports/item/12914-tajikistan-ratifies-agreement-with-russia-on-tajik-labor-migrants.html (last accessed 18 July 2014).

Şarov, I. and Cuşco, A. (2011) 'Moştenirile regimului comunist în perioada post-sovietică: memorie, continuităţi, consecinţe', in S. Musteaţă and I. Caşu (eds) *Fără termen de prescripţie. Analiza investigaţiei crimelor comunismului în Europa*, Chişinău: Cartier.

Sasse, G. (2008) 'The European Neighbourhood Policy: Conditionality Revisited for the EU's Eastern Neighbours', *Europe–Asia Studies*, 60(2): 295–316.

Schiller, N.G. and A. Cağlar (2008) 'Beyond Methodological Ethnicity and Towards City Scale: An Alternative Approach to Local and Transnational Pathways of Migrant Incorporation', in L. Pries (ed.) *Rethinking Transnationalism: The Meso-Link of Organizations*, London: Routledge.

Schiller, N.G., L.G. Basch and C. Blanc-Szanton (1992) 'Towards a Definition of Transnationalism: Introductory Remarks and Research Questions', in N.G. Schiller, L. Basch and C. Blanc-Szanton (eds) *Towards a Transnational Perspective on Migration: Race, Class, Ethnicity, and Nationalism Reconsidered*, New York: The New York Academy of Sciences.

Schöpflin, G. (1993) 'Culture and Identity in Post-Communist Europe', in S. White, J. Batt and P.G. Lewis (eds) *Developments in East European Politics*, Basingstoke: Palgrave Macmillan.

Schöpflin, G. (2000) *Nations, Identity, Power*, London: Hurst.

Scott, J. (2005) 'The EU and "Wider Europe": Toward an Alternative Geopolitics of Regional Cooperation?', *Geopolitics*, 10(3): 429–454.

Scott, J. (2009) 'Bordering and Ordering the European Neighbourhood. A Critical Perspective on EU Territoriality and Geopolitics', *TRAMES A Journal of the Humanities and Social Sciences*, 13(3): 232–247.

Scott, J. (2011) 'Reflections on EU Geopolitics: Consolidation, Neighbourhood and Civil Society in the Reordering of European Space', *Geopolitics*, 16(1): 146–175.

Scott, J.W. and J. Laine (2012) 'Borderwork: Finnish-Russian Co-operation and Civil Society Engagement in the Social Economy of Transformation', *Entrepreneurship & Regional Development*, 24(3–4): 181–197.

Scott, J.W. and I. Liikanen (2010) 'Civil Society and the "Neighbourhood" – Reconciling Supranational, National and Local Agendas', *Journal of European Integration*, 32(5): 232–247.

Scott, J.W. and I. Liikanen (eds) (2011) *European Neighbourhood Through Civil Society Networks? Policies, Practices and Perceptions*, London: Routledge.

Scott, J.W. and H. van Houtum (2009) 'Reflections of EU Territoriality and the "Bordering" of Europe', *Political Geography*, 28(5): 271–273.

Sengupta, A. (2009) *Heartlands of Eurasia: The Geopolitics of Political Space*, Plymouth: Lexington Books.

Ševčenko, I. (1996) *Ukraine between East and West: Essays on Cultural History to the Early Eighteenth Century*, Edmonton: CIUS Press.

Shaffer, B. (2002) *Borders and Brethren: Iran and the Challenge of Azerbaijani Identity*, Cambridge, MA: The MIT Press.

Shakhot'ko, L. (2009) *Model' demograficheskogo razvitiia Respubliki Belarus*, Minsk: Belaruskaya navuka.

Sheffer, G. (2003) *Diaspora Politics: At Home Abroad*, Cambridge: Cambridge University Press.

Shulman, S. (2004) 'The Contours of Civic and Ethnic National Identification in Ukraine', *Europe–Asia Studies*, 56(1): 35–56.

Shymanovich, G. and A. Chubrik (2013) *Predlozhenie rabochei sily v Belarusi: vyzovy dlia ekonomicheskoi politiki*, Minsk: RDP. Online. Available at: www.research.by/p ublications (last accessed 10 February 2013).

Sidorov, D. (2006) 'Post-Imperial Third Romes: Resurrections of a Russian Orthodox Geopolitical Metaphor', *Geopolitics*, 11(2): 317–347.

Silitski, V. (2005) 'Preempting Democracy: The Case of Belarus', *Journal of Democracy*, 16: 83–97.

Slezkine, Y. (1994) 'The USSR as a Communal Apartment, or How a Socialist State Promoted Ethnic Particularism', *Slavic Review*, 2: 414–452.

Smith, A. (2009) *Ethno-Symbolism and Nationalism: A Cultural Approach*, London: Routledge.

Smith, J. (2013) *Red Nations: The Nationalities Experience in and after the USSR*, Cambridge: Cambridge University Press.

Smith, J. and E. Satybaldieva (2015) 'Lessons from Osh: International Responses to the June 2010 Events', *EUCAM Working Paper*.

Smith, K. (2005) 'The Outsiders: the European Neighbourhood Policy', *International Affairs*, 81(4): 757–773.

Sobczynski, M. (2006) 'Studies on Relict Boundaries and Border Landscape in Poland', International Conference 'Borderscapes: Spaces in Conflict/Symbolic Places/Networks of Peace', Trento, Italy, 11–14 June. Online. Available at: www.3unitn.it/events/bor derscapes/download/abstract/SOBCZYNSKI_paper.pdf (last accessed 12 August 2013).

Söderbaum, F. (2013) 'The European Union in Africa. Incoherent Policies, Asymmetrical Partnership, Declining Relevance?', in M. Carbone (ed.) *The European Union as an Actor in Africa: Internal Coherence and External Legitimacy*, Manchester: Manchester University Press, 25–42.

Söderbaum, F. and T.M. Shaw (eds) (2003) *Theories of New Regionalism*, Basingstoke: Palgrave Macmillan.

Soitu, C. and D. Soitu (2011) 'Europeanization at the EU's External Borders: The Case of Romanian-Moldovan Civil Society Cooperation', in J.W. Scott and I. Liikanen (eds) *European Neighbourhood through Civil Society Networks*, Abingdon: Routledge.

Solari, C. (2011) 'Between "Europe" and "Africa". Building the new Ukraine on the Shoulders of Migrant Women', in M.J. Rubchak (ed.) *Mapping Difference. The Many Faces of Women in Contemporary Ukraine*, New York and Oxford: Bergham Books.

Solonenko, I. (ed.) (2012) *European Integration Index for Eastern Partnership Countries*, International Renaissance Foundation and Open Society Foundations, May. Online. Available at: www.eap-index.eu/sites/default/files/pdf (last accessed 20 August 2013).

Stefansson, A. (2004) 'Homecomings to the Future: From Diasporic Mythographies to Social Projects of Return', in F. Markowitz and A. Stefansson (eds) *Homecomings: Unsettling Paths of Return*, New York: Lexington Books.

Stegniy, O. (2012) 'Ukraine and the Eastern Partnership: Lost in Translation?', in E. Korosteleva (ed.) *Eastern Partnership: A New Opportunity for the Neighbours*, Abingdon: Routledge.

Steinkohl, J. (2010) 'Normative Power Rivalry? The European Union, Russian and the Question of Kosovo', *EU Diplomacy Papers* 6, College of Europe, Department of International Relations and Diplomacy Studies. Online. Available at: http://aei.pitt. edu/14315/1/EDP_6_2010_Steinkohl.pdf (last accessed 23 October 2013).

Suny, R. (1993) *The Revenge of the Past: Nationalism, Revolution and the Collapse of the Soviet Union*, Stanford, CA: Stanford University Press.

Supronovich, R. (2012) 'Belarus': migratsionnyi klimat posle krizisa', *Migratsiia*, 21(2): 12–13.

Sushko, O. (2006) 'EU Initiatives for Border Management in the EU's Eastern Neighbourhood', *The International Spectator*, 41(4): 43–53.

Sushko, O. (2010) 'Security Bridge or Vacuum in Post-Orange Ukraine. How Operative is The Euro-Atlantic Integration Toolbox?', *PONARS Eurasia Policy Memo*, 123. Online. Available at: www.gwu.edu/~ieresgwu/assets/docs/pepm_123.pdf (last accessed 15 November 2010).

Suzdal'tsev, A. (2013) 'Novyi vrag'. Online. Available at: http://new.ucpb.org/suzda lczev-novyij-vrag.html (last accessed 3 February 2013).

Swietochowski, T. (1985) *Russian Azerbaijan, 1905–1920. The Shaping of National Identity in a Muslim Community*, Cambridge: Cambridge University Press.

Szporluk, R. (1991) 'The Soviet West or Far Eastern Europe?', *East European Politics and Society*, 5: 466–482.

Szporluk, R. (1997) 'Ukraine: From an Imperial Periphery to a Sovereign State', *Daedalus*, 126(3): 85–119.

Szporluk, R. (2002) 'Why Ukrainians are Ukrainians?', *Eurozine*, 17 September. Online. Available at: www.eurozine.com/articles/2002-09-17-szporluk-en.html (accessed 23 June 2013).

Tassarini, F. (2005) 'Security and Integration in the EU Neighbourhood. The Case for Regionalism', *CEPS Working Documents*, No. 226, July, Centre for European Policy Studies. Online. Available at: http://aei.pitt.edu/6667/1/1251_226.pdf (last accessed 23 October 2013).

Telo, M. (2005) *Europe: A Civilian Power? European Union, Global Governance, World Order*, Basingstoke: Palgrave Macmillan.

Țîcu, O. (2011) 'Border and Territory in the Russian History: A Glance at the Post/ Soviet Period', *Revista de Istorie a Moldovei*, 1–2: 86–114.

Titarenko, L. (2012) 'Sovremennye problemy i osobennosti zenskoi migratsii v Belarusi', *Zhurnal filosofii I sotsial'nykh nauk*, 3–4: 51–55.

Tiuriukanova, Y. (2010) 'Rossiis'kaia migratscionnaia politika v period demograficheskogo spada', *Stenogramma kruglogo stola (chast 2)*. Online. Available at: http://baromig.ru/arrangements/proshedshie/itogi-kruglogo-stola-17-iyunya-2010-goda .php (last accessed 26 August 2013).

Tocci, N. (2012) 'Regional Origins, Global Aspirations. The EU as a Global Conflict Manager Resolution', in S. Wolff and C. Yakinthou (eds) *Conflict Resolution in Divided Societies*, London and New York: Routledge.

Tolipov, F. (2013) 'Uzbekistan-Tajikistan Relations in Limbo', *CACI Analyst*, 16 May. Online. Available at: http://old.cacianalyst.org/?q=node/5775 (last accessed 11 February 2015).

Tolz, V. (2011) *Russia's Own Orient: The Politics of Identity and Oriental Studies in Late Imperial and Early Soviet Periods*, Oxford: Oxford University Press.

Toruńczyk-Ruiz, S. (2008) 'Being Together or Apart? Social Networks and Notions of Belonging Among Recent Polish Migrants in the Netherlands', *CMR Working Paper*, No. 40, Warsaw: Centre of Migration Research. Online. Available at: www. migracje.uw.edu.pl/download/publikacja/615/ (last accessed 22 August 2013).

Trilling, D. (2013) 'Kyrgyzstan & Tajikistan: Another Border Clash, More Conflicting Reports', *Eurasianet.org*, 29 April. Online. Available at: www.eurasianet.org/node/ 66897 (last accessed 11 February 2015).

Troebst, S. (2003): '"Intermarium" and "Wedding to the Sea": Politics of History and Mental Mapping in East Central Europe', *European Review of History: Revue européenne d'histoire*, 10(2): 293–321.

Tulmets, E. (2006) 'Adapting the Experience of Enlargement to the Neighbourhood Policy: The ENP as a Substitute to Enlargement?', in P. Kratchovil (ed.) *The European*

Union and its Neighbourhood: Policies, Problems, Priorities, Prague: Institute of International Relations.

Usmonov, I. (2001). *Dogovor mira* [Treaty of Peace], Dushanbe: Irfon.

Vaculovschi, D., Hârbu, E., Precup, G. and V. Bulat (2010) *Studiul situaţional al forţei de muncă în mediul rural, inclusiv prin prisma de gen. UNIFEM şi PNUD Moldova*, Chişinău.

Valenta, M. and Z. Strabac (2011) 'State-Assisted Integration, But Not For All: Norwegian Welfare Services and Labour Migration from the New EU Member States', *International Social Work*, 54(4): 663–680.

Vaughn Williams, N. (2012) 'Off-Shore Biopolitical Border Security: The EU's Global Response to Migration, Piracy and "Risky Subjects"', in L. Bialasiewicz (ed.) *Europe in the World. EU Geopolitics and the Making of European Space*, Farnham: Ashgate.

Vermeersch, P. (2007) 'A Minority at the Border: EU Enlargement and the Ukrainian Minority in Poland', *East European Politics and Societies*, 21: 475–502.

Vermenych, Y. (2003) *Teoretyko-metodolohichni problemy istorychnoi rehionalistyky v Ukraini*, Kiev: UAN Press.

Virkkunen, J., Fryer, P. and E. Satybaldieva (2015) 'Border Demarcation in the Ferghana Valley: Problem or Solution?', *EUCAM Working Paper*.

Vishnevski', A. (1998) *Serp I Rubl': Konservativnaia Modernizatsia v SSSR*, Moscow: O.G.E.

Vrabie, R. (2009) 'Relatiile Republicii Moldova cu Federatia Rusa', in V. Chirila (ed.) *Evoluţia politicii externe a Republicii Moldova*, Chişinău: Cartidact.

Vyshnevs'kyi, A. (2005) 'Alternativy migratsionnoi strategii', *Demoskop Weekly*, 185–186.

Wæver, O. (1995) 'Securitization and Desecuritization', in R.D. Lipschutz (ed.) *On Security*, New York: Columbia University Press.

Wallace, C. and K. Vincent (2009) 'Recent Migration from the New European Borderlands', in H. Fassmann, M. Haller and D. Lane (eds) *Migration and Mobility in Europe: Trends, Patterns and Control*, Northampton, MA: Edward Elgar.

Walters, W. (2010) 'Migration and Security', in J.P. Burgess (ed.) *The Handbook of New Security Studies*, London: Routledge.

Wierich, A. (2011) 'Solving Problems Where They Are Made? The European Neighbourhood Policy and its Effects on the Context of Other Migration-Related Policies of the European Union', *Perspectives on European Politics and Society*, 12(3): 225–241.

Williams, F. (2008) 'Theorising Migration and Home-based Care in European Welfare States', Paper presented at the Annual Conference of the Canadian Political Science Association, 4–6 June at the University of British Columbia in Vancouver. Online. Available at: www.cpsa-acsp.ca/papers-2008/williams.pdf (last accessed 15 June 2013).

Williams, F. (2011) 'Migration and Care Work in Europe: Making Connections Across the Transnational Political Economy of Care'. Online. Available at: www.social-policy.org.uk/lincoln2011/Williams%20F%20P2.pdf (last accessed 15 June 2013).

Wisniewski, P.D. (2013) 'It is High Time to Start a Real Partnership', Working Paper, Carnegie Moscow Centre.

Wunderlich, D. (2012) 'The Limits of External Governance: Implementing EU External Migration Policy', *Journal of European Public Policy*, 19(9): 1414–1433.

Yakovenko, N. (2002) *'Ukraina mizh Skhodom i Zakhodom': proektcia odniei idei – Paralel'nyj svit. Doslidzhennia z istorii ujavlen' ta idej v Ukraini XVI-XVII st*, Kiev: Krytyka.

Yakovenko, N. (2009) 'Choice of Name versus Choice of Path: The Names of Ukrainian Territories from the Late Sixteenth to the Late Seventeenth Century', in G. Kasianov and Ph. Ther (eds) *A Laboratory of Transnational History: Ukraine and Recent Ukrainian Historiography*, Budapest: CEU Press.

Yefimova-Trilling, N. and Trilling, D. (2012) 'Kyrgyzstan & Tajikistan: Disputed Border Heightens Risk of Conflict', *Eurasianet.org*, 2 August. Online. Available at: www.eurasianet.org/node/65744 (last accessed 11 February 2015).

Yeliseyev, A. (2012) 'How Isolated is Belarus? Analysis of Schengen Countries Consular Statistics (2007–2011)', BISS SA, 01/2012RU, 7 July.

Yeliseyev, A. (2013a) 'Migratsiia. Bol'shoĭ statistichekiĭ obman'. Online. Available at: http://naviny.by/rubrics/society/2013/03/21/ic_articles_116_181209 (last accessed 21 March 2013).

Yeliseyev, A. (2013b) 'Uproshchenie vizovogo rezhima s EC: posledstviĭa I perspektivy'. Online. Available at: http://naviny.by/rubrics/eu/2013/12/04/ic_articles_627_183852 (last accessed 10 December 2013).

Yuval-Davis, N., F. Anthias and E. Kofman (2005) 'Secure Borders and Safe Haven and the Gendered Politics of Belonging: Beyond Social Cohesion', *Ethnic and Racial Studies*, 28(3): 513–535.

Zagorec, V. (2012) 'Vusloviiakh demograficheskikh vyzovov', *Belaruskaya Dumka*, 10: 93–98.

Zagorec, V. and I. Zagorec (2011) 'Methodology of Determining the Extent and Results of External Migration of Population of the Republic of Belarus', *Journal of International Law and International Relations*, 4: 69–76.

Zaleska-Onyshkevych, L. and M. Rewakowicz (eds) (2009) *Contemporary Ukraine on the Cultural Map of Europe*, Armonk, NY and London: M. E. Sharpe.

Zamfirescu, E. (1996) *Mapping Central Europe*, Clingendael: Netherlands Institute for International Relations.

Zdravomyslova, E. (2009) 'Niani: kommertsializatsiiazaboty', in E. Zdravomyslova, A. Rotkirch and A. Temkina (eds) *Novyi byt v sovremennoi Rossii: gendernye issledovaniia povsednevnosti*, St Petersburg: Izdatel'stvo Evropeiskogo universiteta v Sankt-Peterburge.

Zdravomyslova, E., Rotkirch, A. and A. Temkina. (2009) 'Vvedenie. Sozdanie privatnosti kak sfery zaboty, liubvi i naiomnogo truda', in E. Zdravomyslova, A. Rotkirch and A. Temkina (eds) *Novyi byt v sovremennoi Rossii: gendernye issledovaniia povsednevnosti*, St Petersburg: Izdatel'stvo Evropeiskogo universiteta v Sankt-Peterburge.

Zhakevich, V. (2008) 'Migratsionnye nastroeniia v stranakh CIS (po itogam mezdunarodnogo issledovaniia)', *Sotsiologicheskie issledovaniia*, 10: 88–96.

Zharkevich, I. (2010) 'The Role of Civil Society in Promoting Political Accountability in Fragile States: the Case of Tajikistan', *INTRAC*. Online. Available at: www.intrac.org/resources.php?action=resource&id=682 (last accessed 23 February 2014).

Zhurzhenko, T. (2002) 'The Myth of Two Ukraines', *Eurozine*, 17 September. Online. Available at: www.eurozine.com/articles/2002-09-17-zhurzhenko-en.html (accessed 23 June 2013).

Zhurzhenko, T. (2004) 'Cross-border Cooperation and Transformation of Regional Identities in the Ukrainian-Russian Borderlands: Toward a Euroregion "Slobozhanshchyna"?', Part 1, *Nationalities Papers*, 32(1): 207–232.

Zhurzhenko, T. (2005) 'Politics of Border Making and (Cross-)Border Identities', *Eurozine*, 14 January. Online. Available at: www.bmlv.gv.at/pdf_pool/publikationen/ ukraine_zerissen_zw_ost_u_west_m_malek_ukraines_border_t_zhurzhenko.pdf (last accessed 20 January 2011).

Zhurzhenko, T. (2006) 'Regional Cooperation in the Ukrainian–Russian Borderlands: Wider Europe or Post-Soviet Integration?', in J.W. Scott (ed.) *EU Enlargement, Region-Building and Shifting Borders of Inclusion and Exclusion*, Aldershot: Ashgate.

Zhurzhenko, T. (2007) 'Ukraine's Border with Russia Before and After the Orange Revolution'. Online. Available at: www.bmlv.gv.at/pdf_pool/publikationen/ukraine_ zerissen_zw_ost_u_west_m_malek_ukraines_border_t_zhurzhenko.pdf (last accessed 20 January 2011).

Zhurzhenko, T. (2010) *Borderlands into Bordered Lands: Geopolitics of Identity in Post-Soviet Ukraine*, Stuttgart: Ibidem-Verlag.

Zielonka, J. (2006) *Europe as Empire: The Nature of the Enlarged European Union*, Oxford: Oxford University Press.

Zimmer, K. (2008) 'Migrants and Refugees in the Buffer Zone: Asylum Policy in Ukraine', *migrationonline.cz*, Online. Available at: http://aa.ecn.cz/img_upload/6334 c0c7298d6b396d213ccd19be5999/KZimmer_Ukraineasylumandmigrationpolicy.pdf (last accessed 15 September 2010).

Zlotnikau, A. (2004) 'Migratsyinyia pratsesy u Belarusi u kantsy XIX- pachatku XX stagoddia', *Belaruski histarychny chasopis*, 11: 25–32.

Index

For Product Safety Concerns and Information please contact our EU
representative GPSR@taylorandfrancis.com
Taylor & Francis Verlag GmbH, Kaufingerstraße 24, 80331 München, Germany

www.ingramcontent.com/pod-product-compliance
Lightning Source LLC
Chambersburg PA
CBHW060147280326
41932CB00012B/1664